ECONOMICS FOR MANAGEMENT

ECONOMICS FOR MANAGEMENT

(TEXT & CASES)

PROF. S.K. SARANGI
HOD—BUSINESS ADMINISTRATION
&
VICE PRINCIPAL
B.P. Poddar Institute of Management & Technology
Salt Lake, Kolkata.

FIRST EDITION : 2010

Himalaya Publishing House

MUMBAI ● DELHI ● NAGPUR ● BANGALORE ● HYDERABAD ● CHENNAI ● PUNE ● LUCKNOW ● ERNAKULAM ● AHMEDABAD ● BHUBANESWAR ● INDORE

First Edition : 2010

Published by : Mrs. Meena Pandey
for **HIMALAYA PUBLISHING HOUSE PVT. LTD.,**
"Ramdoot", Dr. Bhalerao Marg, Girgaon, **Mumbai - 400 004.**
Phones: 2386 01 70/2386 38 63, Fax: 022-2387 71 78
Email: himpub@vsnl.com
Website: www.himpub.com

Branch Offices:

New Delhi : "Pooja Apartments", 4-B, Murari Lal Street, Ansari Road, Darya Ganj, **New Delhi - 110 002.** Phones: 23270392, 2327863 Fax: 011-23256286

Nagpur : Kundanlal Chandak Industrial Estate, Ghat Road, **Nagpur - 440 018.** Phones: 2738731, 3296733 Telefax : 0712-2721215

Bengaluru : No. 16/1 (Old 12/1), 1st Floor, Next to Hotel Highlands, Madhava Nagar, Race Course Road, **Bengaluru - 560 001.** Phones : 22281541, 22385461, Telefax: 080-22286611

Hyderabad : No. 3-4-184, Lingampally, Besides Raghavendra Swamy Matham,Kachiguda, **Hyderabad - 500 027.** Phone: 040-27560041, 27550139, Mobile:- 09848130433

Chennai : No. 85/50, Bazullah Roda, T. Nagar, **Chennai - 600 017.** Phones: 044-28144004/28144005

Pune : First Floor, "Laksha" Apartment, No. 527, Mehunpura, Shaniwar Peth, (Near Prabhat Theatre), **Pune - 411 030.** Phones: 020-24496323/24496333

Lucknow : C-43, Sector - C, Ali Gunj, **Lucknow - 226 024.** Phone: 0522-2339329

Ahmedabad : 114, "SHAIL", 1st Floor, Opp. Madhu Sudan House, C.G. Road, Navrang Pura, **Ahmedabad – 380 009.** Phone: 079-26560126, Mobile: 09327324149

Ernakulam : 39/104 A, Lakshmi Apartment, Karikkamuri Cross Rd., Ernakulam, **Cochin – 622011.** Phones: 0484-2378012, 2378016, Mob: 09344199799

Bhubaneswar : 5 Station Square, **Bhubaneswar (Orissa) - 751 001.** Mobile - 9861046007, E-mail:- orissa@himpub.com

Indore : Kesardeep Avenue Extension, 73, Narayan Bagh.Flat No. 302, IIIrd Floor, Near Humpty Dumpty School, Narayan Bagh, **Indore (M.P.) - 452 007.** Mob-09301386468

DTP by : Stylish Laser Typesetter, Delhi-110053

Printed by : M.S. Printers, New Delhi-110002

DEDICATED TO THE DIVINE MOTHER

PREFACE

A decade of teaching ECONOMICS in Management Classes and request from students have prompted me to write the Book – ECONOMICS FOR MANAGEMENT – TEXT and CASES. Economics is taught in first three semesters BBA(H) for W.B.TECHNICAL UNIVERSITY and other Technical Universities in India. The Book covers complete syllabi of 3 semesters as MICRO, MACRO and BUSINESS ECONOMICS and is written in simple language and style.There are large number of Case Studies and Solved Numericals to help students to understand the basics and concepts. MBA and PGDM students also will find the Book very useful. The Book contains a complete QUESTION BANK to be useful for students. I am thankful to the Management and Staff of Himalaya Publishing House for accepting my manuscript for publication.

Prof. S.K. Sarangi

CONTENTS

Chapter	*Pages*

ECONOMICS - III : BUSINESS ECONOMICS

ECONOMICS - I
MICRO ECONOMICS

JOAN ROBINSON

The Birth of Monopoly Concept

Joan Robinson

Joan Robinson was the daughter an army General in British army during World War I and a Lecturer of Economics in Cambridge University in 1930s, who was bothered by the assumption of the free market. The free market postulated the existence of an infinite number of sellers and an infinite number of buyers. But Joan Robinson stated that in real life one never came across an infinite number of sellers or producers. The number of producers in any line of manufacture might be sizeable, but by no means countless. Very often they were only a handful.

Joan Robinson developed an alternative concept of the market structure more truthfully reflecting the realities of life. The result was the Economics of imperfect competition, which immediately set the river of economic theory on fire. She showed that even if there were initially a moderately large number of sellers or producers in any branch of production, there was a tendency for this number to reduce. The more efficient and resourceful among the producers gradually weed out the less efficient and less resourceful ones, until a stage arrives when supplies to that particular market come under the grip of a single seller or producer having the single goal of maximising the profitability. And this is made possible through restricting the output and increasing the price of the product. This concept had dealt a lethal blow to the belief fostered by the traditional economic analysis that the free market ensures ideal output and a just price for all. The free market, according to Joan Robinson, ends up in restrictive output and monopolistic price setting.

Thus, the market is not free, the market is not perfect; it is dominated by a few, the monopolists.

A monopoly does not spring overnight, there is a market process, a certain number of entrepreneurs engage against one anothers, confrontation takes place between competing bunches of resources, strategies and skills, temporary success alternating with temporary setbacks. In the final round, one of the entrepreneurs leaves the others behind, lagging rivals dropout, the one left in the field establishes a monopoly. It may be a long process, or a short one, but the emergence of a monopoly in a capitalist system entails a course of toil and application.

But Robinson's depiction of a process through which monopoly gets established is not that essential. An entrepreneur need not prove himself superior to his competitors in the market before gaining the monopoly. A different route may be possible. If one has friends in the right political quarters, a monopoly will be gifted to him on a platter. There are numerous examples of this in India and across the world.

ADAM SMITH, 1723-1790

Born : Kircaldy, Scotland, 1723.

Education : M.A. degree, University of Glasgow, Scotland, 1740, Independent study, Oxford, 1741-1748.

Jobs : Independent study, Edinburgh, 1748-1751, Professor, University of Glasgow, 1751-1764, Tutor for a duke, travelling in Europe, 1764-1766, Independent study, Kircaldy, 1766-776, Commissioner of Customs, Edinburgh, 1777-1790.

Major Publications : *The Theory of Moral Sentiments*, 1759, *An Inquiry into the Nature and Causes of the Wealth of Nations*, 1776.

In 1776, at the age of 53, Adam Smith published an amazing book that would eventually earn him the title "founder of modern economics." The *Wealth of Nations*—still relevant and widely quoted after 200 years—defined the land-scape of economics. Its most revolutionary ideas, illustrated with hundreds of juicy examples, were that people's real incomes, rather than gold or silver, are the measure of a society's wealth and that real incomes would grow through the division of labour, trade, and the use of money.

What personal qualities enabled Smith to write such a classic? What does it take to start a whole new field? Clearly, Smith was bright. After all, he obtained a master's degree at age 17 at a time when few even went to college. But there were other factors that prepared Smith to write his great work. He spent 10 years in independent study, at Oxford and Edinburgh, before obtaining a job as a philosophy professor at the University of Glasgow, his alma mater. After about a dozen successful years at Glasgow, however, he resigned to follow a career path that would take him back to solitary study. In exchange for tutoring a young duke and travelling around Europe for two years, he was given a salary for life. After his tutoring job ended, Smith returned to the small town of his birth, Kircaldy, on the east coast of Scotland, and worked virtually alone for more than 10 years on economics. Thus, Smith spent nearly 25 years in independent study—observing facts, developing theories, imagining how to express the theories—a process that culminated in the *Wealth of Nations*. His intelligence and his love of independently pursuing ideas day after day, year after year are the sources of the *Wealth of Nations*.

Adam Smith is frequently associated with the idea that self-interest, rather than benevolence, should be the basis of society. But an earlier book by Smith, *The Theory of Moral Sentiments*, focused on people's compassion for others, and there is a continuity between this earlier book and the *Wealth of Nations.* Smith recognized the need for cooperation, but reasoned that people's compassion diminishes as they become remote from others in distance, time, or family relationship; and the complexity of a modern economy—the division of labour and the need for resources from all over the world—increases these distances between people, creating the need for alternatives to benevolence. Smith reasoned that self-interest and markets provide that alternative. He wrote that people are

> *...at all times in need of the co-operation and assistance of great multitudes....The woolen coat, for example...is the produce of the joint labour of...[t]he shepherd, the sorter of the wool, the wool-comber or carder, the dyer, the scribbler, the spinner, the weaver, the fuller, the dresser, with many others....[But man's] whole life is scarce sufficient to gain the friendship of a few persons....and it is in vain for him to expect [help from] benevolence only.... It is not from the benevolence of the butcher, the brewer, or the baker, that we expect our dinner, but from their regard to their own interest. We address ourselves, not to their humanity but to their self-love, and never talk to them of our own necessities but of their advantages. [Man is] led by an invisible hand to promote an end which was no part of his intention. Nor is it always the worse for the society that it was no part of it. By pursuing his own interest he frequently promotes that of the society more effectually than when he really intends to promote it.*

Source of quote : Adam Smith, *Wealth of Nations* (New York : Modern Library, 1994), pp. 12, 15, 485.

ALFRED MARSHALL, 1842-1924

Born : Bermondsey (south of London), England, 1842.

Education : Cambridge University, graduated 1865.

Jobs : Professor, University College, Bristol, 1877-1883, Fellow, Oxford University, 1883-1885, Professor of political economy, Cambridge University, 1885-1908.

Major Publications : *Principles of Economics*, 1890, *Money, Credit and Commerce*, 1923.

Alfred Marshall was the first economist to define the powerful unit-free concept called elasticity, for which other economists are eternally grateful. The great economist John Maynard Keynes said, "I do not think Marshall did economists any greater service." Marshall defined elasticity in a remarkable book, *Principles of Economics*, published in 1890, when he was 48 years old. Here is how Marshall put it :

The elasticity of demand *in a market is great or small according as the amount demanded increases much or little for a given fall in price, and diminishes much or little for a given rise in price.*

Marshall's *Principles of Economics* contains many other innovations. The book was used in advanced economics courses for many decades; the economist Milton Friedman was still assigning the book to his students at the University of Chicago in the 1970s.

Why was the book so popular? It demonstrated the tremendous usefulness of the supply and demand model, in which the effects of economic policies are analyzed in a diagram by shifting supply or demand curves and considering their elasticities. Curiously, Marshall chose to make his diagrams the size of postage stamps and place them in small-print footnotes!

Marshall's *Principles of Economics* was not the first book to use demand or supply curves. Nearly 20 years earlier, in 1871, W. Stanley Jevons published a book of similar ideas. But more than anyone else, Marshall developed the supply and demand diagram into a powerful tool for analyzing real-world problems. Many economists credit Marshall with developing the *style* of economic reasoning that is routinely followed in applied economics work today. Marshall taught economists how to think like economists.

What was Alfred Marshall like? He spent much of his life as a professor, lecturing regularly and holding frequent office hours at his home. He trained a whole generation of economists, including John Maynard Keynes. For enjoyment, he loved to hike in the Alps in the summer. He lectured about the material in his *Principles of Economics* many years before the book was published, and he waited until he was over 80 to publish his major work on.macro-economics, which he had lectured about in his 30s! Many have wondered about the reasons for "Marshall's delay," looking into his personal life for answers.

Marshall was born south of London to a family that was not particularly well-off; his father was a dominating figure and forbade Alfred to study mathematics, which Marshall loved but his father did not understand. Rather than I go to Oxford, where his father wanted him to go, Marshall went to Cambridge and financed his education with a loan from one of his uncles.

Marshall did not decide to become an economist until after college. The reason for his choice? He said he saw economics as a way to help the poor and unfortunate in society.

Marshall was the greatest economist of the neoclassical school of the late 19th and early 20th century. The neo-classical school maintained most of the principles of the classical school founded by Adam Smith, but improved on them with the supply and demand model and its underlying foundation.

Marshall's simple, yet broad, definition of economics has itself become a classic. To Marshall,

Political Economy or Economics is a study of mankind in the ordinary business of life; it examines that part of individual and social action which is most closely connected with the attainment and with the use of the material require sites of wellbeing.

Source of quotes : Alfred Marshall, *Principles of Economics*, 8th ed. (New York : Macmillan, 1920), pp. 1, 102.

CHAPTER

1

INTRODUCTION

1. Introduction—Economics
2. Basic Problems of an Economy
3. Working of Price Mechanism
4. Resource Allocation
5. Challenges of Opportunities for Economics

1.0 INTRODUCTION

The English word 'Economics' has been derived from the Greek word 'Oikos' meaning 'house' and 'nomos' meaning the law and order of the stars; and the traditional meaning of economics comes from the Greek word 'Oikonomike' is household management.

Economics as a study of wealth had received great support firm the 'father of economics'—Adam Smith, who together with followers defined economics as the "Science of Wealth".

While A. Marshall in his book 'Principles of Economics' (1890) placed emphasis on human activities rather than on wealth and L. Robbins in 1931 clarified economics as 'Science of Choice', where scarcity inevitable and nothing is plentiful.

P.A. Samuelson (1915) advocated 'Economics is the study of how men and society choose, with or without the use of money, to employ scarce productive resources which could have alternative uses, to produce various commodities over time, and distribute them for consumption".

Economics is a social science. Its basic function is to study how people individuals, households, firms and nations—maximise their gains from their limited resources and opportunities.

Economics studies how households allocate their limited income between various goods and services they consume so that they are able to maximise their total satisfaction.

Economics also studies how producers decide on the commodity to produce, the production technology, location of the firm, market and market segment to cater to price of the product, expenditure on advertising and strategy on facing competition, etc.

It also studies how nations allocate their resources between competing needs of the society so that economic welfare of the society can be maximised.

Economics studies the choice making behaviour of the people and business organisations. Taking appropriate decision or making an appropriate choice in an extremely complex situation is a very complex affair.

Study of Economics helps in utilising analytical tools and techniques, mathematics and statistics and a large number of economic theories in order to make an appropriate decision in a complex situation.

Thus, the analytical tools and techniques, economics laws and theories constitute the body of economics.

The subject matter of economic science consists of the logic, tools and techniques of analysing economic phenomenon, evaluating economic option, optimisation techniques and economic theories.

More specifically, economic laws and tools of economic analysis are now applied a great deal in the process of business decision making. And this has emerged a separate branch of study called Business Economics or Managerial Economics.

Study of economics helps for plentiful income for the individuals and adequate incomes for the state.

In other areas, study of economics helps to increase efficiency and welfare and these areas are education, health and environment.

Political Economics is a study of mankind in the ordinary business of life.

Thus Economics is a social science.

1.1 NATURE AND SIGNIFICANCE OF ECONOMICS

Economics is a social science which studies social and individual behaviour in the pursuit of wealth, with the objective of increasing welfare.

An Economist in interested in the problem of valuation and the process of exchange and price formation in markets.

An economist's interest also extends to wider questions of income and employment generation, growth and distribution, money, trade and taxation in the economy, as well as education, health and environment protection.

Economics theories try to explain economic phenomenon and most theories try to provide predictions. The explanation and predictions provided by economic theory are highly conditional. They are derived from strong simplifying assumptions about human behaviour and economic life. Assumptions are very important to economic theory.

Assumptions are also used to simplify the manifold interdependence of economic life. One man's expenditure is some other man's income. Who in turn spends it generating incomes for still others.

Thus expenditure income chains bind together large parts of the economy.

A part from expenditure income chains, the economy is bound together by interdependence of markets and markets are bound together by the mobility of buyers and sellers.

(a) Macro Economics and Micro Economics Theory has two important branches : Macro Economics and Micro Economics.

Both of these branches deal with human behaviour in relation to wealth.

1.2 INTRODUCTION TO THEORETICAL ECONOMICS

Economics Theory has two important branches Macro economics and Micro economics

(a) Macroeconomics

Macroeconomics deals with the level of output and employment in the economy. Since these determine the level of national income, it is also called income theory. The determination of the level of national income is studies using highly aggregated concepts such as total consumption and total investment in the economy.

(b) Microeconomics

Microeconomics deals with individual human behaviour when faced with choice of human behaviour when faced with choice amidst scarcity. It concentrates on the actions of individuals and well-defined groups of individuals.

Micro economics is interested in individual prices, microeconomics is also called price theory.

Micro economics has two approaches. One which studies all markets simultaneously, whereas, the other studies in formation of price and related behaviour in single markets only.

The latter theory, which is called partial equilibrium analysis was popularised by Marshall.

Macro Economic Theory

Working out of macroeconomic System :

Environmental issues for a business environment are related to the overall economic, social and political atmosphere of the country.

The factors which constitute economics environment of a country include the following factors :

(*i*) Economic Environment Factors (Social, Political & Economical conditions)

1. The type of economics system in the country.
2. General trends in production, employment, income, prices, saving and investment etc.
3. Structure and trends of the working of financial institutions.
4. Magnitude and trends of Foreign Trade.
5. Trends in labour and Capital Markets.
6. Government economic policies, *e.g.*, industrial policy, monetary policy, fiscal policy, price policy etc.
7. Social factors like the value system of society, property rights, customs and habits.
8. Social organisations like trade unions, consumer's co-operatives and producers unions.
9. Political environment is constituted of such factors as political system—democratic, authoritarian, socialist, etc. State Govts' attitudes towards private business, size and working of the public sector and political stability.
10. The degree of openness of the economy and the influence of MNCs on the domestic markets.

A single business firm, small or large is not able to determine and guide the course of economic, social and political factors of the country. However, all the firm together, especially, the great corporate houses may jointly influence the economic and political environment of the country.

Some examples of social, economic and political factors of a country which directly influence the working of a business firm are as follows :

1. A giant multinational company like Coca-Cola is profitably operating in India and China,the both countries having sizeable middle class population with reasonable per capita income. This is socio-economical factor which is very important for the working and growth of any business.
2. In 1976-77, due to the policies of the then Janata Govt. in India, Coca-Cola and IBM Corporation had to leave India. Thus is the political factor which can influence the working of a business organisation.
3. Due to the prolonged disturbances in Assam by the ULFA, and the bodo community and Nagaland agitation in the north-east regions of India, there has been hardly any new business establishment in this part of the country and also of the existing tea companies have reduced their operations.

This is socio-political factor which is also important for the business organisation.

The business managers, therefore, are supposed to be fully aware of the economics, social and political conditions prevailing in the country while taking decision on the wider issues of the business.

(*i*) Therefore, Macroeconomics factors consist of National Income, Economic Growth, Unemployment, Foreign Trade, Taxation Policy, Labour Relations, Distribution system of essential goods, business cycles, Recession etc.

(*ii*) Macroeconomic Issues : The major macroeconomics or environmental issues which figure in business decision making, practically with regard to forward planning and formulation of the business strategy may be described under the following three categories.

(*a*) Issues Related to Macro Variables

General economic trend in the country, rate of inflation, investment climate, trends in the industrial, agricultural outputs, employment status & price trends etc. determine the prospects any business firm.

Therefore, for setting up a new business unit or for expanding the existing business activities, a business manager would analyse the above macro economic parameters.

(*b*) Issues Related to Foreign Trade

A country's economy is greatly influenced by its imports and exports with other countries.

Demand fluctuations in the international market, exchange rate variations, inflows and outflows of foreign capital etc. have direct influence on the country's economic environment and thereby on the functioning of a business firm.

The growth of IT industry in India has been sluggish due to poor demand in USA, particularly after the 11th September 2001 debacle in USA, the country was passing through a great democracy phase.

(*c*) Issues Related to Government Policies

Government politics generally control and regulate the economic activities of a business organisation.

A business enterprise with its profit maximisation objective may result in high social costs in terms of environmental pollution, rise of large slums in cities and towns, etc.

Such social costs bring a firm's interest in conflict with these of the society and also impose social responsibility on the firm.

The government's policies and its various regulatory measures minimise such conflicts.

The forced closure of many polluting industrial units in and around Delhi city and the consequent huge monetary loss in 2000 is a recent example of the result if ignoring the public laws and the social responsibility of the business firm.

Similarly, as a measure of W.B. State Govt. Policies the large number of tanneries in the Easter part of Kolkata city are going to be relocated in the Bantata location.

Pricing Mechanism

Price determination occupies the central stage of economic analysis and of managerial decision making as well. It is because price affects demand and quantity sold in turn affects cost. Thus, price affects profit through its effect on both quantity demanded and total cost.

Hence, pricing a product is a strategic decision factor in working own profit.

Besides, demand and supply factors, other forces behind the price of a commodity are Govt. policies, objectives of producers, market structure (*i.e.* monopoly, oligopoly, monopolistic and perfectly competitive) and so on.

The determination of price is dependent on the competitive structure of the market.

Pricing in public utilities such as electricity, gas, water, telephones and public transportation present a special type problem. In these industries, the nature of technology is such that productions and distribution result in substantial economics of scale. The object of government policy is to protect such utility companies from competition and then subject them to rate control by regulatory commission.

Pricing of search commodities like petroleum products, *i.e.*, LPG, Kerosene, petrol and diesel etc. comes under Administered Pricing Mechanism. These items are subject price control by the central Govt. since they are subsidised.

1.3

(*a*) Economics
- Micro Economics
  Internal to a Business Firm
  - Production
  - Marketing
  - Pricing
  - Profitability
  - HRM
  - Finance
- Macro Economics
  External to a Business Firm
  - GDP
  - Per Capita Income
  - Business Cycles etc.

(*b*) Economics
- Positive What it is
  (explains why inflation occurs)
- Normative Finds Solution
  (finds ways to control rate of inflation)

Study of economics helps understand the following term :

Scarcity → Shortage, less supply & more demand, price increases

Choice → Best of all alternatives

Economic interaction → Exchange of goods and services between people

Organisation → Created and managed by human being, school, college, business firm etc.

Market → A place where buyers and sellers meet and exchange goods/services with prices.

1.4

	Economic Analysis	*Forward Planning*
Individual/Household	Income, Expenditure Disposable Income	Plan for future

Business	Cost, Price, Quality Financial Resources Human Resources	Profitability Market Share, Growth
State/Nation	Human Resource Natural Resource (Land, River, Forest, Mineral Resources) Productive exploitation of above resources	GDP Per Capita Income National Income distribution

2. BASIC PROBLEMS OF AN ECONOMY

Basic problems are :

1. What to produce : To produce more bicycles or more motor cars or to produce more buses or more aeroplanes.

2. How to produce : *i.e.* how to efficiently utilise available resources and produce maximum of a commodity.

3. How to distribute : Having produced more wheat or paddy—how to distribute among all citizens.

For above 3 kinds of issues there are basically 2 types of economies.

***(a)* Market economy :** Goods and services are produced and sold freely. There is competition and price is determined by market equilibrium, India a Market Economy.

***(b)* Command economy :** All decision for production and distribution are taken by govt. Example China, Easter European countries. Broadly speaking, the market economy and the command economy are two alternative approaches to these questions.

In a market economy, most decisions about what, how and for whom to produce are made by individual firm, government and organisation. In a command economy or centrally manned economy, most decisions about what, how, and for whom to produce are made by those who control the governments, which through a central command controls what people do these command economics are few *i.e.*, former USSR, Eastern Europe & China.

Indian economy is a market economy. Basic problem of an economy is to find out the answer to the question, "out of Market Economy or Command Economy, which is better for a country"?

3. PRICE MECHANISM

In market economies prices are freely determined and it is important for determining what is produced, how and for whom.

The roles of price in a market economy are as follows :

(1) Prices serve as signals about what should be produced and consumed, when there are changes in taste or changes in technology.

When more and more people use motor cycles, the price of motor cycle increases. There is less production of cars.

(2) Prices provide incentives to people to alter their production or consumption. A higher demand for motor cycle will allow the firms to produce more. New firms can also enter the scene.

(3) Prices affect the distribution of income or who gets what in the economy. Workers in Motor Cycle firms will earn more and those working in cars mfg. firm will find their income reduced.

Therefore, prices are signals, they provide incentives, and they affect the distribution of income.

4. RESOURCE ALLOCATION

Resources are human resources; Materials resource and capital resource. Economics helps us to economically, effectively and efficiently utilise these resources for production of goods and services required for the citizens.

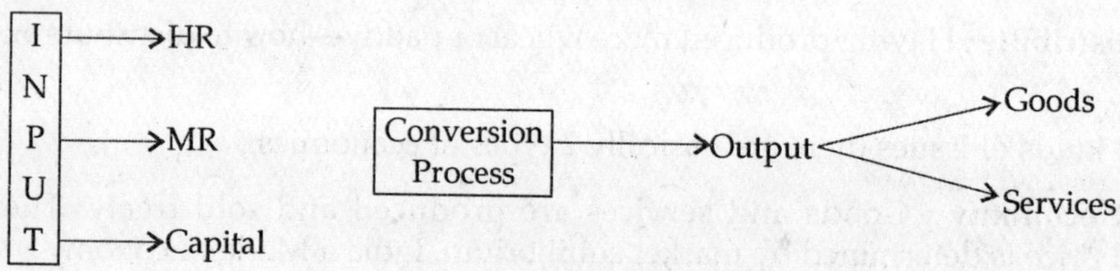

HR = Human Resource & MR = Material Resource

HR may be termed on "Labour" & MR & Capital together as Capital (K)

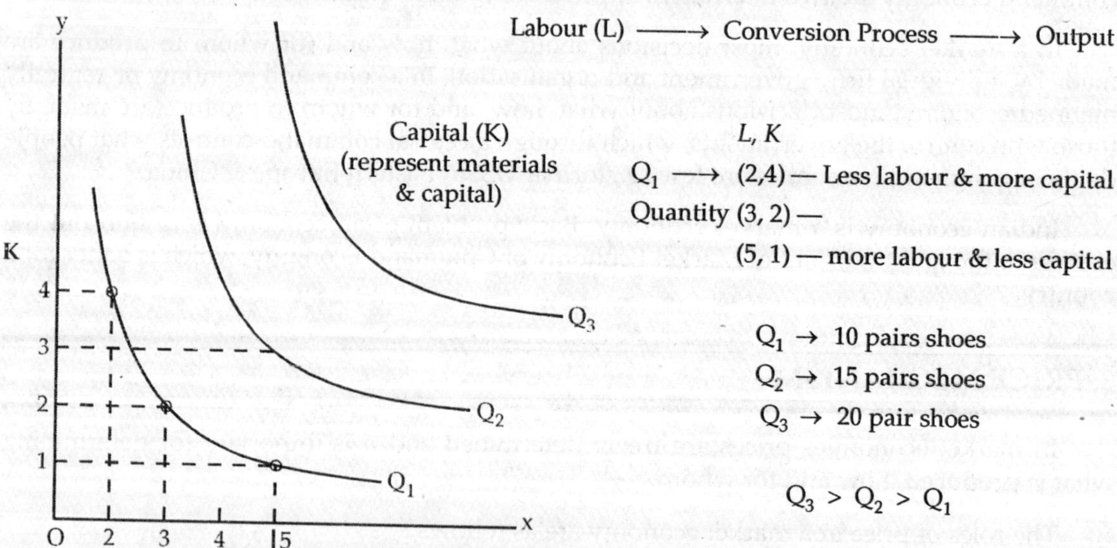

Q_1, Q_2 & Q_3 curves are Isoquant curves.

Fig. Resource Allocation Model

Model → A structural relationship among variables.

Resource allocation should have objectives of target production with available resources with highest productivity at the least unit cost of production.

5. CHALLENGES AND OPPORTUNITIES FOR ECONOMICS

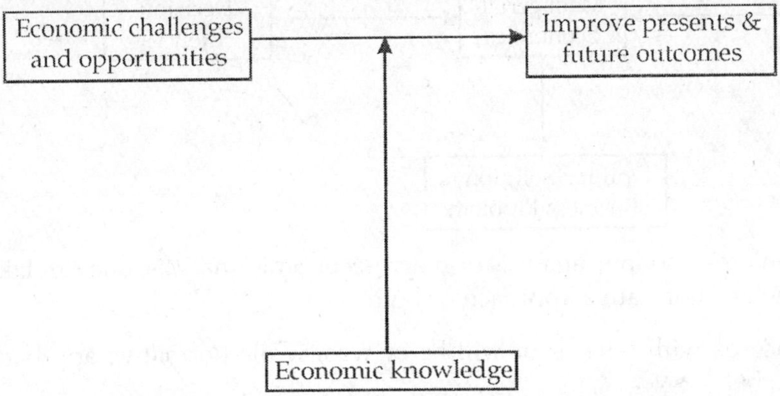

- Descriptions—describing problems & doing economic analysis.
- Explanations—for economic theories
- Predictions—for events
- Recommendations—for solutions & for forward planning

6. INTEGRATION OF ECONOMIC THEORY AND BUSINESS PRACTICE

With the help of economic theory one can understand the actual business behaviour. Economic theory is based on certain assumptions. The conclusions drawn with the help of an economic theory may not generally conform to what actually happens. Managerial economics modifies or extends the theoretical constant of economics to conform to actual business behaviour.

Economic logic, human and behavioural consideration, technological alternatives and environmental factors' have constant the complex considerations to support a business reality and economics has a dominant role to play in business decision making.

Economics and Managerial Economics both deal with identical problems—they both are concerned with problems of scarcity and resource allocation. Since labour and capital resources one always limited for a business firm it must find the best way in which to utilise them for achieving the set goals.

The two main contributions of economics to business economics are :

- to help in understanding the market condition and the general economic environment within which the firm operates.
- To provide a philosophy for understanding and analysing resource allocation problems.

Managerial economics provides a link between traditional economics and the decision sciences for managerial decision making as shown below :

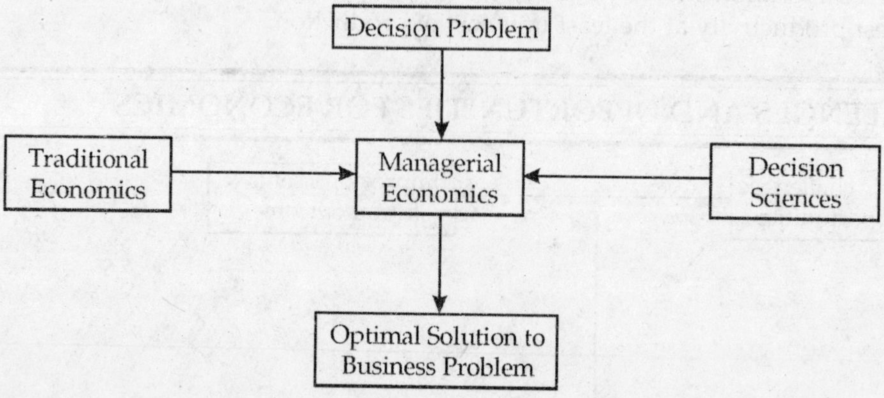

Whether one is using micro-economic analysis or macro-economic analysis, one can take recourse to positive approach or normative approach or both.

Positive approach concerns with what is or will be or was, while normative approach concern with what ought to be.

The positive economic theory attempts to develop hypothesis which explain why it happened. In the case of normative micro-economics, one is concerned with problems like what the objectives and policies or business ought to be and how to go about them. A similar type of analysis at the economy level is unknown as normative macro-economics.

More discussions on Micro & Macro Economics are done elsewhere in this book.

MODEL QUESTIONS

1. What is Economics? How is it helpful for mankind?
2. Describe basic problems of an economy. How is Economics helpful in this respect?
3. What do you understand for the process of Price Mechanism?
4. Elaborate "Resource Allocation Model".
5. What are challenges and opportunities for economics?

CHAPTER

2

ANALYSIS OF DEMAND

ELASTICITY OF DEMAND

Concept & Measurement of Elasticity of Demand, Price, Income & Cross Elasticities, Average Revenue, Marginal Revenue & Elasticity of Demand, Determinants of Elasticity of Demand, Numericals.

DEMAND FORECASTING

Law of Supply, Elasticity of Supply, Static & Dynamic Equilibrium, Effect of Time on Demand, Supply & Price, Short & Long Period Analysis, Case Studies on Elasticity of Demand.

Analysis of Demand, Elasticity of Demand, Revenue Analysis, Demand Forecasting, Elasticity of Supply, Static & Dynamic, Equilibrium, Short & Long Period Analysis, Case Studies on Elasticity of Demand.

1.0 INTRODUCTION

Analysis of demand helps us

(i) understand the behaviour of commodity in demand

(ii) specify a demand function and identify the relevant variables in a business situation

(iii) locate the sources of demand

(iv) identify the nature of demand

1.1 MEANING OF DEMAND

Demand for a commodity refers to the quantity of the commodity which a consumer is willing to purchase per unit of time at a particular price.

Demand for a commodity implies the following :

(a) Desire of the consumer to buy the product

(b) His willingness to buy the product, and

(c) Sufficient purchasing power in his possession to buy the product.

Demand may arise from the following sources :

(a) An individual—for soft drink, cigarettes or footwear—this is individual demand.

(b) A household—for TV, Geyser, Refrigerator etc.—This is household demand.

(c) A market demand—Market demand is aggregate demand. Demand for a commodity by all the individuals and households in the market at a price is the market demand.

1.2 DEMAND FUNCTION

An individual household's demand for a commodity depends on the household's desire for the commodity and its capability to purchase it.

The desire to purchase is revealed by tastes and preferences of the individuals in the household.

The capability to purchase depends on the purchasing power of the household, which is dependent upon the income of the household and the price of the commodity.

Thus, we may say, the quantity demanded (per unit time) for a commodity by a consumer (denoted as Qx) depends upon the following factors :

(i) Price of the Commodity (P_x)

(ii) Prices of Substitutes (P_S) and Complements (P_C)

(iii) Income of the household (I)

(iv) Tastes and preferences of the household (T)

(v) The amount of money annually spent on Sales promotion (A)

(vi) population size or nos. of consumers (N)

A simple mathematical expression for the above is as follows :

$$Qx = f(P_x, P_y, P_z \ldots\ldots P_n, I\,T, A, N)$$

For analysing the demand for goods which are durable, storable and expensive, we may add to the above equation, the variables of *(vii)* consumers' expectations of future prices (E_p) and *(viii)* consumers expected future income (E_y).

The demand function, as given above, is really just a listing of the variables that influence demand.

2. 0 THEORY OF DEMAND

Total sales revenue of a business firm is directly related to the demand for the commodity. If we know the demand curve for a firm's product and the average price set by the firm, we can determine its total revenue, which is just average price multiplied by quantity demanded.

Marginal revenue is the rate of change of total revenue with respect to quantity sold. It indicates to a businessman how total revenue will change if there is a change in the quantity sold of the product.

Mathematically, $\frac{\Delta TR}{\Delta Q}$ *i.e.*, the change in total Revenue (TR) divided by the change in quantity.

A demand curve considers only the price-demand relation, other things remaining the same.

Price-demand relationship may be illustrated in the following diagram known as Demand Curve.

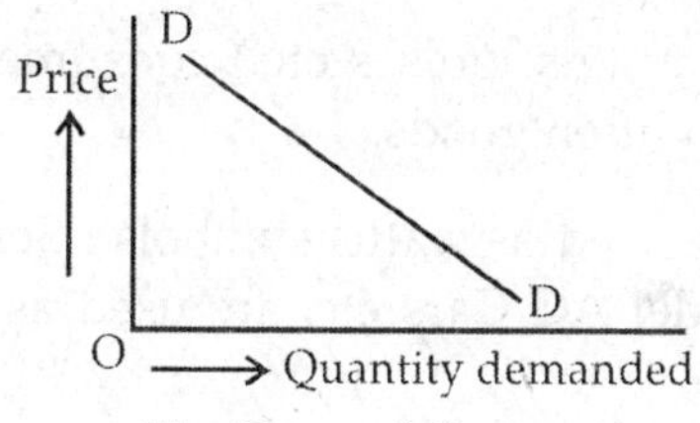

Fig. Demand Curve.

It may be observed from the demand-curve that price of a commodity and the demand for the commodity move in opposite directions.

Market demand for a product is the total volume that would be bought by a defined customer group in a defined geographical area in a defined time period in a defined marketing environment under a defined marketing programme. Thus, market demand is not a fixed number but rather a function of the stated conditions.

2. 1 THE LAW OF DEMAND

The law of demand states that the quantity demanded of a commodity and its price are inversely related, other things remaining constant. That is, if the income of the consumer, prices of the related goods and tastes and preferences of the consumer remain unchanged, the consumer's demand for the good will move opposite to the movement in the price of the good.

If the price of the good increases its quantity demanded decreases, while if price of the good decreases its quantity demanded increases.

The law of demand operates due to the underlying effects of substitution and real income changes.

Any change in the commodity price effects amount demanded of a commodity in two ways :

(i) Substitution effect of a price change

(ii) Income effect of a price change.

2. 2 EXCEPTION TO THE LAW OF DEMAND

(a) Prices of inferior goods in whose case the positive income effect is greater than the negative substitution effect, the law of demand would not hold.

For example, when price of potatoes (main food item for a poor family) decreases significantly, the poor household may like to buy apples (a superior food item for a poor family) out of savings the family derives due to decrease in the price of potatoes, The household increases the consumption of a superior good from the savings by reducing consumption of potatoes.

Thus, decrease in price of potatoes results in decrease in consumption of potatoes.

Such basic food items (*i.e.* grains, pulses etc.) consumed in bulk by the poor families generally fall in the category of Giffen goods.

(b) Commodities which are used as status symbols : Some expensive commodities like polished diamonds, luxury model AC Cars etc. are used as status symbol to display one's wealth.

The quantity demand of these commodities increases with an increase in their prices and decrease with a decrease in their price.

(c) Expectations of change in the price of the commodity :

If a household expects the price of a commodity to increase, it may start purchasing larger quantity of the commodity even at the present enhanced price.

Similarly, if the household expects the price to decrease, it may postpone its purchases.

Thus the law of demand is violated in such cases.

2.3 DEMAND SCHEDULE

A demand schedule at any particular time refers to the series of quantities the consumer is prepared to buy at its different prices.

A demand schedule may be an individual demand schedule or a market demand schedule.

The following table shows the market demand schedule for bananas.

Price of bananas (Rs./dozen)	Quantities demanded of bananas by individual consumers in dozens	Market demand of bananas in dozens
	A B C D E	
10	1 1 3 2 1	8
9	2 5 4 3 2	16
8	3 6 5 3 3	20
6	4 8 6 4 5	27

Thus, market demand is sum total of all consumers' demand.

2.4 CAUSES IN CHANGES IN DEMAND

Increase in demand	*Decrease in demand*
1. Consumers income rise	1. Consumers income falls
2. Changes in tastes and preferences in favour of the commodity	2. Changes in tastes and preferences against the commodity
3. Prices of substitutes rise	3. Prices of substitutes fall
4. Prices of complements fall	4. Prices of complements rise

3.0 DEMAND DISTINCTIONS

Types of demand or nature of demand are known as demand distinctions. Demand for any commodity is determined by its nature. Demand for such commodities which are indispensable for the consumer is not affected significantly by changes in their market conditions.

Opposite will be the case with those commodities which are dispensable or have close substitutes in the market.

Similarly, commodities which are durable have different demand than those which are non-durable.

Use characteristics of different goods also influence demand for them. A good with multiple uses generally has a higher demand than the one with single use.

We can broadly classify the goods in the following categories on the basis of demand distinctions.

***(i)* Direct and Derived Demands :** Direct demand refers to demand for goods meant for final consumption and derived demand is the demand for goods which are needed for further production, *i.e.*, industrial raw-materials, machine tools and equipment etc.

***(ii)* Autonomous and Induced Demand :** All direct demands such as fruits and vegetables are autonomous demands where as demand for cement is derived from the demand for housing and so demand for cement is induced demand.

***(iii)* Durable Goods and Perishable Goods Demand :** Durable goods are considered as assets when purchased and these have replacement demand (due to depreciation) perishable goods satisfy immediate demand and these can not be stocked.

(iv) **New and Replacement Demands :** If the purchase of an item is meant as an addition to the existing stock, it is a new demand. If the purchase of an item is meant for maintaining the old stock, it is replacement demand.

(v) **Industry Demand and Company Demand :** Total demand for Aluminium collapsible tubes for tooth paste packaging is the industry demand and demand for such items for Colgate Palmolive Co. Ltd. is the company demand.

(vi) **Total demand and Market Segment Demand :** Demand for a product for Kolkata market is the Market Segment demand and that for India is total demand.

(vii) **Short-term Demand and Long-term Demand :** Total toilet soap demand is the long term demand whereas glycerine soap demand is only for winter season or short term demand.

Above seven classes are in demand distinction category.

5.3.1 An Analysis of Demand

Demand analysis seeks to identify and measure the forces that determine the volume of sales. It reflects the market share for the company for a particular product.

Demand for a good or service is vital requirement for functioning of any business enterprise, its survival and growth.

Correct information on the demand helps management in planning its requirements for manpower & capital.

Demand estimate is the vital requirement for production planning, inventory planning, capital budgeting, market research, pricing decision and profit planning etc. Demand analysis is one of the areas of economics which has been used most extensively by business managers.

Once demand analysis is done, alternative ways of creating, controlling or managing demand can be inferred.

5.4.0 Elasticity of Demand

Elasticity of demand is a tool to measure the effect of change in any one of the determinants in the demand function *viz.* price, income, preferences, advertising expenses etc.

Elasticity of Demand helps us in understanding demand relationships by providing us a quantitative value for the responsiveness of the quantity demanded to changes in various factors in demand function.

The changes in price of the product, incomes of households, prices of related goods, tastes and preferences, etc. affect quantity demanded of a commodity.

This indicates only the directional impact of changes in the factors influencing demand. The management needs more information than this, *i.e.* it must know the magnitude of the impact of each of these factors on the quantity demanded. The firm is deeply concerned about the impact of these different factors on the quantity demanded of the product.

It is with the understanding of these impacts that the firm can hope to predict its level of sales and sales revenues.

Demand elasticity is simply a measure of relative responsiveness of quantity demanded to changes in one of the determinants, while other determinants assumed unchanged.

Elasticity of Demand (ed) is defined as the ratio of the percentage change in quantity demanded to the percentage change in the demand determinant under consideration.

That is,

$$ed = \frac{\text{Percentage change in quantity demanded of good x}}{\text{Percentage change in determinant z}}$$

Where the parameter Z may be one of the following :

(i) Current Price of the Commodity (P_x)

(ii) Current Price of the related good (P_r)

(iii) Current Income (Y) of consumers

(iv) Expected Price of the Commodity (EP_x) and

(v) Advertisement expenditure (A) etc.

From the demand function, we may notice that certain determinants of demand are completely beyond the control of the firm, *i.e.* income of consumers, numbers of consumers or prices of related goods.

On the other hand, advertising expenses, product price etc. and within the firm's control.

That is the reason why a business firm likes to prefer for price elasticity of demand and advertising elasticity of demand.

We find that it is possible to measure elasticity of demand with respect to each of demand determinants, a scientific quantitative measure for tastes and preferences is not possible and therefore measurement of elasticity is difficult.

5.5.0 Measurement of Elasticity of Demand

We will consider the following Demand Elasticity measurement :

Price Elasticity of Demand
Income Elasticity of Demand
Cross Elasticity of Demand
Expectations Elasticity of Demand
or
Elasticity of Price Expectations
Advertising (or promotional) Elasticity of Demand.

5.5.1 Price Elasticity of Demand (e_p)

Total Sales revenue of a firm equals the price multiplied with quantity demanded. A manager is therefore, interested to know the effect of changes in price and quantity on total revenue.

Price Elasticity of Demand helps him find out that if the percentage increase in price exceeds the percentage decrease in quantity demanded, total revenue will increase. And also if the percentage increase in quantity demanded exceeds percentage decrease in price, total revenue will increase.

Price Elasticity of Demand (e_p)

$$= \frac{\text{Percentage change in quantity demanded}}{\text{Percentage change in price}}$$

$$= \frac{\frac{Q_2 - Q_1}{Q_1} \times 100}{\frac{P_2 - P_1}{P_1} \times 100} = \frac{\frac{\Delta Q}{Q_1}}{\frac{\Delta P}{P_1}} = \frac{\Delta Q}{Q_1} \times \frac{P_1}{\Delta P}$$

$$= \frac{\Delta Q}{Q_1} \times \frac{P_1}{\Delta P}$$

P_1 and Q_1 are initial Price and Quantity

P_2 and Q_2 are changed price and quantity.

Higher the elasticity of demand, greater will be the percentage chance in quantity demanded for every percentage change in price.

For example,

$e_p = 2$, means that 1% change in price will change the quantity demanded by 2%, and

$e_p = 0.5$, means that 1% change in price will change the quantity demanded by 0.5%.

Thus, information about Price elasticity of demand is necessary for a firm for deciding about price change in a certain commodity.

In India, we find Soft Drink Manufacturers Coca-Cola and Pepsi very often use the principle of price elasticity of demand for affecting increases in their total sales revenue.

Since, the elasticity of demand is linked to the law of demand, the coefficient of price elasticity of demand (e_p), will always have a negative sign, *i.e.*, negatively sloping demand curve. In order to avoid confusion in interpretation only the absolute value of e_p is written and the (–) sign is ignored,

(a) Problems on Price Elasticity of Demand

(i) Price of oranges reduces from Rs. 24 to Rs. 18 per dozen when demand increases from 50 to 80 dozens per day in a market. Find the price elasticity of demand for oranges.

Soln. $e_p = \frac{\Delta Q}{\Delta P} . \frac{P_1}{Q_1}$ $\Delta Q = (80 - 50) = 30$ dozens

$$= \frac{30}{6} \times \frac{24}{50} \qquad \Delta P = (24 - 18) = \text{Rs. } 6 \text{ per dozens.}$$

P_1 = Rs. 24/dozen.

$$= \frac{12}{5} = 2.4 \qquad$$ **Ans.** Q_1 = 50 dozens.

(ii) In a particular season, Coca-Cola reduces price per bottle from Rs. 10 to 8, when consumption in a specific locality increases from 15,000 to 20,000 bottles per day.

Find the price elasticity of demand.

Soln. $$e_p = \frac{\Delta Q}{\Delta P} \cdot \frac{P_1}{Q_1}, \qquad \Delta Q = 20{,}000 - 15{,}000 = 5{,}000$$

$$= \frac{5000}{2} \times \frac{10}{15{,}000} = \frac{5}{3} = 1.67 \text{ Ans.}$$

DETERMINANTS OF ELASTICITY OF DEMAND

6.5.2 Reasons for Price Elasticity of Demand

***(i)* Substitutes :** If a product has a large number of close substitutes in the existing price range, demand for the product will be elastic and if the price of product is increased, consumers will prefer to purchase the substitutes products more and will buy the product less.

Pepsi is a close substitute of Coca-Cola and the Cola-Pepsi price-war very often emerges in public.

***(ii)* Share of a Commodity in a Consumer's Budget :** Some goods like common salt and match boxes have a very small share in a consumer's budget, therefore an increase in their prices will not have any appreciable effect on their quantities demanded. In this, demand for these commodities is inelastic.

***(iii)* Type of Commodities—Necessary Vs Luxury goods :** In case of necessary goods like rice and wheat, if prices increase, people will not reduce the quantity of purchase and demand for necessities is inelastic.

But if the prices of luxury goods like cars, Motor-Cycles etc. increase, consumer may like to postpone the purchase and in this case demand of luxuries is price elastic.

***(iv)* Time Period :** Short time and long time period can make a same commodity price-inelastic and price-elastic.

For a Generator supplying power to a factory and using diesel will not reduce the consumption even if price of diesel increases abnormally for a short time period, but in the long run the generator may be converted suitable for a cheaper fuel like Furnace oil in the long time period. Therefore, diesel in the first case is inelastic and in the latter case it is price elastic.

5.6.0 Income Elasticity of Demand (E_y)

Income Elasticity of Demand may be defined as a ratio of percentage change in the quantity demanded to the percentage chance in income of the consumer.

$$E_Y = \frac{\text{Percentage change in quantity demanded}}{\text{Percentage change in income of the consumer}}$$

Let us assume, the commodity is X and Income is Y.

$$\text{Therefore, } E_Y = \frac{\frac{\Delta QX}{QX} \times 100}{\frac{\Delta Y}{Y} \times 100}$$

$$= \frac{\Delta QX}{QX} \cdot \frac{Y}{\Delta Y}$$

$$= \frac{\Delta Q_X}{\Delta Y} \cdot \frac{Y}{QX}$$

A businessman while setting up a fast food restaurant or a beauty parlour will choose localities where a large number of families with high disposable income levels reside.

While, income elasticity of demand is positive for normal commodities since their demand move in the direction of consumers' income, there are some goods like course cereals (*i.e.* coarse rice) whose consumption reduces when consumers' income levels increase and for these goods income elasticity of demand is negative.

***(a)* Problems on Income Elasticity of Demand :**

(i) Ashoke's demand for a commodity increases from 100 units to 200 units in a week, when his income rises from Rs. 2000 to Rs. 3000 per month.

Find his income elasticity of demand.

Soln. $E_y = \frac{\Delta QX}{\Delta Y} \cdot \frac{Y}{QX} = \frac{200-100}{3000-2000} \cdot \frac{2000}{100}$

$$= \frac{100}{1000} \cdot \frac{2000}{100} = 2.$$

(ii) Samir's demand for oranges increases from 50 units to 80 units per week, when his income rises from Rs. 3000 to Rs. 3500 per month, find his income elasticity of demand.

Soln. $E_y = \frac{\Delta QX}{\Delta Y} \cdot \frac{Y}{QX} = \frac{80-50}{3500-3000} \cdot \frac{3000}{50}$

$$= \frac{30}{500} \cdot \frac{3000}{50} = \frac{90}{25} = 3.6$$

5.6.1 Significance of Income Elasticity of Demand

We know that as a result of economic growth, level of national income increases. Since demand for goods and services is positively influenced by the level of national income, economic growth will, therefore, be associated with increase in the sale of normal goods.

If the coefficient of income elasticity of demand is greater than 1, sales of goods and services will grow more than proportionately to the rate of economic growth during the period.

Per capita income growth, for a country is so important that China's per capita income being much higher than that of India's, and for the same reason, China attracts much higher foreign direct investment (FDI) than India.

Therefore, if the per capita income growth is the cause, income elasticity of demand is the effect and both can be termed as the engine for growth.

The knowledge of income elasticity of demand is also useful for forecasting the influence of possible future changes in economic activity on demand.

In the case of measurement of income elasticity, one usually confronts the problem of choosing among various alternative income measures.

The most popular measure of income is the personal disposable income per head.

5.7.0 Cross Elasticity of Demand

The concept of elasticity of demand can be applied in a situation where two commodities are related to each other. The elasticity in this case is called cross elasticity of demand. The concept of cross elasticity of demand is useful in handling inter-commodity demand relation.

Cross elasticity of demand is defined as the ratio of the percentage change in demand for a good to the percentage change in the price of some other good.

In this case, two goods in question are either substitutes or complements to each other.

If two goods X and Y are related,

$$\text{Cross elasticity of demand } \ell xy = \frac{\frac{\Delta Q_x}{Q_x}}{\frac{\Delta P_y}{P_y}}$$

$$= \frac{\Delta Q_x . P_y}{\Delta P_y . Q_x}$$

Examples for substitutes,
Tea and Coffee
Cigarette and Biri
Coca-Cola and Pepsi
& Examples for completary goods,
Sugar and Tea
Petrol and Automobile

For substitute and complementary goods, cross elasticity of demand is positive and negative respectively.

Coca-Cola and Pepsi soft drinks are close substitutes. If the price of Coca-Cola increases, many of its consumers will switch over to the use of Pepsi and the Cross elasticity of demand in such a case will be positive.

For very close substitutes, the greater is the size of cross elasticity coefficient and when two goods are poor substitutes (*i.e.* Tea and Coffee), their cross elasticity is low.

For complementary goods, cross elasticity is negative since the price and demand move in opposite direction. If the price of sugar increases, its demand will reduce and simultaneously, the demand for tea will also fall.

For the perfectly substitutes, the cross elasticity of demand is highly positive and generally tends to infinity; whereas for perfectly complementary goods, the cross-elasticity of demand will be highly negative tending to infinity.

i.e., for Substitutes, for complements, $0 < \ell xy < \alpha$

& for complements $-\alpha < \ell xy < 0$.

For unrelated commodities such as Table Fan and Ceiling Fan, which are neither substitutes nor complements, their cross elasticity of demand will be zero.

(*i*) Price of Coffee increases from Rs. 50 per kilogram to Rs. 70 per kilogram, while demand for tea increases from 5 to 10 kilograms in a locality.

What is the cross-elasticity of demand of tea for coffee?

Soln. ΔP Coffee = 70 – 50 = Rs. 20.

ΔQ tea = 10 – 5 = 5 kgs.

$$\text{Cross } \ell \text{ tea coffee} = \frac{\Delta Q \text{ tea}}{\Delta P \text{ Coffee}} \frac{P \text{ Coffee}}{Q \text{ tea}}$$

$$= \frac{5}{20} \cdot \frac{50}{5} = 2.5$$

5.8.0 Advertising (or Promotional) Elasticity of Demand

How far the demand for a commodity is influenced by advertising efforts and other promotional activities can be measured by advertising elasticity of demand.

Some goods like soft drinks and cosmetics, soaps etc. respond very quickly in terms of their sales in relation to advertising and promotional efforts.

Advertising elasticity does not always coincide with price elasticity, particularly in case of luxury goods which are more advertisement elastic than price elastic.

Advertising elasticity of demand may be defined as the ratio of proportionate change in sales to proportionate change in advertisement expenditure.

Advertising Elasticity of Demand = E_A

$$= \frac{\dfrac{Q_2 - Q_1}{Q_2 + Q_1}}{\dfrac{A_2 - A_1}{A_2 + A_1}},$$

Q and A refer to sales and advertisement expenditure respectively.

$$= \frac{\frac{\Delta Q}{Q_2 + Q_1}}{\frac{\Delta A}{A_2 + A_1}}$$

5.8.1 Factors Influencing Advertising Elasticity of Demand

Sale of different goods reacts differently to same amount of advertisement expenditure.

Even the same commodity may not respond the same way at different levels of advertising expenditure.

This implies that advertising elasticity of demand differs between products and also between different levels of sales of same product.

Following factors influence the advertising elasticity of demand :

(i) **Stage of Product Market :** The advertising elasticity is different for new and old products, and also for products which have, an established and growing markets.

(ii) **Effect of Advertising in Terms of Time :** The time lag in response to advertisement varies. It may be delayed in some cases, depending upon the general economic environment and the advertising media selected. It also depends upon the type of product.

Generally, quick response is obtained for FMCG goods and high time lag for consumer durable goods.

Thus, the difference in time lag of response for various commodities also makes the advertising elasticity of demand different for different goods.

(iii) **Influence of Advertising by Rivals :** The advertising elasticity of demand depends upon the effectiveness of advertising. The latter in turn, depends upon how the other competitors react to the advertising campaign of this firm.

The firm may resort to advertising to defend itself against the other competitors' efforts to promote the sales of their products.

5.9.0 Expectations Elasticity of Demand (or Elasticity of Price Expectations)

The demand for a commodity is affected not only by the Current price but also by the expected future price.

If a consumer believes that price of a particular commodity will rise in future, he will resort to buying more of it now.

Thus, the expectation of a higher price in future increases the demand for the commodity at present. The extent to which demand is affected by price expectation depends upon the elasticity of price expectation.

For example, if there is fear of war breaking out in near future, the price of gold will increase and people will start buying gold in anticipation of further price increase.

The elasticity of price expectation may be defined as the ratio of relative change in expected future price to the relative change in Current Price.

Elasticity of Price Expectation (E_{pe})

$$= \frac{\text{Relative (or percentage) change in expected future price}}{\text{Relative (or percentage) change in current price}}$$

$$= \frac{\frac{\Delta E_p}{E_p}}{\frac{\Delta C_p}{C_p}} = \frac{\Delta E_p}{\Delta C_p} \cdot \frac{C_p}{E_p}$$

where, E_p and C_p are expected and Current prices and ΔE_p and ΔC_p are changes in prices respectively.

The concept of elasticity of price expectations is of great significance in case of speculative trading such as stock market activities.

5.10.0 Demand Forecasting

Demand forecasting is an estimate of the future demand and it is based on the statistical data about past behaviour and relationship of the various determinants. As the future is uncertain, the forecasting of demand can not be accurate.

However, forecasting gives a reliable approximation of future demand.

Forecasts can be both physical and financial in nature, and are used for planning purposes.

Generally, business organisations are interested in both passive and active forecasts and often they predict sales revenues after taking into account changes in a host of policy variables such as prices of substitutes and complements, design, quality and advertising expenses etc.

5.10.1 Purposes of Demand Forecasting

The purposes of demand forecasting will depend on the periods for which it is made.

***(a)* Short-Term Demand Forecasting :** Short-term forecasts may be for seasonal production or short-term purchase policies.

Production of cold creams and glycerine soaps during winter season and production of umbrellas, rain coats and water proof rubber shoes fall in the short term demand forecasts.

***(b)* Long-Term Demand Forecasting :** Long-term demand forecasts are helpful in proper capital planning, *i.e.*, for installing manufacturing facilities and for expanding sales and marketing networks.

Long-term financial planning and man power planning for the future growth of business are dependent on accurate long-term demand forecasts.

Generally, long-term demand forecasts for a product of a company may be for a period of 3 to 5 years, but in certain cases it can even be for 10 years.

Long-term demand forecasting is thus useful in determining capital expenditure in planning raw material requirement, financial requirement and determining the size and scope of R & D Programme.

5.10.2 Types of Demand Forecasts

***(i)* Economic and Non-economic Forecasts :** Profitability and Return on Investment are economic forecasts whereas social, political forecasts are non-economic forecasts.

***(ii)* Micro and Macro Forecasts :** Micro forecasts are for the firm level whereas macro forecasts are for the industry level.

***(iii)* Active and Passive Forecasts :** Forecast results are put into planning in case of active fore casts and when they are not utilised they are passive forecasts.

***(iv)* Short-term and Long-term Forecasts :** These have been discussed before.

5.10.3 Methods of Demand Forecasting

Initially when some business managers attempted to forecast the demand for their products, they depended on their personal judgement and past-experience and made intelligent guesses about future demand and sale prospects for their products.

In course of time, however, specialist took over and used increasingly sophisticated statistical techniques and mathematical formulae to clarify demand relationships and arrive at accurate demand forecasting.

The following are some of the methods employed for demand forecasting.

***(a)* Survey of Buyers Intentions :** A direct method of demand fore-casting for a short period is to find out what consumers prefer and intend to buy.

For this, a company may undertake surveys of what buyer's plan to buy during a forthcoming period say a year.

The opinion survey can take the form of interview of the buyers.

The survey method is useful when the bulk of the sale is to a few industrial buyers.

***(b)* Collective Opinion Survey :** In this method, opinions of many top executives of companies connected with purchase or sale of the product are collected and compiled.

This method is based on first hand information of the consumers.

***(c)* Survey of Experts' Opinion :** A company may engage experts in the field of market research and demand forecasting to analyse the past and present economic conditions, undertake sample surveys of the market, carry out opinion polls and then forecast demand. Delphi Method used by Rand Corporation, USA uses opinions of a panel of experts not known to each other. A co-ordinator of the company collects individual opinions and combine them to arrive at a conclusion. The Delphi method is primarily used to forecast the demand for new products. Though it provides valuable insights, it is rather expensive as the experts may charge high fees for their opinions.

(d) **Market Experiments :** A company may conduct studies and experiments to find out the behaviour of consumers under actual or controlled market conditions.

In this method, a company may assess the important demand determinants like price, advertisements, expenditure, product design etc.

(e) **Trend Projections :** Every company has accumulated data on the sales of its products for the past many years. This firm arranges such sales data chronologically and then prepare time series relating to sales to represent the pattern of effective demand for a particular product.

The time series is used to prepare a trend line which is projected into the future.

Following two methods are used for trend projections :

(i) The method of moving averages

(ii) The method of least squares

Methods of Demand Forecasting

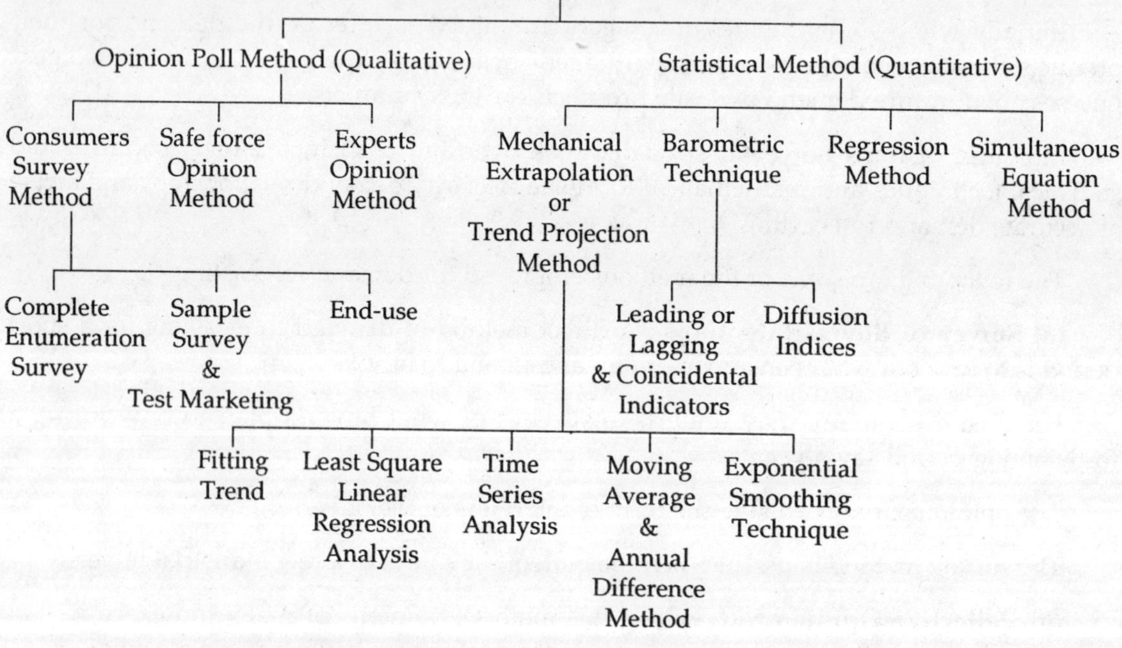

(i) The method of moving averages : It is a simple method involving calculations of moving averages for 3-4 years. period to find out the trend.

In this way, the firm calculates the moving averages or the trend of demand which is plotted on a graph with horizontal axis representing the years. From the graphical presentation, demand forecasting is projected through the extension of curve for the years ahead.

(ii) The method of least squares : It is more scientific than moving averages method and is most commonly used.

It uses the straight line equation $Y = a + bx$

where, Y = Demand for the product a & b are constants.

X = Determinant or the variable on which Y depends.

Say, Agricultural production/demand (Y) depends on quantity of rainfall (x) A straight line known as "the line of best fit is used and we try to minimise the sum of squares of deviations between the observed and fitted value of data.

(f) **Regression Analysis :** This method is based on demand forecasting on certain economic indicators such as

Personal disposable income
Demands for agricultural equipment
Demands for building materials

After collecting above information, one is concerned in establishing the relationship between the demand for a product and the particular economic indicator through the method of least squares and derives the regression equation.

The linear relationship is expressed by the equation.

$$Y = a + bx$$

where Y = Demand for the product

X = Economic indicator.

Once, the equation is derived, the value of Y is estimated for any value of x.

There are however two major limitations to regression analysis.

(i) It is not easy to locate an appropriate economic indicator for demand forecasting of a particular product.

(ii) The regression analysis is not applicable for a new product as no past sales data are available.

5.10.4 Determinants of Demand Forecast

Goods can be broadly classified into three categories.

(a) Capital Goods—Equipment, Machinery

(b) Durable Consumer Goods—Automobiles, TV Sets, Refrigerator.

(c) Consumer Goods (non-durable)—Soft drinks, Cigarettes, Biscuits.

A. Demand Forecasting for Capital Goods

Demand for capital goods are of two kinds :

(a) Replacement Demand

(b) New Demand

Demand forecasting for capital goods has to consider the following factors.

(i) Extent of excess capacity in the industry using the capital goods.

(ii) Forecast of demand for the commodity which the capital good is capable of producing.

(iii) Existing inventory of capital good.

(iv) Age distribution of existing stock.

(v) The rate of obsolescence.

(vi) The availability of funds and cost of funds to a firm planning for capital goods.

(vii) The nature of tax/duties applicable on re-equipment.

(viii) The prices of substitutes and complementary goods.

(ix) The market structure within which the capital goods operate.

After collecting the above information, a firm can take the help of regression analysis to forecast the demand for capital goods in question.

B. Demand Forecasting for Consumer-durable Goods

Demands for consumer durable goods are of 2 kinds.

(a) Replacement demand

(b) New demand

Demand forecasting for consumer-durable goods has to consider the following factors.

(i) Changes in size and characteristics of population

(ii) Saturation limit of the market

(iii) Existing stock and age distribution

(iv) Replacement demand Vs New demand

(v) Income levels of Consumers

(vi) Consumer Credit outstanding

(vii) Tastes and preferences of Consumers

(viii) Advertising efforts.

After collecting above information, a firm can resort to the Survey of Consumer plan and then the data can be fed into a regression model to forecast the demand for the Consumer durable goods, Econometric model consisting of a mathematical equations of independent and dependent variables is used for demand forecast for consumer durable goods.

C. Demand Forecasting for Consumer Goods

These include those items which can be used only once, *e.g.*, Soft drink, Cigarettes, Confectionery etc.

Demand for Consumer goods is basically influenced by the following factors :

Population and its characteristics (i.e. culture, habits) Income level, purchasing power or disposable income, price of goods, Advertising efforts.

Size and characteristics of population for consumer goods demand are very important and it is commonly known as demography, and refers to the total population, income groups, social status, age and sex imposition, urban rural ratio, geographical characteristics, level of education etc.

Demand for consumer goods is influenced by all the above factors.

With the help of demographic variables, demand for each market segment can be estimated as distinct from the total market demand.

5.11.0 Demand Forecast—Industry Examples

The estimated demand for a product determines the maximum amount of its output. Every business firm needs to make a forecast of sales before deciding the quantity to be produced.

A proper demand or sales forecast helps in preparing appropriate production schedules so as to avoid overstocking and delays in meeting demand.

In the long-run, demand forecasts facilitate capacity planning.

Before introducing a new product in the market, it is always desirable to first forecast its demand.

For example, Hindustan Unilever Ltd. made extensive demand forecast, before introducing any of their consumer product such as Close Up Toothpaste and Lux or Life Buoy toilet soaps.

Forecasting demand for new products is important for two reasons. First, when a businessman wants to introduce new products for diversification and growth, he needs an estimate of likely demand. Secondly, every product has a life span and a firm has to go in for new products when old products decay and die out.

5.11.1 Demand Interrelationships

The demand for some products is interrelated positively or negatively. Positively, demand for one product (say, socks) increases with increase in the demand for another product (say, shoes). Such products are known as complementary products. Examples of these products are also pen and ink.

On the other hand, in case of substitute products increase in the demand for one product results in a fall in the demand for another product, *e.g.* Cigarette and Biri, or Biri and Tobacco.

Demand interrelationships are influenced by random and seasonal fluctuations in demand.

Some products face seasonal fluctuations in demand. For example, ice cream, fans, coolers etc. are much more in demand during summer than in winter.

In the off-season months, the plant and equipment remain partly unutilised.

In order to avoid this wastage of resources, a firm may undertake production of other products which have peak demand in different seasons.

For example, a fan manufacturer may during the winter undertake production and sale of room heaters.

This will provide cost effectiveness in production.

Thus, a combination (mix) of products can be designed to minimise costs associated with idle resources.

Also, there may be interrelationships between products from the supply side. Some firms combine production of two or more products which use the same basic raw-materials.

For example, many Vanaspati manufacturers produce washing soaps to make profitable use of left over waste of Vanaspati.

Similarly, a Sugar Mill may add another product to make use of molasses.

5.12.0 Revenue Analysis, Total Revenue, Marginal Revenue, Average Revenue

Revenue Analysis :

Revenue is the money a seller receives by selling a product provide to a customer.

Total Revenue (TR) is the amount money a seller receives from a customer by selling a Product quantity (Q) at Price (P).

Therefore TR = P.Q.

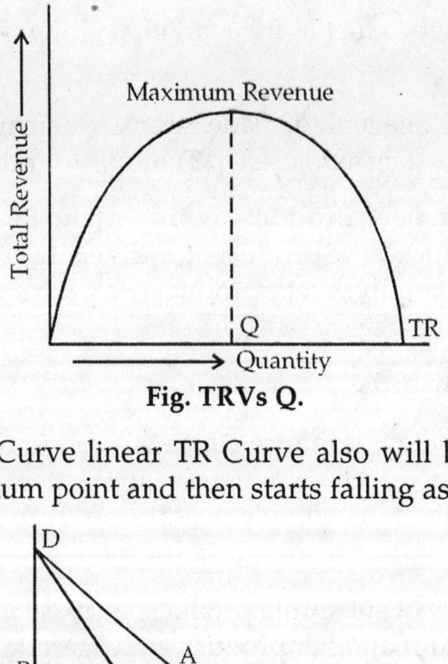

Fig. TRVs Q.

For a market Demand Curve linear TR Curve also will be linear and initially slopes upwards, reaches the maximum point and then starts falling as shown in above figure.

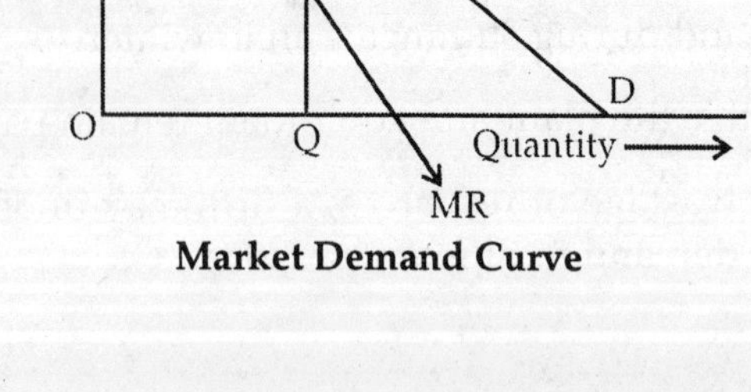

Market Demand Curve

For a Price P on Market Demand Curve and Quantity Q, total revenue TR = Area of rectangle OPAQ.

Marginal Revenue (MR)

Marginal Revenue is the change in total revenue resulting from selling an additional unit of the product.

Marginal Revenue is the slope of the total revenue curve at any level of quantity.

In order to sell an additional quantity of product its price must fall, and the Marginal revenue will be equal to the price of extra unit (P_{n+1}) minus the loss from selling all previous units at the new lower price.

On the above Market Demand Curve, MR Curve is drawn as above.

Extend the mid point of AP by joining with D till it touches the X axis quantity line.

MR Curve has the negative slope like Demand Curve and is also a straight line like Demand Curve (DC).

Relation between Total Revenue (TR), Marginal Revenue (MR) and Price Elasticity of Demand (e).

(i) For demand is elastic, $e > 1$, TR Curve has a positive slope and an increase in price will result in decrease in TR while a decrease in price will result in an increase in TR.

(ii) For demand is inelastic, $e < 1$, an increase in price leads to an increase in TR and a decrease in price leads to a decrease in TR.

(iii) For demand has price elasticity $e = 1$, TR is not affected by an change in price and $MR = 0$.

(iv) $MR = P\left(1 - \frac{1}{e}\right)$.

Usefulness of Elasticity of Demand Concept in Business.

The concept of elasticity of demand is useful for the business in the following ways :

(a) Elasticity measures help the management in fixing the prices of goods.

(b) The concept is also important for a multi-product unit for fixing the production target, for various goods by estimating likely demands and income elasticity in a market segment.

(c) The price elasticity of demand as well as cross elasticity would determine the substitution between goods and hence are useful in fixing the output mix for production plan.

The Law of Supply

Supply of a commodity refers to the various quantities of the commodity which a seller is willing and able to sell at different prices in a given market, at a point of time, other things remaining the same.

Since higher money income is necessary to induce producers to produce more, the amount supplied therefore increases when producers get a higher price for their product, other things being equal.

The quantity supplied depends on cost of production, producers' objectives, state of technology and prices of other goods in a market.

However, the law of supply takes into account only the most important determinant of supply, *i.e.* price of the commodity.

Therefore, the law of supply states that "other things remaining constant more of a commodity is supplied at a higher price and less of it is supplied at a lower price.

The supply schedule when represented graphically is known as the supply curve as shown in the following diagram.

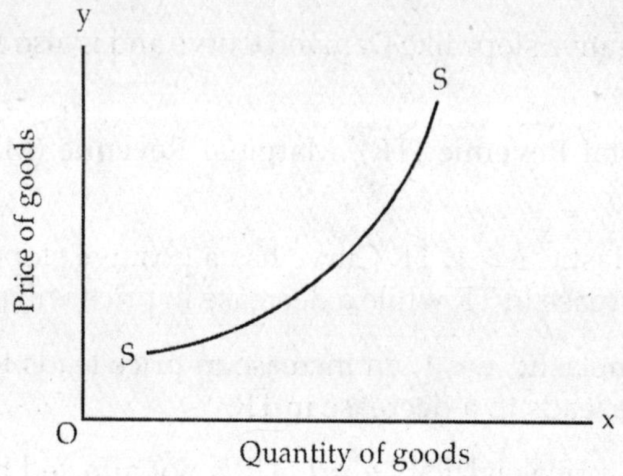

The supply curve shows the maximum amount of the goods which the firm would be willing to sell at each possible price of the goods, under given conditions of supply.

Elasticity of Supply

Elasticity of supply of a commodity is defined as the responsiveness of quantity supplied to a unit change in price of that commodity

Elastic

When the quantity supplied change more than proportionately to the change in price, the supply to be elastic.

Inelastic

If the change in price leads to less than proportionate change in quantity supplied, the supply tends to be inelastic.

For example, if 1 percent change in the price of sugar leads to 5 percent change in its quantity supplied, the supply of sugar is said to be elastic.

On the other hand, if 1 percent change in the price of common salt leads to 0.5 percent change in its quantity supplied, the common salt supply is said to be inelastic.

Kinds of Supply Elasticity

The two limiting cases of supply elasticity are

(*i*) Elasticity of supply equal to infinity and

(*ii*) Absolutely inelastic supply or zero supply

Another way of stating the range of supply elasticity is that elasticity of supply can be greater than, equal to, or less than unity.

The different kinds of supply elasticities are given in the following table :

When elasticity of supply is	*It is called*
(*i*) Equal to infinity	Perfectly Elastic
(*ii*) More than 1 but not infinity	Relatively Elastic
(*iii*) Equal to 1	Unitary Elastic
(*iv*) Less than 1 but not zero	Relatively inelastic
(*v*) Equal to Zero	Perfectly inelastic

S_1S_1 is the infinitely elastic or perfectly elastic supply curve as shown in the graph, S_2S_2 is the case of zero elasticity or perfectly inelastic supply curve as shown in the graph. The quantity

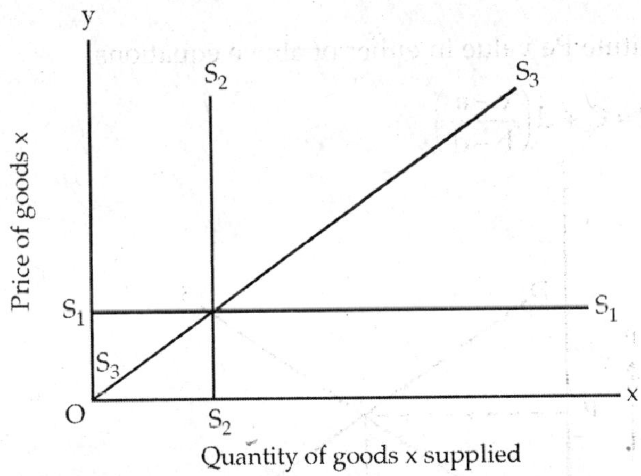

supplied does not change when prices change. S_3S_3 is the curve showing the case of unitary elastic, *i.e.*, when the quantity supplied changes in the same proportion as the change in price. Here the supply curve has unit elasticity.

E_s is the elasticity of supply (*i.e.* a measure) is given as—

$$E_s = \frac{\text{Relative change inquantity supplied of the commodity}}{\text{Relative change in the price of commodity}}$$

$$= \frac{4Q}{Q} \div \frac{4P}{P} = \frac{4Q}{Q} \times \frac{P}{4P} = \frac{4Q}{4P} \times \frac{P}{Q}$$

where, E_s = Elasticity of supply of the goods

Q = Original quantity supplied of the goods

ΔQ = change in quantity supplied of the goods

P = Original Price of commodity

ΔP = Change in Price

When the supply curve is a curved line, its elasticity at any point can be measured by drawing a tangent to the supply curve at that point.

2.4 *(a)* Demand and Supply Curves

Demand curve
$Qd = a + bP$ P = Price, a = constant, $b < 0$ (–)ve

Supply Curve
$Qs = C + dP$ P = Price, C = constant, $d > 0$ (+)ve

At equilibrium
$Qd = Qs = Qe$ $\therefore a + bP = C + dP$
Qe = Quantity at equilibrium or $P(b - d) = (c - a)$

P_e = Price at equilibrium $\therefore P_e = \dfrac{c-a}{b-d}$

To find Qe, Substitute Pe value in either of above equations

$$Qs = Qe = C + dP = C + d\left(\frac{c-a}{b-d}\right)$$

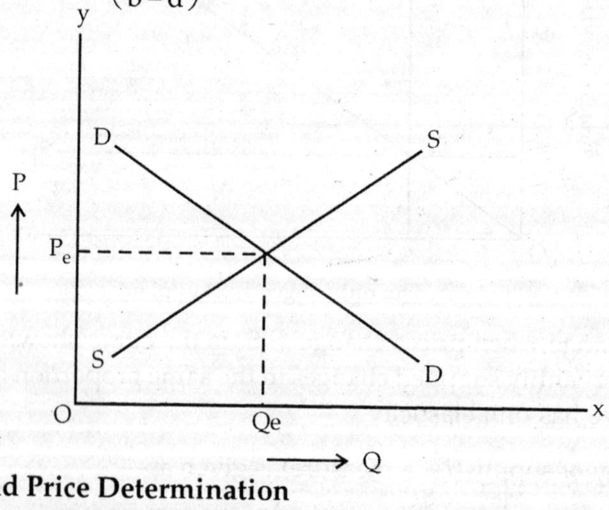

2.4.0 Equilibrium and Price Determination

Static and Dynamic Equilibrium

The quantity demanded of a goods increases when its price decreases and when the price of the goods increases its quantity demanded decreases. It we draw this phenomena in the following graph; The figure becomes as follows :

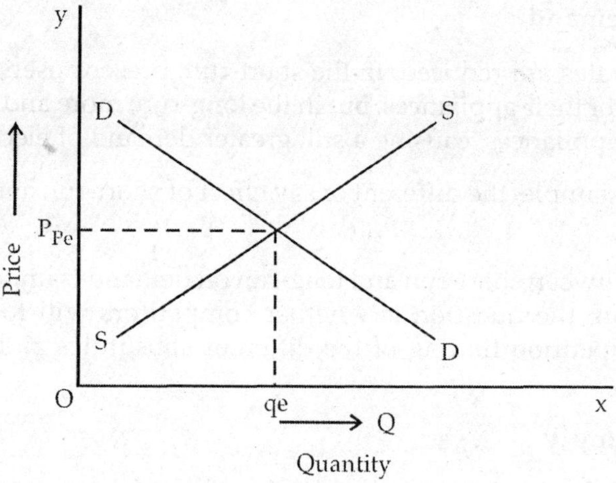

DD and SS are demand and supply lines respectively. The point of intersection of DD and SS lines at E gives the equilibrium price pe and the quantity exchanged at the equilibrium price is qe.

Thus the demand supply cross, in the simple market model provides the equilibrium price and sales.

Equilibrium in the above market model has been established at the point where supply equals demand.

***(i)* Static Equilibrium :** Static concerns itself with the simultaneous and instantaneous or timeless determination of economic variables by mutually interdependent relations.

In the example discussed above, we have utilised the concept of static equilibrium or static state. Here the equilibrium price is that at which demand equals supply. This approach to equilibrium is called static.

In static equilibrium, the values of endogenous variables instantaneously derive from the exogenously given data. Thus in our market model the height and shape of the DD and SS curves reflect the exogenous influences. From these curve, the equilibrium price and sales are instantaneously derived.

***(ii)* Dynamic State :** When time entire the situation, it is called dynamic.

When exogenous variables change over time, each time period will exhibit a unique static equilibrium. By stringing together these static equilibria over time, we can create a picture of the equilibrium growth path of endogenous variables corresponding to the growth path of exogenous variables.

Thus we can study growth through the comparative static method, this is the simplest type or dynamic state.

2.4 *(b)* Effect of Time on Demand

Effect of time on supply

Effect of time on price

Effect of Time on Demand

If the electricity rates are reduced, in the short-run, present users of electric appliances will make greater use of their appliances, but in the long-run; more and more people might be induced to use these appliances, causing a still greater demand of electricity.

From the above example, the different or say effect of short-run and long-run on demand is quite clear.

The distinction between short-run and long-run on demand is important in a competitive situation. In short-run, the question is whether competitors will follow suit, whereas in long-run, due to competition finding of the different substitutes and other complex effect may follow.

Effect of Time on Supply

The supply curve for market period will be vertical, *i.e.*, supply remain fixed whatever the price. The market period supply curve is not applicable in all cases.

It is particularly important in the case of perishable goods which are difficult or say impossible to store and the demand for which is subject to short-run fluctuations.

For example, in place, the supply of ice in summer on any given morning is fixed. A sudden shift in the demand due to unexpected hot day can not influence the supply of ice on that particular day.

In case of short-run period the supply curve would be sloping line, moving upward from left to right there by indicating that with price increase supply also increases.

In long, period, supply curve will tend to have a flatter slope than the short period supply curve indicating that with a price increase the supply tend to be larger than in the short-run period.

Effect on Time on Price

Now let us see that how price can be found out in different time period, given a change in demand.

In the market period, and upward shift (towards right) in the demand curve would result in an immediate rise in price as there will be no increase in supply.

But under short-run period of the production is more causing a fall in price due to increased output.

Further under long-run period, with more machines installed, the output would increase still further and thus the price would further drop.

On the other hand, a downward shift (towards left side) in demand curve would not immediately affect the quantity supplied but the price would drop sharply, followed by some recovery as reduced output in the short period.

In the long period firm would see more profitable use for their plants as they would be able to replace the worn out machines. This will reduce output still further and permits some recovery in price.

The following figure shows the demand of a commodity where SS, S_1S_1, S_2S_2 represent the market period, short-run period and long run period supply curve. Suppose the demand for the commodity in the market shifts to D_1D_1, Now, immediately, supply of commodity can not be increased and hence market or momentary equilibrium is established at price OP_1.

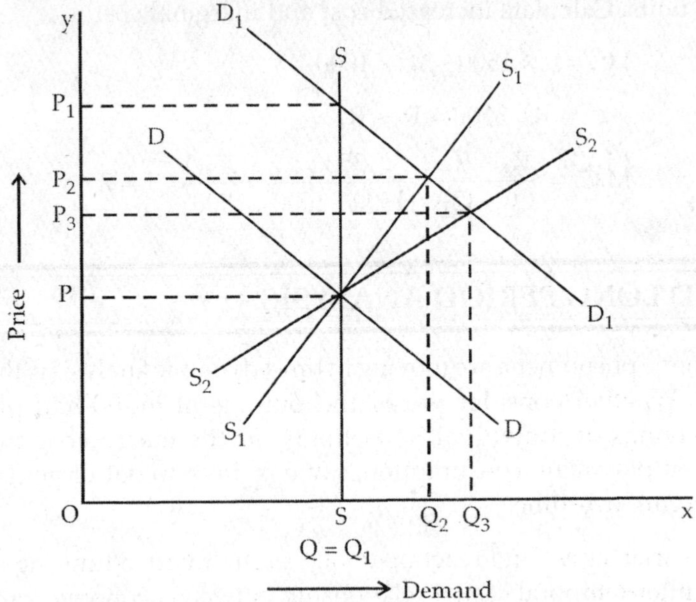

Fig. Effect on Time on Price.

In the short-run, the supply of commodity can be increased by using more intensively the existing equipment for longer hours. As a result the price drops to OP_2.

In the case of long run, supply can be fully adjusted to meet the changed demand conditions. Now firm would come for additional manufacture with additional equipment. Thus supply increases further, and the price is still lower OP_3.

***(i)* Marginal Pricing :** Let us define some related terms. An average cost means total amount received from sales divided by the number of units sold

i.e., $$\text{A.C.} = \frac{\text{T.C.}}{Q}$$

Total cost means total amount received. It can be obtained by multiplying number of units with price *i.e.* T.R = Q × P.

***(ii)* Increment Cost :** This is the additional cost earned by selling an additional (marginal) unit of production.

This means that it is the total cost when one more or less unit is sold.

In actual practice, it is rare that output increased by one unit. The extra cost earned on additional output which is due to additional input can be determined by finding out the change in total cost as result of this output.

Thus, $$\text{M.C.} = \frac{R_2 - R_1}{Q_2 - Q_1}$$

. R_1, R_2 are total cost before and after Price Q_1, and Q_2 is the quantity before and after.

Example

Suppose the price of a product is reduced from Rs. 10 to Rs. 9 due to this, sale increases from 1000 to 1500 units. Calculate increased cost and marginal cost.

Solution : I.C. = 9 × 1500 – 10 × 1000

= Rs. 3500 = $R_2 - R_1$

$$\text{M.C.} = \frac{R_2 - R_1}{Q_2 - Q_1} = \frac{3500}{1500 - 1000} = \frac{3500}{500} = \text{Rs. } 7.$$

2.5 SHORT AND LONG PERIOD ANALYSIS

Since all economic phenomena are moving in time, dynamic analysis is the realistic method of studying them. Whether consider prices and outputs of individual produced, income, consumption or savings of individual households, or the macro economic variables like aggregate income employment, consumption, savings, investment or general price level, all variably keep changing overtime.

Most of these variables act and react upon one another with a time lag and this bring out the importance of inter-temporal casual relationship between economic variables.

A dynamic theory shows in the course or time a condition of economic system has grown out of its condition in the previous period of time. It is the form of analysis which has central importance for the study of the process of economic development be the short-run or long-run processes.

Most of the discussion pertaining to price determination in carried out in a static framework. However, Marshal has considered the important of time element in determining the equilibrium of firm and industries in his analysis. He has discussed how the supply of a commodity changes in the short-run and long-run when a change in its demand takes place and a new equilibrium position is established. In other words, Marshal takes into account the processes of change. Thus his discussion on the time element in the theory of price determination contained in his opinion open principally of Economics falls in the domain of dynamic analysis.

2.6 STATIC AND DYNAMIC STATES

A system is dynamic if its behaviour over time is determined by functional equation in which variables at different points of time are involved in an essential way.

It is clear from the above definitions that time plays an important role in a dynamic system. This is due to the reason that the values of economic variables in such a system depend partly on their values at past moments of time. Therefore, dynamic analysis traces the time path of economic variables and involves variables and their lagged values.

Another important point is that the variables at different points of time must enter into the problem in an essential way.

As per Samuelson, if one year the crop is high, because of favourable weather, the next year low and so forth, the system will be static even though until stationary.

On the other hand, a truly dynamical system may be completely casual, in the sense that its behaviour depends only upon the initial conditions and the time which has elasped. The calender date not entering into the process.

From the above discussion it can be concluded that statical system can be converted into a dynamic system by simply dating the various variables.

However, it should be remembered that, for a system to become dynamic, the variables should have different dates attached to them.

CASE STUDIES

Theory of Demand—Elasticity of Demand

A Case Study : How does theory of demand apply to the Airlines fares for domestic destinations?

Ans : The globalisation and liberalisation have increased competition among domestic Airlines, like Indian Airlines, Jet Airways and Sahara, Air Deccan—including King Fisher Air line.

Since the demand for air travel is elastic, lower fares will surely increase total revenue. Somehow if the fares are kept proximity to AC-2 Tier or Ist Class Railway fares especially for Metro to Metro or Metro to large industrial towns/tourist spots, many middle class families/ persons would prefer to travel by air lines in order to save time.

Now-a-days, unsafe conditions in railway journeys will also prompt middle class people to take to airlines travels provided the air fares are matched close to those of AC-2 tier or Ist class railway fares.

When the airlines are flying with many empty seats, the additional costs of carrying extra passengers is very little.

So, revenue increases faster than costs and so also profits rise.

Case Study - 2

Let us say, Sahara Airlines is capable of carrying 10,000 passengers per month on a particular route at a fixed cost of Rs.3.00 Lac.

The variable cost per passenger is Rs. 10 and the fare is Rs. 50 per trip.

If presently, it is able to carry 8000 passengers, *i.e.* 20% of its capacity is idle.

At present, its total earning is

Rs. 50 × 8,000 = Rs 4.00 Lac.

Its total cost = Rs. 3.00 Lac + Rs. 10 × 8,000

= 3.80 Lac

So, its profit = Rs. 4.00 Lac – 3.80 Lac

= Rs. 20,000.

Now, suppose it reduced its fare to Rs 45. As a result it is able to carry all 10,000 passengers and thus fly to full capacity.

Now, its total revenue = Rs. 45 × 10,000 = Rs. 4.50 Lac

and total cost = Rs. 3.00 Lac + Rs. 10 × 10,000 = Rs. 4.00 Lac

So, its profit will be Rs. 50,000, which amount is 250% than previous profit.

Case Study - 3

Elasticity of demand and following case examples :

Automation

The effect of the use of machinery or employment largely depends on the elasticity of demand for the commodity produced by the firm.

Suppose, a firm introduce a labour saving automation process which makes 100 workers redundant.

However, a part of cost reduction due to impact of automation is passed on to the consumers in the form of lower price of the product.

If the demand for the product is elastic, a small price cut will lead to more than proportionate increase in demand.

As result, output many increase to such an extent that 100 unemployment workers are reabsorbed by the firm.

However, if the demand is inelastic, only very few workers may be re-employed, because, the increase in the volume of firms business will be small.

Case Study - 4

Trade union's wage bargaining

The capacity of trade union to raise wages depends on the elasticity of demand for the product in which labour is employed as a major output.

If wages are permitted to rise, cost and price will also rise.

If the demand for the product is inelastic, the entire rise in cost in passed on to the consumers.

Since the demand is inelastic, sales will not fall due to rise in price, and thus a wage rise is economically feasible in the food industries, where most of the food item such as potato, cereals and agricultural commodities are highly demand inelastic.

In case, of bumper crops due to good monsoon. The supply is more and prices of most of the agricultural commodities become lower.

Due to the nature of demand inelasticity, there is sharp fall in the revenue of farmers.

Therefore, the government has to come to help the farmers by declaring the protection price or its should start purchasing directly from the farmers in order the keep the price stable.

Case Study - 5

Demand Elasticity and the Manufacturer—Pricing policy

It is necessary for a manufacturer to know something about elasticity of demand for his product.

If the manufacturer is considering an increase in output, he knows that in order to sell the increased output he must reduce the price.

But, if the demand is inelastic, the quantity demanded will not rise much.

So, he will find that his total revenue from the sale will fall.

If will be better for him to leave and think as they originally are.

A profit maximising firm will never choose to lower its price in the elastic range of its demand curve, as such a price decrease would decrease total revenue and at the same time increase costs, since output would be rising.

The result would be a dramatic decrease in profits.

This explains, *why a monopolist who is a price maker never operates on the inelastic part of his demand or average revenue curve.*

If, demand is highly elastic, a reduction in price many cause total revenue to rise on the elastic part of the demand or average revenue curve.

In this case, he may decide to increase his output and then it will be profitable.

A manger can make use of the concept of price elasticity of demand for the following questions :

(i) What will be the impact on sales of a 5% increase in price?

(ii) How large a price reduction is necessary to increase sales by 10%.

(iii) Given marginal cost and price elasticity, information, what is the profit maximising price?

Q. 1. Give a very clear concept of demand curve.

Ans. Law of demand states that everything else remaining constant, quantity demanded and price are inversely proportional.

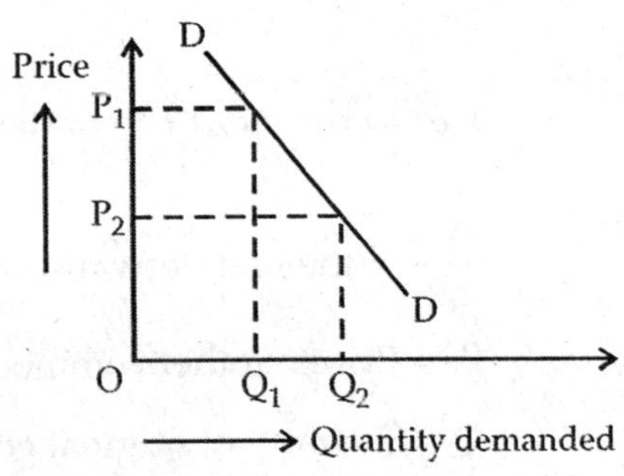

In other words, when quantity demanded is lower (at Q_1 in graph), price is higher at P_1 and when, quantity demanded is higher at Q_2 (in graph) price is P_2.

Due to the law of demand condition, demand curve has negative slope and it slopes downward right.

Q. 2. Give exception to the law of demand.

Ans. The law of demand holds good for all normal goods but in case of inferior goods for whose positive income effect is stronger than negative substitute effect to give combined effect as positive effect so that the law of demand is violated, such goods are Giffen goods. Potatoes and coarse cereals are exception to the law of demand and are Giffen goods.

Q. 3. What do you mean by related goods?

Ans. Related goods are either substitutes or complement Tea and Coffee, Coca-Cola and pepsicola are substitute commodities for whose cross price elasticity of demand is positive *i.e.* any change in quantity demanded and change in price will move in the same direction. Complements are these goods for whose cross price elasticities are negative.

Complements are those goods for whose cross price elasticity is negative. Car and petrol, pen and ink are complementary goods for whose cross prise elasticity is negative. If price of petrol increases, car demand reduces.

Q. 4. Give the concept of normal and inferior goods.

Ans. The law of demand holds good for all normal goods, *i.e.*, quantity demanded and price are inversely proportional everything else remaining same. Example—Ball pens, tariffs of phone calls and TV sets etc. hold the law of demand. For these commodities, quantity demanded have increased manifold since last decade and price have also come down drastically.

Inferior goods are those goods for whose positive income effect is of a lower magnitude than the negative substitution effect, the law of demand still holds good.

Most of the agricultural commodities are in the category of inferior goods.

Q. 5. Give three different measures of price elasticity of demand.

Ans. $e_d = \dfrac{\text{Percentage change in the quantity demanded}}{\text{Percentage change in the demand determinants}}$

Thus e_p = price elasticity of demand = $\dfrac{P\ 4Q}{Q\ \Delta P}$

and e_y = income elasticity of demand = $\dfrac{Y\ 4Q}{Q\ \Delta Y}$

and e_c = cross elasticity of demand = $\dfrac{\Delta Q\ P_0}{\Delta P_0\ Q}$

$\dfrac{\Delta Q}{\Delta P_0}$ = the first derivative of the demand equation w.r.t. price

P_0 = Price of other commodity

Q = Quantity of original commodity

The coefficient of cross elasticity can be zero, positive or negative. It is zero, in case of unrelated goods like tractors and motor cars. It is positive if the two commodities are substitutes. And it is negative if the two goods are complementary.

PROBABLE QUESTIONS

1. Define price elasticity of demand and distinguish its various types.

   Discuss the role of price elasticity of demand in managerial decisions.
2. What is price elasticity of demand? How is it measured? What is its significance in business?
3. How are the price elasticity, cross elasticity and advertising elasticity of demand measured?
4. Explain the concept of income elasticity of demand and explain its role in business decisions.
5. What is the cross elasticity of demand? Is it positive for the substitutes?
6. Define elasticity of price expectations? Does the concept provide any useful information to Management?
7. What are determinants of demand forecast for various goods?

   Discuss about various factors to be considered for demand forecasting of capital goods, consumer durable goods and consumers goods.
8. What is the importance of demand forecasting?

   What methods would you use for forecasting demand for *(a)* Soft drinks and *(b)* Colour TV Sets and *(c)* Two-wheeler automobiles for a metro city in India.
9. Discuss about the important factors you would consider for forecasting the demand for *(a)* Cars, *(b)* Cement, *(c)* Detergent powder, *(d)* Refrigerator, *(e)* Readymade garments for a metro city in India.
10. Given the demand function $Q = 10 - 2P$

    (a) Prepare a demand schedule and draw the demand curve

    (b) Derive the total and marginal revenue schedules.

    (c) Calculate the elasticity of demand for the decrease in price from Rs. 3 to Rs. 2.

CHAPTER 3

PRODUCTION FUNCTION

- Economic Region & Optimum Factor Combination
- Expansion Path
- Ridgelines
- Production Function
- Isoquant/ISO Cost
- LSOM
- MRTS
- Leontief Production Function (Fixed Proportion Production Function)
- Law of Variable Proportion (Law of Diminishing Return)
- Returns to Scale (Increasing, Constant & Decreasing)
- Economies of Scale & Diseconomies of Scale (Internal & External)

The production function is a purely technical relation which connects factor inputs and outputs. It described the lower of proportions, that is, the transformation of factor inputs into products (outputs) at any particular time period.

The Production function represents the technology of a firm of an industry, or of the economy as a whole. The production function includes all the technically efficient methods of production.

A method of production (process, activity) is a combination of factor inputs required for the production of one unit of output. Usually a commodity may be produced by various methods of production.

For example, a unit of commodity x may be produced by the following process :

	Process P_1	Process P_2	Process P_3
Labour Units	2	3	1
Capital Units	3	2	4

Activities may be presented graphically as follows :

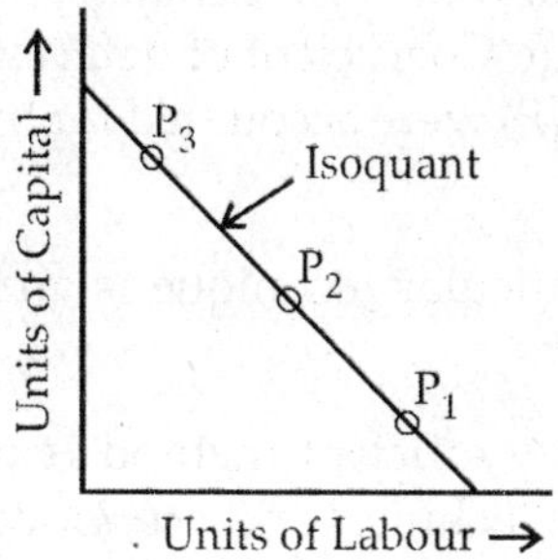

Linear of Isoquant

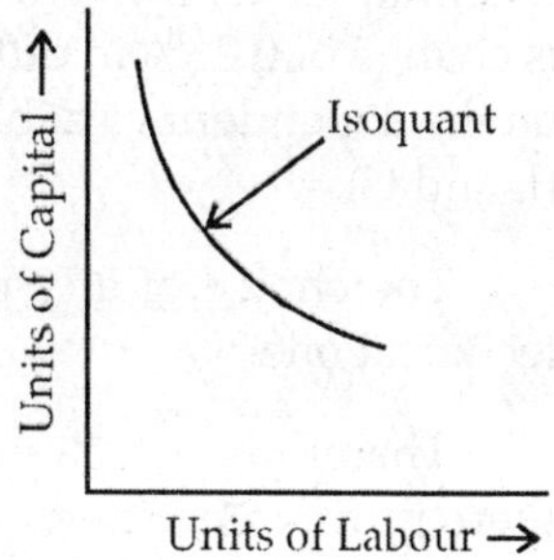

Convex Isoquant

Labour

Along the Isoquant Curve, same quantity of output with varying combinations of Labour & capital.

If a process uses less of some factor and more of some other factor, compared to other process, then these two processes can be directly compared on the criterion of technical efficiency.

The type of process to be chosen for production depends upon the prices of factors. The Theory of Production describes the laws of Production.

Higher is the economic efficiency, greater can be the profitability of the mfg. unit.

The efficiency of production also depends upon long term changes like *(a)* technical progress or improvements in technology, *(b)* economics of large scale production and *(c)* capital labour substitution or the degree of mechanization.

The basic analytical device for analysing all the above ingredients of economic efficiency is the concept of production function which, is the systematic relationship between inputs and outputs.

Production function along with the related analytic concept of isoquant is used to find the least cost (most efficient) combination of inputs.

The study of the production function is concerned with establishing the maximum output from a given set of inputs and with a given state of technology.

The Production function can be stated in the general form of an equation.

$$Y = f(x_1, x_2, \text{etc.})$$

where Y = the units of output, a function of two or more inputs, say labour and capital x_1 = Units of labour and x_2 = Units of capital.

The method of estimating the production function is the method of least square. A popular production function derived by Mr. Cobb and Mr. Douglas **(Cobb—Douglas method)** is as follows.

$P = BL^aC^{1-a}$ P = Total output,

L = Index labour employment in mfg. unit.

C = Index of fixed capital in mfg. unit, a and 1 – a an elasticities of production in percentages.

Typically in a place, this eqn. becomes

$$P = 1.01\ L^{0.75}c^{0.26}R_2^{0.94}$$

This shows that by 1% change in labour input (L) is associated by 0.75% change in output when capital *(c)* is fixed. Likewise, by 1% change in capital *(c)* when labour (L) is constant there is change of 0.26% in output. Coefficient of determination R_2 shows that 94% of the variations on the dependent variable (P) were accounted for by the variations in the independent variable (L and C).

The choice of any particular technique is an economic one, based on prices, and not a technical one.

Therefore, a technically efficient method is not necessarily economically efficient, and there is difference between technical and economic efficiency.

(i) Isoquant

This includes all the technically efficient methods for producing a given level of output. The production Isoquant may assume various shapes depending on the degree of substitutability of factors.

The simplest production function relates one output to two inputs as shown in figure. The alternative methods of different combinations of two factors of production that can yield the same output and the resulting curve is called an isoquant. It shows that a given quantity of output can be produced with the varying proportion of labour and capital.

(a) **Isoquant :** This type assumes perfect substitutability of factors of production, a given commodity may be produced by using only capital, or only labour, or by an infinite combination of Labour and Capital.

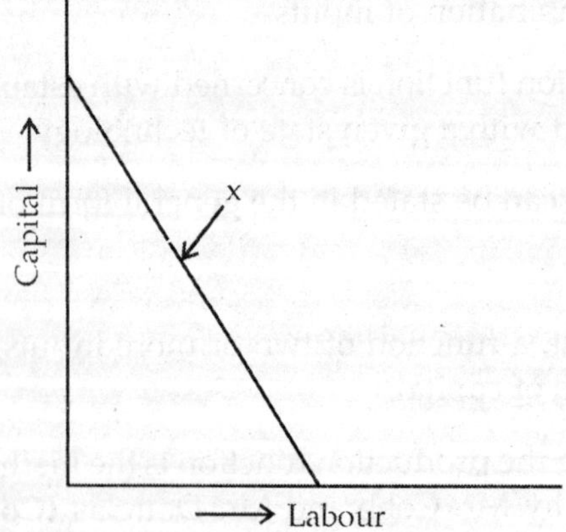

Definition of Isoquant

Various alternative methods using different combinations of two factors of production that can yield same output are represented in a curve known as "Isoquant". All points on the curve represent the same quantity of output.

So, Isoquant represents all the combinations of the two factors of Production that yield the same output.

The slope of Isoquant curve shows the rate at which capital can be substituted for labour and vice versa, while the output quantity is unchanged.

The rate is called *MARGINAL RATE OF TECHNICAL SUBSTITUTION (MRTS).*

***(a)* Isoquants :** Isoquants are a geometric representation of the production function. The same level of output can be produced by various combinations of factor inputs.

The Curve which is the locus of all possible combination is called Isoquant or Iso-product Curve.

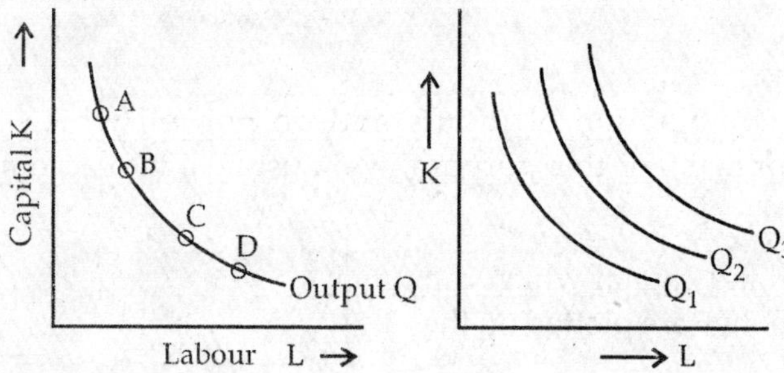

various quantities of output Q_1, Q_2, Q_3

A, B, C, D
represent various
combinations of K & L
to give same output = Q

***(b)* MRTS :** Marginal Rate of Technical Substitution MRTS is defined as the rate at which two factors (K & L) are substituted for each other.

Say 10 pairs of shoes can be produced in following ways.

Q	K	L
10	8	2
10	4	4
10	2	8

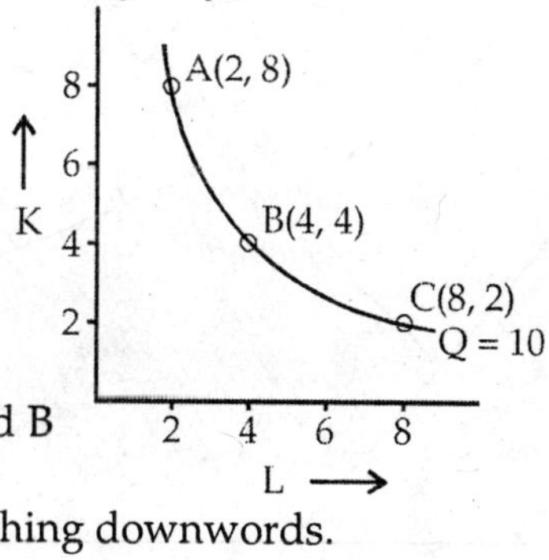

MRTS of labour for capital bet. Points A and B

$= -\left[\frac{\Delta K}{\Delta L}\right] = \frac{4}{2} = -2$ (–)ve, since it is diminishing downwords.

MRTS bet. B & C $= -\left[\frac{\Delta K}{\Delta L}\right] = \frac{2-4}{8-4} = -\frac{2}{4} = -\frac{1}{2}$

MRTS has decreased because capital and labour are perfect substitutes for each other.

(ii) Isoquant & MRTS

The Slope of Isoquant Curve

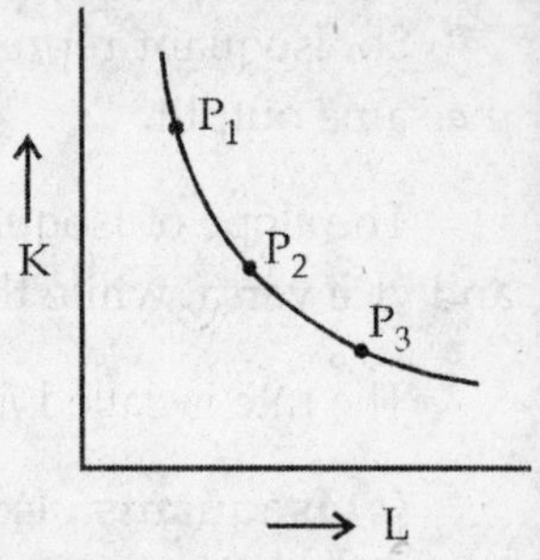

P_1, P_2, P_3 are processes (or methods) using various combinations of capital and labour to result in same quantity of output.

The slope of the isoquant curve shows the rate at which capital can be substituted for labour and *vice-versa*, keeping the level of output unchanged.

This rate is called Marginal rate of technical substitution (MRTS).

The point at which this rate is equal to ratio between the prices of inputs represents the optimum combination of inputs.

(iii) Isocost Curves

Isoquants deal with physical combination of inputs and do not tell which input combinations are most efficient or optimal. For this purpose, we must take into account the input prices.

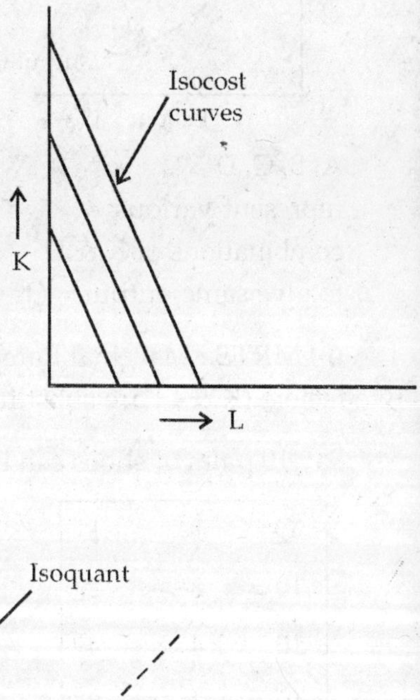

The various quantities of labour and capital which can be obtained from a given amount of money are plotted on the chart, showing Isocost Curves.

An iso cost line shows all combinations of Inputs that can be employed for a given cost. Isocost lines are parallel, *i.e.*, slope of each line $-\frac{PL}{PK}$ since that represent the rate at which input L can be substituted by input K while output is unchanged.

(iv) Isoquant

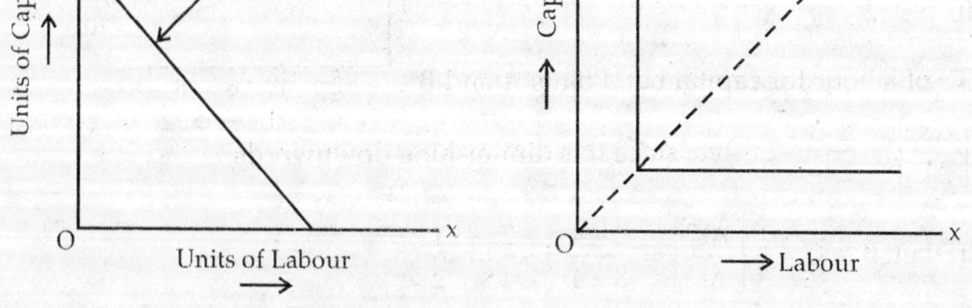

(a) **Linear Isoquant** *(b)* **Input-output Isoquant**

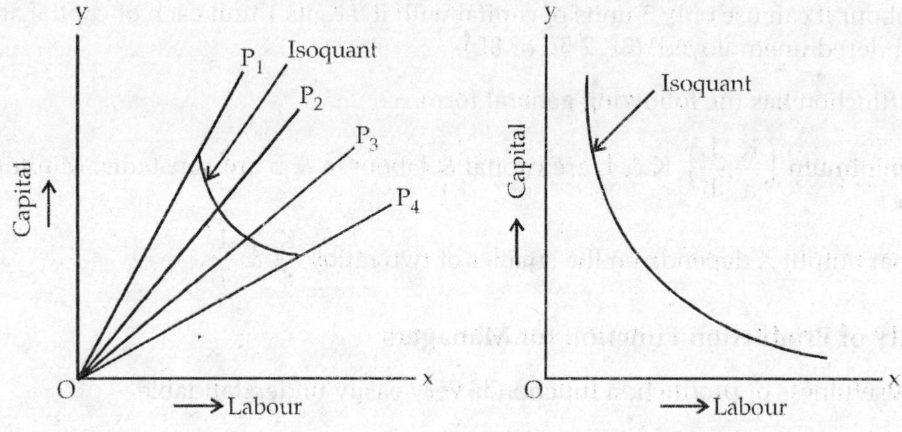

(c) **Linear Programming Isoquant** (d) **Convex Isoquant**

TYPES OF ISOQUANT

(v) LSOM—Leontief Static Open Model

(a) Input-Output Isoquant

(i) This assumes strict complementarity (that is, *zero* substitutability) of the factor of Production.

There is only one method of production for any one commodity. The isoquant takes the shape of a right angle. This type of, isoquant is also called. 'Leontief Isoquant' after Leontief, who invented the input output analysis.

In this case K & L are not substitutive

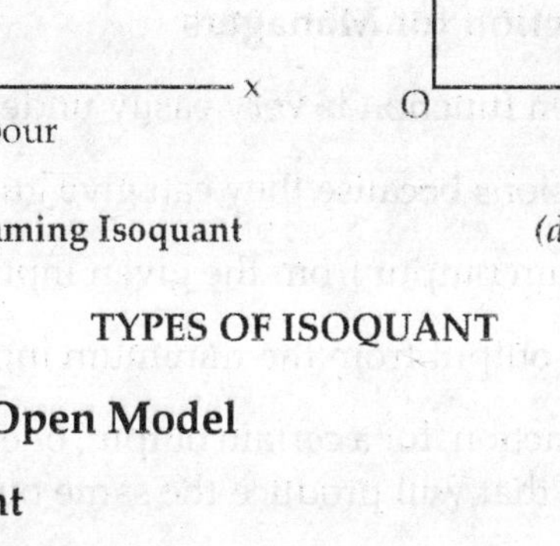

(b) Leontief Production function and Fixed Proportion Production Function

This production function is based on the condition that there is a fixed proportion in which the various factor are to be used in the production process.

If an input is available in a greater quantity than required by this proportion, the additional quantity will be redundant, while it is available in lesser quantity than needed by the proportion, then the other input will be rendered redundant.

For example, if for a particular process 10 labour and 4 capital units are required, and if the firm has 12 labour and 4 capital units, it will find 2 units of labour unused, while if it had 9 units of labour it can use only 3 units of capital with it, *i.e.*, its 1 unit each of capital and labour will be rendered unemployed. (3K 7.5L or 8L).

This function has the following general form.

X = minimum $\left(\frac{K}{a}, \frac{L}{b}\right)$ K & L are capital & labour, a & b are constants. Minimum word implies that output X depends on the smaller of two ratios $\frac{K}{a}$ & $\frac{L}{b}$.

(vi) Utility of Production Function for Managers

The usefulness of production function is very easily understandable.

It is helpful in making decisions because they can give guidance in two directions.

(i) How to obtain maximum output from the given input.

(ii) How to obtain a given output from the minimum input.

From a given production function, for a certain output, one can derive all the combinations of the two factors of production that will produce the same output.

Using Linear programming method, the production function can be easily estimated.

(vii) Production Management

Production management implies planning, organising, directing and controlling the activities of the production function which is concerned with the conversion of raw materials into finished products.

Production management deals with decision making related to production processes so that the resulting good or service is produced according to specifications in the amounts and by the schedule demanded and at minimum cost.

Production management covers only the manufacturing organisations while operations management has a much wider scope consisting of both manufacturing and service organisations such as Banks, Insurance, Hospitals and Transport Companies etc.

(viii) Production Economics

Production economics is a branch of micro-economics. It is concerned with the analysis of the allocation and use of resources in production processes within individual business firm. It Involves the study of costs and returns associated with production functions.

Production economics is defined as "the application of the principles of micro-economics in a commercial enterprise."

Production economics clarifies the concepts of costs, returns, input-output relationship and resource allocation for cost reduction or profit maximisation. Production economics enables the business manager to respond correctly to change in wage rates, interest rates, prices and other such variables.

Production economics is helpful in finding correct answers to the following questions :

(i) What is efficient production?

(ii) What is optimum level of output?

(iii) How to determine the most economical amount of input?

(iv) How should a business firm respond to a change in the price of its product?

(v) How should a firm respond to a change in wage rate or interest rate?

(vi) How does technological change influence cost and output?

(ix) Scope of Production Economics

The economics of production deals with vital issues that influence the viability and rofitability of a manufacturing concern. Some of these issues are as follows :

(a) determination of plant capacity

(b) location of physical facilities

(c) layout of physical facilities

(d) design of product and product mix

(e) process design

(f) number of shifts working

(g) material handling facilities

(h) maintenance practices

(i) control of quantity etc.

(x) Economic Efficiency, Unit Total Cost

Production economics is mainly concerned with the firm's problem of attaining and maintaining unit costs of production at the minimum level.

It explains the effect of technological change, economics of scale, and unit costs of production etc. Production economics is concerned with the problem of economic efficiency or cost effectiveness of production.

The goal of production economics is effective design and operation of production system so as to maximise economic efficiency or to minimise cost of production per unit,

Economic efficiency or cost effectiveness depends upon two factors :

(a) quantities inputs and outputs, and

(b) prices of inputs and outputs.

Suppose, a factory produces 1,20,000 wrist watches per annum (Q = 1,20,000). The price of labour is Rs. 60,000 per annum (*i.e.* the annual wage 60,000) and the factory uses 100 man years (it employs 100 workers throughout the year *i.e.* Ni = 100). Then we get

$$\text{Unit labour Cost} = \frac{60,000}{1,20,000/100} = \text{Rs. } 50/-$$

Similarly, we can calculate the unit cost for every other input and then add them together to obtain the unit total cost *i.e.*,

$$\text{Unit total cost} = \frac{\sum C_1 N_1}{Q}$$

The lower is the unit total cost, higher is the economic efficiency or more cost effective is the production.

***(xi)* The Law of Variable Proportions**

The laws of production describe the technically possible ways of increasing the level of production. Output may increase in various ways.

Output can be increased by changing all factors of production. Clearly this is possible only in the long-run. Thus the laws of return to scale refer to the long-run analysis of production.

In the short-run output may be increased by using more of the variable factor(s), while capital (and possibly other factor as well) are kept constant.

The marginal product of the variable factor(s) will decline eventually as more and more quantities of this factor are combined with the other constant factors.

The expansion of output with one factor (at least) constant is described by the of (eventually) diminishing return of the variable factor, which is often referred to as the law of variable proportions.

Example : Production Function with one variable Input.

Nos. of Labour Units	*Total Physical Product*	*Average Physical Product*	*Marginal Physical Product*
(1)	(2)	(3)	(4)
		= (2) ÷ (1)	
1	100	100	100
2	210	105	110
3	330	110	120
4	430	107.5	100
5	520	104	90
6	600	100	80
7	670	95.7	70
8	720	90	50
9	750	83.3	30
10	760	76	10

In the above table, it is assumed labour is the only variable input.

This law states that as more and more of one factor input is employed, all other input quantities constant, a point will eventually be reached where additional quantities of varying input will yield diminishing marginal contributions to total product.

This is the law of variable proportions and this *is* a familiar economic assumption which under lies the short-run production function.

(xii) Law of Diminishing Return

The law of diminishing returns states that as more and more of the variable input is added to the fixed factor base, the increase to total output after some point will decline progressively with each additional unit of variable factor.

(xiii) Optimum Combination of Inputs

Our objective is to maximise output within a cost constaint. *To Satisfy the cost constraint we can select a point on the Isocost line* (but can not select a point right to it) maximisation of output we have to find an isoquant which satisfies the need to search for the *highest Isoquant which will be tangent to Isocost line.*

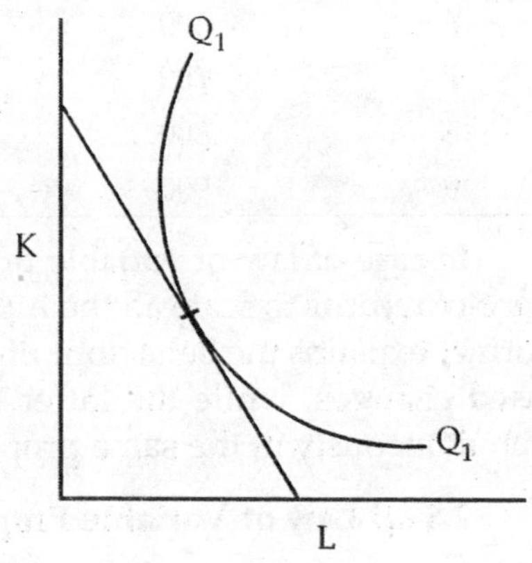

Tangent ensures attainment of highest Isoquant subject to a cost constraint isoquant Q_1 satisfies the cost constraint and yields maximum output.

Mathematically, maximisation of production within a cost constraint requires one condition to be fulfilled, *i.e., the slope of Isoquant should be equal to the slope of ISO cost curve*. Therefore, the point at which production of a given *quantity of output is possible at the least cost, must ensure equality between slope of Isocost line and the slope of Isoquant* (*i.e.* MRTS) at that point.

The above condition ensures maximisation of output within the cost constraint.

The law of diminishing returns is also referred to as the "law of variable proportion" which implies that as additional units of variable factors are added to a given quantity of all other factors, the increment to output attributable to each of the additional units of the variable factor will increase at first, decrease later, and eventually become negative,

The law of diminishing returns is strictly a short run phenomenon.

2.8 RETURNS TO SCALE

Returns to scale is a long-run phenomenon where we can change all inputs simultaneously. Under this concept, the behaviour of output is studied when all factors of products are changed in the same direction and in the same proportion,

(a) Increasing return to Scale : If output increase more than proportionate to the increase in all inputs.

(b) Constant returns to Scale : If all inputs are increased by the same proportion, output will also increase by the same proportion.

(c) **Decreasing returns to Scale :** If increase in output is less than proportionate to the increase in all inputs.

The three kinds of returns to scale can be illustrated with the help of following example :

Table : Returns to Scale in a Manufacturing Unit

Unit of labour	*Units of capital (Rs. '000)*	*Percentage increase in labour and capital*	*Total Product ('00 units)*	*Percentage increase in total product*	*Return to scale*
(1)	*(2)*	*(3)*	*(4)*	*(5)*	*(6)*
1	100	—	100	—	—
2	200	100%	220	120%	
3	300	50%	350	59%	Increasing
4	400	33.33%	500	42.9%	
5	500	25%	625	25%	Constant
6	600	20%	750	20%	
7	700	16.66%	860	14.66%	
8	800	14.29%	940	9.3%	Decreasing
9	900	12.5%	1,000	6.4%	

In case of law of variable proportions some of the inputs are held constant, while in the case of returns to scale all the inputs are chanced in the same proportion. This means that the former explains the behaviour of output when the proportion in which different factors are all used changes, while the latter explains the behaviour of output when all inputs change simultaneously in the same proportion.

2.8 *(a)* Law of Variable Proportion

or

Law of diminishing Return

Above tables of L, TPP, APP, MPP are graphically expressed as follows :

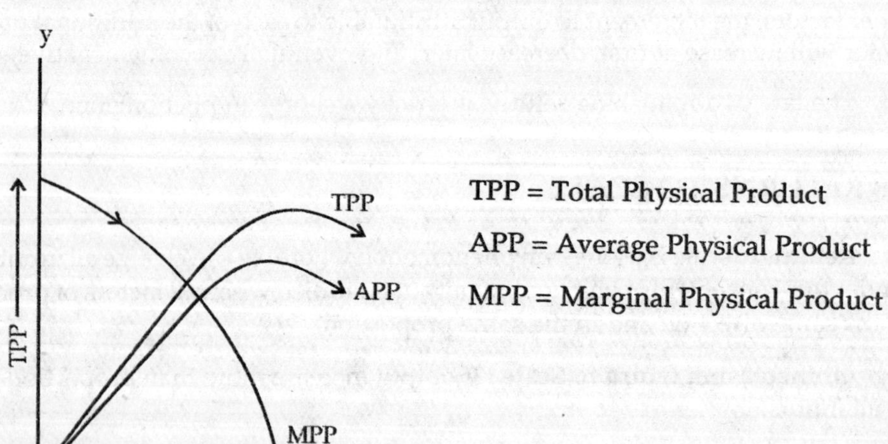

(i) Economies of Scales (Internal & External Economies and Diseconomies)

(a) Meaning and Analysis of Economies of Scale

Economies of Scale means economies which arise from the firm increasing its plant size.

Economies of Scale may also arise from an increase in the number of plants of a firm, irrespective of whether the firm continues to produce the same product in the new plants or diversifies.

In general, such Inter-plant economies of scale are of the same nature as the single-plants (intra-plant) economies, although the importance of each type of scale economies may be different with an increase of the scale of operation of the firm via the installation of additional plants.

Pecuniary (concerning) economies are economics realised from paying lower prices for the factors used in the production and distribution of the product, due to bulk-buying by the firm as its size increases.

Such monetary economics do not imply an actual decrease in the quantity of inputs used but accrue to the firm from lower prices paid for raw materials (bough at a distant due to large volume of the purchase), lower interest rates (and lower cost of finance in general) as the size of the firm increases.

Real economics are those associated with a reduction in the physical quantity of inputs, raw materials, various types of labour and various types of capital (fixed or working capital).

(b) We may distinguish the following main types of real economies :

(i) production economies *(ii)* selling or marketing economies *(iii)* managerial economies *(iv)* transports and storage economies *(v)* Pecuniary Economies.

(i) Production economies of Scale :

Production economies may arise from :

(a) Labour economies : These are achieved as the scale of output increases due to specialisation, time-saving, automation of the production process and cumulative volume.

(b) Technical economies : These are associated with the fixed capital which includes all types of machinery and other equipment.

The main technical economies arise from :

(1) Specialisation of capital equipment and high degree of mechanisation for large scale of output.

(2) Set-up Costs.

(3) Initial fixed costs.

(4) Capacity requirement—this means stand by equipment necessary" to avoid disruption of production in case of break-down.

(5) *Inventory economies.*

Stocks of raw materials do increase with scale but not proportionately, Randon fluctuations in the supply of such inputs are smoothed out with stocks whose size need change by less than the size of the firm.

***(ii)* Selling or Marketing Economics**

Selling economies are associated with the distribution of the product of a firm. The main types of economics arise from the following :

(1) Advertising economies

(2) Special arrangements with exclusive dealers and distributors.

Large firms can enter exclusive agreements with distributors, who undertake the obligation of maintaining good service department.

This is usual for motor-car & two-wheeler and household goods (Refrigerator, TVs etc.)

***(iii)* Managerial Economies**

Managerial costs are partly production costs and partly selling costs.

Managerial economies arise from the following :

***(a)* Specialisation of Management :** *i.e.*, each managerial function is specialised, production. Finance, Marketing, Personnel etc. are specialised.

***(b)* Decentralisation of Decision-making Process :** The decentralisation of decision-making in large firms has been found very effective in the increase of efficiency of management. With decentralisation the flow of information within the firm is reduced and thus distortions and delays of this information in the various sections of the firm is to a large extent avoided.

Decentralisation of the decision-making process is one of the main means of Increasing the efficiency of management in large scale plants and of avoiding managerial diseconomies in still larger plants.

***(c)* Mechanisation of Managerial Functions :** Large Scale firms are able to achieve high degree of mechanisation in managerial functions by telephones, telex, fax, dictaphone, E-mail, Videocon conferencing, Internets, voice mails etc., computers with various softwares etc.

***(iv)* Transport and Storage Economies**

Transport and storage costs are incurred partly on the production side and partly on the selling side of the firm.

Costs of constructing large Tanks, warehouses become less as the size increases.

Similarly large firms are capable of maintaining their own transports for transport of raw materials and finished products and thus may be able to reduce costs.

Also, large firms may adopt cheaper modes of transport such as cable trolleys, conveyors, trollies on rails, water ways transport using ships, steamers and burges etc. and these methods of transport will reduce the transportation costs.

(v) Pecuniary Economics of Scale

These are economics accruing to a large firm due to discounts that it can obtain due to its large scale operations.

The larger firm may achieve

(1) Lower prices of its raw materials, bought at special discounts from its suppliers.

2.9 ECONOMY OF SCALE/DISECONOMY OF SCALE

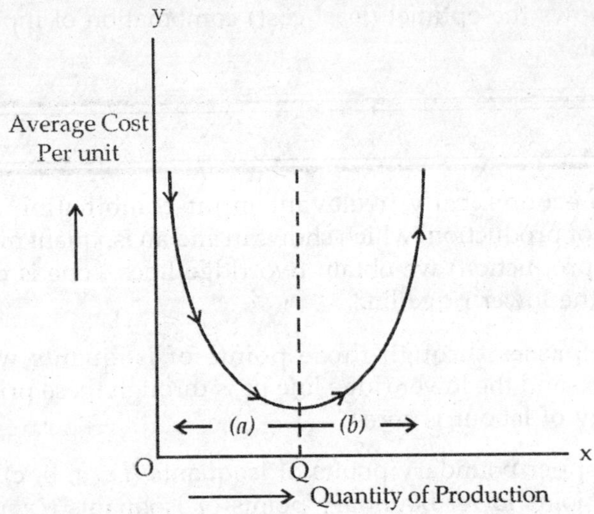

(a) Economy of scale, *i.e.,* of the optimum capacity of production for which average cost per unit of production is the least.

(b) As production capacity increases beyond "Q" diseconomy of scale starts, *i.e.,* average cost per unit production increase due to managerial inefficiency and other factors.

Expansion Path

The expansion path is the curve along which the firm expands output when factor prices remain constant.

The expansion path indicates how factor proportions change when output (or expenditure) changes keeping factor prices unchanged.

On the expansion path MRTS remain constant, since the factor price ratio is constant.

Q_1, Q_2, Q_3 are 3 isoquants KL, K'L', K"L" are tangent to Q_1, Q_2, Q_3 represent Isocost lines.

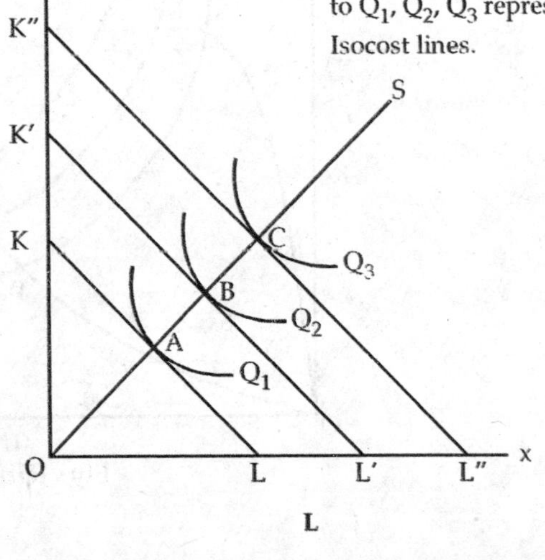

KL, K'L', K"L" Iso cost lines represent minimum cost of producing three output levels MRTS at A, B, C points are equal. OS is the expansion path which gives a locus of points along which MRTS constant and equal to factor price ratio.

Expansion path is made up of points of efficient (least cost) combinations of input factors, *i.e.*, it is the locus of efficient combination of the inputs.

On the expansion path, MRTS remains constant, since the factor price ratio is constant.

The expansion path gives the firm its cost structure and the long run total cost curve is derived from the expansion path.

The expansion path shows the optimal (least-cost) combination of input to be used to produce each level of output.

3.1 RIDGE LINES

Ridge lines eliminate economically irrelevant input combination and incompass economically feasible range of production (which shows in and an isoquant map, an isoquants for a particular method of production) we obtain two ridge lines—one is called the upper ridge line and the other is the lower ridge line.

The upper ridge line passes through those points of isoquants whose marginal productivity of capital is zero and the lower ridge line pass through these prints or isoquants where marginal productivity of labour is zero.

The line that connect upper boundary points of isoquants (*i.e.* a, b, c) is called upper ridge line and the line that joins lower boundary points or isoquants (*i.e.* p, q, r) is called lower ridge line.

The regions above the upper ridge line "abc" and below the lower ridge line "pqr" are economically inefficient as compared to the area within the two ridge lines cba opqr".

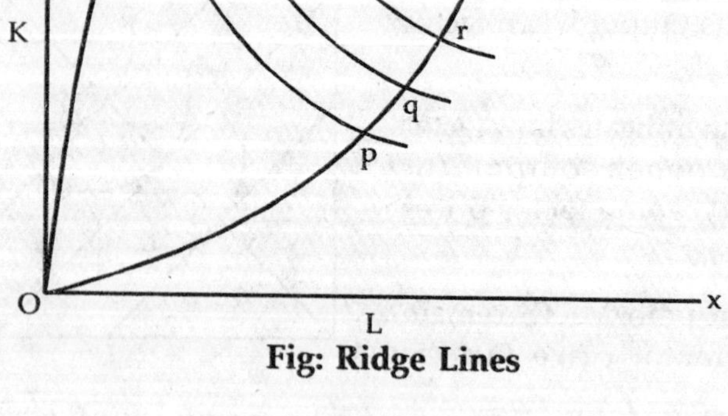

Fig: Ridge Lines

As shown in the diagram oabc—Upper Ridge Line & opqr—Lower Ridge Line.

PROBABLE QUESTIONS

1. *(a)* Define Isoquant and Iso cost curves.

   (b) What is ISOM?
2. *(a)* What do you understand by "MRTS"?

   (b) Explain Fixed Proportion Production function.
3. *(a)* Define and explain "Law of variable proportion".

   (b) How is it different from "Return to scale"?
4. *(a)* Explain various "Return to scale" with examples.

   (b) What are various "Economies of Scale"?
5. *(a)* Explain the concept of economy and diseconomy of scale.

   (b) Write notes on—

   (i) Expansion Path

   (ii) Ridge lines.

CHAPTER 4

THEORY OF COST

- Significance of Cost Analysis
- Role of Cost in Managerial Decision-Making
- Various Cost Concepts
- Marginal Cost and Elasticity of Demand
- Cost and Output Relations
- Short-Run Cost Curves
- Long-Run Average Cost Curves
- Cost and Size of the Plant
- Economies of Scale
- Economies of Scope

1.0 SIGNIFICANCE OF COST ANALYSES

Cost Analysis helps the Management

(i) draw a distinction between those cost elements that are relevant for managerial decision making and these elements which are not useful for this purpose.

(ii) understand the basic difference between the various cost concepts.

(iii) analyse the behaviour of cost.

(iv) comprehend the different sources of economics of scale.

(v) Specify the appropriate method of measuring cost-output relation in specific cases.

1.1 ROLE OF COST IN MANAGERIAL DECISION-MAKING

Study of costs is essential for making a choice among the competing production plans. Production decisions are not possible without their respective cost considerations. Since the productive resources are scarce with any firm and also since these have alternative uses, the use of these resources involves sacrifice and cost. The management will have to analyse these sacrifices or costs whenever it decides to use the resources.

Secondly, no estimate of profit is possible without the knowledge of costs involved.

An useful cost analysis requires the management to :

(a) anticipate future condition as precisely as possible.

(b) have clarity about the various cost concepts.

(c) have a clear understanding of alternative plans and the type of costs involved.

(d) decide about the valuation of an asset.

(e) ascertain at the outset whether the cost-analysis is being done for the control or appraisal purposes.

(f) decide about the method of cost-estimation.

Each Management, in addition to above, has to identify the following determinants important for its business.

(a) Plant size

(b) Percentage utilisation of the Plant capacity

(c) Technology

(d) Prices of various inputs like raw materials, auxiliary materials, labour & power etc.

(e) Lot size

(f) Stability of Production level

(g) Management and labour efficiency

The management must look at the impact of above factors on certain activity and also supplement by adding other deteminants that are relevant, for the particular situation.

Further, Management is vitally concerned with future costs for the simple reason that they are the only costs over which managers can exercise any control. Historical costs are of no interest to management except as basis for evaluating past operations.

1.2 COST CONCEPTS RELEVANT FOR MANAGERIAL DECISIONS AND CORPORATE PLANNING

Managerial decisions involve a selection between alternative courses of action. Costs play a very prominent role in such decisions as it helps in specifying various alternatives in terms of their quantitative values. These quantitative values provide indication to the management about the economically most desirable choice, because non-quantitative factors, like labour relations, goodwill etc. may also influence the decisions. Yet, information on quantified costs is necessary for taking a final decision.

Following cost concepts are relevant for managerial decisions and corporate Planning :

(i) **Future Costs :** Managerial decisions are concerned with future. Historical costs provides a basis for prediction, but for decision making and corporate planning only those costs which are expected to be incurred in future are relevant.

(ii) **Incremental Costs :** These are added costs and thus are avoidable costs.

These are costs which would not be incurred if a particular project is not undertaken.

(iii) **Imputed Costs (Implicit cost) :** These are theoretical costs which are not recognised by the accounting system, but are of practical relevance for decision-making.

For example, a firm by using its own capital within the business is foregoing the income it would have received had it lent the capital to an outside agency. Whereas, in accounting system interest is recognised as a cost only if it is actually paid, but in managerial decision making this cost is to be taken into account.

(iv) **Opportunity Costs :** An opportunity cost is a cost resulting from alternative opportunity that has been forsaken. The opportunity cost of a good or service is measured in terms of revenue which could have been earned by employing it in some other alternative use.

For example, the land of a dilapidated and fully depreciated building, if used for the expansion of an existing plant, the rental value of the land should be included to its opportunity cost.

A garage space in a posh locality of a metro city, if used for business purpose, *i.e.* doctors chamber" or "Beauty Parlour" would provide much higher earning to the owner, compared to renting it out for car park.

(v) **Sunk Cost :** A "sunk cost" is defined as the one for which the expenditure has been incurred in the past and which will not be affected by the particular decisions under consideration now. The opposite of the sunk costs are the "incremental costs" which require an additional outlay of cash if new decisions are implemented.

Since sunk costs do not change, they are irrelevant for decision making while incremental costs are the relevant ones.

(vi) **Common costs or costs of multiple product (or joint cost) :** Multiple Product output is the normal pattern, or production and for determining the Production cost of individual items allocation of common overhead expenses are made by adopting proper statistical methods

which reveal the relationship between overhead expenses and output of various products. In operating Railway Services, the cost of station, track, equipment and staff etc. are common costs (or/indirect cost).

Common costs are indirect costs.

In the case of joint product, whose product mix can not be changed, separate costs of products can not be determined and the products have to be considered together. But then the pricing of separate products would be on the basis market conditions.

***(vii)* Marginal Costs and Incremental Costs :** Marginal costs are closely related with incremental costs.

Marginal cost deals with unit-by-unit changes in output, whereas incremental cost is not restricted to 'a unit change.'

Marginal cost is the amount added to total cost by a unit increase in output. Incremental cost is related to change in any number of units of out put or even change in its quantity.

Marginal cost as a concept is particularly superior to incremental cost, when dealing with decision like

(a) selecting optimum level of output,

(b) selecting optimum combination of inputs.

Incremental costs are superior to marginal costs in case if discrete alternatives are to be compared.

For example one can compare two technical processes through incremental cost.

1.3 MARGINAL COST AND ELASTICITY OF DEMAND

(a) When elasticity of demand is greater than one, the marginal cost is (+) ve and total cost rises as price falls

(b) When elasticity of demand is equal to one, the marginal cost is zero and a change in price will not change the total cost.

(c) When elasticity of demand is less then one, marginal cost is (–) ve and total cost falls as price falls.

Marginal cost is earned by selling an additional (marginal) unit of production.

Avg. Cost (AC) = Marginal Cost (MC) $\times \frac{e}{e-1}$ $\quad \therefore$ AC = MC $\times \frac{e}{e-1}$

and MC = AC $\times \frac{e-1}{e}$ $\quad$ MC = AC $\times \frac{e-1}{e}$

$e = \frac{AC}{AC-MC}$ $\quad$ e = elasticity of demand.

Elasticity of demand = $e = \frac{AC}{AC-MC}$ and MC = AC $\times \frac{e-1}{e}$

***(viii)* Total Costs :**

T = TFC + TVC

TC = Total Costs

TFC = Total Fixed Costs

TVC = Total Variable Costs

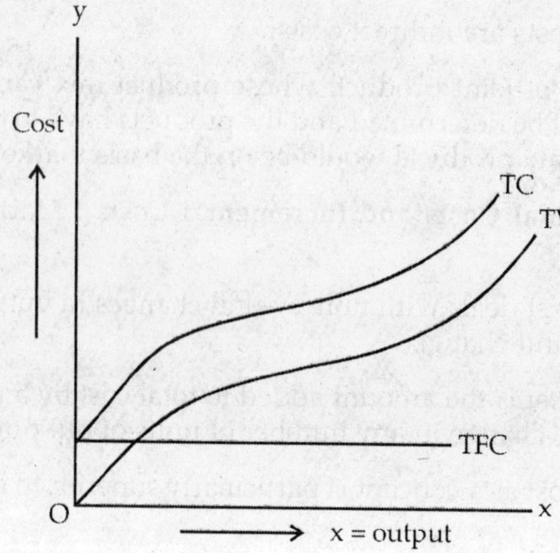

The Fixed Costs include :

(a) Salaries of staff & executives

(b) Depreciation of Plant and equipment

(c) Expenses for building depreciation and repair

(d) Interest on Capital borrowed

(e) Overhead expenses

The variable costs include :

(a) Cost of raw materials

(b) Cost of auxiliary items

(c) Cost of labour

(d) Cost of power

(e) Cost of packing materials

(f) Cost of maintenance & spares

***(ix)* Social Costs :** Costs due to pollution and congestion on the parts of society are the social costs.

Social cost is the total cost to the society on account of production of a good.

2.0 COST AND OUTPUT

Total cost of a firm is the sum-total of all the explicit plus implicit expenditures incurred for producing a given level of output.

It represents the money value of the total resources required for production of goods and services by the firm.

Average cost is the cost per unit of output, assuming the production of each unit of output incurs the same cost.

Average cost equals the total cost divided by the number of units produced.

Total cost equals total fixed costs and total variable costs.

Description of fixed & variable costs have been given before.

Management control is exercised to keep the variable costs lower.

$$\text{Productivity (P)} = \frac{\text{Output (0)}}{\text{Input (1)}}$$

Productivity is the ratio between the output of goods and services and the input of resources consumed in the process of production.

Output implies total production while input means land, labour, capital and management.

Productivity is a measure of how efficiently an organisation has used its resources.

Productivity is all about the efficient use of inputs, producing more output with the same resources or produce the same output with less resources.

High productivity results in low unit cost for good or services.

Productivity is not only the rate of production of material goods, but its concept is extended to services also, *e.g.*, banking, transportation, insurance firms.

The performance aspects of quality and effectiveness have also been integrated into productivity.

Optimisation of inputs, process and output requires modern technologies of both production and quality.

The efficiency of the production system also depends upon marketing.

Therefore, productivity of the business system embraces marketing also.

Efficient design, development, transfer of products and services and cost control measures etc. call for involvement of both management and labour through out the organisation.

Productivity can be viewed from different perspectives. We may refer to the productivity of a nation, of an industry, of an enterprise or of an individual employee. A nation can be productive only when its Institutions and people are productive.

Higher productivity leads to economic growth and social progress. It is only by improving productivity that employees can get better wages and working conditions and more employment opportunity."

Higher productivity brings lower prices for consumers and higher dividend for shareholders. It improves the exports and foreign exchange reserves of a country. Thus, productivity is the key to prosperity.

Higher productivity is of special significance in a developing country like India.

Mass poverty and unemployment can not be eliminated without increasing productivity in agriculture, industry and all other areas of human activity.

COST AND OUTPUT

Cost comprises of the *(i)* money value represented by the material used to make the product *(ii)* wages of the workers and *(iii)* other indirect costs attributable to its manufacture.

The excess value or market price over the costs incurred in producing the product represents the margin of profit.

In order to make the product more profitable, there should be a constant search for reducing the output costs.

Reduced output costs means one or more of the following advantages :

(i) Increase the margin of profit

(ii) Reduce the wastages.

2.1 Following table gives the relationship of output with total cost, average cost and marginal cost :

Units of Output	*Fixed Cost—Rs.*	*Variable Cost—Rs.*	*Total Cost Rs.*	*Marginal Cost—Rs.*	*Avg. Cost 4 ÷ 1 Rs.*	*Avg. Fixed Cost 2 ÷ 1 Rs.*	*Avg. Variable Cost 3 ÷ 1 Rs.*
(1)	*(2)*	*(3)*	*(4)*	*(5)*	*(6)*	*(7)*	*(8)*
0	176	0	176	—	—	—	—
1	176	75	251	75	251	176	75
2	176	130	306	55	153	88	65
3	176	175	351	45	117	59	58
4	176	209	385	34	96	44	52
5	176	238	414	29	83	35	48
6	176	265	441	27	74	29	44
7	176	289	465	24	66	25	41
8	176	312	488	23	61	22	39
9	176	328	504	16	56	20	36
10	176	344	520	16	52	18	34

Values in the above table are arbitrary. On studying the above table, following points are noteworthy :

(i) Average cost is equal to total cost divided by number of units output.

(ii) The total cost is equal to the sum of fixed cost and all the marginal costs. For examples, for 4 units output, total cost Rs. 385 = 176 + 75 + 55 + 45 + 34.

(iii) Where marginal cost is falling, total cost will rise at a declining rate, but on other side; where marginal cost is rising, total cost will also rise at an increasing rate.

(iv) When marginal cost is lower than average cost, average cost will be falling. For example, upto the 10 units output as above. This will be so irrespective of the fact whether the marginal cost is rising or falling.

Let us have the following additional figures added to the above table :

(1)	*(2)*	*(3)*	*(4)*	*(5)*	*(6)*	*(7)*	*(8)*
	Rs.	*Rs.*	*Rs.*	*Rs.*	*Rs.*	*Rs.*	*Rs.*
11	176	367	543	23	49	16	33
12	176	400	576	33	48	15	33
13	176	448	624	48	48	14	34
14	176	510	686	62	49	13	36
15	176	600	776	90	52	12	40

(v) For example, for an output of 11 and 12 units, the marginal cost is rising, but the average cost is falling.

(vi) When the marginal cost first falls and then rises, *i.e.*, the marginal cost curve is U-shaped, the marginal cost will be equal to the average cost at a point where the average cost is the minimum. For example, at an output of 13 units, the cost is lowest at Rs. 48 where the marginal cost is also Rs. 48.

(vii) When the marginal cost is greater than the average cost, the average cost will rise, for example, for output of 14 and 15 units.

(viii) If the marginal cost is below the average variable cost latter must be falling. This can be verified for 11 units output.

(ix) If the marginal cost is higher than the average variable cost, the latter must be rising, this is verified for output levels of 13, 14 and 15 units.

(x) If marginal cost first falls and then rises, it will be equal to the average variable cost at a point, where the average variable cost, is minimum. This is seen for an output of 12 units where marginal cost and average variable cost are equal to Rs. 33.

The above analysis can easily be given graphically as follows :

(a) When MC falls, AC also falls. Table shows from 1 to 10 units.

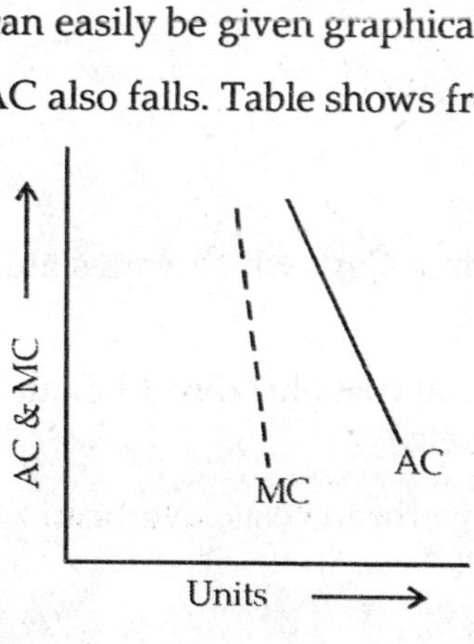

MC = Marginal Cost

AC = Average Cost

(b) When MC and AC are constant. Table gives at for 13 output units.

(c) When AC increases MC also increases. For example from 13 to 15 units output.

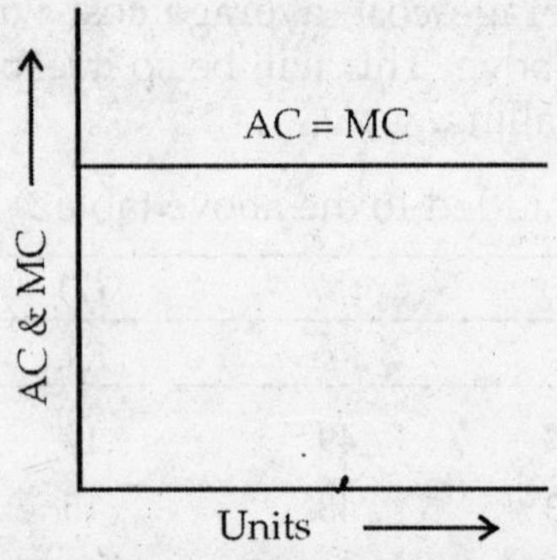

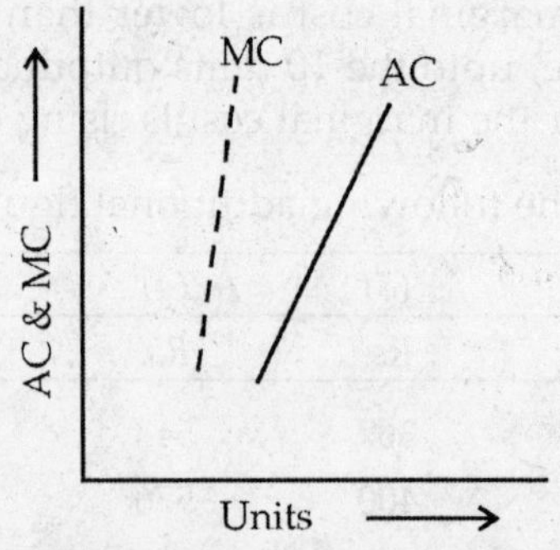

(d) If we plot a graph between units of output and AC and MC, we get a U-shaped curve, both curves intersecting at the lower AC value and the value for MC must be equal to AC at this point. Point O is the point of intersection and MC is equal to AC at this point.

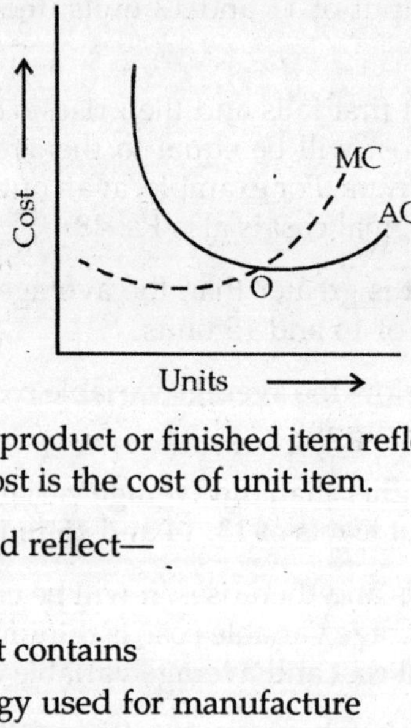

(e) **Product Cost :** Price of a product or finished item reflects the overall expenditure on its manufacture plus profit. Unit cost is the cost of unit item.

The cost of a product should reflect—

—Its quality

—The volume of material it contains

—The production technology used for manufacture

—The quality of workmanship

—The use of Product.

I. Elements of Cost :

(i) **Direct Cost :** It is also called Prime Cost, which varies almost proportionately with the volume of production.

Direct cost includes direct material cost plus direct labour cost plus direct expenses (fuels, electricity and packaging etc.).

(ii) **Indirect Cost :** It is also called overhead costs, overhead expenditures are expenses other than direct expenses.

Indirect cost includes indirect material cost *(i.e.,* tools and fixtures used for production) plus indirect labour cost plus indirect expenses (such as advertisement, telephone, rent and insurance and travelling expenses etc.)

We shall write down all costs in the following ways :

Prime Cost = Direct labour + Direct material + other Direct Expenses

Manufacturing Cost (Factory Cost) = Prime Cost + Factory Overhead.

Production Cost or Unit cost = Manufacturing Cost + Establishment Cost.

Establishment Cost = Office Administration + Advertisement and Distribution

Selling Price = Production Cost + Profit

Factory overhead = Indirect labour + Indirect material + Other indirect expenses (all in the factory).

(f) **Equilibrium of a Firm :** A consumer is said to be in equilibrium when he spends his limited income on different goods in such a way that he gets maximum satisfaction. Likewise a producer is said to reach equilibrium when he combines the different factors of production so that he produces maximum output at minimum cost. Just as the consumer attempts to maximise his satisfaction and the producer attempts to maximise his outputs, similarly a firm while selling the products attempts to maximise its profit. A firm is said to be in equilibrium when a firm produces that output and fixes that price at which it secures maximum profit. We make certain basic assumption for explaining the equilibrium of the firm.

(i) The firm is said to have only one aim or goal, *i.e.,* get maximum possible profit, it is not satisfied with only normal profit or fair profit.

(ii) The firm is said to have full knowledge of the position where profit is maximum. By a series of experiments, the firm has found out the point at which it can secure maximum profit.

These two assumptions may not hold good in real life, for business firms may be satisfied with whatever profits they are securing. Besides they may not be in a position to change the output and their prices continuously and find out the position of maximum profit.

If a firm goes for maximum profit it will not produce even a single unit of product at a loss. To maximise profit a firm should produce and sell up to the point at which the revenue from the last unit (marginal revenue) is equal to the cost of the last unit (marginal cost). Beyond this point of equality of marginal revenue and marginal cost, the firm will experience losses because additional cost will be more than additional revenue received. Thus the basic condition of a firm's equilibrium is that the firm should stop at the point of equality of marginal cost and marginal revenue (MC = MR).

In case of a monopoly firm's marginal revenue is at a lower level than the price. Therefore, marginal cost is lower than the price. In summary form, it is

MC = MR (in equilibrium)

MR < Price (for monopoly firm).

MC < Price or Price > MC

In graphical representation it is as shown in below Figure.

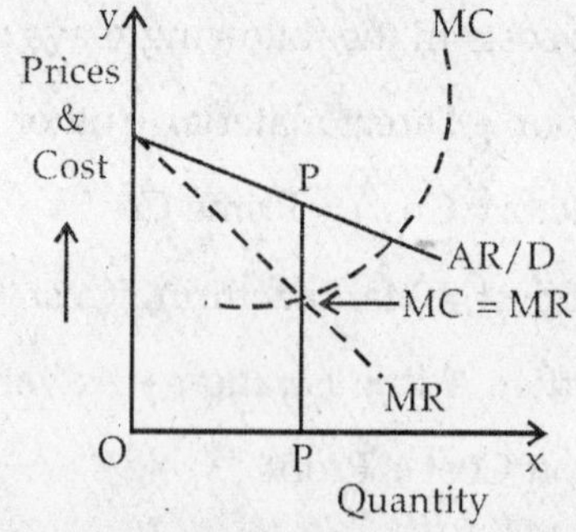

Explicit (or Paid out) and Implicit (or Imputed) Costs

Explicit costs are those expenses which are actually paid by the firm. These costs appear in the accounting records. On the other hand, implicit or imputed costs are the theoretical costs in the sense that they go unrecognised by the accounting system. These costs may be defined as the earnings of those employed resources which belong to the owner himself.

For example, the interest payment on borrowed funds is an explicit cost and it is entered in the books of account. But the amount of interest which the employer could have earned (and which he forgoes when he uses his capital in his firm) is his implicit cost.

2.3 PRIVATE AND SOCIAL COSTS

Economic costs can be calculated at two levels, micro-level and macro-level. The micro-level economic costs relate to functioning of a firm as a production-unit, while the macro-level economic costs are the ones that are generated by the decision of the firm but are paid by the society and not the firm.

For example, if the decision of a firm to expand its output leads to increase in its costs, this is private cost. Whereas, if it also leads to certain cost to the society, may be in the nature of higher doses of pollution, or greater congestion, these costs which are external to the firm are social costs from the society's point of view.

2.4 ACCOUNTING AND ECONOMIC COSTS

Accounting costs are the actual or outlay costs. These costs relate to the past, these are generally sunk costs. The accounting costs are useful for managing taxation needs as well as to calculate profit or loss or the firm.

Economic costs relate to future and are in the nature of the incremental costs both the imputed and the explicit costs as well as the opportunity costs.

Since the only costs that matter for business decision are future costs, it is the economic costs that are used for decision making.

2.5 ECONOMIC RENT

The difference between actual and opportunity cost is called Economic Rent or Economic Profit. Opportunity costs or alternative costs are the return from the second best use of the firm's resources which the firm forgoes in order to avail of the return from the best use of the resources.

Short-Run Cost Curve

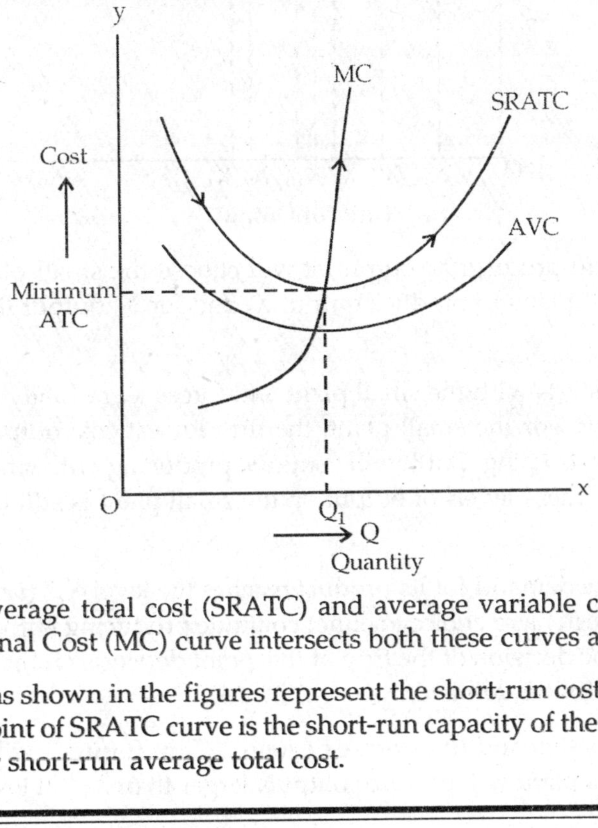

The short-run average total cost (SRATC) and average variable cost (AVC) are almost U-shaped. The Marginal Cost (MC) curve intersects both these curves at their lowest points.

The cost functions shown in the figures represent the short-run cost, incurred by majority of firm. The lowest point of SRATC curve is the short-run capacity of the firm any change from this will result higher short-run average total cost.

3.0 COST AND SIZE OF THE PLANT

The long-run cost output relationship can be shown with the help of a long-run cost curve. *The long-run average cost curve is derived from short run cost curves.* Each point on the long-run average cost curve corresponds to a point on a short-run cost curve, which is tangent to the long-run curve at that point.

For example, figure below :

A firm faces a choice of three methods of production, each with a different plant sizes, small, medium and large.

These plants operate with the average costs SAC_1, SAC_2, and SAC_3 respectively as shown in the figure.

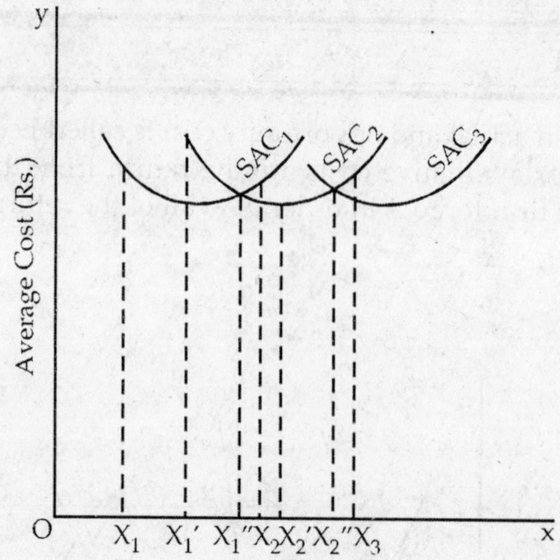

If the firm plans to produce X_1 output, it will choose the small plant. It will choose the medium size plant if it plans to produce output X_2 and for X_3 output it will choose the large size plant.

Now, if the firm starts with the small plant and forces a gradually increasing demand, it will increase its output. For the small plant, the firm lowest cost output level is X_1, beyond which average cost starts rising. But it will continue producing with small plant even beyond X_1, as average cost for these levels of output on the small plant is still lower than that on the medium plant.

It is only when the demand for its product reaches the level X_1'' (*i.e.*, point of intersection of SAC_1 & SAC_2) the firm has a choice to either continue producing with small plant or use the medium size plant. The decision of the firm at this point depends on the cost but on the firm's expectation about the future demand.

If the firm expects demand to increase beyond X_1'', in future it will choose the medium size plant, because this plant will produce outputs larger than X_1'' at lower average cost than that of the small plant.

The firm will face the similar decision problem when it reaches the level X_2''.

Thus from the above example, we can assume that there are many plant sizes, each suitable for a certain level of output, we will get as many SAC curves intersecting each other. As the number of plant sizes increases, the points of intersection of SAC curves will come closer.

And, it we assume that there are a large number of plant sizes the intersection points will be so near to each other that we get almost a continuous curve known as long-run Average cost curve (LAC curve).

This is also known as Envelope curve as it envelopes the short-run Average Cost Curves.

This is further shown in the following Fig.

Cost and Size of the Plant

An optimum size of plant may be defined as the one that leads to the most efficient utilisation of resources. Given technology, there has to be one level of output and the size of plant which results in the least cost output.

Graphically, this unique least cost plant size can be shown below :

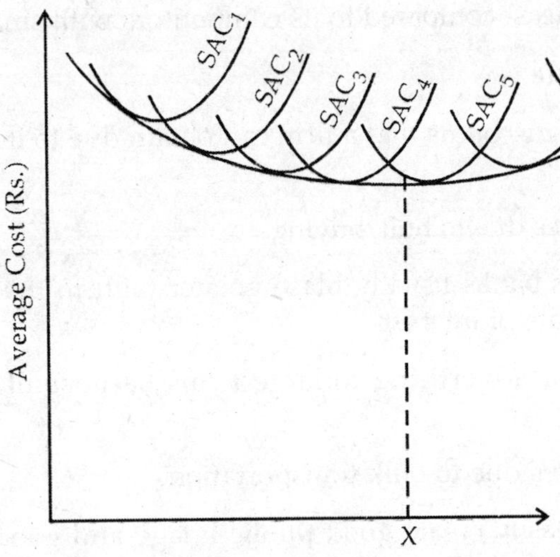

Units of Output

The U-shapedness of the LAC Curve reflects the laws of returns of scale.

According to these laws, the cost per unit of production decreases as plant size increases due to the economies of scale which the larger plant sizes make possible.

But the economies of scale exist only up to a certain size of plant, known as the **optimum plant size,** where all possible economies of scale are fully exploited.

Beyond the optimum plant size, diseconomies of scale arise due to management inefficiencies.

As plant size increase beyond a limit, the control, the feedback of information at different levels and decision making process becomes less efficient.

The makes the LAC curve turn upwards.

In the above graph, "X" is the point of optimum output and the corresponding plant size is the optimum plant size.

(a) Economics of Large Plant Size

Large Corporate Houses take the advantage economics of large plant size and set-up grand size plant to obtain economics of scale of operation.

For many types of equipment both initial and running costs increase less rapidly than capacity. Tanks, Blast furnaces and other static and mobile containers are examples of this form of economy.

Any container whose external dimensions are doubled has its volume increased eight times, but the area of its surface walls would have increased only four times. This reduces material costs and, where appropriate, heat loss is the minimum.

Moreover," the management and labour inputs required to operate a large plant are seldom proportionately greater than that required for a smaller size plant. Also, costs incurred for R & D market research, development of product design etc. are shared for a large size plant and the unit output costs are the least compared to its competitors with smaller size plants.'

(b) Pecuniary Economies of Scale

These economies include the discounts that a firm can obtain due to its large size. These discounts may be in the nature of :

(i) Lower raw material prices due to bulk buying.

(ii) Lower cost of capital, as banks usually place greater faith in the large firms, and, therefore charge lower rate of interest.

(iii) Offers of lower rates for advertising to large firms because of their large scale advertising.

(iv) Lower transportation rates due to bulk transportation.

(v) A large scale firm can easily create good public image and goodwill which form valuable intangible assets for the organisation.

(vi) Due to above benefits, it is able to attract highly qualified and competent professionals and skilled personnel for the over-all benefit of the organisation.

3.0 *(c)* The Analysis of Economies of Scale

Economies of scale are of two kinds :

Internal economies

External economies.

Internal Economies of Scale : These are which arise from the firm increasing its plant size.

External Economies of Scale : These are which arise outside the firm, from improvement (or deterioration) of the environment. Internal economies relate only to the long-run and determine the shape of the long-run cost curve, the external economies affect the position of the short-run and long-run cost curve. Internal economies are categorised into Real economies and Pecuniary economies.

Real economies arise when the quantity of inputs used decreases for a given level of output. Pecuniary economies has been discussed under point *(b)* before.

Real economies include the following :

(i) **Production economies :** These arise from labour fixed capital and inventory requirement of the firm.

3.4 ECONOMIES OF SCALE

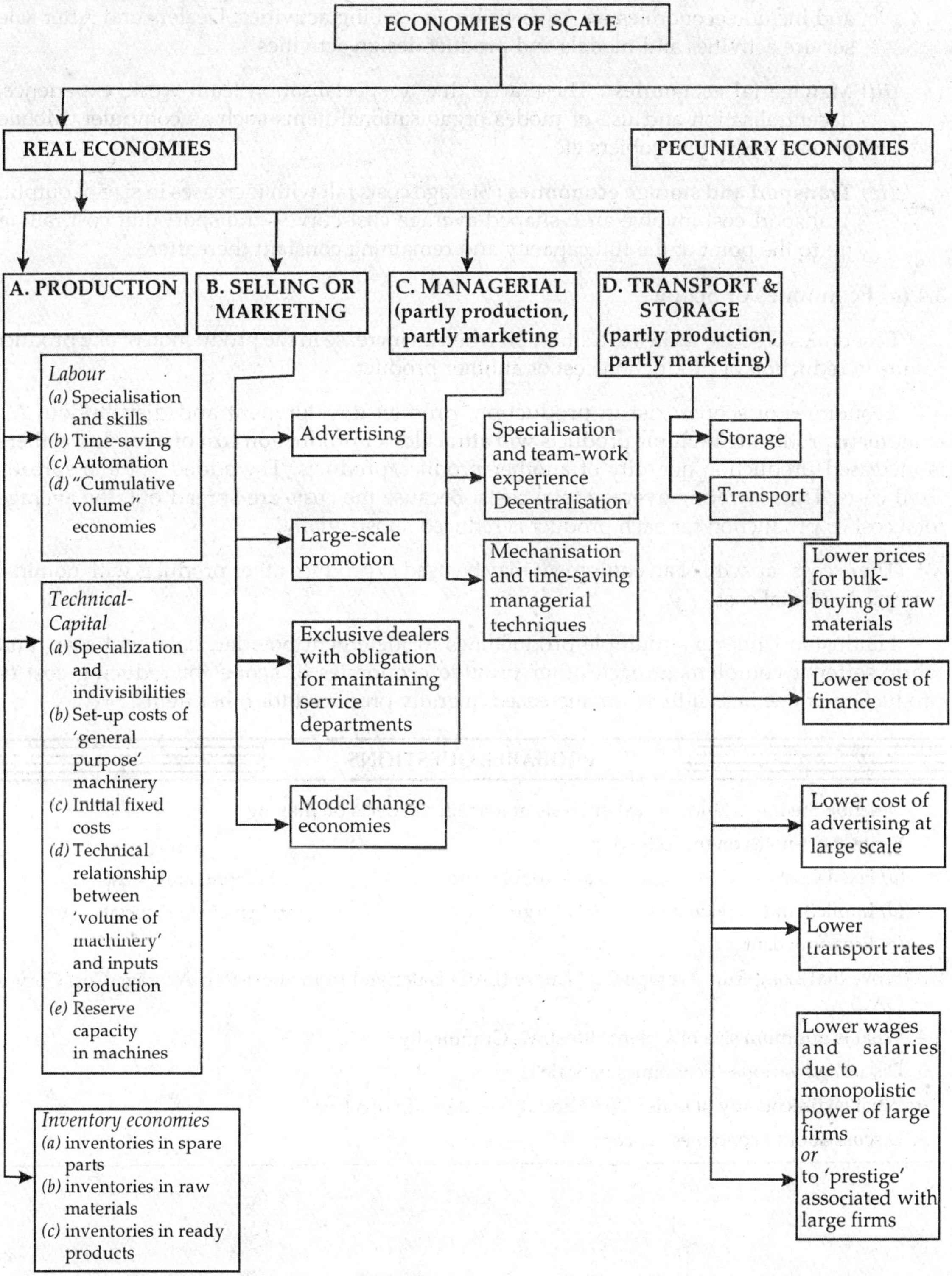

Source : Koutsoyiannis, A, *"Modern Micro Economics,"* Second Edition, Macmillan Publications, p. 127.

(ii) **Marketing economies :** These are associated with marketing activities of the firm and include economies on Advertising and selling activities, Dealers and After sale service activities and models and product design activities.

(iii) **Managerial economies :** These arise due to specialisation team work, experience, decentralisation and use of modes organisational items such as computer, Mobile phones and photo copiers etc.

(iv) **Transport and storage economies :** Storage costs fall with increases in size of output. Transport cost involve an L-shaped average cost curve—transport unit cost falling up to the point of the full capacity and remaining constant thereafter.

3.4 *(a)* Economies of Scope

Economies of scope relates to a situation when an increase in the production of one product results in reduction of production cost of another product.

Economies of scope exist in production, product development and distribution. An equipment producing multiple products will attract lower production cost of a product if there is increased production quantity of another product/products. The added volume spreads fixed costs. Thus lowering average total costs. Because the costs are spread out, the average total cost or production for each product is reduced substantially.

The excess capacity of an equipment may be used to produce other products with nominal increase in capital cost.

Hindustan Unilever's multiple productlines for detergent powder, detergent soap, and fabric softener complement each other provide economies of scope for reducing cost of production of one item if there are increased quantity produced for other items.

PROBABLE QUESTIONS

1. Describe the importance of cost analysis in managerial decision making.
2. Write short-notes on the following :
   (a) Fixed Cost *(b)* Variable cost *(c)* Opportunity cost
   (d) Implicit and Explicit cost *(e)* Marginal cost *(f)* Private and social cost
   (g) Economic rent
3. Prove that Long-Run Average Cost Curve (LAC) is derived from Short-Run Average Cost Curves (SAC)
4. What is optimum size of a plant? Illustrate Graphically.
5. Discuss on various "Economies of Scale".
6. What is diseconomy of scale? Write about "equilibrium of a firm".
7. Discuss about Economies of scope.

CHAPTER 5

ANALYSIS OF COMPETITION, COMPETITIVE SITUATION

- Market Structure
- Business Decisions
- Objectives of a Firm
- Perfect Competition—Short-Run and Long-Run
- Monopoly and Perfect Competition
- Monopoly Power
- Equilibrium of a Firm
- Perfect Competition—Features
- Monopoly—Features and Causes
- Monopolistic Competition
- Equilibrium of a Firm in Monopolistic Competition
- Price Discrimination
- Conditions for Price Discrimination
- Price Leadership—Types and Advantages
- Lerner's Monopoly Power
- Three Degrees of Price Discrimination
- Various Cost Curves and Relationships
- Perfect Competition—Short-Run and Long-Run Equilibrium

- Monopoly—Short-Run and Long-Run Equilibrium
- Monopolistic—Short-Run and Long-Run Equilibrium
- Price and Marginal Cost
- Cost Curves with Conditions of Profit and Loss
- Cost Curves with Break Even Point and Short Down Point
- Price Discrimination—Conditions and Practical Applications
- Oligopoly—Features, Absolute and Limited Monopoly Compared
- Oligopoly Curves and Kinked Demand Curves Monopolistic Competition—Curves

1. MARKET

What is a Market?

Market is an area over which buyers and sellers are in close touch with one another either directly or through dealers, that the price obtainable in one part of the market affects the prices paid in other parts.

Market has four basic components :

(i) **Consumers :** There should be buyers of the product. For example, in a country where whole population is poor, these can handly be a market for luxuries like cars, VCR etc.

(ii) **Sellers :** Unless a commodity is offered for sale in the market there is no question of anybody buying the commodity. Therefore, any market, the existence of sellers is another necessity.

(iii) **A Commodity :** Each commodity has a separate market, in the sense that every commodity has separate set of buyers and sellers. So, for a market we consider only those buyers and sellers who come in close contact with each other for the same good.

(iv) **A Price :** The exchange of commody between the buyer and sellers occurs at a particular price which is mutually agreeable to both the buyers and sellers of the commodity.

2. ANALYSIS OF COMPETITION, KINDS OF COMPETITIVE SITUATION

(a) Pure Competition

Pure competition is said to exist when only two conditions exist.

(i) There are large number of buyers and sellers of the product.

(ii) The products of the firms must be homogenous.

(b) Perfect Competition

Perfect competition is supposed to fulfil some additional condition like

(i) Perfect knowledge of the market with both the buyers and sellers.

(ii) Perfect mobility of consumers and goods.

(iii) No obstacles exist against the entry or exist of the firm.

(iv) There is no transport cost.

However, the line of distinction between the perfect and pure competition is very thin. This holds true form the point of view of managerial decision making.

Both pure monopoly and pure competition are rare to find. The examples of other market forms are more commonly observed. For instance, for the defence requirements. The Govt. is a monopolistic buyer, while doctors well-known price discriminators enjoy monopoly situation.

However, the majority of enterprises fall into the category of monopolistic competitors.

Competing neighbourhood retail stores are typically monopolistic competitors, as each has growth of loyal customers for some reason or the other.

2. *(a)* Kinds of Competitive Situations

Various kinds of competition are as follows :

(a) Predatory competition, *(b)* Cut-Throat competition, *(c)* Destructive competition, *(d)* Effective or Workable competition, *(e)* Potential competition.

(a) Predatory Competition

Some sellers are motivated by an urge to obtain future monopoly power and profit and engage in predatory competition.

In case of predatory competition, a seller cuts price of product for the sole purpose of eliminating a competitor.

The seller either cuts price uniformly, or cuts price on a particular brand or temporarily cuts price in one zone while maintains the price in other zones.

(b) Cut-Throat Competition

This is a market situation where sellers in order to survive reduce prices to a point where no seller is in a position to recover his cost and earn fair return on investment.

In other words, there is a price war between sellers, which arises due to the existence of idle capacity with the producer and the presence of high fixed cost. Continuing with such a situation for a long time is ruinous for the business.

During the last decade, in India, there has been price wars leading to cut throat competition in item like Pcs, photo copiers audio cassettes and writing instruments like pens.

In such type of competition, the manufactures attempt to introduce technical and innovative measures in the manufacturing operations, and measures like cost control, inventory control, productivity and incentive schemes for improving labour efficiency etc.

(c) Destructive Competition

There may be a situation where a firm suffers from idle capacity and the problem of recovery of its paid cost. Such a situation may lead firms to successively cut prices and ultimately land in a situation where none of them is able to recover costs and earn a fair return on his investments.

In the seventies and eighties of the last century, there existed such type of competition in the automobile sector and some brands of cars like Standard Herald, completely went out of existence.

(d) Effective or Workable Competition

A competitive situation among sellers (though not perfectly competitive) offering real alternative to consumers sufficient to compel sellers to offer better quality, service and price significantly to attract consumers.

In this competition, different sellers are seen as attractive by a consumer. The sellers' price and output policies are aimed at attracting as large a number of consumers as possible.

(e) Potential Competition

It is a situation where producers do not overcharge from those whom they sell and do not overpay those from whom they buy. The precondition for such a competition to exist is the freedom of entry or exist.

When any supernormal profits are earned, these invite the threat of entry.

While when even normal profits are not possible, there is the possibility of some existing firm leaving the industry/locality.

2*(f)* **Market Structure**

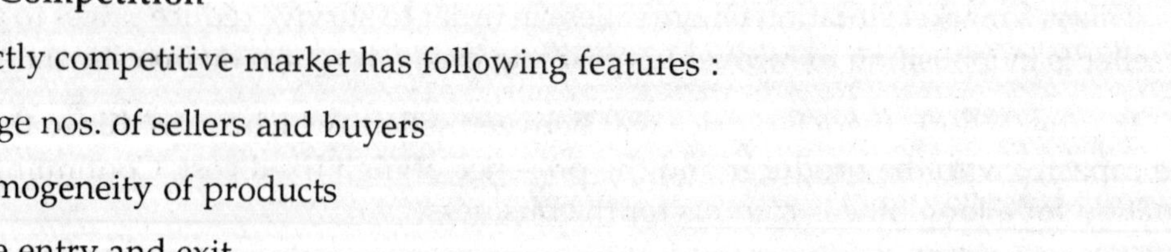

2*(g)* Perfect Competition

A perfectly competitive market has following features :

(i) Large nos. of sellers and buyers

(ii) Homogeneity of products

(iii) Free entry and exit

(iv) Perfect knowledge about the market

(v) Collusion among sellers completely absent.

Under such a market condition, each firm acts as a price taker *i.e.* it can have no price policy.

Price is determined for all firms of identical products at the intersection of supply, demand curves.

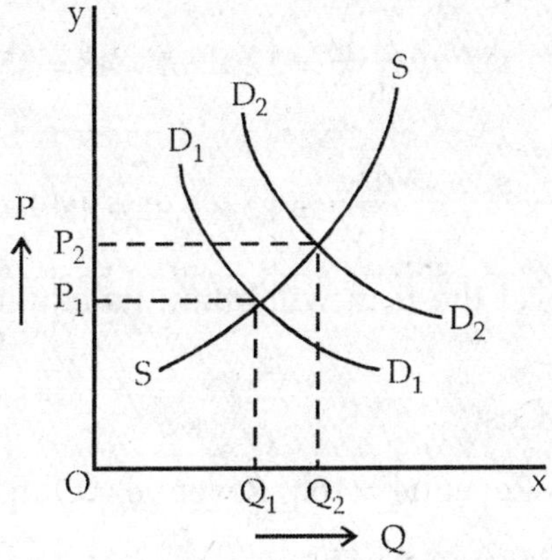

Each firm will adjust its output so that marginal cost is equal to market price (marginal revenue) and demand curve is perfectly elastic.

In the Short-Run

A firm may earn higher profit since price may be greater than average cost.

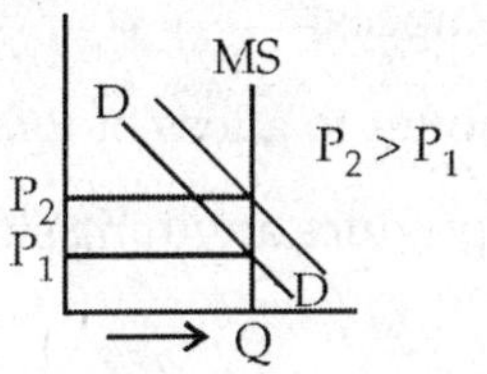

MS—Short-run supply curve
SS—Long-run supply curve
DD—Demand curve
P = Price, Q = Quantity

But in the Long-Run Equilibrium

Each firm will earn only normal profits.

For profit maximisation MR = MC → Usual Condition

Numerical 1

A competitive firm in the short-run can sell all its output at a fixed price of Rs. 10 per piece.

The cost function (in Rs.) of the firm is

$$C = 2q^3 - 24q^2 + 80q + 85$$

(i) What is the profit maximising output level?

(ii) What is the maximum amount of profits?

Solution : $C = 2q^3 - 24q^2 + 80q + 85$

So, $MC = \frac{dc}{dq} = 6q^2 - 48\,q + 80$

For equilibrium

$$P \text{ (Price)} = MC \text{ (MC = MR = Price)} = 6q^2 - 48q + 80 = 10$$

or $6q^2 - 48q + 70 = 0$ Solving for q we get q = 6.1 or 1.92

or $3q^2 - 24q + 35 = 0$

At the second order condition

$$\frac{d^2c}{dq^2} = 12q - 48$$

At $q = 6.1$ $\frac{d^2c}{dq^2} = 12 \times 6.1 - 48 = 25.2 > 0$

and At $q = 1.92$ $\frac{d^2c}{dq^2} = 12 \times 1.92 - 48 = -24.96 < 0$

So, at 6.1 units output level the firm will attain its equilibrium, *i.e.*, its profits will be maximised.

$\therefore$ Profit = π = Revenue – Cost

q = output, P = Price, R = Revenue = 10q, Revenue = Output × Price = q × 10

$= 10q - (2q^3 - 24q^2 + 8q + 85)$

for $q = 6.1$ $= 10 \times 6.1\ (2(6.1)^3 - 24(6.1)^2 + 8 \times 6.1 + 85)$

$= -72.92$ (in Rupees)

So, Maximum profit amount to a loss of Rs. 72.92.

Hence, the firm will not produce anything since it is losing at the profit-maximising output level.

And the firm can improve upon its profit level by influencing its product price.

2. *(h)* Monopoly

Monopoly is a market situation which is diametrically opposite to that of perfect competition. There is a single seller/producer.

In monopoly, the firm is a price maker and can increase his sales only by cutting price.

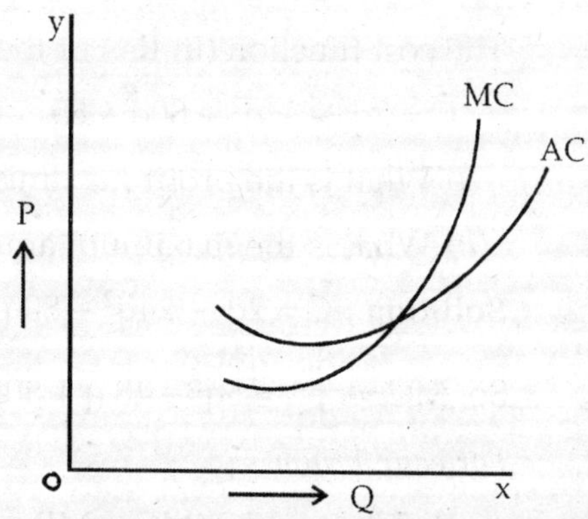

A perfect competitor adjusts his output level for a given price level in order to maximise profit. But a monopolist is at liberty to vary either output or price to reach an equilibrium, but not both at the same time.

A monopolist is expected to have U shaped AC and MC curves. But profits are not evitable even for monopoly.

Monopolists may have costs and revenues condition that result in temporary losses or normal profits. Having a monopoly does not guarantee profits. Whether or not there can be profits depends upon whether or not there are customers who are willing to pay, prices high enough to exceed production costs.

This is the reason, most public bus services in India run at a loss. Example most state Bus services and state electricity boards run at losses.

If the monopolist incurs a short-run loss and there is no plant size that will result in profit (or at least no loss) the monopoly will go out of business.

Multi Plant Monopoly

The manager determines a plant size of different size that will lead to profit. The firm thus adjusts to a plant size in such a manner that new MR equals long-run MC. This is multiplant monopoly.

2. *(i)* Perfect Competition and Monopoly Compared

1. Under competition, variation in output has no effect on price and therefore MR is equal to price.

   But if monopolist wants to sell more, he must reduce price and therefore MR < P for every output level.

2. Monopoly price is higher than competitive price and monopoly output is lower than competitive output.

3. Under perfect competition, the firm in the long-run makes only normal profits but under monopoly the firm can get super normal profits even in the long-run.

4. Monopoly power = $\frac{P - MC}{P}$ under perfect competition P = MC and Seller's monopoly power is zero. But under monopoly MC = MR, P > MR, *i.e.* P > MC.

Numerical 2

A monopolist faces a demand curve $P = 100 - 2q$ and has the cost curve $C = Q^3 - 3q^2 + 50q$ 10 [where P = price, C = total cost].

Determine the profit—maximising output of the firm.

Profit = Revenue − Total Cost

Solution : Hence Profit $= \pi = (100 - 2q)q - [q^3 - 3q^2 + 50q + 10]$

q = Quantity = Output

or $\pi = 100\,q - 2q^2 - q^3 + 3q^2 - 50q - 10$

$= -q^3 + q^2 + 50q - 10$

For profits to be maximum

$$\frac{d\pi}{dq} = 0 = -3q^2 + 2q + 50$$

or $3q^2 - 2q + 50 = 0$

i.e. $\therefore\ q = 4.8$ or $q = -4.2$

Take q = 4.8

Ignore –4.2 since (–)ve sign

Thus profit maximising price P = 100 – 2 × 4.8

= 90.4 at **q = 4.8**

2. *(j)* A.P. Learner has devised a formula for measuring the degree of monopoly power

L_1 = Lerner Index

$$= \frac{P - MC}{P} = \frac{1}{e_p}$$

$$\text{Since } MR = AR\left(1 - \frac{1}{e_p}\right)$$

Thus, as e_p decreases, L_1 increase, *i.e., the more inelastic the demand curve the greater will be the monopoly power.*

So, A monopolists demand curve is inelastic.

$$\text{Hence } L_1 = \frac{P - MC}{P} \text{ at equilibrium output level}$$

$$= \frac{90.4 - 90.3}{90.4} = \frac{0.1}{90.4} = 0.0011 \text{ (approx.)}$$

$$MC = \frac{dc}{dq} = (q^3 - 3q^2 + 50q + 10) \quad \text{at } q = 4.8$$

$$= 3q^2 - 6q + 50 \quad \text{at } q = 4.8$$

$$= 3(4.8)^2 - 6(4.8) + 50$$

$$= 90.3$$

Numerical 3

The average price of a ball pen is Rs. 10/unit. Because of large number of mfrs, this price is not affected by a new entrant, A mfr. estimates that monthly total cost including a normal profit is given by TC = 1000 + 2Q + 0.01Q². To maximise total profit, how many ball pens should be produced each month? In the short run, how much economic profit will the business earn each month?

Solution : Taking derivative of total cost equation gives the marginal cost equation.

$MC = \frac{dTC}{dQ} = 2 + 0.02Q$, Profit is maximised by equating price and marginal cost. Thus profit maximising output is given by soln. to 10 = 2 + 0.02 Q.

$\therefore$ Q = 400 per month

Economic Profit = Total Revenue – Total Cost

$$= TR - TC = 10 \times 400 - [1{,}000 + 2Q + 0.01Q^2]$$

Put Q = 400, $= \text{Rs. } 600$

Thus, in short-run economic profit = Rs. 600 per month.

Numerical 4

A bicycle mfr. faces a horizontal demand curve. The firm's total costs are given by TVC = $150Q - 20Q^2 + Q^3$, Q = Quantity, TVC = Total Variable Cost

Below what price should the firm shut down operations?

Solution : Marginal cost is the derivative of total cost w.r.t. Quantity (Q).

Thus, $$MC = \frac{dTVC}{dQ} = 150 - 40Q + 3Q^2$$

and Average variable cost equation is given by

$$AVC = \frac{TVC}{Q} = \frac{150Q - 20Q^2 + Q^3}{Q} = 150 - 40Q + 3Q^2$$

The shut down point is where price equal minimum average variable cost.

But Profit maximisation requires that price also equal marginal cost.

Thus, by setting MC = AVC

The result is $150 - 40Q + 3Q^2 = 150 - 70Q + Q^2$

Rearranging terms gives $2Q^2 - 20Q = 0$

$$\text{or } 2Q(Q - 10) = 0$$

$$\text{or } Q = 0, Q = 10$$

Substituting Q = 10 into marginal cost equation becomes P = MC = 150 – 40(10) + 3(100) = 50

and Q = 0 substituting P = 150—this is not valid since Q = 0

The relevant solution is non zero output. Thus, if price falls below Rs. 50 per unit, the firm should shut down.

2. *(k)* Business Decisions

Decisions is about identifying the alternatives and choosing the best of these alternatives. Tangible decision is about quantifying. The choice, *i.e.*, quantum of profit, sales turnover etc., where as intangible decision is goodwill and industrial relation etc.

The diagram for decision-making is given below :

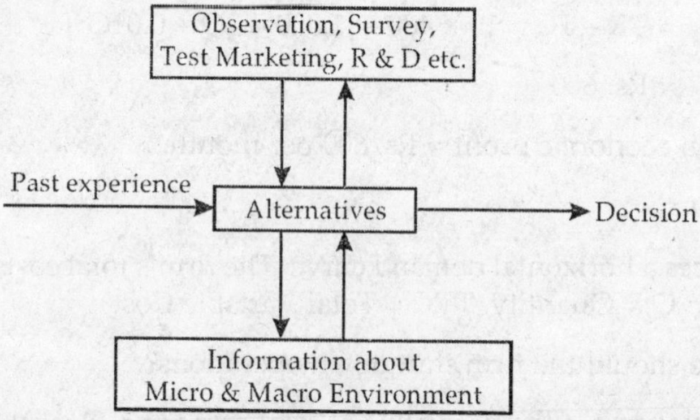

Micro environment may consists of Company's Production, Marketing Finance, Human Resource etc., whereas Macro environment many consist of external environment, *i.e.*, social, legal, Economical, Political and Technological aspects.

2. *(l)* Objectives of a Firm

According P.F. Drucker, a business firm may have 8 objectives, *i.e.*, physical resource, Financial resource, Human resource, Productivity, Marketing, Innovation, Profitability and social responsibility.

In Principles of Management we generally consider four objectives of a business firm, *i.e.*, sales maximisation, profit maximisation, growth rate maximisation and social responsibility.

3. EQUILIBRIUM OF A FIRM

For a firm, the price at which the quantity demanded of the product equals its quantity supplied is called its equilibrium price, and the corresponding quantity as its equilibrium quantity.

When a firm sells equilibrium quantity (Q_e) at equilibrium price (P_e), the firm is said to be in equilibrium.

Equilibrium is a situation best suited to the firm, given the circumstances.

Any effort to sell at a price higher than the equilibrium price would be frustrated by competitors, while no rational firm would like to sell at a price lower than what it could get.

If we assume that firms always attempt to maximise profits, the basic economic theory of the firm provides a framework for the determination of price.

If the production and sale of an additional unit of product adds more to revenue than to costs, profit is increased and thus that unit should be produced and sold.

If the additional unit of output involves larger costs than revenue, if should not be produced.

In other words, the firm continues to increase output until the marginal revenue (MR) is larger than marginal cost (MC).

Thus, the firm is in equilibrium only when MR = MC.

However, the rule that MR = MC maximises profits does not directly determine the price that the firm should charge for the product.

The determination of appropriate price depends upon the type of market structure in which the product is being sold.

4. PERFECT COMPETITION : FEATURES

Main features of a perfectly competitive market is characterised by :

(i) A very large number of relatively small buyers and sellers.

A single buyer's or seller's actions can not, therefore, have any perceptible influence on market price. The firm is, thus, a price taken and quantity adjuster.

(ii) There is no product differentiation, *i.e.*, homogeneous products.

(iii) The firms are free to enter or leave the industry, *i.e.*, only the efficient firms exist at any point of time.

(iv) The firms in the industry do not collide with each other, *i.e.*, each firm takes its independent action.

(v) The factor of production must be free to enter or leave the industry, *i.e.*, in the perfectly competitive market there should be perfect mobility of products.

(vi) Each buyer and seller operates under conditions of certainty, being endowed with complete knowledge of prices, quantities, costs and demand.

Although some of the assumptions of the perfectly competitive model may be unrealistic, use of the model in economic theory has been increasing recently for two quite different reasons.

(a) The perfect competition model can be used as an ideal or yard stick against which all other models can be compared and evaluated.

(b) This model has been quite accurate in explaining and predicting behaviour of the market and the firm under certain circumstances.

5. MONOPOLY : MONOPOLISTIC COMPETITION

A pure monopoly exists if one and only one firm produces and sells a particular commodity in the market. No other seller can enter the market, else monopoly would cease to exist. Thus, in case of pure monopoly by definition the firm and industry coincide, the single firm producing the product is itself both the firm and the industry. There are no direct competitors or rivals. But this does not always guarantee success, it only ensures that the monopolist is price maker who can set the price to the best of his advantage without fear of new firms entering the market to compete away his profits.

Further, the product which the monopolist sells is distinct in the sense that no close or perfect substitute exists for this product.

Thus, the policies of a monopolist would be constrained by the availability of reasonably adequate substitute goods. For example, the Railways in India are a public monopoly, but there are different substitutes available for the purpose, *e.g.*, road transport, airways, sea/river transport etc.

These different substitutes, however, cannot be regarded as close substitutes of railways services.

(a) **Main features of monopoly are :**

Only one producer with no direct competitor/rival and some amount of competition exists from indirect competition may exist from the substitutes, and that monopolist is a price maker.

The elasticity of demand for the product determines the level up to which the Monopolist can raise the price while cost conditions determine the level down to which the monopolist can lower this price.

The monopoly is not a permanent phenomenon. The firm which is a monopoly now, may not remain or monopoly in future if :-

—Close substitutes emerge,

—Demand pattern of the consumers undergoes a change,

—New Firms are able to enter the industry, or

—Govt. intervenes to control the monopoly.

(b) **Causes of Monopoly :** (or the Origin of Monopoly)

The causes of monopoly may be legal or technological or both :

Following are main causes that laid to a monopoly situation.

(i) Patent rights for the products or the production process give legal monopoly rights to firms.

(ii) Govt. policies such as granting licences or imposing foreign trade restrictions (like quotas etc.) result in creating monopolies.

(iii) Ownership and control of some strategic raw materials.

(iv) Exclusive knowledge of technology by the firm.

(v) It may be that size of market can accommodate only a single firm.

The technology might be such that only a large output can reap the economics of scale. In such a case, none firms will mean that none of the firms would be able to exploit the economics. Such a monopoly is known as "natural monopoly".

6. MONOPOLISTIC COMPETITION

(a) Meaning and main features :

Monopolistic competition refers to a situation where there are many sellers of a differentiated product. There is competition which is keen, though not perfect, between many firms making very similar products. In other words, it is a situation where there is competition among many sellers producing close substitutes but not perfect substitutes. That is the products are differentiated and each seller can independently dictate about its own price-output policies.

Following are main characteristics of a monopolistically competitive situation :

(i) **Many Number of Sellers :** In case of monopolistic competition the number of sellers in "many and small enough". They are many in number but no seller is big enough to influence the market price which is determined by the interaction of industry demand and supply. Each seller pursues its independent course of action.

(ii) **Product Differentiation :** One of the main features of monopolistic competition is product differentiation. There are many firms producing a particular product, but each firm introduces its product in such a way that its product is not the same as being sold by other. The basis for this differentiation may take the form of quality difference, advertisement patent rights trade marks etc.

Thus, the differentiation of products makes the products of different firms heterogeneous.

In this case, the products of one firm encounters close substitutes from the other firms and, therefore, their close-elasticity is quite high.

(iii) **Advertisement** is used as an instrument to impress upon the consumers the superiority of the product. Out of two types of advertisements, *i.e.*, informative type which is used for new products and other type, *i.e.*, manipulative advertisement is aimed to create a psychological preference in favour of the product.

(iv) **Patent Rights and Trade Marks :** There are certain brand names which command a goodwill in the market, *i.e.*, HLL, Godrej, Tata etc. The goodwill creates preferences of the consumers in favour of popular brands and is thus an instrument in product differentiation.

(v) **Quality Differentiation :** The monopolistic competitor tries to distinguish his product on the side of production by introducing changes in its quality.

This is done with the help of craftsmanship and changes in shape, design, size, colour etc. of the product. These changes in quality are undertaken in accordance with the tastes and preferences of the consumers.

(vi) **Freedom of Entry of the New Firms and Exit of the Old Firms :** In monopolistic competition there are many small firms each producing a close substitutes. In the long run, therefore, there cannot be any restrictions on entry or exit of the firms.

(vii) **Higher Elasticity of Demand :** Due to differentiated product, the individual firm possesses some monopoly power, and therefore, its demand curve is more elastic than the perfectly competitive firm.

This means, that a small decrease in the price of the product may lead to a large increase in the demand for this product, assuming the prices of other firms remaining the same.

7. EQUILIBRIUM OF A FIRM IN MONOPOLISTIC COMPETITION

Equilibrium of the firms under monopolistic competition follows the general practice of short period and long period analysis.

(a) Short-Run :

Short-run equilibrium of the firm is based on the following assumptions.

(i) These are large number of sellers, each acting independently and each having some monopoly power due to its product differentiation.

(ii) Each firm has an elastic demand curve.

(iii) Entry and exit of firms is not permitted (by the very definition of short period)

(iv) The short-run cost curves of each firm differ from each other.

Given these assumptions, each firm aims at that level of price and output which maximises its profits,) The equilibrium price and output of a monopolistically competitive firm is determined at the point where its marginal cost equals marginal revenue.

(b) Long-run Equilibrium :

If firms in monopolistic competition are observed to be making economic profits, other firms will be tempted to enter the market. However there is a cost barrier to be overcome, because the new firm must spend enough on R & D to come up with a differentiated product, and then spend enough on advertising and promotion to penetrate the market.

Thus entry is not completely free, but is relatively easy.

Since the firm is in equilibrium, it has no incentive to change the price, but the abnormal profits will attract new competitors into the market, as a result of which the supply of the product will increase and the market share of the existing firm will decline. This will change the demand and reduce abnormal profits.

This state will continue till new firms find the profits attractive.

Now, there will be no further entry into the industry, since profits are just normal.

The equilibrium is stable as the firm will be a loser if it either raises or lowers the price.

8. DISCRIMINATING MONOPOLY OR PRICE DISCRIMINATION

(a) Meaning of Price Discrimination

Price discrimination is said to exist when the same product is sold at different prices to different buyers.

The product is basically the same but may have slight difference.

For example, a cinema theatre has different charges on the basis of location of seats, though the same movie is shown at a particular time.

Similarly, for different classes in trains and aircrafts different fares are charged though all passengers are performing the same journey.

No doubt, the comforts differ between classes, but they are generally not in proportion to the form differences.

(*b*) Conditions when price discrimination is possible

(*i*) **Difference in Price Elasticities :** Depending on the preference of buyers, their income, their location and the case of availability of substitutes, the product has different elasticity with different customers. Whenever the elasticities of demand differ between buyers they can charge different prices for the same good.

(*ii*) **Market Segmentation :** It must be possible to divide the market into sub-markets with different price elasticities of the customers. A different price can then be fixed for each market segment, *e.g.*, doctors charging different fees from rich and poor of the same locality.

(*iii*) **Effective Separation of Sub-markets :** There must be effective separation of different market segments in the sense that no reselling can take place from the low price market to the a high price market.

Otherwise the products of the firm would start flowing to high price market via the low price market, thus raising price in the latter and lowering it in the former. This will obviously defeat the purpose of price discrimination.

(*iv*) Various brands of a certain article, which in fact are almost alike, may be sold as different Qualities, and these are sold under different labels and names which induce the rich and snobbish buyers to separate themselves from poor buyers.

Each monopolist competitor practices product differentiation, and it tries to find loyal customers in the area as well as distant market.

Under monopolistic competition, in the long-run all firms tend to be at an equal price level for the same type of product and even the inefficient firms may stay in the market on the strength of their product differentiation.

Under monopolistic competition, the resources are inefficiently utilised to keep excess capacity by that competitors deliberately and therefore, the firms keep their average costs and selling prices high, Since any change in price by a firm under monopolistic competition invites counter moves from its rivals, the firms normally maintain their price levels.

Example : Various small companies manufacturing Pens.

8. (*c*) Price Leadership

If changes are usually or always introduced by a firm and usually or always followed with similar price changes by other sellers, price competition may be said to involve Price Leadership.

Oligopoly is a situation where a few large compete against each other and there is an element of interdependence in the decision of these firms. Each in the oligopoly recognises this interdependency.

A major policy change on the part of one firm will have immediate effect on its competitors and the competitors are then likely to react with their counter strategies.

Oligopoly tends to reduce the freedom of action a firm has in taking its price decision because the firm is not sure of the reactions of its rivals. One way to come out of this uncertainty and regain some measure of initiative is to reduce the cross-elasticity of demand between one's own product and that of one's rivals with the help of product differentiation.

An equal popular alternative for the firm is to deliberately choose a pattern of price parallelism, *i.e.*, one firm taking the initiative role or leadership.

Example : Scooter-Bajaj Auto/LML, TVS, Motor Cycles, Hero-Honda, Kinetic and Escort etc.

Imperfect Collusion—Price Leadership Model

Among the competing business firms mutual distruct and unwilling to surrender their sovereignty, make the collusion imperfect.

Most important form of imperfect collusion is price leadership. These kinds of price leadership are given below :

8. *(d)* Types of Price leadership

There are three kinds of price leadership :

(i) **Dominant/Firm Price Leadership :** A large firm is the dominant firm (high market share) for the product can resort to price leadership, *i.e.*, the large firm fixes the price and other small firms act as price-takers. Example-SAIL *vis-a-vis* Tata Steel.

(ii) **Collusive Price leadership :** Collusive price leadership may emerge in oligopoly as a result of an explicit or a tacit collusion.

The leader may be the larger firm in the group and the small firms follow the price change initiated by the dominant firm.

Example : Price Cartel through Manufacturers' Association.

(iii) **Barometric Price Leadership :** Barometric price leadership gets its name from the fact that one firm acts as a "barometer", reflecting changing market condition or costs of production that require a change in price.

A firm with small market share but an efficient user may act as a barometric leader and is in the best position to judge the changes in demand and cost conditions that its price change is in the best interest of the group.

Since the barometric leader has very little power to impose his decisions on other firms in the industry, leadership may thus be short lived.

Example : Tata Steel has lower market share than SAIL, but it is the lowest cost steel producer in the world.

8. *(e)* Advantages of Price Leadership

(i) The most important advantage of price leadership is that by this method the firms opt out of the uncertainty surrounding pricing decisions in oligopoly.

There is interdependence between the firm's own behaviour and the behaviour of its rivals.

Firms choose a parallel price rather than resort to undercutting each other.

This process facilitates development of new products and improvement in quality.

(ii) Price leadership eliminates the possibility of a price war.

(iii) Price leadership involves mutual understanding between the oligopoly firms and is the most convenient strategy for oligopoly firms to stay and grow together.

8. *(f)* Elasticity of Supply

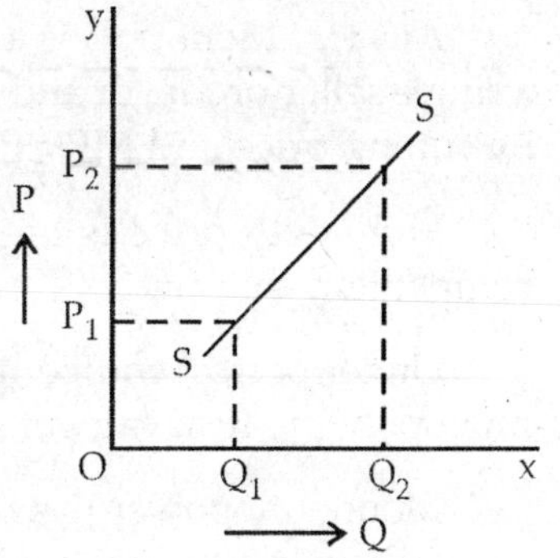

Supply curve has positive slope and slopes upward right.

If the quantity demanded increase the prices increases and subsequently price increases. In figure, $Q_2 > Q_1$ & $P_2 > P_1$ Elasticity of Surplus, $E_s = \frac{P}{Q_s}\frac{\Delta Q_s}{\Delta P}$, P = Initial Price, Q_s = Initial quantity Supplied, ΔQ_s = Change in quantity supplied and ΔP = Change in price.

Q. Give Relationship between Marginal Revenue and Price elasticity of demand.

Ans : $$MR = P\left[1 - \frac{1}{e_p}\right]$$

MR = Marginal Revenue, P = Market Price or the Product and e_p = The price elasticity or demand for the product.

The above formula is very useful when the demand function has a known constant price elasticity.

Business managers must estimate the value of MR in order to arrive to decision about price and output.

8. *(g)* Write A.P. Lerner's Monopoly Power

Ans : A.P. Lerner has advised a formula for measuring the degree of monopoly power

$$L_1 = \text{Lerner Index} = \frac{P - MC}{P} = \frac{1}{e_p}$$

$$\text{Since } MR = AR\left(1 - \frac{1}{e_p}\right)$$

Thus, as e_p decreases, L_1 increases, *i.e.*, the more in elastic the demand curve the greater will be the monopoly power.

$$\text{Hence } L_1 = \frac{P - MC}{P}$$

Under perfect competition, P = MC and seller's monopoly power is zero, but under monopoly

MC = MR P > MR and P > MC

9. Various Concepts

(a) Monopoly and Monopoly power

(b) Price discrimination and different forms of price discrimination

(c) Three degrees of price discrimination.

Ans : *(a)* Monopoly is a market situation which is opposite of perfect competition. There is a single seller producer and in monopoly a firm is a price maker and can increase his sales only by cutting price and MR< P for every output level.

Monopoly price is higher than competitive price and monopoly output is lower than competition output.

Under perfect competition, the firm in the long-run makes only normal profits but under monopoly the firm can get super-normal profits even in the long run.

Monopoly power has been explained under question no. q.no. 8 before.

(b) **Price discrimination** is said to exist when the same product is sold at different prices to different buyers. The product is basically the same but may have slight difference in packaging or otherwise.

The necessary conditions which must be fulfilled for the implementation of price discrimination are as follows :

(1) The markets must be divided into different price elasticities.

(2) There must be effective separation of sub markets so that no resulting can take place from a low price market can take place from a low price market to a high price market.

Examples : Various classes of Railways and cinema theatre classes.

(c) Under monopoly condition, there are three different types of price discrimination, *i.e.*, price discrimination of the **first degree, second degree,** and **the third degree.**

Under the **first degree of discrimination** the monopolist is able to sell each separate unit of the output at a different price to the same buyer.

Example : Specialist physician charges higher fees when the visits patients house, than the fees at his clinic.

Under the **second degree,** goods are divided into different blocks of units for each block a different price is charged.

Example : Mangoes and Apples in blocks as per quality with the same seller.

And under the **third degree,** the seller divides buyers according to their income, location, types of uses etc, and charges different prices for each group of consumers.

Example : Price difference in an elite locality and in a general market (*i.e.* say new market and college street market in Kolkata).

10. Cost curves showing TVC, AVC, FC, VC and TC etc.

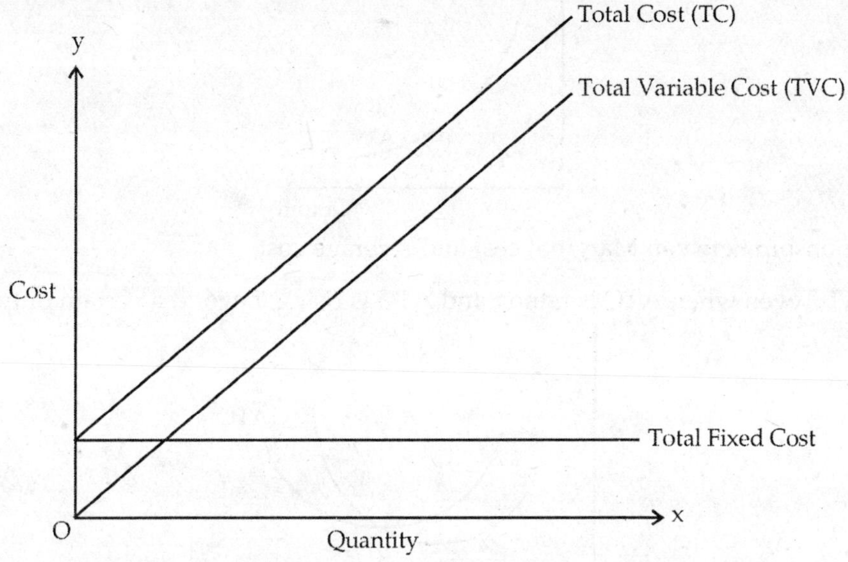

Total cost is an integration of total fixed cost and total variable cost.

Total variable cost represents the total cost of all variable inputs employed in a particular production process.

The slope of the total cost curve is related to return to scale concept.

Total fixed cost is the total cost of all the fixed inputs employed in a particular production process. TFC is represented by a horizontal straight line.

Average cost (AC) is defined on total cost of production divided by the total number output produced.

$$AC = \frac{TC}{Q}$$

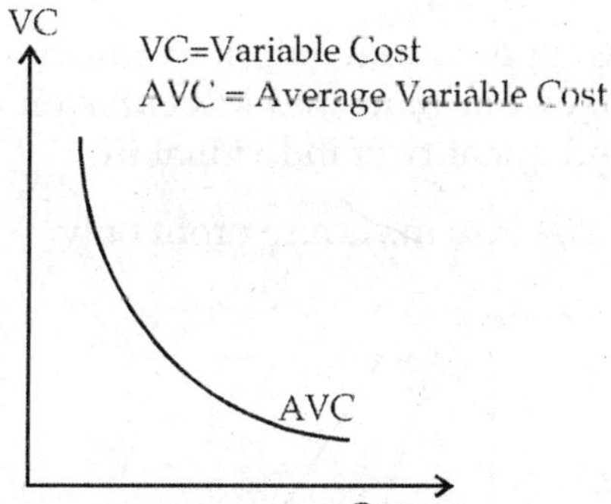

Fig. Relationship VC & AVC.

Average fixed cost (AFC) is the amount of fixed cost required to produce a single unit of production and is calculated by

$$AFC = \frac{TFC}{Q}$$

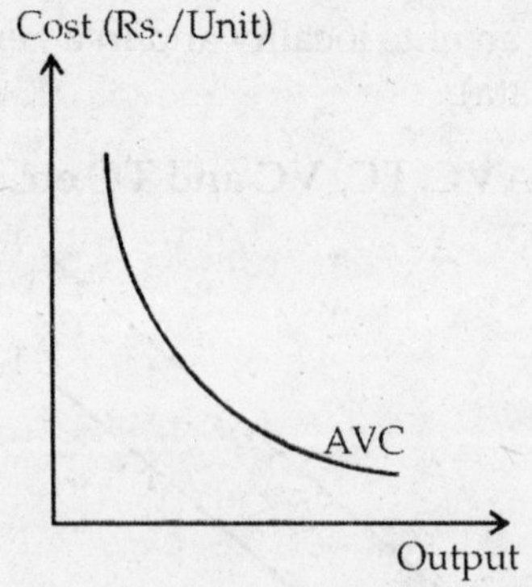

& Relationship between Marginal cost and Average cost

MC< ATC even when ATC is falling and ATC is rising, beyond a certain output.

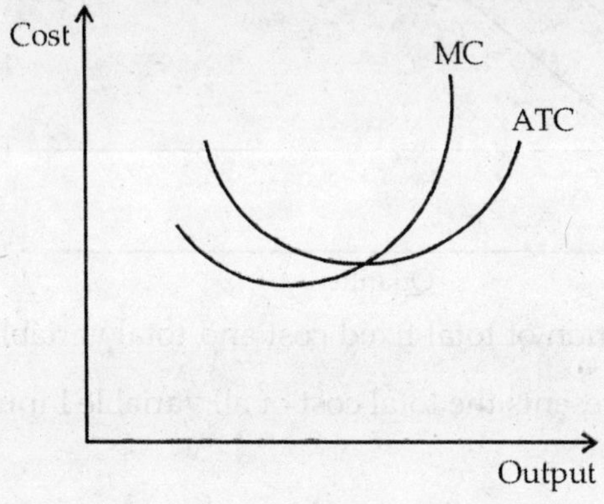

11. *(a)* Perfect competition—short run and long run equilibrium

(b) Monopoly—short run and long run equilibrium

(c) Monopolistic—short run and long run equilibrium

(a) See on page no. 104 & 105

(b) Monopoly—Short run and long run equilibrium :

To find out profit maximising price and output of any monopoly firm, we need to know the characteristics of MC curve on one hand and MR curve on the other, because that curves determine equilibrium price and quantity of individual firm.

The objective of a monopolist is to maximise profit only.

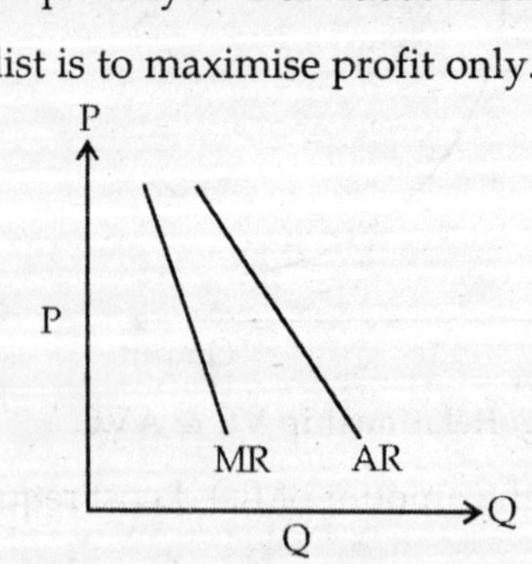

For a monopolist, the slopes of marginal cost curve and average cost curve will remain the same as under perfect competition, while average and marginal revenue curves are different from that of perfect competition.

For a monopolist the demand curve and AR curve are the same and MR curve is downward sloping.

Following conditions should satisfy for Monopolist's profit maximisation.

M **(Ist order condition)**

and Slope of MC > Slope of MR **(Second order condition).**

(c) (i) Short-Run Equilibrium—Monopolistic Competition

Any firm under mono polistic competition faces negatively sloped demand curve, as the products manufactured by different firm under different brand names are close substitutes and hence, the customers find an option to switch over to other brands, if a firm makes any upward revision in price.

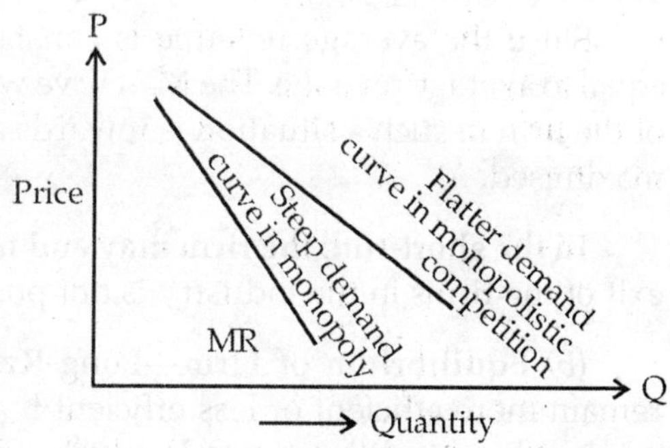

For monopolistic competition MC & AC curves are as usual U-shaped.

For Profit maximisation

MC = MR and Slope of MC Curve > Slope of MR curve

Therefore, the short run equilibrium under monopolistic competition, is exactly the same as the short-run equilibrium under monopoly.

(2) Long-Run Equilibrium Monopolistic Competition

In the absence of entry barriers, the new firms will easily enter into the industry and as a result, total demand for the product will be distributed among more number of firms each of which produces a differentiated product.

So, now demand of each individual firm will decrease causing a left ward parallel shift in their respective AC Curve.

Entry of new firm will continue to shift until super normal profits disappear.

Similarly, loss will encourage some firm to exit leading to a right ward parallel shift in AR curve.

Shift in AR (either left or right ward) continues fill the firm arrive at a no profit no loss "situation."

12. Short-run and long-run equilibrium of the perfectly competitive firms

(a) Equilibrium of a Firm—Short-Run in Perfect Competition.

In a situation of perfect competition each firm is relatively insignificant so that no one or them can affect price noticeably. If any firm raises the price of its product above market price,

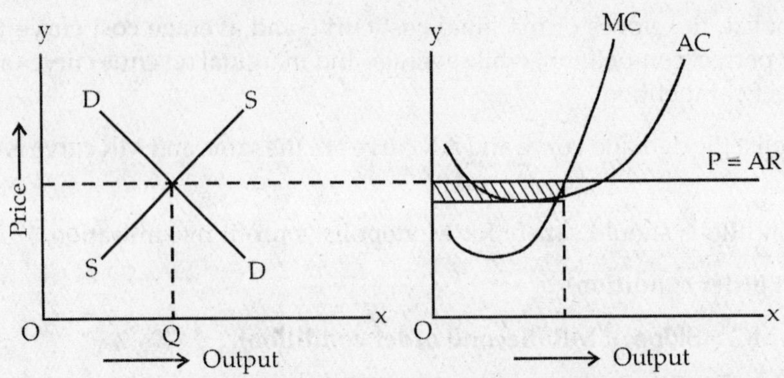

it will be unable to sell anything whereas the firm gains nothing but cutting the price below the market price because it can sell any amount or the prevailing price.

Thus in a competitive situation, all firms get the same price.

Since the average revenue is constant, the marginal revenue will also be constant and equal to average revenue. The MR curve will coincide with the horizontal AR curve. The decision of the firm in such a situation is towards adjusting its output to the given price so that profit is maximised.

In the short-run, the firm may end up making either profit or loss as in the short entry or exit of the firms in the industry is not possible.

***(b)* Equilibrium of Firm—Long-Run**—in perfect competition. In this case no firm can remain more efficient or less efficient than others in the long-run. The long-run the situation represents a condition towards which a purely competitive market would find to move in the long-run.

In case of long-run also AR and MR curves are a horizontal straight line at the level of price (P).

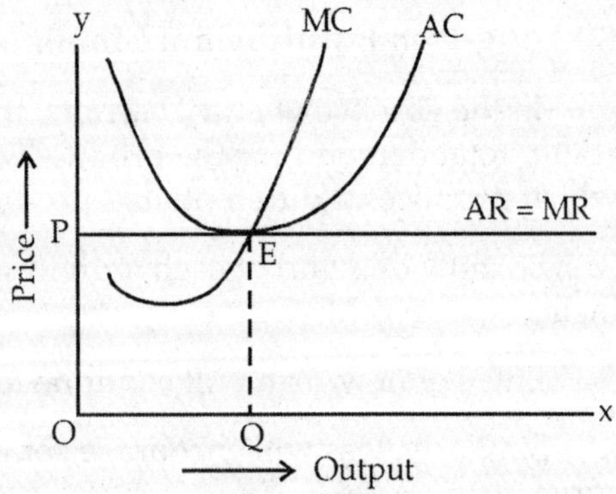

Thus, in the long-run a perfectly competitive situation a firm's demand curve, average revenue curve and marginal revenue curve are all horizontals and coincide with each other. In long-run, the firms make normal profits or losses because at equilibrium the firm is producing at that level of output where the average revenue equals its average cost.

Thus, in long-run, P = AR = MR = AC = MC, *i.e.*, **in long-run the firm produces at its most efficient level of output where average costs are minimised.**

***(c)* Short-Run and the Long-Run**

Short-run is the period of time during which it is not possible to change all inputs to production, only some inputs, such as labour may be changed.

Long-run is the minimum period of time during which all inputs to production can be changed.

Economists frequently use capital as an example of a factor that does not change in the short-run and they use labour as an example of a factor that can change in short run.

(d) Price Equals Marginal Cost

If firms are maximising profits, then they choose a quantity (Q) such that price (Market price) equals the Marginal Cost (MC).

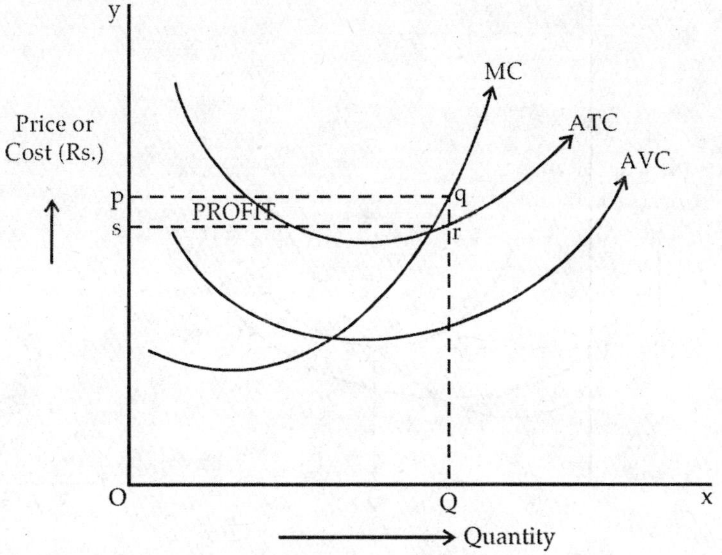

Fig. Cost Curve Diagram.

Thus, as shown in the graph, the profit maximising quantity (Q) is produced which is obtained by the intersection of price (Market Price) line and the marginal cost curve.

(e) Showing Profits on the Cost Curve Diagram

Quantity (Q) × Price (P) = Total Revenue and Point 'r' gives the average total cost for the quantity (Q) produced. Rectangle pqQO represent the total revenue and rectangle SrQO represents the total average cost for producing quantity (Q). Therefore, profits are represented by the rectangle pqrs, *i.e.*, Total revenue P × Q – Total Cost Q × ATC.

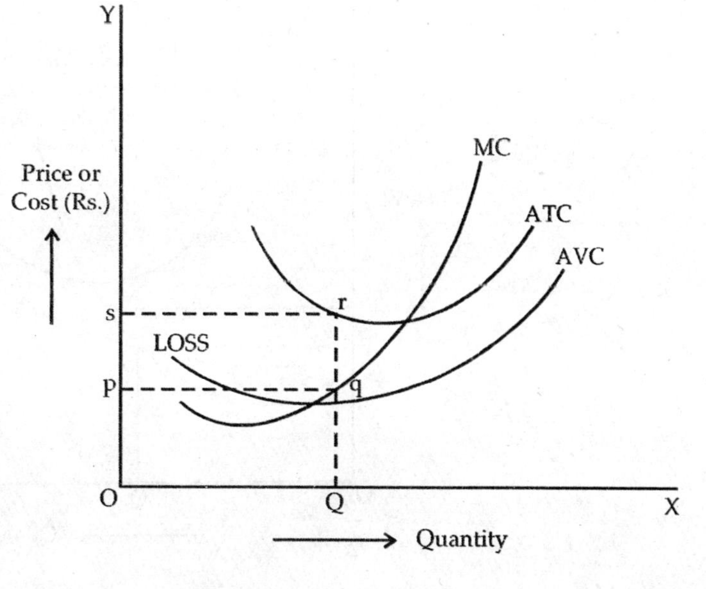

(f) Showing a Loss on the Cost Curve Diagram

Here, the market price is lower than previous diagram. The market price line intersects price or the marginal cost curve at a cost point below the average total cost curve. Thus the area of the total cost rectangle is larger than the area of the total revenue rectangle.

(g) Showing Break Even Point on the Cost Curve Diagram

When there is no profit and no loss as shown in the diagram, *i.e.*, pqQO rectangle represents total revenue and total average cost for producing quantity (Q).

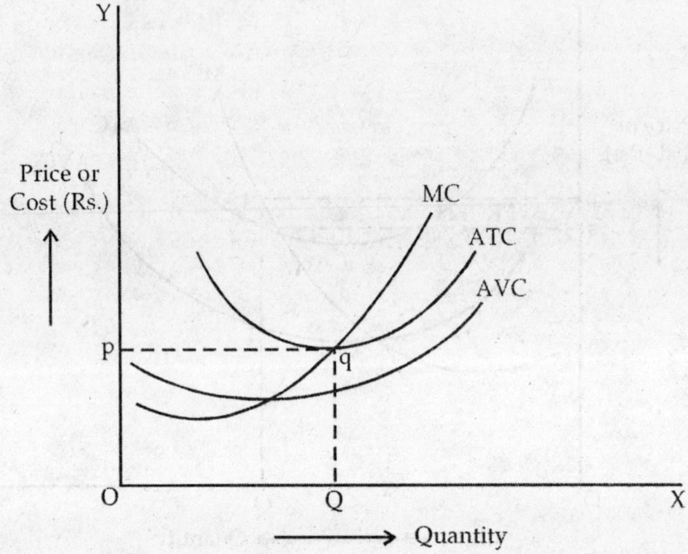

Here P = ATC

i.e. Price equals the minimum of average total cost.

(h) Showing a Shutdown Point on the Cost Curve Diagram

When price (p_1) is a above average variable cost, the firm should keep producing even if profits are negative. But, if price (p_2) is less than average variable cost, losses will be smaller if

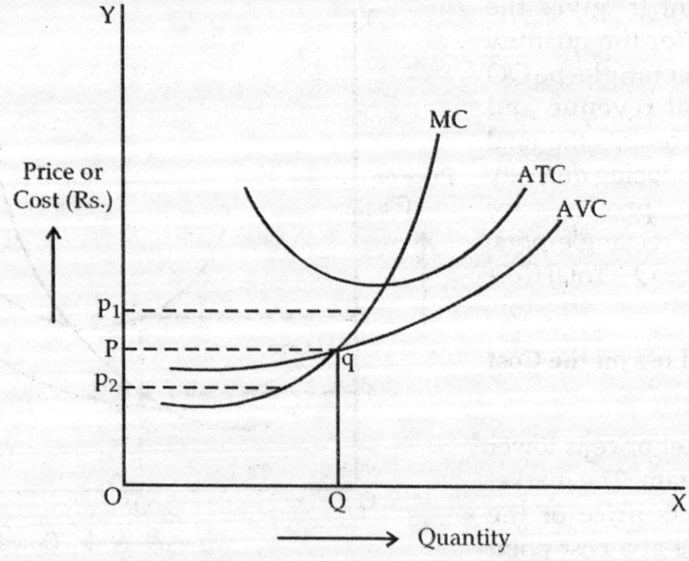

the firm shuts down and stop producing. Hence, the shutdown point is when price equals average variable cost.

∴ At Shutdown Point P = AVC

Note → Shutdown Point → P = Minimum AVC & Break Even Point → P = Minimum ATC

13. PRICE DISCRIMINATION

(a) Conditions necessary for price discrimination to operate are as follows :

1. The firm must be able to set its price. Thus price discrimination will be impossible under perfect competition, where firms are price takers.
2. The markets must be separate. Consumers in the low priced market must not be able to resell the produce in the high priced market.
3. Demand elasticity must differ in each market. The firm will charge the higher price in the market where demand is less elastic, and thus less sensitive to a price rise.

(b) Practical application for price discrimination are the following advantage for the firm :

1. Price discrimination will allow the firm to earn higher revenue from any given level of sales.
2. A firm adopting price discrimination may be able to use it to drive competitions out of business. If a firm has monopoly in one market (*i.e.* say home market), it may be able to charge a high price due to relatively inelastic demand, and thus make high profits.
3. If the firm is under oligopoly in another market (*i.e.* say export market), it may use the high profits in the first market to subsidise a very low price in the oligopoly market, thus forcing its competitiors out of business.
4. Maximising output for the firm will be at a price P = MC = MR.

14. OLIGOPOLY

(a) Features of an oligopolistic market?

Ans : Features of an oligopolistic market are as follows :

(1) There are only a small number of firms who continue the market share.

(2) These firms are selling products which are either standardised or differentiated.

(3) Standardised products exist in the homogeneous oligopoly market.

Example : Ceiling Fan market's standard product with few manufacturers.

(4) Differentiated products are sold in the differentiated oligopoly market.

Example : Motor cycles market heavily differentiated products with few manufactures like Hero Honda, Bajaj Auto, TVS, and Kinetic etc.

(5) Standardised product market is also called homogeneous oligopoly in which a firm has to depend heavily on the price policies of its rivals.

(6) In differentiated oligopoly, each seller tries to differentiate the product firm other sellers, and heavily spend on sales promotion. Here, each firm has an independent demand function and demand curve, showing the impact of price spreads.

***(b)* Difference between absolute monopoly limited monopoly**

Absolute monopoly has following features :

(1) A single seller

(2) No close substitutes

(3) Closed entry

(4) Price maker

(5) Possibility of price discrimination.

Absolute monopoly is the opposite of perfect competition.

The extreme form of absolute monopoly does not exist in real sense. Therefore, it is an extreme model of market structure.

In the real sense, it is the imperfect competition which dominates the market structure.

The main form of imperfect competition is monopolistic competition which is the combination of monopoly and perfect competition.

Some elements of monopoly exists in monopolistic competition and hence, monopolistic competition is called limited monopoly.

***(c)* Monopolistic or Limited Monopoly**

Features of monopolistic competition or **limited monopoly** are as follows :

(1) Large number of buyers and sellers

(2) Differentiated products

(3) Free entry and exit

(4) Prices in the long-run almost equal

(5) Non-price competition.

***(d)* Oligopoly**

Oligopoly with product differentiation

(i) Firm producers 0 × units and sells at OP Price, earn only normal profit. (refer diagram next page)

(ii) At Ox* units production the average cost in the least, therefore without resorting to price war a firm can differentiate its product & sells at price P* corresponding Ox* larger unit produced and earning total large profit.

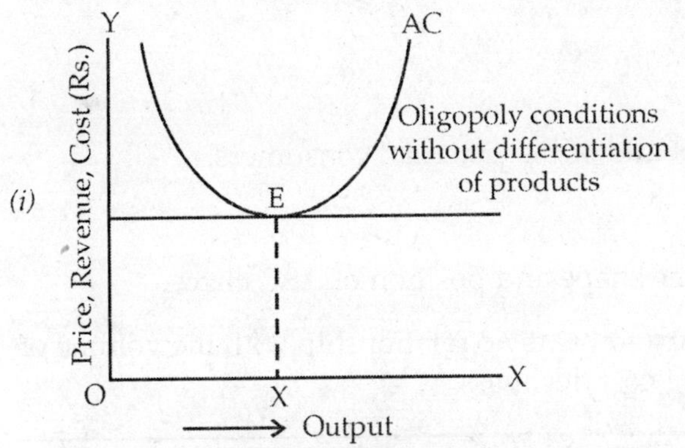

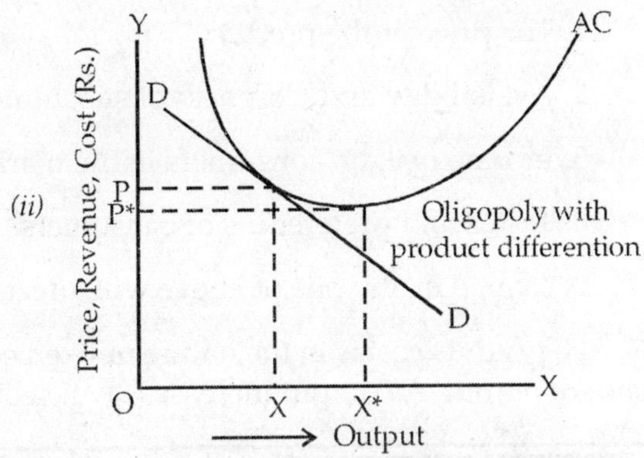

***(e)* Kinked Demand Curve** (under oligopoly) Kinked demand curve was used by Paul M. Sweez to explain price rigidity Kinked demand curve concept explains that each oligopoly will act and react in a way that keeps conditions tolerable for all members of the industry.

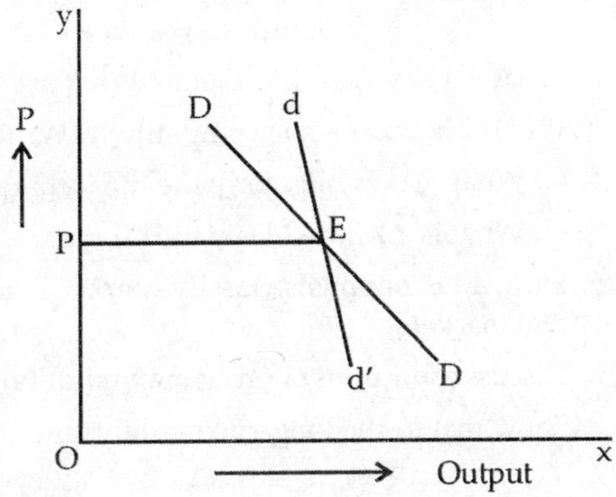

Such a situation is most likely to occur where products are quite similar and the prices are same. If one firm decides to sell at higher price, and competitors do not follow this scheme, the firm loses its customers to its rivals. The oligopoly firm realises that it is better to accommodate rivals rather than start a price war.

Graph shows firm's demand curve DD and market supply curve dEd' intersects at E.

If an oligopolier reduces price, he expects his competition to follow suit, while no competitor will follow him when he raises price. The relevant demand curve for the firm is DEd' (with a kink at E). For price reduction below P the share of market demand curve d'E is relevant as the counter moves by rivals will keep market share of firm constant.

This is **Kinked demand curve.**

***(f)* Monopolistic Competition**

The shape and position of selling cost curve are as follows :

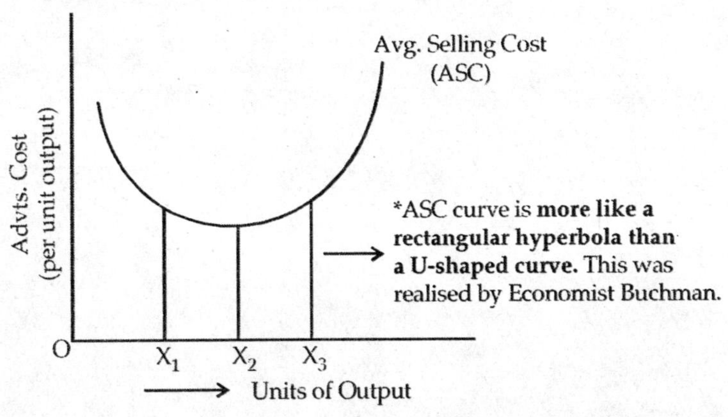

1. The price of the product
2. Availability and closeness of substitute
3. Income of extg. consumers in the market and of the potential consumers.
4. Tastes and preferences of consumers.

A change in any one of above will affect, the shape and position of ASC curve.

Here advts cost is in the nature of fixed cost and bears no relationship with the volume of sales of output. As output increases, avg. selling cost decliness.

PROBABLE QUESTIONS

1. (*a*) What are the objectives of a firm?
   (*b*) Discuss the conditions of Profit maximisation.
   (*c*) Under what conditions would a firm decide to stop production?
2. What is Price Discrimination? What are its various types?
3. What is Monopolistic competition? Write down its characteristics.
4. (*a*) What makes oligopoly the most characteristic form of industrial market?
   (*b*) What is a Kinded Demand Curve?
5. How do Economists classify market structure? How do these market structures compare with the real markets?
6. Discuss conditions of profit maximisation utilising the Total Cost, Marginal Cost and Revenue curves.
7. Show that in the long-run equilibrium
   AR =MR =LAC = SAC.
8. (*a*) Explain how the sales and Pricing Policy of Monopoly is derived from the market demand curve.
   (*b*) What are 1st, 2nd and 3rd degrees Price discrimination?
9. (*a*) Define monopolistic competition. How does it differ from perfect competition and Monopoly?
   (*b*) What is Product Differentiation?
10. (*a*) Discuss short-run and long-run equilibrium under perfect competition.
    (*b*) Show Profit & Loss separately on Cost Curve Diagrams.

CHAPTER 6

FACTOR PRICING—I

- Marginal Productivity Theory
- Marginal Physical Product
- Marginal Revenue Product
- Value of Marginal Product
- Supply of Inputs
- Determination of Wage Rates under Perfect Competition and Monopoly
- Subsistence Theory of Wage
- Modern Theory of Wage Determination
- Exploitation of Labour
- Rent Concept—Ricardian and Modern Theories of Rent
- Quasi-rent

Factor Pricing—I Marginal Productivity Theory and demand for factors.
Nature of supply of factor inputs
Determination of wage rates under
Perfect Competition and Monopoly
Exploitation of labour
Rent—Concept : Ricardian and modern Theories of rent, Quasi-rent.

1. *(a)* Marginal Product or Marginal Physical Product (MPP)

Addition to total output by employing an additional unit of a factor (quantity of other factors remaining unchanged) is called the marginal physical product of that factor. For example, if by employing 16th unit of labour hour the output of good X increases from 1000 units to 1050 units, the MPP of 16th unit is 50 units of good X. Since the marginal product is measured in physical terms it is also called marginal physical product.

(b) Marginal Revenue Product (MRP)

In case we measure the contribution of output of the additional unit of the factor in term of its revenue contribution, it is called marginal revenue product. MRP is derived by multiplying MPP with the marginal revenue got from the sale of the produced good.

From the above example, if the 50 units of additional output contributed by the 16th unit of labour are sold in the market at Rs 100 per unit of good, then MRP of labour is Rs 100 × 50 = Rs. 5000.

It is written $MRP_{labour} = MPP_{labour} \times MR_{good}$

(c) Value of Marginal Product (VMP)

VMP measures the addition to revenue resulting from a unit increase in the quantity of the productive factor (quantity of all other factors remaining constant). The difference between MRP and VMP basically lies in their methods of measurement. In case of VMP,

$$VMP_{labour} = MPP_{labour} \times Price_{good}$$

(d) MRP and VMP

The relationship between the units of a variable factor with their marginal revenue product and the value of marginal product are shown in the following table.

(e)

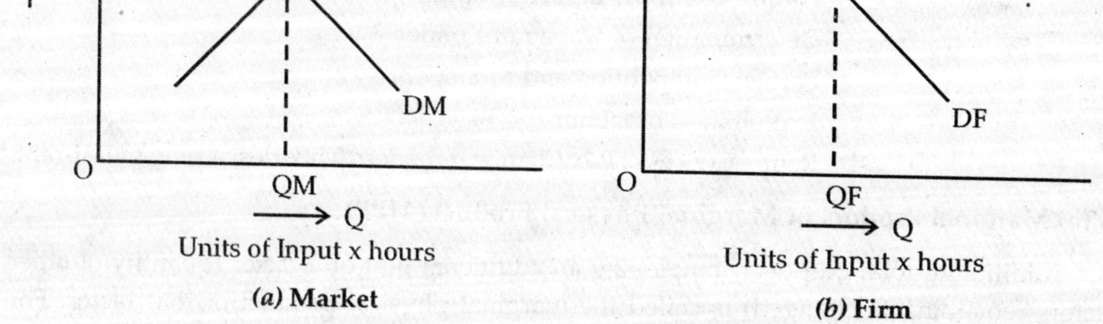

(a) **Market** *(b)* **Firm**

Table 1

Units of Variable Factor (x)	*Total output of Good X (Units Q_n)*	*Marginal Physical Product (MPP_x)*	*Marginal Revenue Product $MRP_x = MPP_x + MR_x$ MR = Rs. 10*	*Value of Marginal Product VMP = $MPP_x \times P_x$*	*Marginal Resource Cost (MRC_x) $P_x = 100$*
(1)	(2)	(3)	(4)	(5)	(6)
1	10	10	100	100	100
2	35	25	250	250	100
3	55	20	200	200	100
4	70	15	150	150	100
5	80	10	100	100	100
6	85	5	50	50	100

Marginal Physical Product (col 3) increases initially and then starts falling. The firm can sell as much output as it produces at a given price Px = Rs 10; MRP also shows the same behaviour as VMP, *i.e.*, it increases initially and then declines (colns 4 & 5). If the price at which the firm sells its output remaings the same irrespective of the amount sold, price equals its marginal revenue and MRP equals VMP.

But if the commodity market is imperfectly competitive, *i.e.*, the firm can sell greater amount only by reducing its price (*i.e.* monopoly condition), then the marginal revenue (MR) will be less than Price. ($MR < P_x$). VMP will therefore be more than MRP in an imperfectly competitive commodity market.

In the above table, by comparing coln (4) and (6), we can say that the firm should employ only 5 units of factor as by employing the 6th unit it gets less revenue than it pays to the factor.

MRC (Marginal Resource Cost) refers to changes in cost associated with a unit change in input while MC is change in cost due unit change in output.

In the graph *(a)* as shown above, MC = P (Market price) of input, of unit of inputs which is determined by the intersection of its market demand and supply curves.

Since the firm is buying an input in a perfectly competitive market accepts the input price as given, the supply curve of the input to the firm is, therefore horizontal and the input price equals its MC (curve SF in graph *(b)*).

The firm's demand curve for the input is given by the portion of the MRP curve for the input where MRP is decreasing DF, in graph *(b)*. This is so because, the firm employs additional units of input only when its price declines.

The profit maximising condition for utilising the input is to employ the input up to the point where the MRP of input is equal to MRC of the input (Point of intersection of DF and SF in graph *(b)*). The profit maximising quantity or the input the firm should employ as shown OQF in graph *(b)*.

2. The Supply of Inputs

The supply of ingredient inputs produced in other industries in simple to analyse. The short-run supply curve of such inputs will be the aggregate of the individual firms marginal cost curves in the input producing industry.

In the long-run, the "optimal average costs" of the input producing industry will define the input supply curve. Thus, the supply curve of inputs produced in other industries is defined by their production costs.

(a) Factors and agents of production

Factors of production such as land, labour and capital and productive agents such as entrepreneurs have no production costs. Their supply is either fixed in quantity or quality or is governed by subjective costs. Based upon the conditions surrounding the supply of their services, the prices received by their inputs are claimed as rent, wages, interest and profit.

These terms carry a special meaning in economics which are explained in this chapter under " Theory of Income Distribution".

(b) Determination of wage rates under perfect competition and monopoly and Exploitation of labour :

Under perfect competition wage rates are determined by supply and demand factors. The wage rates under monopoly are discussed under the capitalist economy according to the theory of Karl Marx. The Marxian Theory also explain the exploitation of labour.

In the advanced economies, people prefer to work less and enjoy more leisure at very high wage rates. Wage is a payment made by the producer to the labour for the services rendered by him in the production process. **"Money wage"** is the amount of money paid to the labour at a regular time interval, whereas **"Real wage"** includes money wage plus incidental benefits such as "free meal", "free medical facility" and "free transport" etc.

***(i)* The subsistence theory of wage :** This theory states that wages are determined by a natural law the operation of which necessarily brings them down to the level of the bare necessities of life. If wages exceed this minimum or subsistence level, labourers will multiply and population will increase causing an increase in labour supply. This increase in labour supply will in term bring down the wage level once again to the level of subsistence.

If on the other hand, wages fall short of the minimum or subsistance level, labourers will die causing a contraction in labour supply. This fall in supply, will in turn, push up the wage level once again to the level of subsistence.

Hence, in the **long run, the wage rate** would invariably get adjusted at the subsistance level.

David Ricardo was of the view that the **subsistance level or wages would be absolutely constant and rigidly fixed for all time. For this reason, the German economist "Lassle" called the subsistence wage theory the "Iron Law of Wages".**

***(ii)* Marginal Productivity theory of wage determination :** This theory is a specific case of the generalised marginal productivity theory of distribution. According to this theory, wages are determined by the marginal productivity of labour and equal it at the point of equilibrium.

The wage which the last employed labourer receives must form the norm for all labourers of the same skill and ability, since for the same service it is impossible to pay unequal wages.

The exponents of marginal productivity theory of wage (*i.e.*, JB Clerk, Stanley Jevons & Alfred Marshall etc) were of the view that the importance of labour for the employer depends on the labour's physical productivity. This theory is superior to subsistence wage theory.

***(iii)* Modern Theory of Wage Determination :** This theory states that "Equilibrium wage rate and the level of employment are determined by the point of intersection of the demand for labour curve and the supply of labour curve.

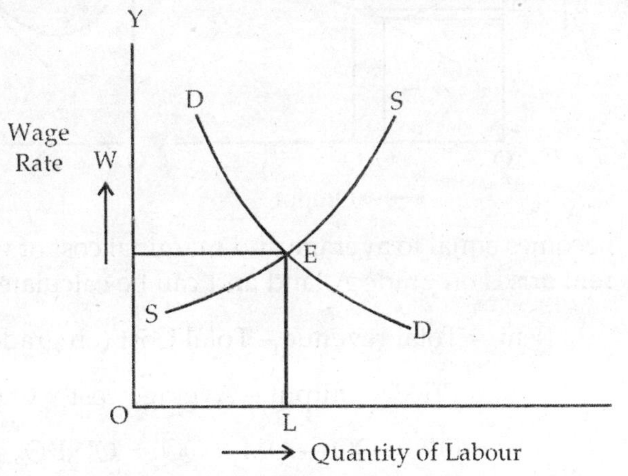

In the equilibrium, the wage rate OW will be established in the market and at this wage rate, the quantity of labour demanded and supplied will be OL.

(c) Rent

The price paid to any resource, when it is fixed in supply is called rent. Rent is the price paid to all free gifts of nature which are called land in economics. Such ingredients have no supply costs. They command a price only because they are scarce and are fixed in supply.

Classical economists regarded rent as the return to the factor of production "land".

David Ricardo had defined rent as follows :

Rent is that portion of the produce of the earth which is paid to the landlord for the original and indestructible powers of the soil.

Marshall and other economists have defined rent to include all free gifts of nature.

As per modern economists, **formal definition of rent is as follows :**

Economic rent may be defined as any payment to a unit of factor of production, which is in excess of the minimum amount necessary to keep that factor in its present occupation.

For example, if an Engineer's minimum salary is Rs. 10,000 per month and he earn Rs. 11,000 per month then he is getting a surplus income of Rs. 1000 and this will be his rent. Thus, rent can be earned by any factor of production.

***(i)* The Ricardian Theory of Rent :** Rent under extensive cultivation.

In a place grade A superior quality and Grade B inferior quality of land for wheat cultivation. Initially, when population is less, land A is brought under cultivation. Since, under perfect competition, the price to be determined is equal to both marginal cost and average cost, the price of wheat is equal to OP_1. At this price there is no rent on grade A land when population rises and grade B Land is brought under cultivation. The new price of wheat

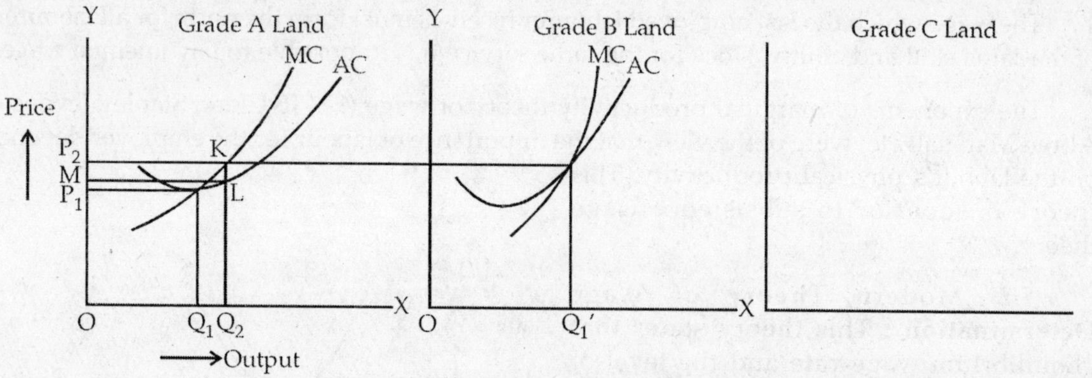

becomes equal to average and marginal cost of wheat on grade B land. It is thus OP_2 and now rent arises on grade A land and can be calculated as follows :

Rent = Total revenue – Total Cost (on grade A land)

= Price × Output – Average cost × Output (on grade A land)

$= OP_2 \times OQ_2 - OM \times OQ_2 = OP_2KQ_2 - OMLQ_2$

$= P_2KLM.$

Thus, rent on grade A land is equal to P_2KLM.

***(ii)* The Ricardian theory of Rent :** Rent under intensive cultivation.

Ricardian Theory can also be used to explain the emergence of rent in case of intensive cultivation, *i.e.*, on the same plot of land, application of successive doses of labour and capital will bring forth a progressively diminishing output. As more and more does of labour and capital are employed on that plot of land, a state is finally reached where a particular dose (which represents a particular combination of labour and capital) **brings forth output just equal to its cost this is known as marginal dose. All earlier doses will yield rent.** This will be equal to the surplus output enjoyed by every super-marginal dose over the marginal dose.

***(iii)* Assumption of the Ricardian Theory of Rent :** Main assumptions of this Theory are as follows :

(1) Ricardo assumed the existence of a marginal land or no-rent land. The rent on the superior lands is measured upwards from this no rent land.

(2) Ricardo assumed that land has certain original and indestructible powers and rent is a payment for the use of these powers.

(3) Ricardo assumed that rent arose on account of the differences in the quality of various lands. If lands were homogeneous and uniform quality rent would not have arisen.

***(iv)* Modern Theory of Rent :** The modern concept of rent differs from Ricardo's concept in that *whereas according to Ricardo's opinion rent can be earned only by land, the modern economists argue that it can be earned by any factor of production.* However, a deeper analysis of the question of economic rent would reveal that the modern concept of rent is a refined and generalised form of Ricardo's concept.

Richardo's analysis is based on the use of land for cultivation but if the landlord prefers to rent out his land for other purpose which yields higher earning than in cultivation, then rent is surplus over and above what is necessary to keep it in its present use.

The minimum payment that has to be made to a particular factor of production to retain it in its present use is known as **transfer earning.**

The modern concept and definition of rent is "Rent is the difference between the actual earning of a factor of production and its transfer earnings.

Thus,

Rent = Present earnings – Transfer earnings

In most cases, the actual earnings of a factor of production contain both transfer earnings and rent.

A house owner in a business locality can rent out his garage for a beauty parlour and can earn much higher amount than renting it out as a garage for car. Thus, the difference between actual and opportunity costs is called economic rent or economic profit.

***(v)* Quasi Rent :** The quasi rent is a surplus that a producer receives in the short period over his variable costs from the sale of his output.

Quasi – Rent = Total Revenue – Total Variable Cost.

If a producer can not earn profit but can manage to recover the variable costs in the short period, he will be satisfied. In case, the price of his product does not ensure the recovery of the variable costs, he will stop production. If his actual revenue exceeds the total variable cost, then this difference (TR – TVC) is of the nature of a surplus and may be considered as the quasi-rent earned by the producer.

In the long period, all factor of production are variable. Therefore, under perfect competition in the long period when total revenue and total cost are equal, quasi-rent is not earned.

In case the quasi-rent is greater than the fixed cost, the firm earns profit, it is less than the fixed cost, the firm suffers a loss and wen quasi-rent is just equal to the fixed cost the firm earn only the normal profit.

***(vi)* Effect of Price on Rent :** If price rises, rent also rises and if price falls, rent also falls. So price has effect on rent but reverse is not true, *i.e.*, rent no effect on price. Therefore, price determines rent, but price is not determined by rent.

PROBABLE QUESTIONS

1. *(a)* Illustrate the relationships between Marginal Physical Product, Marginal Revenue Product and Value of Marginal Product.

   (b) What do you understand by "the profit maximixing quantity of input"?

2. *(a)* Describe the determination of wage rates under perfect competition and monopoly.

   (b) What is "Exploitation of Labour"?

3. (*a*) Highlight the subsistence theory of wage.
   (*b*) What is Marginal Productivity theory of wage?
   (*c*) Describe the modern theory of wage.
4. (*a*) Describe the Ricardian theory of rent.
   (*b*) What are the assumption on this theory?
5. (*a*) Describe modern theory of rent.
   (*b*) What is "Transfer Earning"?
   (*c*) Write notes on "Quasi-rent".

CHAPTER 7

FACTOR PRICING—II

Interest is earned from capital or reward from liquidity.

- Theories of Interest
- Classical Theory
- Loanable Funds Theory
- Keynes's Liquidity Preference Theory
- Modern Theory of Interest

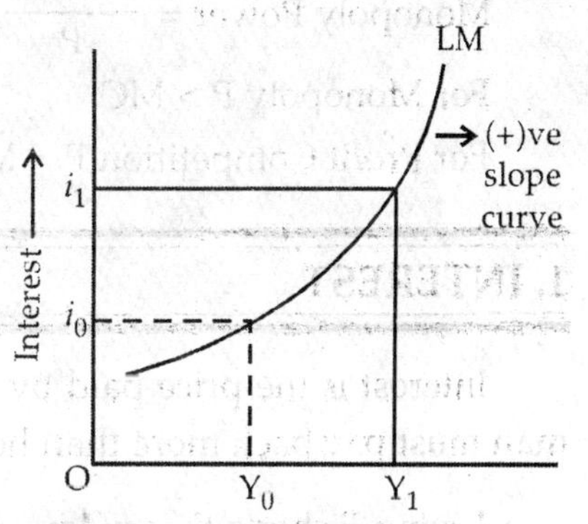

(1) LM curve represents monetary equilibrium condition and if income increases 'i' increases. If 'i' increases, people will keep more fixed deposits in banks, banks will give more credit to industries, more income will generate.

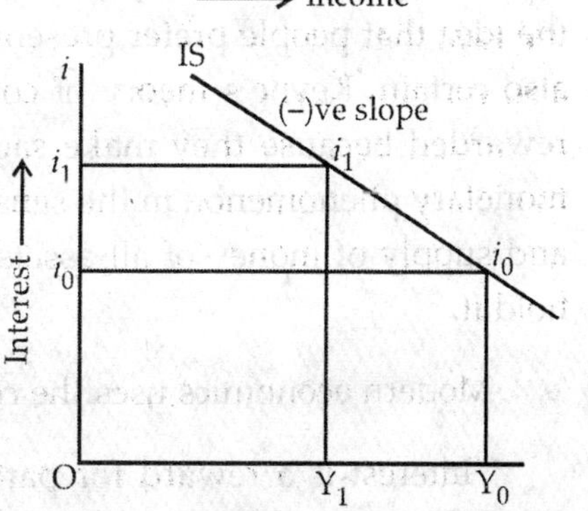

(2) IS curve represents product market equilibrium IS = Investment spending; when 'i' increases, investment spending low and income level is also low.

(3) Profit = TR – TC

$$\underset{\text{Economic Profit}}{\pi_E} = \underset{\text{Accountant Profit}}{\pi_A} - OC \qquad \pi_A > \pi_E$$

OC = opportunity cost, *i.e.* income foregone, which a business man could expect from second best alternative use of his resource.

(4) Functions of Profit →
- Operational Efficiency
- Source of Internal Finance
- Helps in interfirm comparison

(5) Theories of Profit —
- Walker theory
- Clerk's dynamic theory
- F.H. Knight's theory

(6) Monopoly Profit increases due to —
- Economy of scale
- Ownership of critical raw material (Arab Countries)
- M & A strategy L.N. Mittal—Largest capacity steel producer in the world.

$$\text{Monopoly Power} = \frac{P - MC}{P}$$

For Monopoly P > MC

For Profit Competition P = M → Monopoly Power = 0

1. INTEREST

Interest is the price paid by the borrower to the lender for the use of loanable funds. A man must pay back more than he borrowed, otherwise the lender will feel himself cheated.

Lrving Fisher's theory known as the "Time Preference Theory" of interest, is based on the idea that people prefer present income to future income even when the future income is also certain. Keyne's theory of consumption function stated that the lenders deserve to be rewarded because they make sacrifice when they save. In Keyner's opinion interest is a monetary phenomenon in the sense that the rate of interest is determined by the demand for and supply of money of all assets, money is the most liquid and therefore, people want to hold it.

Modern economics uses the concept of interest in the following statement.

"Interest is a reward for parting with the liquidity; in other words, a reward for not hoarding".

2. VARIOUS THEORIES OF INTEREST

***(i)* The Classical Theory :** According to the classical theory of interest, the rate of interest is determined by the interaction of demand for and supply of capital.

The classical theory of interest is the saving and investment theory of interest.

Since the rate of interest is explained in term of demand for and supply of real capital the theory suggests that whereas the demand for capital is made only for investment purposes and varies inversely with the rate of interest, the source of supply of capital is income which people withhold from consumption.

The classical economist assumed that saving is functionally related to the rate of interest and varies directly with it. The intersection of the demand and supply schedules determines the rate of interest.

The diagram highlights the determination of rate of interest under the classical approach.

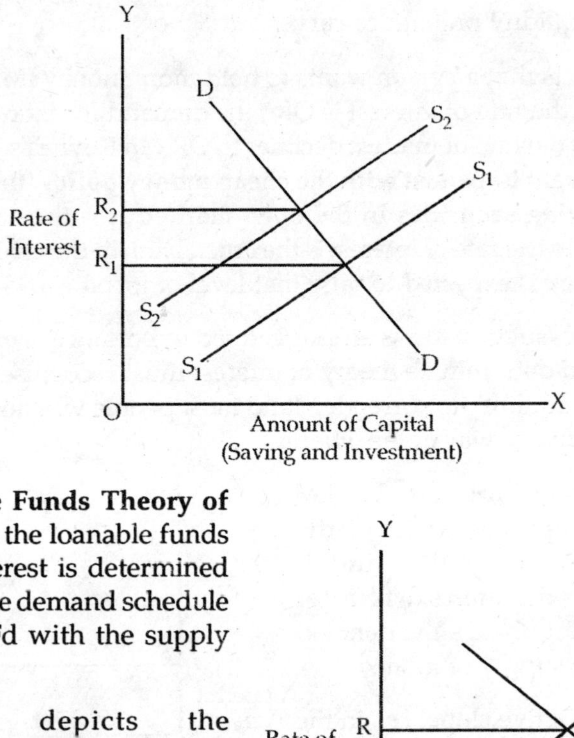

***(ii)* The Loanable Funds Theory of Interest :** According to the loanable funds theory, the rate of interest is determined by the intersection of the demand schedule for loanable funds, LFd with the supply schedule LFs.

The diagram depicts the determination of rate of interest under loanable funds approach. (OR= rate of interest) Intersection schedules gives the 'natural rate of interest.'

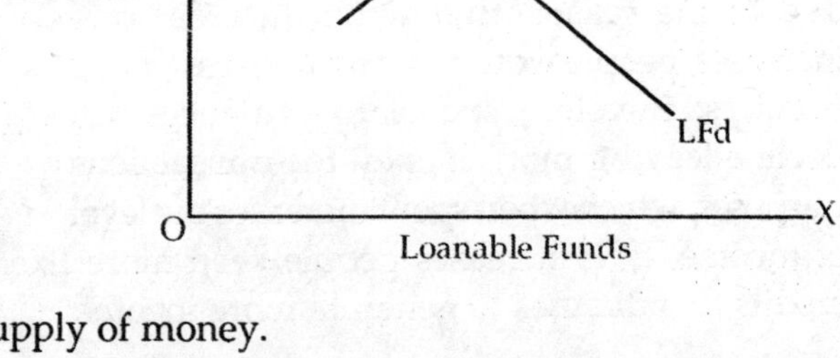

***(iii)* Keynes's Liquidity Preference Theory :** According to Keynes, interest is the price of money loans. His analysis of interest runs in terms of demand for and supply of money.

The diagram depicts the determination of interest under liquidity preference approach.

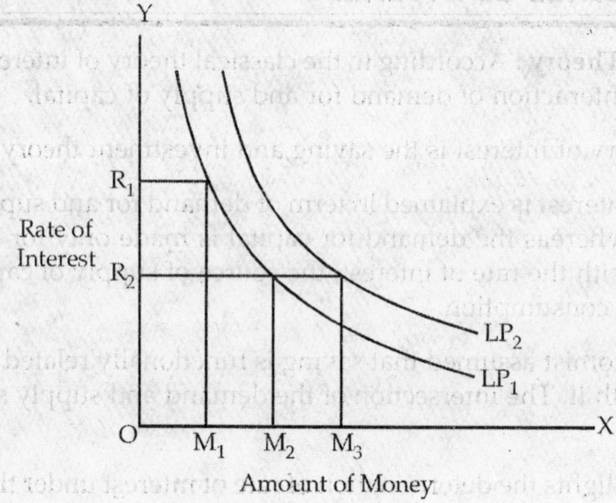

LP_1 and LP_2 are liquidity preference curves.

The diagram depicts that a person wants to hold more money (M_2 & M_3) at lower rate of interest (R_2) and when the rate of interest is QR_1, the demand for money balances OM_1 and it increases to OM_2 when the rate of interest declines to OR_2. In Keynes's Theory of interest if the monetary authorities want to **persist with the cheap money policy, they should increase the money supply by buying securities in the open market.** It is thus clear that in Keynesian economics a reduction in the rate of interest is the crucial link in the chain by which an increase in the quantity of money is expected to raise that level of income and also of employment.

However, the critics suggest this is an exaggerated importance of expectations in Keynes's theory. A complete and determinate theory of interest must recognise this fact that "without saving there can be no liquidity to surrender "and most people will not borrow money unless they find it productive in one way or the other.

***(iv)* Modern Theory of Interest :** The LM Curve is a graphic representation of the monetary equilibrium condition and it specifies the level of income interest which, for different rates of interest, makes the demand for money equal to the supply of money.

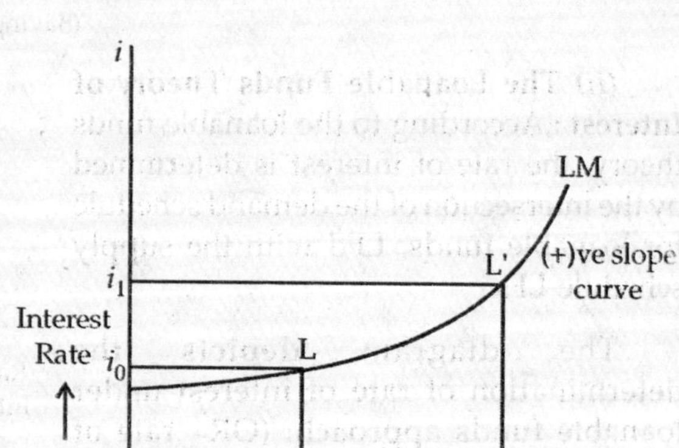

LM curve has a positive slope, *i.e.*, in the money market Y and i vary directly. This is due to the reason that when interest rate increases, people would like to hold less of idle balances. Therefore, speculative balances will decline leaving more money for transactions purposes, which when spent increases the level of income. If 'i' increases people keep more fixed deposits in banks, which will give more credits to industries to generate more income.

In the process of selecting arbitrary rate of interest rates and finding the level of income at which saving is equal to investment indicated by the interest rate, are can trace out a curve called the "IS Curve". Thus the IS curve connects all points at the plane that represent possible combination of Y and i that make S (Saving) equal to I (Investment) and that give equilibrium income levels.

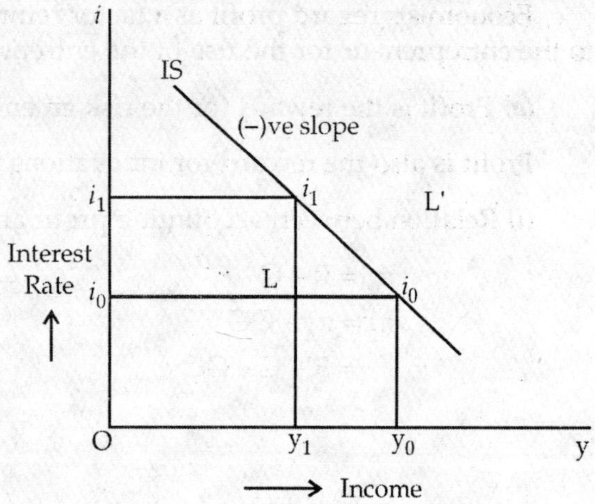

From this, we arrive at the following definition of the IS Curve, the IS curve is a graphic representation of the product market equilibrium condition that planned investment be equal to saving and it shows the level of income that will yield equality of planned investment and saving at different possible interest rates. As the IS Curve slopes downward from left to right, *i.e.*, y and i vary inversely. When interest rates are relatively high, investment spending will be relatively low and thus the level of income would also the low. At lower rates of interest, investment spending will increase leading to higher income levels.

PROFIT

1. Profits and Importance of Profits

Peter Drucker has suggested eight important areas of business objectives.

1. Marketing
2. Innovation
3. Human Organisation
4. Physical Resources
5. Financial Resources
6. Productivity
7. Social Responsibility
8. Profit Requirement.

Profit requirement for a business organisation is so vital for its survival and growth that the management is concerned with making around efforts in the efficient implementation and control of the above first seven areas of business objectives for the maximisation of the ultimate objectives *i.e.* profit.

2. Meaning and Nature of Profit

For an Accountant, profit means the net income from the business. It is calculated by deducting from the total receipts the total expenditure incurred in a business ventures.

Economists regard profit as a factor return like wages, interest and rent. Profit is a return to the entrepreneur for the use of the entrepreneurial ability.

(a) Profit is the reward for the risk an entrepreneur takes in a business.

Profit is also the reward for innovations in production method, products, marketing etc.

(i) Relation between accounting profit and economic profit.

$$\pi_A = R - C$$
$$\pi_E = \pi_A - OC$$
$$= R - C - OC$$

π_A = Accounting Profit
π_E = Economic Profit
R = Revenue
C = Explicit Costs (Paid out costs)
OC = Opportunity Costs

Opportunity cost is the income foregone which a business could expect from the second best alternative use of his resources.

Since every decision involves a sacrifice of alternatives, the opportunity costs are implied in any decision-making.

If opportunity costs are considered then economic profit would find to be less than accounting profit.

3. Functions of Profit

(i) Profit is a measures of the operational efficiency of the firm.

(ii) Profit is the premium that covers up the cost or staying in business replacement, obsolescence, risk and uncertainty.

(iii) Profit is the courses of internal finance. The net retained earning is used to finance expansion and replacement programme.

(iv) Commercial profitability is an established criteria of project evaluation or appraisal.

(v) Profit reflects the income earning capacity of the firm and thus determines if the firm is capable of discharging social responsibility or not.

(vi) Inter firm comparison, inter industry comparison or product line comparison are all facilitated by the index of profit.

No business firm can function today without having a profit policy because plays a crucial role to help decision-making.

4. Economists Theories of Profit

***(a)* Walker's Theory of Profit :** According to F.A Walker profit is the rent of "exceptional abilities that an entrepreneur may possess" over others. Just as rent is the difference between the yields of the least and the most fertile lands, profit is the difference between the earning, of the least and the most efficient entrepreneurs.

***(b)* Clark's Dynamic Theory of Profit :** According to J.B. Clark, profits arise in a dynamic economy.

A dynamic economy is characterised by *(i)* increase in population *(ii)* increase in capital *(iii)* Multiplication of consumer wants.

The entrepreneurs who take successfully the advantages of changing conditions in a dynamic company make profit.

(c) Knight's Theory of Profit: According to F.H. Knight, profit is the refresh to uncertainty bearing. Profit arises from the decisions taken and implemented under the conditions of uncertainty. In his view, the profits may arise as a result of decisions concerning the state of market *e.g.* decisions which result in increasing the degree of monopoly, decisions with respect to holding stocks, and decisions taken to introduce a new technique. According to Knight, profit is the reward for an entrepreneur for his skill for uncertainty bearing. Uncertainties are those risks which are not insurable with an insurance company and they arise from factors like competition, market condition, technological changes and govt. policies change.

(d) Monopoly Profit: Monopoly may arise due to *(i)* economies of scale *(ii)* sole ownership of certain crucial raw materials *(iii)* legal sanction and protection *(iv)* Margers and taken overs.

A monopolist may earn "Monopolist profit" and maintain it in the long-run by using its monopoly powers. Monopoly Power has been described before.

$$\text{Monopoly Power} = \frac{P - MC}{P}, \text{ for Monopoly } P > MC$$

PROBABLE QUESTIONS

1. *(a)* **What is innovation theory of profit?**

   (b) **Distinguish between Accounts' Profit and Economist's Profit.**
2. *(a)* **Discuss Knight's theory of profit.**

   (b) **Highlight JB Clark's contribution to theory of profit.**
3. *(a)* **What are various functions of profit?**

   (b) **Discuss nature and importance of profit.**
4. *(a)* **Discuss about Keyne's contribution to theory of interest.**

   (b) **Distinguish between gross and net interest.**
5. **How did Ricardo explain the determination of the rate of interest?**
6. **What is marginal productivity theory of interest?**

QUESTION BANK

(Economics)—I

BBA-104

Module for objective (multiple choice) questions

Answer any ten by writing appropriate answer in box.

1. Economics is

   (a) Applied behaviour *(b)* Social Science *(c)* Financial in character

2. Micro economics is concerned with

   (a) Functioning of a business *(b)* A state's economy *(c)* Per capita income

3. Macro economics is concerned with

   (a) Functioning of a business *(b)* Pricing of a commodity *(c)* Per capita income

4. Elasticity of Demand means

   (a) Percentage change in quantity demanded

   (b) Percentage change in quantity demanded with respect to percentage change in demand determinants.

   (c) Percentage change in price of a commodity with respect to percentage change in quantity demanded.

5. Cross elasticity of demand is positive

   (a) For substitute goods *(b)* For complementary goods *(c)* Neither of above

6. Giffen goods

   (a) violate the Law of Demand *(b)* are inferior commodities *(c)* are luxury goods.

7. Competitive situation

   (a) is not desirable in an economy

   (b) may be perfect or imperfect

   (c) neither of above

8. A monopolist can

   (a) increase his sale or price *(b)* only increase his profit *(c)* do neither of above

9. Under a perfectly competitive situation a firm's AR curve and MR curve are identical

   (a) True *(b)* False *(c)* Not known

10. Isoquant is used to study
    (*a*) for maximising output (*b*) for cost minimising behaviour
    (*c*) for deriving optimum profit
11. Law of variable proportion is applicable
    (*a*) Long-term situation (*b*) Short-term situation (*c*) Neither of above
12. "Returns to scale" is a
    (*a*) Long from phenomenon (*b*) Short-term phenomenon (*c*) Neither of above
13. Price discrimination take place
    (*a*) When price is variable (*b*) When price is increased
    (*c*) When same good is sold at different prices to the same buyer.
14. Profit maximising out put takes place when
    (*a*) Price equals marginal cost
    (*b*) Total cost equals marginal revenue
    (*c*) Average cost equals total cost
15. Monolistic competition is same as
    (*a*) Monopoly situation (*b*) Perfect competition (*c*) Neither of above
16. Break Even Point occurs when
    (*a*) Maximum profit is generated (*b*) There is no profit and no loss
    (*c*) Maximum output is obtained
17. Economic profit is
    (*a*) Higher than Accountant's profit (*b*) Equal to Accountant's profit
    (*c*) Less than Accountant's profit
18. Barometric price leadership takes place
    (*a*) Under perfect competition (*b*) Under monopoly situation
    (*c*) Under oligopoly situation
19. The Ridge lines form the boundaries for
    (*a*) the most profitable regions (*b*) the economic region of production
    (*c*) maximising output region
20. Explain path indicates
    (*a*) Optimum combination of factors of production at a particular output level
    (*b*) Maximum combination of factors of production at the maximum output level
    (*c*) Neither of above
21. Short Run AC curve of a firm is
    (*a*) A straight line (*b*) Concave shaped (*c*) U shaped
22. LAC Curve is derived from
    (*a*) MR Curve (*b*) SAC Curve (*c*) Neither of above

23. A monopolist prefers to operate under
    (*a*) In elastic zone (*b*) Elastic zone (*c*) Equilibrium condition
24. Labour exploitation rate is
    (*a*) the least rate of wage payment to labour
    (*b*) the difference between marginal revenue product
    (*c*) the non payment of wage to labour.

Module for short questions
Answer any three questions 3 × 5 = 15 marks
(Answer within 50 words)

1. Define Economics and discuss Marshall's attempts at defining Economics.
2. Economics studies "Choice amidst scarcity" discuss.
3. Distinguish between Micro and Macro Economics.
4. Define "Law of Demand" and examine the exception.
5. What factors influence the elasticity of demand?
6. Write about characteristics and utility of ISO quant curves.
7. What is MRTS?
8. What is LSOM?
9. What are objectives of a firm?
10. Discuss the condition of profit maximisation.
11. Under what conditions will a firm decide not to produce?
12. What is price discrimination? Discuss its various types.
13. What is Monopolistic competition? Briefly write about its characteristics.
14. What makes Oligopoly the most characteristic form of industrial market?
15. What is Kinded demand curve?
16. What do you mean by "Labour exploitation rate"?
17. Briefly discuss about Keyne's Theory of Interest.
18. What is marginal productivity theory of interest?
19. Define Rent and Quasi-rent.
20. Discuss Marshall's theory of profit.
21. Distinguish between Accountant's profit and Economist's profit.
22. Show graphically BEP analysis.
23. Why there is no supply curve under monopoly?
24. Discuss graphically the Ridge lines.
25. What is the significance of "Expansion Path?
26. How is Oligopoly situation beneficial for customers?
27. How is monopoly power measured?
28. What is innovation Theory of profit?

Module for Long Questions
(Answer within 500 words)
Answer any three 3 × 15 = 45 Marks

1. *(a)* Define Economics. Discuss Marshall's attempts at defining Economics.

   (b) Economics studies "choice amidst scarcity "Justify".

2. Distinguish between the concerns of Micro economics and Macro economies.

3. *(a)* State and justify "Law of Demand' and examine the exceptions with examples

   (b) What is the price elasticity of demand? How can it be measured?

4. Elaborate with examples about the factors that influence the elasticity of demand.

5. *(a)* What are Isoquants ISO costs and MRTS?

   (b) Show how isoquants can be used to study the cost minimising behaviour of the firm.

6. *(a)* What is LSOM?

   (b) State the Law of variable Proportion.

   (c) What is the significance of cobb-Doughlas production function?

7. *(a)* Write about the significance of short-run and long-run cost curves.

   (b) What are refers to scale"? Discuss various determinants of returns to scale.

8. *(a)* How do Economists classify market structures?

   (b) How do these market structures compare with the real markets? Classify the real markets.

9. *(a)* What are the objectives of a firm?

   (b) Discuss about the importance of cost management for a business firm.

10. Explain BEP analysis graphically and mathematically.

11. *(a)* Discuss condition of profit maximisation utilising the total cost, Marginal cost and Revenue curves.

    (b) Under what conditions will a firm decide not to produce?

12. *(a)* State the condition for Profit maximising producing by a firm in perfect competition.

    (b) Show that in the long run equilibrium

    AR = MR= LAC = SAC

13. Evaluate the cost and economic efficiency of perfectly competitive markets. How do they benefit the consumers?

14. *(a)* What is monopoly? Explain how the sales and pricing policy of monopoly is derived from the market demand curve.

    (b) What are 1st, 2nd and 3rd degree Price discrimination?

15. *(a)* Define monopolistic competition. How does it differ from Perfect competition and Monopoly?

    (b) What is product differentiation?

16. *(a)* What makes obligopoly the most characteristic form of industrial markets?

    (b) Evaluate the significance of the Kinked demand hypotheses.

17. (a) Evaluate subsistance theory and marginal productivity theory of wages.
    (b) What is labour exploitation rate?
18. (a) Distinguish between gross and net interest. How did Ricardo explain the determination of the rate interest?
    (b) Discuss about Keyne's contribution to theory of interest.
19. (a) Define Rent" Explain Ricardo's Theory of rent.
    (b) Explain Marshall concept of quasi-rent.
20. (a) Distinguish between the accountant's and economist's concepts of profits.
    (b) Discuss Marshall's and Knight's Theories of profits.
21. Write short notes on any three.
    (1) Giffen goods and law of demand
    (2) Cross elasticity of demand
    (3) Demand determinants
    (4) Demand distinction categories
    (5) Economics of scale
    (6) Ridge points and Ridge lines
    (7) Expansion Path
    (8) Price leadership
    (9) Objectives of a firm
    (10) Equilibrium of a firm
    (11) Angle of incidence and Margin of safety
    (12) Isoquants and MRTS
    (13) Marginal cost, average total cost and average variable cost curves.
    (14) Shutdown point
    (15) Monopoly and Monopolistic competition
    (16) Discriminating Monopoly
    (17) MR on a kinked demand curve
    (18) Labour exploitation rate
    (19) Gross and Net Interest
    (20) Quasi-rent
    (21) Innovation theory of profit
    (22) Risk and uncertainty.

ECONOMICS - II
MACRO ECONOMICS

DAVID RICARDO, 1772-1823

Born : London, 1772.

Education : Never attended college.

Jobs : Stockbroker. 1786-1815, Member of Parliament, 1819-1823.

Major Publications : *The High Price of Bullion*, 1810; *On the Principles of Political Economy and Taxation*, 1871 : *A Plan for a National Bank*, 1824.

David Ricardo did not go to college. Instead, he went to work as a stockbroker at age 14 and eventually accumulated a vast fortune, including a beautiful country estate. Although Ricardo did not get interested in economics until he was 27, did not write on economics until he was 37, and then died young at age 51, he became one of the most influential economists of all time.

Ricardo continued the tradition of Adam Smith. In fact, he got interested in economics after reading Smith's *Wealth of Nations* during a vacation. But Ricardo greatly extended and improved on Smith's theories and made them more precise. Along with Smith and Robert Malthus—who was Ricardo's close friend but frequent intellectual opponent—Ricardo is considered by historians to be in the classical school, which argued for laissez-faire, free trade, and competitive markets in 18th and 19th-century Britain.

Ricardo grappled with three of the most important policy issues in economics : inflation, taxes, and international trade. Both his first book, published in 1810, and his last book published the year after his death, focused on inflation and what the government should do to keep inflation low.

Taxes were the subject of about one-third of the chapters of his major economics treatise, *On the Principles of Political Economy and Taxation.* In analyzing the effects of taxes—whether on corn, rent, land, gold, houses, profits or wages—Ricardo emphasized how taxes affected people's incentives, and in particular the incentive to save for the future. He wrote :

There are no taxes which have not a tendency to lessen the power to accumulate.... It should be the policy of governments... never to lay such taxes as will inevitably fall on capital : since by so doing, they impair the funds for the maintenance of labour, and thereby diminish the future production of the country.

But perhaps Ricardo's most famous contribution is to international trade—in particular, his theory of comparative advantage. Ricardo used this theory to argue for repeal of the restrictions on agricultural imports known as the corn laws. Although he had a seat in the Parliament from which to argue his free trade position, it was not until 20 years after his death that the corn laws were repealed.

Ricardo's theory of comparative advantage is a good example of how he improved on the work of Adam Smith. Here is how Ricardo described comparative advantage in 1817 :

Under a system of perfectly free commerce, each country naturally devotes its capital and labour to such employments as are most beneficial to each.... it will appear then, that a country possessing very considerable advantages in machinery and skill, and which may therefore be enabled to manufacture commodities with much less labour than her neighbours, may, in return for such commodities, import a portion of the corn required for its consumption, even if its land were more fertile, and corn could be grown with less labour than in the country from winch it was imported. Two men can both make shoes and hats, and one is superior to the other in both employments : hut in making hats, he can only exceed his competitor by one-fifth or 20 per cent, and in making shoes he can excel him by one-third or 33 per cent;—will it not be for the interest of both, that the superior man should employ himself exclusively in making shoes, and the inferior man in making hats?

Ricardo then went on to compare his more powerful comparative advantage result with Adam Smith's simple examples where each country had an absolute advantage over the other in producing one good versus another good.

Source of quotes : David Ricardo, *On the Principles of Political Economy and Taxation,* 1817, pp. 136, 152-153, in *The Works and Correspondence of David Ricardo.* ed. Piero Sraffa (Cambridge University Press, 1962).

JOHN MAYNARD KEYNES, 1883-1946

Born : Cambridge, England, 1883.

Education : Cambridge University, graduated 1906.

Jobs : India Office, London, 1906-1909, Cambridge University, 1909-1915, British Treasury, 1915-1919, Cambridge University. 1919-1946.

Major Publications : *The Economic Consequences of the Peace,* 1919; *A Tract on Monetary Reform,* 1923; *A Treatise on Money,* 1930 : *The General Theory of Employment, Interest and Money,* 1936.

John Maynard Keynes—the inventor of the marginal propensity to consume and of the broader idea that a decline in aggregate demand could bring the economy below its potential—was one of the greatest economists of all time, of similar stature to Adam Smith, David Ricardo, and Alfred Marshall. Keynes put forth the marginal propensity to consume and the multiplier in *The Genera! Theory of Employment, Interest and Money.* Written in the midst of the Great Depression, it provided an explanation for a worldwide tragedy that prevailing economic theory—with its microeconomic emphasis, as represented by Marshall's *Principles of Economics*—hardly addressed. Keynes's ideas spread rapidly and had a lasting influence; referring to them as the "Keynesian revolution" is no exaggeration. Many elements of Keynes's theory are contained in this and the previous chapter of this text.

Much of the *General Theory* is difficult to read. As Keynes put it. "This book is chiefly addressed to my fellow economists." But Keynes's well-developed writing skills emerge in some of the less technical passages, especially those on speculation and expectations in financial markets.

The *General Theory* is a highly theoretical book with very little data. In fact, until Keynes demonstrated the importance of aggregate demand very little data were available on aggregate income, consumption, or investment. But Keynes did give factual evidence about the marginal propensity to consume and the multiplier. He recognized that existing aggregate data for Britain were not sufficiently accurate to estimate the marginal propensity to consume, so he provided estimates for the United States using preliminary data that were soon to be published for the first time by Simon Kuznets of Harvard University. Keynes writes :

At present, however, our statistics are not accurate enough.... The best for the purposes, of which I am aware, are Mr. Kuznets' figures for the United States.... though they are, nevertheless, very precarious.... If single years are taken in isolation, the results look rather wild. But if they are grouped in pairs, the multiplier seems to have been less than 3 and probably fairly stable in the neighbourhood of 2.5. This suggests a marginal propensity to consume not exceeding 60 to 70 per cent....

Note that Keynes's estimates of the MPC are very close to the example used in this chapter.

The *General Theory* was not Keynes's only book. Keynes gained notoriety in his thirties for a best-selling book called *The Economic Consequences of the Peace,* written in only two months during the summer of 1919. As an economic adviser to the British government. Keynes accompanied the prime minister to the Versailles Peace Conference in 1919 at the end of World War I. It was at that peace conference that the victors demanded heavy reparations from Germany, harming the German economy and thereby helping Hitler in his rise to power. In his 1919 book. Keynes predicted serious harm from the stiff reparations and ridiculed the heads of government at the conference, including his own prime minister, Lloyd George, and the American president Woodrow Wilson.

Keynes's *Tract on Monetary Reform* written in 1923 US focused more on inflation than did the *General Theory.* Although Keynes has been criticized for not dealing with inflations in the *General Theory,* his earlier writings suggest that, if he had lived longer, he may have weighed in against the forces that led to the high inflation of the late 1960s and 1970s.

Source of quote : John Maynard Keynes, *The General Theory of Employment, Interest and Money,* first edition (1936), *in The Collected Writings of John Maynard Keynes,* Vol. VII (Cambridge : Cambridge University Press), pp. 154-155.

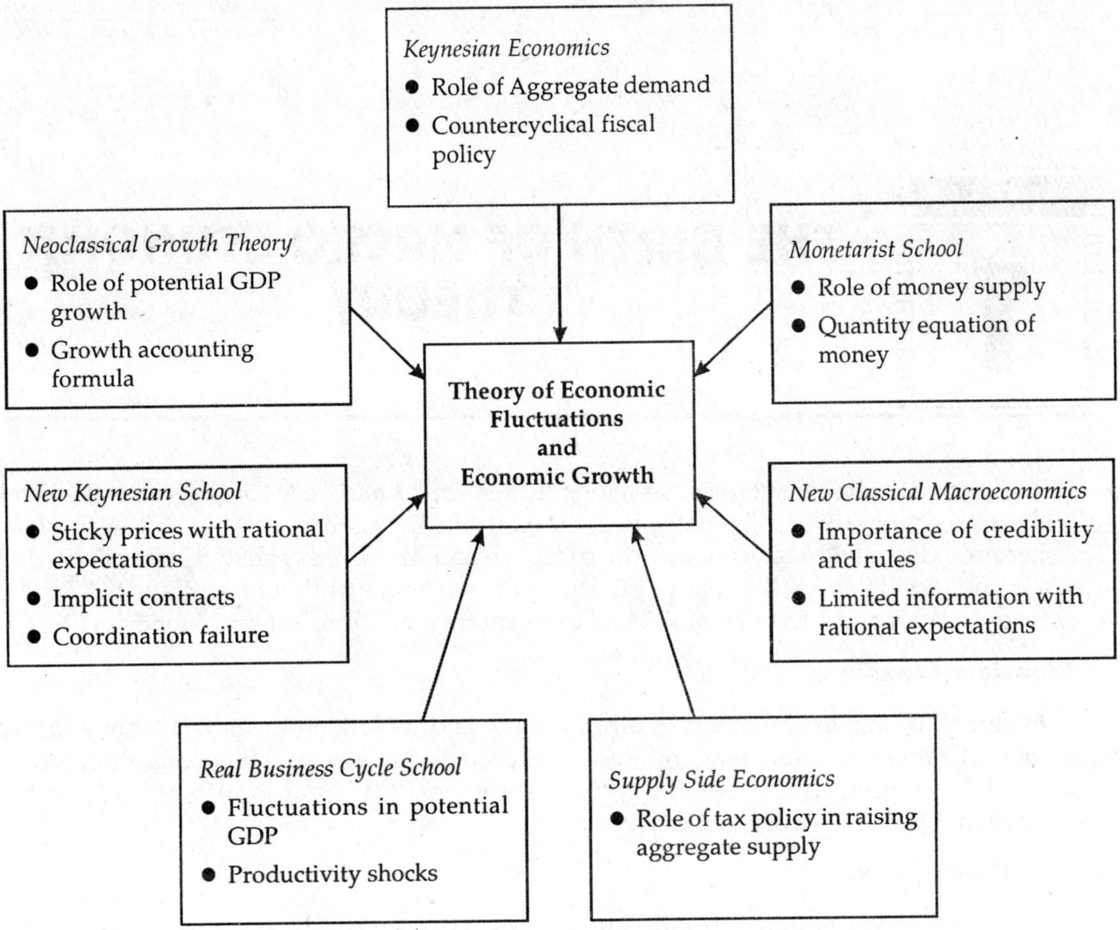

Fig. Spheres of Influence in Macroeconomic Thought

Different schools of thought have influenced the development of macroeconomics. Keynesian economics, the monetarist school, and neoclassical growth theory developed between the 1930s and the 1960s. New classical macroeconomics, the new Keynesian school, the real business cycle school, and supply side economics represent more recent developments. There has been—and still is—heated debate and controversy among the different groups.

CHAPTER 1

THE BIRTH OF MACRO ECONOMIC THEORY

The study of macroeconomics has a long history, but it had been formalised at the hands of J.M. Keynes in the 1930s. Great classical thinkers like D. Ricardo, A. Marshall, A.C. Pigou, I. Fisher provided a body of economic doctrines which J.M. Keynes called 'classical'. Modern macroeconomics dates back to the publications of two books authored by Keynes "Treatise on Money" (1930) and "The General Theory of Employment, Interest and Money" (1936).

1. Monetary Economics

Evolution of money. Function of Money, Bank and its functions, Indian Money Market Commercial Banks need and functions, Reserve Bank of India, need and functions. Price Indices Uses and limitation, inflation—Cost Push, Demand Pull, Causes effects and control, Devaluation, Quantity theory of Money.

1. Evolution of Money

Under the barter system, an individual produces some goods in greater quantity than what he could consume so as to exchange the surplus with another person for something he needed in return. The economy based upon this system of exchange is called the barter economy.

The difficulties with the barter system are :

***(a)* Lack of Common Measure Value :** Different commodities are of different values. There is no common measure of value under the barter system. If a cow is to be exchanged for wheat, it is difficult to decide in what proportion the two items are to be exchanged.

***(b)* Indivisibility of Commodities :** There are many goods which are individual. Transaction is unthinkable for obtaining a pair of shoe in exchange of a horse.

With innumerable and diversified human wants, people started looking for a more convenient form of exchange, that is, sale and purchase with the help of money. Money is commodity which is accepted customarily without any special test of quality and quantity.

According to Kent, money is anything which is commonly used and generally accepted as a medium of exchange.

2. Functions of Money

There are three functions of Money :

(a) Primary Function

***(i)* Medium of Exchange :** This is the central function of money. Money as a medium of exchange is used for sale and purchase of goods and services.

***(ii)* Measure of Value :** In measuring value in exchange, money serves as a common measure of value, *i.e.*, money measures the value of economic goods. Since money is generally acceptable, it works as a common denominator into which the values of all goods and services are expressed.

In a money economy, it is a simple matter to as certain in the relative exchange value of goods by comparing their market prices is term of monetary units.

Thus, money acts as a yard stick or standard measure of value to which all other things can be compared.

In 1923-24, when prices rose substantially in Germany, exchange was entered into with US dollar and Swiss Franc, but the actual payment was made in German Marks.

Here, the Marks served as the unit of account (a measure of value) while US dollar or Swiss Franc served as the medium of exchange.

But, in general, money perform both these functions at the same time.

(b) Secondary Functions

***(i)* Standard of Deferred Payments :** Under credit transactions, instant payments are not made and debtors promise that they will make payment on some future date. Therefore, money facilitates credit transactions.

***(ii)* Store of Value :** The wealth can be stored in the form of money. It has got both liquidation and purchasing power. Liquidity function of money ensures that goods and services can be purchased by money.

This function of money enables people to save a part of their current income and store it for future use.

***(iii)* Transfer of Value :** Money helps us to transfer values from one person to another and from one place to another up to any amount due to its general acceptability.

(c) Contingent Function

***(i)* Equalisation of Marginal Utilities and Productivity :** One can maximise the utility of his limited resources by equalising the marginal utilities of the various commodities. For equalising these marginal utilities, money plays an important role, as the price of all the commodities are expressed in terms of money. Likewise, a producer can maximise the production by equalising the marginal productivities of factors of production.

(ii) **Distribution of National Income :** Money facilitates the distribution of national income among the various factors on the basis of their marginal productivities. It is simple to decide the remunerations of various factors in the form of wages, rents, interest and profits with the help of money. These are the rewards of labour, land, capital and entrepreneur respectively.

(iii) **Liquidity :** Money being the most liquid asset can be converted into any type of asset according to choice of the holder. Liquidity of money raises the mobility and productivity of the capital.

(iv) **Basis of Credit :** The important of credit has increased manifold and cheques, bills of exchange and promissory notes etc. are the instruments used extensively everywhere. Money is the basis of credit, since circulation of credit instruments is not possible in the absence of money.

(v) **Guarantor of Solvency :** It is necessary for a firm or a bank to have sound asset position with sufficient liquidity to serve as the guarantor of its solvency. Money imparts liquidity to all types of wealth.

(vi) **Best Utilisation of Resource :** To spend the cumulative purchasing power in the best manner in future, it is necessary to give at monetary shape. Thus, money also acts as carrier of decision.

3. Quantity Theory of Money

Money performs the function of medium of exchange. Its value is reflected in the amount of goods and services which it helps to buy. Thus, the value of money refers to its exchange value or purchasing power.

The quantity theory of money explains the value of money or price level in term of changes in the quantity of money in the economy. However, sometime increases in the quantity of money may not increase demand. Under these situation, increase in money supply may not increase the price level.

These situations are as follows :

(1) The proportionate increase in output exceeds the proportionate increase in the quantity of money supply.

(2) There is decrease in population.

(3) Taste and preference go against the commodities.

(4) There is an anticipation of a fall in the price in future.

Several economists have expounded different theories to explain the relationship between the price level and quantity of money. The theory was first propounded by an Italian economist Davan Zatti. Two approaches to the quantity theory, namely cash transaction and Cambridge cash balance approach are explained here.

A. Cash Transaction Version of Quantity Theory

Fisher's equation known as "equation of exchange" is written as the equality of supply of money and the demand for money.

$$MV = PT \quad \text{or} \quad P = M\frac{V}{T}$$

where, M is quantity of money in circulation

V stands for the transaction velocity of circulation

P stands for the general price level

T stands for the value of trade or the total number of transaction during a given period of time.

The above equation is also known as cash transaction version of quantity theory.

On account of sharp criticisms by some monetary expert, Fisher extended his original equation of exchange to incorporate volume of bank deposits (M') and its velocity of circulation V').

The extended equation can be written as

$$MV + M'V' = PT$$

On the basis of this equation of exchange, Fisher concluded that other things remaining equal, as the **quantity of money in circulations rises, the price level rises in direct proportion.**

This is show by the equation,

$$P = \frac{MV + M'V'}{T}$$

In above equation, if M = Rs. 500, M' = Rs. 1,000, V = 4. Then for T = Rs. 3,500, the price level can be calculated as under.

$$P = \frac{MV + M'V'}{T} = \frac{\text{Rs. } 500 \times 4 + \text{Rs. } 1{,}000 \times 5}{\text{Rs. } 3{,}500} = \text{Rs. } 2.$$

Hence, the value of money can be determined by a 1/P or T/(MV + M'V').

In this case, the value of money is ½ or 0.5. If V, V' and T remain constant, then the money supply in the Fisher's equation is doubled, when other variables constant, the value of money will become half.

Fisher's equation of quantity theory assumes that 'V' and 'T' remain constant during the short period. The velocity of circulation (V) is assumed to be institutionally constant on the ground that the factors that determine the behaviour of 'V', such as size of population, turnover rate, availability of goods, payment habits. The prosperity to consume, future expectation of prices, rates of interest etc. remain more or less unchanged during the short period.

Fisher assumes a long period of time, since in the short period, change in quantity of money (M) may change the price level (P).

B. Cambridge Cash Balance Approach

Fisher's approach was based on the medium of exchange function of money, emphasising the demand side of money. Some English economists of the 20th century following the lead of Marshal popularised a slightly different version of the quantity theory. Since these economists, namely, Pigou, Robertson and Keynes belonged to the cambridge university, this theory has come to be known as the Cambridge approach or Cash Balance Approach of the quantity theory money.

According do this approach, the value of money or the price level depends upon the demand for money. Here, the demand for money arises not on account of transactions but for the purpose of being a store of value. The usefulness of money as a medium of exchange is recognised but their function has been relegated to a secondary position.

However, among the above two approaches there are different notion of money. In the cash transactions approach, money is expected to circulate, *i.e.*, it emphasises velocity of circulation. In the cash balance approach money is kept as idle balance to have command over future goods.

Marshall Equation

The demand for money according to Marshall is the demand for cash balances. Instead of explaining price level with reference to total volume of trade, it is conceived with the level of income.

Marshall's equation is

$$M = KY$$

where, M = total money supply at a point of time

and Y = the level of national income

and K = is the proportion of income which people want to hold in the form of money.

C. Pigou Equation

The original version of the cash balance equation developed by A.C. pigou is as follows :

$$P = \frac{KR}{M}$$

where, P = the purchasing power of money or value of money

K = stands for proportion of total real income which the community desires to hold in the form of money

M = total supply of money at a point of time and

R = total real income or resources of the economy.

Pigou's equation shows that the value of money (P) changes inversely in response to changes in the supply of money (M). The value of money (P) can be calculated by dividing the amount of goods and services which people wish to purchase (KR) by the total supply of money (M). Pigou's equation can be written as $\frac{1}{P} = \frac{M}{KR}$ where $\frac{1}{P}$ is the price level.

D. Keynes Equation

Noted economist Keynes gave cash balance equation, which has a reference only to consumer goods. According to him, people hold money to buy only consumer goods and services.

His equation is n = PK or $P = \frac{n}{K}$

were n = total supply of money in circulation

P = general price level of consumption goods

K = the proportion of consumption goods for which the purchasing power is kept by the people in the form of cash.

Further, Keynes expanded his equation to include bank deposits.

We have $n = P(K + rK')$

or $\frac{n}{(K + rK')}$

where r = indicates the proporation of cash resources of banks to their public deposits.

and K′ = stand for the proportion of consumption units that the people keep in the form of bank deposits.

The value of 'r' depends upon the monetary policy of the central bank and practices followed by the banks regarding the maintenance of reserves.

4. Indian Money Market

Like in any market, certain goods are traded in the money market too. The good that is brought and sold in the money market is money or near-money financial assets. The money market is a market for short-term money and financial assets that are close substitutes for money.

Financial assets of long-term maturity is very much the domain of investors of the capital market where these long-term securities are traded.

Short term is generally for a period of one year.

It is the money market which meets short term requirements of borrowers and provide profitable avenues to the lenders.

(a) The objectives of money market in India are as follows :

(1) an equilibrating mechanism for evening out short-term deficits and surpluses.

(2) a focal point for central bank invention for influencing liquidity of the economy.

(3) an access to the users of short term money to meet their requirement at reasonable pricc.

The **short term money market** in India consists of markets for inter bank call and short notice money, treasury bills, commercial bills, commercial papers, certificates of deposits and inter bank participation. All these markets are closely inter linked.

The major participants in the money market are the commercial banks, financial institution, corporation and individuals.

The larger the number of participants, greater will be the depth of the market.

Trading in the money market is conducted over telephone followed by written confirmation from both the borrower and the lender.

(b) Sources of supply and demand for funds in the money market.

The major sources of supply of funds are :

(1) Investment Institutions like LIC, GIC, UTI and mutual funds.

(2) Cooperative Bank—Seasonal nature of their lending operation coupled with limited avenues for gainful employment of their funds induces them to access the money market.

(3) Cash rich corporate bodies and public sector undertakings.

The major sources of demand for funds are commercial banks constitute the major borrowers of funds in the money market.

While demands for funds vary considerably over a relatively long period, it is the changes in the supply of funds in the shorter term that determines the condition in the money market.

(c) Major instruments in the money Market

(1) Treasury Bills : A treasury bill is basically an instrument of short-term borrowing by the central government.

The banks make use of these bills essentially for parking surplus funds for very short periods.

These 91 days bills are rediscounted by the Reserve Bank of India.

In view of low yield, this instrument has ceased to be of relevance to the money market.

(2) Commercial Bills : Bills of exchange are drawn by the seller (called drawer) on the buyer (called drawee) for the value of goods delivered to him. Such bills are called trade bills. On acceptance by commercial banks trade bills are called commercial bills.

The bank on due date would receive the face value (maturity value) from the drawee.

The bill market is a vital segment of the money market.

(3) Certificates of Deposits (CD) : Certificate of deposit is a document of title to a time deposit. It is distinguished from a conventional time deposits in respect of its free negotiability and hence marketability.

CDs can widen the range of money market instruments offering investors greater flexibility in the employment of their short term surpluses and following the rationalisation of interest rates on short term deposits.

Being a negotiable instrument, CD can be transferred by endorsement and delivery but only after the expiry of 45 days from the date of issue to the primary investor.

(4) Commercial Paper (CP) : CPs are negotiable money market instruments issued by well-rated companies to raise short term working capital requirement directly from the market instead of borrowing from the banks. CPs issued as unsecured instance of promissory notes on a discount to face value basis.

The issuer promises to pay to the buyer some fixed amount on some future date by pledges no assets.

CPs can be issued directly through banks/merchant banks (called dealers).

5. Devaluation

Devaluation is reduction in value of home currency with respect to a leading foreign currency, *i.e.*, US dollar or Pound Sterling or Japanese yen etc.

Maintenance of stable exchange rate is an essential condition for the creation of international confidence and promotion of smooth international trade on the largest scale possible. Instability in exchange rate might lead to undesirable effect such as weakening of the value of currency in the world market, speculation and even flight of capital abroad.

Due to unfavourable balance of payment and poor foreign exchange reserve, the home currency in under server strain and IMF or International Monetary Fund may insist for reducing the value of home currency with respect to a leading foreign currency.

Devaluation is decided by the Central Bank in percentage, *i.e.*, if in a certain year and time Us 1 dollar = Rs. 50 and India currency is devalued @ 10% then US 1 dollar = Rs. 55.

Devaluation encourages exports and discourages import of goods and services for a country.

If devaluation is the cause and effects is increase in exports which helps the country to solve the balance of payments to some extent.

Most countries opt for devaluation of currency when they face adverse BOP.

While depreciation is the reduction in the external value or the currency as a result of market forces, devaluations is the lowering of the value of the currency by the govt.

For devaluation to be successful, the following condition have to be met : The elasticity demand for the country's exports as well as imports should be greater than unity, there should be an increasing demand for the goods exported in the international markets.

5. *(a)* Monetary Aggregates M_1, M_2, M_3, M_4 & M_0 :

Extent of Money

The RBI generally measures the extent of money and credit available in the economy at a given time.

The following indices are generally used for the purpose.

M_1 = This represents money supply with the public. M_1 has two components *(a)* currency with the public and *(b)* deposits of publics with the banks.

Currency with the public is the sum total of notes in circulation and circulation of rupee coins and small coins minus the cash on hand with banks.

Deposits of the public with banks is the sum total of demand deposits with banks and other deposits of the public with the RBI.

M_2 = This represents total of M_1 Plus Post Office savings and bank deposits.

M_3 = It is the sum total of M_2 and the time deposits with banks.

M_4 = This represents M_3 plus total post office deposits.

M_1 is called "narrow money" while M_3 is called "broad money". Ms represents the aggregate monetary resources or the money stock of the entire banking sector.

M_0—Cash in circulation with the public and cash held by, banks and building societies, plus bank's operational balances with the Central Bank.

M_0, M_1, M_2, M_3, M_4 are monetary aggregates.

6. Monetary Policy and Fiscal Policy

Two types of policies are pursued by a country to combat inflation and recession (*i.e.* inflationary and deflationary tendencies) in the economy.

These are called stabilisation policies, which include (1) Monetary Policy and (2) Fiscal Policy.

(1) Monetary Policy

It refers to the credit control measures adopted by the Central Bank (in India... Reserve Bank of India).

These are Quantitative or general controls and Qualitative or Selective controls.

Quantitative or general controls include bank rate variations, open market operations and varying reserve ratios. They aim at regulating the overall level of credit in the economy through the commercial banks. Bank rates is the minimum lending rate at which the central bank discounts bills and securities held by commercial banks.

By raising bank interest rate the Central Bank makes borrowing costlier. This reduces the money supply in the economy, resulting in the reduction in demand for goods and services and this checks the price rise.

Also the Central Bank sells securities in the open market and thereby reduces reserves of commercial banks which reduces credit in the market and this reduction in money supply helps in checking price rise. Changes in reserve ratio can help combat inflation.

The part of deposits which a commercial bank has statutorily to keep with the central bank as deposit is called the reserve fund.

In order to reduce the credit by the commercial banks, many a time the central bank increases the percentage of deposits. Increase in reserve ratio reduces the bank advances, thereby reducing demand for goods and services, and checks price rise.

Selective credit controls are used to encourage or discourage specific types of credit for particular purposes.

In order to check the speculative activity in the economy, the central bank changes the margin requirements to be charged by commercial banks on these activities.

In recessionary conditions, the central bank should use monetary policies in the opposite direction to control reversionary forces. The central bank should lower the bank interest rate, thus, making borrowings by commercial banks cheaper, which in turn lower their lending rates, resulting in greater demand for credit.

This would encourage investment, output, employment, income and demand.

Consequently, prices would start rising.

Similarly, in open market, the central bank should buy securities thereby raising money supply in the economy, whose impact would also be an increase in investment, output, employment, income and prices.

The central bank can also use the instrument of reserve ratio to combat recessionary conditions.

Lowering reserve ratio would lower reserves of commercial banks which would encourage greater lending, thus reviving economic activity.

2. Fiscal Policy

Fiscal Policy refers to the deliberate changing of taxes and governmental spending for the purpose of keeping the actual GNP close to the potential full employment GNP. If the potential GNP is exceeded it causes inflation, while if the actual GNP falls short of the potential it causes recessionary conditions.

Recovery and Prosperity Phases : When inflation, is due to excess purchasing power in relation to the amount of goods and services available in the economy, the basic remedy for controlling inflationary conditions is to drain away excess purchasing power. In such a case, fiscal policy should aim at taking the rupees out of the income-expenditure stream. As a result of this the aggregate demand will reduce, leading to control of price rise.

This is done in two ways :

(a) To restrain or reduce government spending and create a surplus budget (where tax revenue exceeds government expenditure).

The cut back on government expenditures would reduce aggregate demand originating in the public sector.

(b) To increase taxes on business and consumers without increasing government expenditure. Its impact would also be to create surplus budget and dampen the aggregate demand.

However, both the approaches can also be used simultaneously.

Recession : To combat recessionary conditions, just the opposite of fiscal policy measures need to be adopted.

The government should aim to generate fiscal deficit by either increasing government expenditure, or decreasing taxes or both.

In recession, the economy suffers from unemployment as well as low level of output and aggregate demand.

To give boost to aggregate demand, there is need to pump purchasing power in the economy. By increasing the aggregate demand, the unused capacity and unemployed labour can be employed.

3. Banking System

***(i)* Introduction :** A commercial bank is a profit seeking business firm, dealing in money or rather dealing in claims to money. It is a financial institution that creates demand deposits which are subject to withdrawal by the owner on demand and subject to transfer to a third party by means of a cheque. In this respect it differs from all other financial institutions.

Moreover, deposits in a commercial bank circulate as money while deposits in other financial institutions do not.

In fact, the greater part of money supply is the direct consequence of the money creating activities of commercial banks :

(a) *Definition of a Bank* : A bank is an establishment for the custody of money, which it pays out on a consumer's order.

A bank is defined as an institution whose debts (bank deposits) are widely accepted in settlement of other people's debts to each other.

The Banking companies Act, 1949 defines a bank, "which transacts the business of banking which means the accepting, for the purpose of lending or investment, of deposits of money from the public, repayable on demand or otherwise and withdrawable by cheque, draft, order or otherwise."

***(ii)* Functions of Commercial Banks :** Major functions of a commercial bank may be categorised into *(a)* Banking Functions, *(b)* Non-banking functions

***(a)* Banking Functions**

The main banking functions are as follows :

1. *Acceptance of Deposits from Public* : The primary function of commercial banks is to accept deposits from the public. Deposits are in the form of Saving Accounts, Current Accounts and in fixed deposits accounts.

   The banks pool the scattered savings of the public and serve as the reservoir of savings.

2. *Making Loans and Advances* : It extends loans and advances out of the money which comes by way of deposits to business and entrepreneurs against approved securities.

   A bank advances to customers in the forms of overdrafts discounting bills, money-at-call and short notice, loans and various forms of direct loans to traders and manufacturers.

3. *Use of Cheque System* : Commercial banks also render important services by providing an expensive medium of exchange such as cheques. It is very convenient to use cheques for setting debts in the business transactions.

(b) Non-banking Functions

Non-banking functions are classified as Agency, Services and General Utility Services.

(c) Agency Services

Banks perform certain functions for and on behalf of their customers, which are as under.

(i) To collect or make payments for bills, cheques, promissory notes, interest, dividends, rents, subscriptions, insurance premia etc. For these services, some charges are usually levied by the banks.

(ii) To remit funds on behalf of the clients by drafts or mail or telegraphic transfers.

(iii) To act as executor, trustee and attorney for the customer's will.

(iv) Some banks also act as Depository Participant for their customers to facilitate working of Dematerialisation of share process.

(d) General Utility Services

Following general utility services are performed by commercial banks :

(i) Letters of credit are issued in favour of their customers for business transactions.

(ii) Bank drafts and traveller's cheques are issued in order to provide facilities for transfer of funds.

(iii) Banks may deal in foreign exchange or finance foreign trade by accepting or collecting foreign bills of exchange.

(iv) Banks may act as referees with respect to the financial standing and business reputation of customers.

(v) Sometimes, public issues of shares and debentures etc. are underwritten by banks.

(vi) Some banks arrange for safe deposit vaults, so that customers may keep their valuables in safe custody.

(iii) Central Bank

In different countries, central banks are known by different names. For instance, for USA, it is the Federal Reserve Bank, for U.K. it is the Bank of England and for India, it is the Reserve Bank of India (RBI).

A central bank is an institution whose main function is to help, control and stabilise the monetary and banking system of the country in the national economic interest.

The central bank regulates the activities of commercial banks, integrates them and direct their policies according to the best national economic interest.

Following are the major functions of the central bank.

(i) It issues the currency notes for the country.

(ii) It is the custodian of foreign exchange reserve of the country.

(iii) It serves as the banker to the government.

(iv) It serves on banker to commercial banks.

(v) It serves as the monetary authority for the country and regulates the credit creation activity of each and every bank and also performs the function of a controller of credit.

(vi) It serves as a leader of the banking system, and supervises the activities of all the banks in the country.

(vii) It helps to promote the economic development of the country.

(iv) Banks and Financial Institutions

Introduction

Finance is as crucial to an enterprise as is blood to the human body. The requirement of finance is inevitable for setting up a new enterprise.

Money is not easily available for setting up a business unit in India and entrepreneurs invariably borrow from relatives and friends, sell the jewellery of the family or the property or borrow from money lenders at exorbitant rate of interest for starting new enterprises.

Development of financial Institutions in India for lending finance for new business was necessitated.

Also credits started flowing for industries and businesses after the nationalisation of banks in 1969.

***(a)* Banks**

Funding patterns of the commercial banks at the time of independence of India were heavily tilted in favour of large industry and trade.

***(b)* RBI and Commercial Banks**

Central Bank : The Reserve Bank of India (RBI), is the Banker to the Government of India. RBI monitors and controls the activities of all the commercial banks as mentioned above.

RBI announces norms for Banks and Financial Institutions and other financial agencies from time to time in the form monetary policy.

***(c)* RBI control over Commercial Banks and Financial Institutions (FIs)**

RBI's controls affect the total quantity of credit and country's economy generally.

These general controls with which commercial banks and FIs are concerned are the following :

(a) *Bank Rate :* This is also called the discount rate which refers to the rate at which RBI lends money to commercial Banks. During the inflationary period, the bank rate is enhanced so as to increase the rates of interest on loans. This gives a dampening effect on the borrowers.

The reverse course of action is advised by RBI during the period of recession.

(i) Availability of liberal credit for some business groups : RBI advises commercial Banks to advance liberal credits to special groups or priority sectors like small scale industries, co-operatives, self-employed persons, small shop owners and transport operators etc.

(ii) FIs : FIs like IFCI, IDBI and SFCs obtain funds from RBI for financing various economic activities.

(b) *Cash Reserve Ratio (CRR)* : Under the RBI Act, 1935, every commercial bank has to keep a certain minimum cash reserve with RBI. RBI normally varies CRR between 3 and 15 per cent of commercial banks demand and time deposits.

CRR is a powerful instrument under the control of RBI.

An increase in CRR would reduce the available funds for banks credit and a reduction would have the opposite effect.

(c) *Statutory Liquidity Ratio (SLR)* : In addition to CRR, every commercial bank should keep a certain percentage of its total demand and time deposits with RBI in the form of cash gold and securities.

Maintenance of adequate liquid asset is a basic principle of sound banking.

As per Banking Regulation Act, 1949 each Commercial Bank is required to maintain a minimum ratio of liquid assets as per periodical direction of RBI.

Enhancement of CRR and SLR reduce the capability of commercial banks to expand credit to business and industry and thus create anti-inflationary situation.

(d) *Refinance Policy* : The system of refinance provided By RBI to commercial banks affects their credit.

RBI changes the system from time to time to allow or disallow certain flow by banks.

The scope of refinance as an instrument of credit control depends on the liquidity position of the commercial banks.

Commercial banks depend on RBI to a great extend for the subsidised refinance of agricultural and rural credit.

(d) Indian Banking System

Banking in India is carried out by the Reserve Bank of India and; Public Sector Commercial Banks including State Bank of India and other banks mentioned in this chapter

The Reserve Bank of India (RBI) : RBI was established by the Reserve Bank of India Act, 1934 and is now the central reserve bank of this country.

The main functions of RBI are the following :

(i) To act as depositing of the Government of India cash balances and as its financial agent and treasurer in general.

(ii) To manage, supervise and direct the currency of the country; and to maintain the currency reserve.

(iii) As the treasurer or cashier of the country to manage different remittance of the Government and to act generally as a banker of the Government.

(iv) To manage the public debt of the country.

The other peculiarity of RBI is that it is not expected to do commercial business, but generally acts as a Banker's Bank.

RBI not only manages the currency reserve but also controls the reserves of the Commercial Banks with the result that they manipulate the currency in the interest of the Country's credit.

Through the RBI Act of 1948, all the shares of the bank were transferred to the Central Government free from all trusts, liabilities and encumbrances.

Functions of a Commercial Bank : A commercial bank performs several important functions. It receives deposits both on current account and savings account and also term fixed deposits.

Money thus received is used for providing loans which enable business and other economic activities to be performed.

The function of discounting bills and promissory notes is profitable operation of the bank and constitutes a useful service to its customers.

Other functions of a commercial bank consists of issuing of drafts letters of credit, circular notes, and acting as acceptor on behalf of its customers of bills drawn on the authority of letters of credit buying or securities, making periodical payments on customers' orders, acting as Executors and Trustees and receiving in safe custody valuables and securities from customers.

(e) Role of Indian Banking System

This section deals with the role of Indian Commercial Banks.

Indian commercial banks have played a significant role in this economic development of the country, especially in terms of branch expansion, deport mobilisation credit expansion, promotion of small and medium business and entrepreneurs.

The major roles played by the commercial banks are for the mobilisation of savings and deposits and allocation of finance for business.

Many banks have undertaken new schemes such as investment banking, securities—trading and insurance business in order to successfully compete with non-banking companies.

The administered interest rates for banks were deregulated in the nineties and the banking sector reforms facilitated the creation of a competitive environment, especially in the face of globalisation which started operating in India and world wide.

MACRO ECONOMIC THEORY INFLATION

1. Meaning of Inflation

Inflation is a situation of substantial and rapid general increase in the level of prices and consequent determination in the value of money over a period of time.

The behaviour of general prices is measured through price indices.

Inflation is statistically measured in terms of percentage increase in the price index as rate per cent per month or a year.

Usually, the wholesale price index (WPI) numbers are used to measure inflation.

Alternatively, the consumer price index (CPI) or the cost of living index number may be used to measure the rate of inflation.

Thus, inflation is defined as a state in which the value of money is falling and prices of goods and services are rising.

2. Inflation Rate

Prof. Rowan's formula : Prof. Rowan suggests the following formula to measure the percentage rate of inflation.

$$= \frac{4P(t)}{P(t-1)} \times 100$$

where $\Delta P(t) = P(t) - P(t-1)$, P = the price level and t, (t − 1) are the periods of calendar time to which the observations are made.

3. WPL & CPI—Inflation Rates, Price Indices

The wholesale price index WPI—based inflation rate had touched a record low of 0.27% in the 3rd week of March, 2009.

But the consumers are facing the price rises for food, vegetable and other daily consumable items. Price of potato had increased from Rs. 6 kg to Rs. 10 Kg during mid Feb. to mid March 09. This means that even if the rate of inflation has lowered, it has not reflected in the prices of daily consumable items.

In India, the inflation rate in determined on Wholesale Price Index—WPI.

On the contrary, Consumer Price Index (CPI) is determined on the prices of daily consumable items and in this case, the weightage of food items is much higher than industry produced items like fuel, electricity, steel and cement etc.

The food item have a weightage of 57% in CPI, while their weightage in WPI is just above 15%.

Due to reduction in demand, the fuel, electricity, steel etc. prices have reduced from of 48% inflation rate of 5.5 % inflation rate from April 2008, to Jan., 2009. But during this period inflation rate for food items have increased 1½ times to 11.48 % overall, then together have brought down the rate of inflation in March 09.

4. Application of Rowan's Formula

Table 1 : Inflation Rate in India 2001-01—2002-04

Year	*WPI*	$\frac{4P(t)}{P(t-1)} \times 100$	*Inflation Rate*
2000-01	257	—	—
2001-02	281	$\frac{281-257}{257} \times 100 = \frac{2400}{257}$	= 9.3%
2002-03	289	$\frac{289-281}{281} \times 100 = \frac{800}{281}$	= 2.9%
2003-04	316	$\frac{316-289}{289} \times 100 = \frac{2700}{289}$	= 9.3%

Thus, the common feature of inflation is a price rise, the degree of which may be measured by price indices.

5. Theories on Inflation

(a) As per some economists' views—Inflation is a pure monetary phenomenon.

(b) Other economists believe—Inflation is a post full employment phenomenon.

(a) Inflation as pure monetary phenomenon, according to this theory, other things, being equal, if money supply increases, there is inflation or rise in prices.

Fisherian equation follows :

$$P = \frac{MV}{T}$$

Assuming V and T to be constant, P rises directly in proportion to the increase in money supply (M).

Economists such as Milton Friedman, Hawtrey and Golden Weiser who looked upon inflation as a purely monetary phenomenon, firmly believed in the quantity theory of money.

(b) Inflation as a Post-Full Employment Phenomenon. Economists such as Pigou and Keynes regarded inflation as phenomenon of full employment.

The Keynesian theory of inflation in based on the concept of full employment. In the Keynesian view, rising prices in all situations can not be termed inflation. In a situation of under employment, when an increase in money supply and rising prices are accompanied by an expansion of output and employment, inflation does not occur.

Sometime, due to bottlenecks, in the economy, an increase in money supply may cause prices to rise more than the expansion of output and employment. This is know as semi-inflation or bottleneck inflation.

Once full employment level is reached, the entire increase in money supply is reflected by rising prices, a case of a true inflation.

Inflation occurs in a situation where there is an increase in demand expressed through more money spending but no corresponding increase in production either due to bottlenecks operating in the economy or because the economy or has already reached the full employment level.

Keynes has mentioned the following four related terms while discussing the concept of inflation.

1. Reflation
2. Inflation
3. Disinflation
4. Deflation

Using, a business cycle model like the following figure, we may clarify above terms as under.

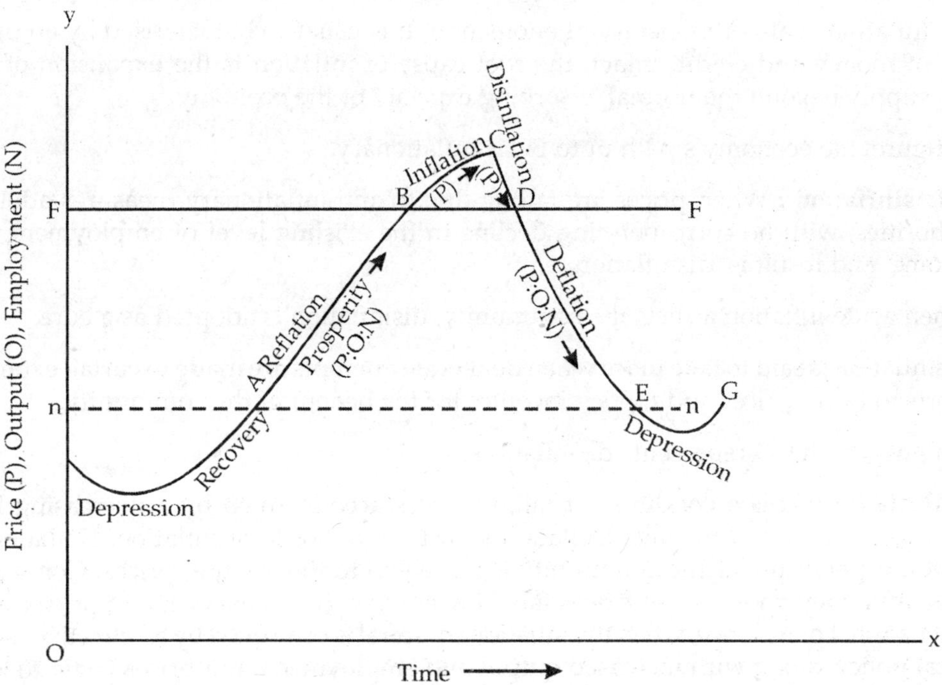

Fig. The Model of a Trade Cycle.

1. Reflation : It is a situation of rising prices, deliberately undertaken to relieve a depression with rising prices, employment, output and income also increase till the economy reaches the full employment ceiling.

In above figure, FF line represents the full employment ceiling and represents the normal path. In the beginning when the economy is at a point of below full employment equilibrium, an increase in money supply leads the economy to more on the path or AB.

However, till the economy reaches the point B, Price rise in accompanied by the expansion of employment and output, the situation, is, thus, described as "semi-inflation or 'reflation."

2. Inflation : It occurs when prices rise after the stage of full employment is reached in the economy, with no corresponding rise in employment and output.

The followings are the main characteristics of inflation :

(a) Inflation is a long term operating dynamic process.

(b) Inflation is a process of persistently rising price level.

(c) Inflationary price rise is persistent and is irreversible within a short time; thus, it should be distinguished from a price rise which may occur temporarily, due to short-term security or during a cyclical upswing.

(d) A cyclical movement is not inflation. Inflation is a rising trend in the price level.

(e) Inflation is fostered by the interaction of a multitude of economic factors.

(f) Inflation is a post-full employment phenomenon.

(g) Inflation is also a monetary phenomenon. It is usually characterised by an overflow of money and credit. Infact, the root cause of inflation is the expansion of money supply beyond the normal absorbing capacity of the economy.

In figure, the economy's path upto BC is inflationary.

3. Disinflation : When prices are falling due to anti-inflationary measures adopted by the authorities, with no corresponding decline in the existing level of employment, output and income, and result is 'disinflation.'

When acute inflation afflicts the community, disinflation is adopted as a cure.

Disinflation is said to take place when deliberate attempts are made to curtail expenditure of all sorts to lower prices and money incomes for the benefit of the community.

In figure, path CD represents disinflation.

4. Deflation : It is a condition of falling prices accompanied by a decreasing level of employment, output and income. Deflation is just the opposite of inflation. Deflation occur when total expenditure of the community is not equal to the existing prices. Consequently, the value of money goes up and prices fall. However, each and every fall in price cannot be called deflation. For instance, when the inflationary spiral is controlled by an effective monetary and fiscal policy, along with increased output and employment, and prices begin to fall, it is not called deflation.

The process of reversing inflation without either creating unemployment or reducing output is called "disinflation" and not "deflation".

Deflation is an under employment phenomenon. In Figure, the path DEG shows deflation.

5. Types of Inflation :

(i) Moderate—Single digit inflation

(ii) Galloping—2 or 3 digit inflation over 10% inflation is galloping type.

(iii) Hyper inflation.

Prices rise every moment and no limit to which price will rise over 1000 per cent in a year, it is called a Hyper inflation.

Two schools of though on cause of inflation.

***(i)* Demand-Pull Inflation**

Prices rise in response to an excess of aggregate demand over existing supply of goods and services. Inflation might be caused in the first place, by an increase of quantity of money, when the economy is operating at full employment level.

Demand-pull inflation (or demand inflation) is defined as a situation where the total monetary demand persistently exceeds the total supply of goods and services at current prices so that prices are pulled upwards by the continuous upward shift of the aggregate demand function.

***(ii)* Cost-Push Inflation**

The second group of economists believe that the process of inflation is initiated not by an excess of general demand but by an increase in costs, as factors of production try to increase their share of the total product by raising their prices.

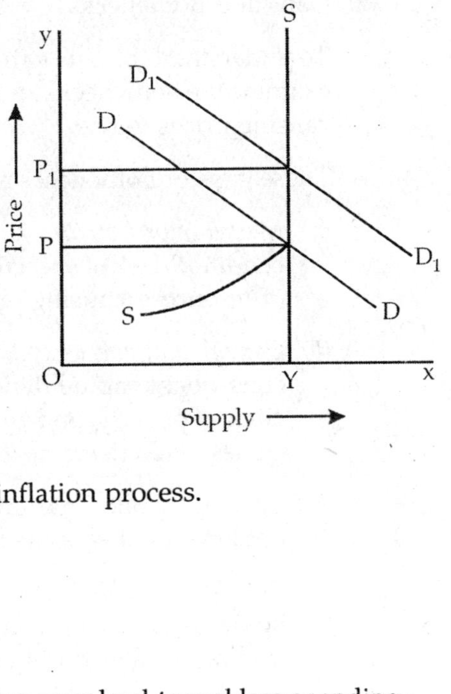

Thus, a rise in prices is initiated by the growing factor costs. Therefore, such a price rise is termed as 'cost push' inflation as prices are being pushed up by the rising factor costs.

Cost-push inflation or cost inflation is induced by the wage inflation process.

Cost-push inflation may also be induced by profit inflation process.

6. Causes of Inflation :

(i) Over expansion of money supply.

(ii) Expansion of Bank credit.

(iii) Deficit financing—High dose of deficit financing may lead to reckless spending.

(iv) Ordinary Monetary Factors

Among other monetary factors, influencing the price trend in an economy, the major ones are listed below :

(a) *High non-development expenditure* : High spending for the defence and non-development purposes.

(b) *Huge Plan Investment* : This may result in an excess demand in the capital goods sector, raising industrial prices.

(c) *Black Money* : This causes lavish spending causing excess demand of goods and services resulting in price rise.

(d) *High Indirect Taxes :* High excise duties and custom duties imposed by Govt. on raw materials and essential goods will result in price rise.

(v) Non-Monetary Factors

(a) High population growth

(b) *Natural calamities :* These include droughts, floods, earthquake causing failure of agricultural crops.

(c) Hoarding

(d) Monopolies—unfair trade practices by big industrial houses result in price rise

(e) Under utilisation of resources

(vi) Gaps and Bottlenecks

To understand the true nature of inflation in an under developed country, we should examine the bottlenecks and gaps of various types which obstruct the normal growth, causing prices to rise.

These gaps or bottlenecks are listed below :

(a) *Market Imperfections :* Rigid social and institutional structures, ignorance of market condition, lack of specialisation and training may not allow an optimum utilisation of resources, causing price rise.

(b) *Capital Bottlenecks :* On account of a new low rate of capital formation and consequent capital deficiency, an underdeveloped country is caught in vicious circle of poverty, and any excessive money supply instead of breaking this vicious circles tends to create a chronic inflationary spiral.

Thus in a poor nation, there is inflation because by virtue of its internal bottlenecks, it is prone to chromic inflation.

(c) *Entrepreneurial Bottlenecks :* Entrepreneurs in under-developed countries lack skill, boldness and risk-taking, lack still, boldness and risk taking ability, they prefer trading or safer traditional investment rather than attempt risky innovation.

Large amount of private investments in unproductive fields like land, jewellery etc., which is a gross socio-economic waste, starves the developing economy of its much needed capital resources.

Thus, increased money supply or savings in terms of money makes little impact on real output resulting in price rise.

(d) *Food Bottleneck :* Due to slow growth of agriculture, over pressure of growing population on land, primitive methods of cultivation, lack of adequate irrigation facilities, and other reasons, agricultural production fails to keep pace with growing population's demand, this food bottleneck creates problem of price rise in food grains and this becomes the cornerstone in the whole price structure in the developing economies.

(e) *Infrastructural Bottlenecks :* These refer to inadequate power supply facilities, transport facilities, communication facilities which restrict the growth of industrial, agricultural and commercial sectors and cause underutilisation of resources resulting in price rise in goods and services.

(f) *Foreign Exchange Bottleneck :* Developing economies suffer from a fundamental structural disequilibrium in the balance of payment due to large gap between imports and exports and hence suffer from foreign exchange scarcity.

This eventually leads to a heavy price rise of exportable commodities in the domestic market.

(g) *Resources Gap :* Owing to backward socio-economic structure in a less developed country, its govt. always finds it difficult to raise sufficient resources through taxation, public borrowings and profit of state enterprises, to meet the ever increasing public expenditure.

As such under the pressure of resources gap, the govt. has to resort to high amount of deficit financing which cause price rises, and this makes economy inflation prone.

7. Inflation Versus Delation :

Both inflation and deflation are socially bad, but inflation may be considered to be the lesser of the two-evils.

Inflation is unjust because it affects different classes of people in society indifferent ways and in different degree. It breaks public morale since it is demoralising. It promotes speculation and hoarding.

Inflation erodes real savings by deterioration in the value of money.

On the other hand, deflation is inexpedient and therefore, not advisable. It is inexpedient for the following reasons :

(i) Delation means falling prices in general which adversely affect the marginal efficiency of capital. Consequently, investment volume tends to contract causing unemployment to increase.

(ii) It inflicts on society the harsh punishment of mass unemployment. Money income of community diminishes and, therefore, even though people's purchasing power is increased due to falling prices, they are unable to buy goods in the required quantities.

Thus, aggregate demand falls, profit falls, producers suffer heavy losses.

This clearly shows that though inflation is unjust, it is better than deflation.

Keynes showed a preference for inflation, because it is the lesser of two evils.

Deflation increases the level of unemployment in the economy, whereas inflation at least implies that all factors are employed in some way or another.

Inflation in a post-employment phenomenon whereas deflation is an under-employment phenomenon aggravating the problem of unemployment.

8. The Control of Inflation :

Following broad categories of instruments are used to control inflation in modern economy.

(i) Monetary policy (ii) Fiscal policy

(iii) Direct control (iv) Miscellaneous measures

***(i)* Monetary policy :** Inflation is primarily a monetary phenomenon. Hence, the most logical solution to check the flow of money supply by devising appropriate monetary policy and carefully implementing monetary measures.

Monetary policy used to control inflation is based on assumption that a rise in prices is due to excess of monetary demand for goods and services by the people because easy bank credit is available to them.

Monetary policy thus, pertains to banking and credit availability or loans to firms and households, interest rates, public debt and its management and the monetary standard.

Central Bank or RBI generally uses three quantitative weapons.

(a) Bank rate may be raised.

(b) Open market sales operation may be undertaken.

(c) The cash reserve ratio (CRR) may be increased.

***(ii)* Fiscal Policy :** Fiscal policy is budgetary policy in relation to taxation, public borrowing and public expenditure. Change in the total expenditure can be effected by fiscal measures.

These would involve increase in taxation, and decreases in government spending.

The government counteracts an increase in private spending and reduces total outlays.

An effective programme to minimise inflation, should combine fiscal and monetary policies.

***(iii)* Direct Controls :** Direct controls refer to the regulatory measures undertaken to convert an open inflation into a repressed one.

Such regulatory measures involve the use of direct control on prices and rationing of sector goods.

The function of price control is to fix a legal ceiling, beyond which the prices of particular goods may not increase, thus inflation is suppressed.

In case, of severe scarcity of certain goods like food grains, the govt. has to enforce rationing along with price control.

The advantages of direct controls are that they can be introduced or changed quickly and easily and hence the effects of these changes are rapid.

***(iv)* Miscellaneous Measures :** Other measures may be that production of certain articles of necessity, at the expense of luxury goods, can also serve as an anti-inflationary measure, since they will help to keep prices from rising.

During galloping inflation, it may be necessary to apply a wage-profit freeze; *i.e.* ceilings on wages and profits are enforced.

Relaxation of restrictions on imports a may also helps to increase supplies and keep the prices under limits.

In an overpopulated country like India, it is also essential to check the growth of population through an effective family planning programme, since this will control the demand on goods and services.

PROBABLE QUESTIONS

1. What is inflation? What are its effects on the various classes of people?
2. What are the causes of inflation?
3. Distinguish between inflation and deflation, "Inflation is unjust and inflation is in expendient, of the two perhaps deflation is the worst" elucidate.
4. What measures are taken to control inflation?
5. What are various types of Inflation? Distinguish between "Demand-Pull " and "Cost-Push" inflation?
6. *(a)* Is inflation harmful to economic development.

   (b) Distinguish between Inflation and Reflation.

   (c) Distinguish between deflation and disinflation.
7. What are various function of money?
8. Describe quantity theory of money.
9. *(a)* Write on importance of commercial banks and their function.

   (b) What is the role of RBI? Describe function of RBI.

CHAPTER 2

NATIONAL INCOME

1. National Income — Concepts and Definition
2. Product and Money Flow and National Income
3. National Income, GDP, GNP, NNP etc.
4. Measurement of National Income
5. Measurement of National Income in India
6. Personal Income, Disposable Income and Per Capita Income
7. *(a)* Circular Flow of Income in a Four-Sector Economy

   (b) Factors Affecting the Size a Nation's Income

   (c) Approaches to Measure National Income

1. NATIONAL INCOME — BASIC CONCEPTS AND DEFINITION

National income is the final outcome of all economic activities of a nation valued in terms of money.

National income is the most important macro economic variable and determinant of the business level and environment of a country.

The level of national income determines the level of aggregate demand for goods and services.

A relevant component of national income is a factor variable considered in demand forecasting.

Conceptually, national income is the money value of the end result of all economic activities of the nation.

Economic activities include production by farmers, production by firms in industrial sector, production of goods and services by the government enterprises, and services produced by business intermediaries (wholesalers and retailers banks and other financial organisations, universities, colleges and hospitals etc.

On the other hand, non-economic activities include spiritual, psychological, social and political services, which produce goods and services that do not have any economic value.

2. PRODUCT AND MONEY FLOWS AND NATIONAL INCOME

While economic activities generate flow of goods and services, on the one hand, they generate money flows, on the other, in the form of factor payment wages, interest, rent, profits and earnings of self employed.

Thus, national income may also be obtained by adding the factor earnings and adjusting the sum for indirect taxes and subsidies.

Thus, national income refers to the money value of the entire final goods and services resulting from all economic activities of the country.

National income also includes employer's contribution to the social security and welfares funds for the benefit of employees, profits of public enterprises and services of own occupied houses.

3. NATIONAL INCOME

One of the most important concepts in all economic systems is the national income. Technically, it is called the gross national product (GNP). Economic growth is symptomised by an upward movement in GNP as the key variable. So, GNP measures the economic performance. A more reliable indicator of economic performance is per capita income.

(a) Economic Activity : A Circular Flow

Money, goods and factor services (also known as economic inputs flow through the economy in a curricular manner as shown below.

There are three major transactors (Govt., Business and households) and two basic kinds of markets (resource and Product markets).

A business buys land, labour and capital from resource markets and pays rents, wages and interest for the resources.

Households contribute land, labour, capital and entrepreneurial talent to resource markets in exchange for income.

In product markets, households spend money for consumer goods and services and Govt. provides, these goods and services, such as law court, police, municipal service, health service

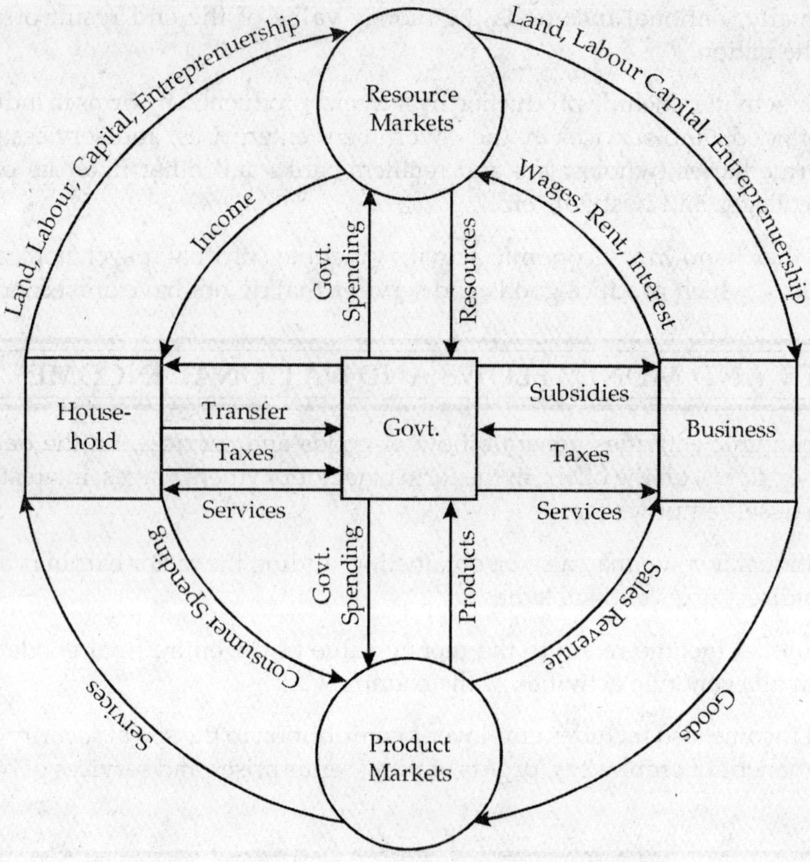

Fig. The Circular Flow of Economic Activity.

to households and business. In turn, it receives taxes from them. It also uses the markets to purchase resources and products (*i.e.* medicines for hospital and services of school teachers) paying for them from its tax resources.

So, business, Govt. and households are interdependent. Each of these three groups help create and maintain economic activity in a process that continues over and over again.

There are three ways of arriving at the estimate of national income. The three methods give us identical results.

The circular flow diagram identifies two basic unit or an economy, *i.e.*, producers and consumers.

In a modern economy, total production is divided into three main categories, *i.e.*, **consumption goods** (like bread, butter, rice, clothing etc.) **investment** (or capital) **goods** like coal, electricity etc. and **services** such as postal, railways, banking etc.

Consumption goods are for consumption by households. Durable goods like motor cars etc. are produced in a year and consumed for number of years say 15 years. But other services like hair cuts, or perishable goods like vegetables, there is hardly any difference between the time of production and consumption.

Investment goods are divided into three parts fixed capital (Plant & Machinery land) circulating capital (Raw Materials, Finishing products) and Residential Housing.

(b) Measurement (Estimation) of National Income

Output method, Income method and the expenditure method, *i.e.*, three methods for measurement of national income.

The output method is known as product method. The product method uses the approach to add up the market values of all output produced by business firms. In order to estimate total output of society, we have to add up the money values of different types of production such as tonnes of steel, barrels of oil, numbers of motor cars etc. We have to express the market value of every commodity (or service) in terms of money because the units of measurement are different for different commodities.

This approach measures the circular flow by going directly to producers and is illustrated by the middle or the circular flow diagram as shown before.

4. MEASUREMENT OF NATIONAL INCOME

(a) Gross National Product (GNP)

GNP is defined as the value of all final goods and services produced during a specific period, usually one year, plus incomes earned abroad by the nationals minus incomes earned locally by the foreigners.

GNP is the most comprehensive measure of the nations' productive activities.

GNP = GNI (Gross National Income)

GNP is estimated on the basis of product flows, GNI is estimated on the basis of money income flows (*i.e.* wages, profits, rent, interest etc.)

(b) Gross Domestic Product (GDP)

GDP is defined as the market value of all final goods and services produced in the domestic economy during a period of one year, plus income earned locally by the foreigners, minus incomes earned abroad by the nationals.

In case of GNP, the incomes earned by the nationals abroad are added and incomes earned locally by the foreigners are deducted from the market value of domestically produced goods and services.

In case of GDP, the process is reverse—incomes earned locally foreigners are added and incomes earned abroad by the nationals are deducted from the total value of domestically produced goods and services.

(c) Net National Product (NNP)

NNP is defined as GNP less depreciation

GNP = GNP – Depreciation

Depreciation is that part of total productive assets which is used to replace the capital worn, out in the process of creating GNP. Depreciation is the term used to denote the worn out or used up capital. An estimated value of depreciation is deducted from the GNP to arrive at NNP.

(d) National Income

Some Accounting Relationships.

(i) Accounting Identities at Market Price :

GNP = GNI (Gross National Income)

GDP = GNP less Net Income from Abroad

NNP = GNP less Depreciation

NDP = (Net Domestic Product) = NNP less net incomes from abroad.

(e) Method of Measuring National Income

National Income may be measured by the following three methods :

(i) **Net Product Method :** When the entire national economy is considered as an aggregate of producing units.

(ii) **Factor Income Method :** When the national economy is considered as combination of factor owners and users. National Income = Rent + Wages + Interest + Profit.

(iii) **Expenditure Method :** When national economy is viewed as a collection of spending units.

5. Measurement of National Income in India

After independence, a National Income Committee (NIC) headed by PC Mahalanobis had recommended setting up an organisation for collecting necessary data for estimating national income and thus the Directorate of National Sample Survey was formed.

NIC's methodology for estimating national income was followed till 1967, till such time when the Central Statistical Organisation (CSO) took over the responsibility.

Better availability of relevant data facilitated CSO to adopt improved methodology and procedure for estimating national income.

For estimation of national income from the commodity producing sectors, *i.e.*, Agricultural and Manufacturing Sectors, and 'Income method' for the service sectors which include trade, commerce, transport and government services. The national income is estimated at both constant and current prices.

CSO has adopted the following 15 Sectors of the national economy for estimation of the national income.

1. Agriculture
2. Foresty
3. Fishing
4. Mining and quarrying
5. Large scale manufacturing
6. Small scale manufacturing

7. Construction
8. Electricity, gas and water supply
9. Transport
10. Communication
11. Real estate and dwellings
12. Public Administration
13. Defence
14. Other services
15. External Transactions.

Centre of Monitoring Indian Economy (CMIE) publishes periodically basic statistics relating to Indian Economy.

6. *(A)* PERSONAL INCOME, *(B)* DISPOSABLE INCOME AND *(C)* PER CAPITA INCOME

(a) Personal Income

The total of incomes received by the inhabitants of a nation including the income of non-profit institutions, is usually called personal income.

In any given year, the total amount of income earned and the total amount of income received (personal income) are almost certain to be different because there are many income categories which represent income earned but not actually received by the households.

On the other hand, some incomes which are currently received are not currently earned, like transfer payments (pensions benefits, interest on govt. Bonds etc.).

Thus, personal income is calculated by subtracting from national income these types of income which are earned but not received and adding those types which are received but not currently earned.

Therefore,

Personal Income = National Income – (Govt. income from property and entrepreneurship + corporate income tax + Retained earnings + Social security contribution) + transfer payments.

(b) Disposable Income

It is common knowledge that the households do not have whole of the income earned at their disposal. A part of its is taken away by the government as personal taxes such as personal income taxes, personal property taxes, in-heritance and wealth tax etc. Disposable personal income is, therefore, simply personal income less all kinds of personal taxes.

That is

Disposable Personal income – Personal Income – Personal taxes

(c) Per Capita Income

$$\text{Per Capital Income (PCI)} = \frac{Y}{P}\frac{\text{National Income}}{\text{Population}}$$

$$\text{For a developing economy } \frac{\Delta Y}{Y} > \frac{\Delta P}{P}$$

whereas, for a poor economy $\frac{\Delta Y}{Y} < \frac{\Delta P}{P}$.

Per Capita Income, is an important parameter for the country's economic growth.

For 2004-05, India's GDP $ 702.95 billion & population of 1.08 billion. Therefore, Per Capita Income (PCI) = $\frac{702.95}{1.08}$ = $ 651.

GDP at factor cost is shown above, which is marginally higher than gross National Income.

Thus Per Capita income is nothing but the country's average level of productivity. If the per capita income in the US is higher, that simply means that the average American is more productive than an average Indian.

The country's per capita income increases whenever the per capita income of an additional worker is more than the average.

Per capita income is also expressed in terms of Per Capita GNP (PPP) basis. Purchase power parity is 'PPP' which means if foreign exchange rate in 2006 is $1 (US) = Rs. 45, when Rs. 45 can buy many things in India US $1 hardly can buy anything in USA.

Per Capita GNP (PPP) in 2003 for India US $ 2880 and that for China US $ 4980 (*i.e.* 1.7 times of India's) purchase power parity basis.

Per Capita Income

Per Capita Income is useful for measuring the country's economic standing whether economically it is an advanced or a backward country.

According to U.N. criteria, countries having a capita income below 500 Us dollar a year are clarified as underdeveloped countries.

Moreover, growth of per capita income is taken as an index of the country's economic development over a period of time.

In India since 1955, the Central Statistical Organisation regularly compiles estimates of national income and per capita income of the country.

Per capita income refers to the average per head in the country. It is measured by dividing the national income by the total population of the country.

$$\text{Thus, Per Capita Income} = \frac{\text{National Income}}{\text{Total Population}}$$

The measurement of per capita income for India on the basis of the following information furnished by the Economic Survey 1981-82 of the Govt. of India :

1. India's national income at current prices was Rs. 1,04,201 crores in the year 1980-81.
2. India's population for that year was estimated to be 67.8 crores.

Thus, India's per capita income (1980-81)

$$= \frac{\text{Rs. } 1,04,201 \text{ crore}}{67.8} = \text{Rs. } 1,536.9 \text{ at current prices.}$$

Personal Income

National income denotes the total income accruing the factors of production. It does not directly represent the total income individuals received. Indeed, it represents the aggregate income flow to households from various sectors.

To understand precisely difference between the national income and personal income, one should know that the entire income which is accrued to the factors of production is actually not paid to individuals owning the factors of product. Some portion of this income is deducted in the form of corporate taxes or retains as undistributed or retained profits. All these constitute a part of the factor income, but these are not received by the owners as their personal income.

The total income of individuals always includes an amount that can not be termed as payment for factor services rendered. Gift's, pension, relief payments are example of such payments.

They are known as transfer payments. Corporate taxes, undistributed profits and retained profits result in the difference between national income and personal income.

Thus, Personal income = NNP at Factor Cost – Corporate Taxes – Undistributed Profits + Transfer Payments.

Disposable Income

It is the total income that remains in the hands of individuals to spend. It differs from personal income by direct taxes that individuals pay, so, it is calculated after deducting personal taxes from personal income.

Thus, Disposable Income = Personal Income – Personal Taxes.

7. *(a)* Circular Flow

The Circular flow of income in a four sector economy is shown in Figure.

***(b)* Factors Affecting the Size of a Nation's Income**

The quantity and quality of the factor endowment of a nation play an important role in determining the size of the national income. If a nation possesses large amounts of natural resources and skilled manpower, it is termed rich. Broadly speaking, natural resources, human resources, capital resources and self sufficiency are the factors that affect the size of the national income.

(a) **Natural resources :** These include minerals mined from the earth, agricultural potential, and energy resources (including oil, gas, hydroelectric, thermal, and wind power).

(b) **Human resources :** If a nation has a large literate population, which is capable and knowledgeable in wealth creating processes, the nation will have a large national income.

(c) **Capital resources :** To have a good national income, a nation must create and conserve capital resources. This includes not only tools, plants and machinery, factories, mines, domestic dwellings, schools and colleges, but also infrastructure facilities like roads, railways, airports, seaports and communication facilities.

(*d*) **Self-sufficiency :** A nation cannot have large national income if its citizens are not self-supporting and self-sufficient. Government should encourage entrepreneurial activities that increase self-sufficiency.

7. (*c*) Approaches to Measure National Income (Mathematical Approach)

There are three ways to measure national income : product approach, income approach and expenditure approach.

Product Approach

In this approach, national income is measured by calculating the total value of the final output of a country. All goods and services produced in the country comprise the final output. The amount of each of these goods and services produced in a given year is denoted by Q_1, Q_2, Q_3---Q_n and their respective market prices are denoted by P_1, P_2, P_3----P_n.

The products of quantities or services produced and their respective prices are added up to arrive at the national income. Mathematically this can be represented as

$$NI = P_1Q_1 + P_2Q_2, + P_3Q_3 + ----P_nQ_n.$$

$$\text{Or } NI = \sum_i P_iQ_i$$

Income Approach

The annual flow of factor earnings in the form of wages, rents, interest and profits accrued from labor, land, capital and organisation respectively are taken into account in the income approach. All these factors contribute to the production of the final output. The value of the final output can also be expressed as the total income of factors used in the production process such as building or land, capital, households and organizations.

Mathematically, this can be expressed as

$$P_iQ_i = W_i + R_i + I_i + P_i,$$

where W, R, I and P stand for wages, rent, interest and profits respectively.

$$NI = \sum_i P_iQ_i$$

Expenditure Approach

In expenditure approach, national income is measured by aggregating the flow of total expenditures on the final goods and services in an economy. Any economy broadly consists of households, business firms and government. Household expenditures can be measured by aggregating their expenditures on the various goods and services purchased. Similarly for the other two sectors, their expenditures can be measured. So, the national income will be equal to sum of expenditures of all three sectors. Mathematically this can be expressed as

$Y = E_n + E_b + E_g$, where E_n, E_b and E_g denote the annual flow of expenditures by the household, business and government sectors respectively.

All three approaches discussed above yield the same results. They provide alternative methods to measure the national income.

PROBABLE QUESTIONS

1. What is National Income? Write about basic concepts.
2. Define and Co-relates

   GNP & GDP

   NNP & GNP

   How is National Income measured?
3. What is the relevance of national income statistics in business decisions? What kind of business decisions are influenced by the change in national income?
4. How is National Income for India estimated?
5. Describe the circular flow of economic activation to estimate national income.
6. Define National Income. How is it measured.
7. Write relationships at GDP, GNP & NNP.
8. Write notes on Personal Income, Disposable Income and Per Capita Income.
9. What factors affect the size of a National Income?
10. What is CSO? How does it measure National Income in India?

CHAPTER

3

PUBLIC FINANCE

Public Revenue, Public Expenditure, Public Debt, Fiscal Policy, Deficit Financing, Indian Public Finance—sources of central and state government revenues, importance of public expenditure in India, heads of public expenditure, budget, need and types, VAT, MODVAT.

1. **Public Finance :** Public finance is that branch of economics which studies how the public bodies at national, state or local levels raise their revenues and how they spend them. Thus, it is the investigation into the nature and principles of public expenditure and public revenue.

Public finance in concerned with raising the revenues, incurring expenditures on different items and the principles and policies relating to these matters.

2. Public finance is broadly classified into following four parts Public Expenditure, Public Revenue, Debt and Financial Administration.

(a) Public Expenditure

The Government of every country perform basically two types of function. Obligatory functions include maintenance of law and defence of the country to ensure peace.

Other functions like building of roads, bridges, hospitals, schools & college etc. and to develop infrastructure for promoting business and economic activity in the country are included under optional functions. To perform these functions the government incurs expenditure. Here, we study principles, the effects on different sectors, problems and control of expenditure by public authorities.

As the govt. is responsible to the public, it must take utmost care to spend the public money for maximum public welfare. For this, the expenditure plans of the govt. must follow certain principles or canons.

The five canons of public expenditure are as follows :

(1) Canons of benefit : The canon of benefit is really the most important canon of public expenditure. This principle requires that the amount and pattern of public expenditure should be planned in a manner that maximises social benefit.

The principles of maximum social advantage is similar to the principle of maximum satisfaction.

In the words of Pigeou, "Expenditure should be pushed in all directions up to the point at which satisfaction obtained from the last shilling expended is equal to the satisfaction cost in respect of the last shilling called up on government service".

For maximum social advantage, every unit or public expenditure should enable the entrepreneur to get the maximum output at the minimum cost.

(2) Canon of Economy : This canon states that the govt. being trustee of the public funds, should spend money in an economical way with utmost care. The government should not spend more than necessary on a particular item of expenditure.

The main aim of this canon is to avoid extravagance and wastes of all kinds, by checking duplication and overlapping of expenditure.

(3) Canon of Sanction : This canon implies that the expenditure should not be incurred unless it has been sanctioned by an appropriate authority.

The sanction of proper authority is necessary to see that the expenditure for which sanction is required, aims at bringing about maximum social advantage.

(4) Canon of Surplus : According to this canon, the state must avoid resorting to deficit financing. It is dangerous and may involve the risk of economic disaster.

A surplus in budget may be justified during inflation on an anti-inflationary measure. But this policy may prove to be disastrous in a period of deficit financing may be recommended.

(5) Cannon of Elasticity : In addition to above four canons, the additional canon followed is **canon of elasticity.** This canon maintains that the government should be able to change the public expenditure with greater ease to suit the circumstances.

Thus, public expenditure should be elastic or flexible, increasing during periods of emergency and decreasing during periods of normalcy.

The proportion of public expenditure to the national income in India today is one of the highest in developing countries in world over the last five decades in India, the proportion of developmental expenditure in total public expenditure has shown a phenomenal rise.

(b) Public Revenue

The government after planning its expenditure, attempts to raise the resources, to finance the expenditure. The income of the government through all its sources is known as public revenue.

Taxation is the most important source of public revenue.

Commercial revenue, administrative revenue and gifts as well as grants are other sources of public revenue.

(1) Commercial Revenue : The revenue received by the government from the sale of goods and services by the public enterprises is called commercial revenue.

The payments for the services of railways, airlines, posts and telegraph, electricity, etc. are included in this category.

The revenue of the government from its commercial activity depends on the range of these activities and the price policy.

(2) Administrative Revenue : The characteristic of administrative revenue is that they generally arise as a by product of the administration of a control function of government. These are fees, licence fees, special assessment, fines and penalties and for features etc.

(3) Gifts and Grants : Gifts and grants include voluntary contributions from private individuals or non-governmental or governmental donors or international agencies to the government fund for specific purposes, such as relief fund, foreign grants to fight against some diseases etc.

(4) Taxation : Tax is the primary source of public revenue. Tax is a compulsory contribution imposed by a public authority, irrespective of the exact amount of service rendered to the tax payer in return.

Thus, a tax is a compulsory contribution from the people to the state, against which no specific benefits can be expected from the exchequer.

Tax revenue collections are generally spent by the state in the common interest of all.

Taxes are broadly classified as direct and indirect taxes. Direct taxes are these taxes which are levied on the property and incomes of person & businesses, who pay them directly to the government.

Income tax, wealth tax, corporation tax, gift tax, toll tax and estate duty etc. are important examples of direct taxes.

Indirect taxes are imposed on commodities and services, sales tax, Excise duty, custom duty and entertainment tax etc. are important examples of indirect taxes.

(c) Public Debt

Like individual, the public bodies also borrow funds from the public to meet their obligation, particularly under abnormal situation like war, famine, floods or natural calamities.

Under these situations, the expenditure of the govt. exceeds its revenue : The deficit may be met by govt. through borrowing from public.

The govt. may even borrow funds from the public under normal circumstances for promoting the economic development of the country.

Public debt deals with the principles and methods of raising debts from public and their repayment and management of public debt.

Taxation policy may fail to mobilise enough resources in the developing countries due to low level of per capita income. Some times, it may not even be considered to be just. Some people recommend public borrowing for financing of low gestation development projects, the benefit of which may not be available to the present generation.

Public borrowing may be used to check non essential private consumption expenditure. The govt. may issue debenture, bonds etc. with attractive rates of interest for this purpose.

When the government fails to collect sufficient resources, it may resort to compulsory savings, public borrowing will be successful only when debts are collected from the idle balances with the people.

If borrowing leads to a fall in current consumption or is financed, through cut in investment, it may not have desired effects.

2. Objectives of Fiscal Policy in Developing Countries

The objectives of fiscal policy vary from country to country, according to the level of economic development. While it aims to maintain full employment and to stabilise the growth rate in developed countries, the aim of fiscal policy in the developing countries is to reconcile the conflicting objective of accelerating the rate of capital formation and economic growth, equitable distribution of income and wealth, increasing job opportunities and price stability.

Thus main objective of fiscal policy are mobilisation of Resources, Economic development and growth, expansion of employment, reduction in disparities of income, price stability and correcting disequilibrium in "Balance of Payments".

(d) Financial Administration

Under this branch, we study the problem of financial management, *i.e.*, how the govt. controls its financial operations. **It covers matters like preparation and sanction of various types of budgets** as well as **development finance, auditing of government** accounts etc.

Thus, in a developing country like India public finance means the way. Govt. collects revenue and the manner it spends it for the maximum benefit of the society taking into consideration the principles and theories of political science and economics. Public finance operations have far reaching effects on the grounds of achievement of social objectives, equitable distribution of income and wealth, production, employment and economic activity, economic stability and maintaining balance of payments etc.

3. Comparison between Monetary Policy and Fiscal Policy

Both Monetary policy and Fiscal policy can be used to check depression or to curb inflation. However, fiscal policy is more successful in curbing inflation. Neither monetary policy nor fiscal policy alone can provide the means for sufficient stabilization programme. Instead, each is essential and must be used to supplement the other. Hence, fiscal policy does not provide a complete substitute for sound monetary policy.

The effects of fiscal policy are more direct, as it involves shaping of the tax structure, determination of the amount of tax revenue and volume as well as direction of public expenditure.

The effects of Fiscal policy are direct, while those of monetary policy are indirect in nature.

Fiscal policy operations should be free from political pressures, as far as possible so that the central bank may use initiative and discretion in its monetary policy.

For monetary policy to be effective, the monetary authority must have an effective say in regulating money supply and then a reasonable degree of controle over the creation of reserve money.

4. Indian Public Finance, Central and State Governments Revenues

The constitutional set up of a country may be unitary or federal. Under the former, there is only one government, the central government which is all powerful and takes decision in all matter's while in the latter, there is central government as well as state governments.

India has adopted federal types of government in which the central and state governments work together for the welfare of the people.

The centre deals with matters of national and international concern, like defence, external affairs, issue of currency, etc. The rest of the activities come under the jurisdiction of the state.

The functions and powers of the centre and the state governments are clearley defined in the Indian constitution under the Union List and the State List respectively. The concurrent list gives such function which can be performed by the centre as well as the state governments.

In India, responsibility as well as resources are allocated between the centre and the state governments. However, the maintenance of financial relation between the centre and the states becomes the most difficult problem due to multiplicity of taxing and spending authorities in a federation.

The structure of federal finance comprises of two essential components.

- One is regarding the division of power between the central and the state governments in respect of raising and disbursing of public funds.
- The second relates to the transfer of funds from the centre to the various states.

1. The Principles of Federal Finance : B.P. Adarkar has laid down the following principles to govern the functioning of the Federal Finance System.

(a) *Independence and Responsibility :* Complete autonomy of financial operations must be extended to centre as well as state governments to render their normal activities for the promotion of social and economic advancement. In other words, central government and state governments should be able to obtain sufficient funds for the achievement of their legitimate aspirations.

(b) *Elasticity :* Besides adequacy, there should be elasticity in the financial resources. Each layer of the government should be able to expand the resources in response to the growing needs and responsibilities so that it may discharge its obligation and function without any difficulty.

(c) *Administrative Efficiency :* The successful operation of the federal system requires minimisation of the cases of fraud and tax evasion. Administrative cost should be reduced to minimum.

5. Sources of Revenue of Central Government

Items 82 to 92(*a*) in the Union List in the Seventh Schedule of the Constitution refer to the sources of the Union Government. The Union List (List 1) contains 12 items of taxation. These are as follows :

(i) Taxes on income other than agriculture income

(ii) Duties on custom including export duties.

(iii) Excise duties on tobacco and other goods manufactured in India except alcoholic liquors for human consumption, opium and narcotics.

(iv) Corporate tax

(v) Taxes on capital value of the assets exclusive of agricultural land, of individuals and companies and taxes on the capital of companies.

(vi) Estate duty in respect of property other than agricultural land.

(vii) Terminal taxes on goods or passengers carried by railways sea or air, taxes on railway fares and freights.

(viii) Stamp duty in respect of negotiable instruments and policies of insurance.

(ix) Taxes on sale and purchase of newspapers and advertisements published therein.

(x) Taxes other than stamp duties on transactions in stock exchanges and future markets.

(xi) Taxes on the sale or purchase of goods other than newspapers, where such sale or purchase takes place in the course of into state trade or commerce.

(xii) Fees taken in the Supreme Court.

6. The Central Taxes may be Clarified into four Categories.

(a) **Taxes and duties accruing wholly to the Central Government.** These taxes and duties include custom duties comprising of export duties, corporate taxes, on the capital value of the assets exclusive of agricultural land of individual and companies etc.

(b) **Taxes and duties levied and collected by the Central Government, but proceeds shared with the states.** Article 268 of the Constitution provides for the sharing of the proceeds of central tax on income and union excise duties with the states in a prescribed manner.

(c) **Taxes and duties levied and collected by the Central Government, but proceeds wholly distributed among the states.** According to Article 266(2) of the Constitution proceeds of estate and **succession** duties in respect of property other than agricultural land, terminal taxes on railways fares and freights, taxes on sale or purchase of goods including newspapers in the course of into state trade or commerce etc.

(d) **Taxes and duties levied by the centre, but collected and appropriated by the states.** The Central Government fixes rates of taxes and states collect and appropriate the proceeds.

7. Sources of Revenue of State Government

In the Seventh Schedule of the Indian Constitution, items 45 to 63 in the state list refer to the tax sources of the statues. These items are :

(i) Land revenue, including the assessment and collection of revenue.

(ii) Taxes on agricultural income, on land and building.

(iii) Duties in respect of succession to agricultural land.

(iv) Estate duty in respect of agricultural land.

(v) Taxes on lands and buildings.

(vi) Taxes on mineral rights, subject to any limitation imposed by the Parliament.

(vii) Excise duties on alcohalic liquors for human consumption, opium and other narcotics.

(viii) Taxes on the entry of goods into a local area for consumption or sale.

(ix) Taxes on the consumption and sale of electricity.

(x) Taxes on the sale or purchase of goods other than newspapers.

(xi) Taxes on goods and passengers carried by road or inland waterways.

(xii) Taxes on vehicles.

(xiii) Taxes on animals and boats.

(xiv) Tool taxes.

(xv) Taxes on profession trades and employment.

(xvi) Capitation taxes.

(xvii) Taxes on luxuries including entertainment, ammusements, betting and gambling.

(xviii) Stamp duties in respect of document other than that subject to stamp duty by the Union Government.

(xix) Fees in respect of any of the matters in the state list, but excluding court fees.

Thus, the state list contains 19 items and the entire proceeds collected from the above mentioned taxes are credited to the consolidated fund of the respective states and utilised for meeting their expenditures.

Besides these independent tax sources, they have share in some specific union taxes also.

Articles 274 protects and safeguards the financial interest in the study against any possible encroachment by the union in their revenue reserves.

8. Importance of Public Expenditure in India

Early classical thinkers favoured minimum state interference in the economic life of the country and opposed any increase in the government expenditure. In their opinion, the public expenditure should be kept at the minimum possible level and the state should not spend more than what is necessary for the performance of its responsibility. In the words of H. Parnell, "every particle of expense that is incurred beyond what necessity absolutely requires for the preservation of social order and for the protection, against foreign attack is waste and unjust and oppressive imposition upon public."

In the new millennium, with the emergence of the welfare state in a democratic system in India, there has been a spectacular expansion in the activities and the function of the state both intensively as well as extensively. As a result, there has been a phenomental rise in the public expenditure. This trend is expected to continue in future also.

The welfare state in the present century promotes economic, political and social well-being of the citizen of the country. Therefore, to achieve satisfactory performance in these activities there should be direct functional relationship between the state activities and the growth of public expenditure.

Also, the rise in the population in India would necessitate the increase in the size of public expenditure for meeting the growing needs of the population, such as educational, health care and other social infrastructure facilities.

9. Heads of Public Expenditure

During the course of economic development, government expenditure rises more than proportionately with per capita community output. Thus, the income elasticity of demand for public expenditure exceeds one. The government has to incur rising expenditure to deal with complexities in economic life, as economy develops.

The following three heads require the rising public expenditure.

(i) Maintenance and enforcement or law and order, internally and externally (*e.g.* expenditure on defence, external affairs, police and justice etc).

(ii) Participation in material production (*e.g.* expenditure on economic services like industry, transport, communication, agriculture, irrigation and water etc.)

(iii) Provision of social services (*e.g.* expenditure on education, medical services and public health and water supply etc)

Total outlay in the public sector in India increased from Rs. 1960 crores during the 1st Five Year Plan to Rs. 4,34,100 crores during the Eighth Five Year Plan.

This enormous rise in public expenditure has been on account of

- **Growth in Population :** *i.e.* increase in population from 36.1 crore in 1951 to 84.4 crore in 1991 on account of heads like education, healthcare and maintenance of law and order etc.

- **Rise in National Income :** The ratio of public expenditure to the national income rises considerably in response to rise in the per capita income during the early period of its development.

- **Urbanisation :** The increased process of urbanisation during the Five Year plan periods required more public expenditure on transportation, housing and maintenance of law and order.

- **Administration :** Since Independence, increased administration including over staffing, revision of pay scales and annual increments, have put heavy expenditure on administration.

- **Development Projects :** Development projects under various five year plans require huge investment both in financial and real terms.

The public expenditure should be incurred in a responsible and rational manner to ensure that the funds are efficiently and effectively deployed to serve the large interests.

Priority in the allocation of funds assumes a special importance. Further, the productivity of the investment undertaken by the government should be improved so as to generate funds for further development.

10. Budget, Needs and Types

The Indian Constitution provides that *(i)* no tax can be levied or collected except by the authority of law, *(ii)* no expenditure can be incurred from public funds and *(iii)* the executive authorities must spend public money only in the manner sanctioned by the Parliament in the case of the Union and by the State Legislature in a state.

In deference to the provision of the Constitution, the Indian Govt. has been preparing annual budgets, placing them before Parliament, getting its approval and spending and raising, revenues as stipulated in the annual budgets.

The work of preparing the Union budget in the month of August every year and finalisation, it is presented to the Parliament on the last day of February. The budget is generally presented by the Finance Minister in the name of the President of India.

The budget speech of the Finance Minister is of great importance and is eagerly awaited by the finance and business circles as it contains information about fresh taxes and proposals relating to expenditure. No discussion is allowed on the date of presentation of the budget. Discussion follows on later dates and then the budget demands are put to a vote. When the budget is passed by the Parliament, it goes to the President for his assent. The tax proposals of the budgets are embodied in another bill which is passed as the Finance Act of the year.

There is another type of budget known as Interim Budget" which may be introduced later in year to increase taxation and expenditure at the time of any financial crisis.

Sometimes, there may be slight modifications of taxation and expenditure without the formality of introducing a revised budget.

The annual budget is divided into two parts *viz. (a)* Revenue budget and *(b)* Capital budget.

The revenue budgets deals with revenue receipts, which include receipts from taxes, interest receipts and dividends and profits and revenue expenditure which is mainly on administration.

The Capital budget is the statement of all capital expenditure and capital receipts which include market loans, external aid, deposits and provident funds.

For Budgetary control and Budgets of a business enterprise :

Budgetary Control : Budgetary control is a plan of operation based on a forecast of sale, income and expenditure which deals with departmental budgets framed on the basis of policy requirements and the responsibilities of executives. This activity also calls for a constant comparison of the actual with the budgeting results.

Budgetary control is a means of effective management control.

The primary object of a budget is to ensure the optimum utilisation of available funds for the purpose of producing at minimum cost and selling in a competitive market at maximum profit.

Budgets are broadly of following types :

(a) **Revenue and expense budgets :** Sales budget and operating expense budget

(b) **Time, space, materials and manpower budgets :** Budget for labour hours, M/c hours and material units etc.

(c) **Capital expenditure budgets :** Financial plan for capital expenditure, expansion / growth etc.

(d) **Cash budgets :** Forecast of the cash receipts/Expenses.

(e) **Master operating budgets :** Forecast of income statement and forecast of balance sheet.

11. VAT & MODVAT

Vat is a centrally directed value added tax in lieu of Sales Tax with effect from 2006. Vat has been introduced with the initiative from the Ministry of Finance Govt. of India and with the support of concerned states.

The Central Govt. had set aside in last 2006 budget Rs. 5000 crore for fear of compensating the losses incurred by the joining states in the first year of introduction of the new system. But the amount of compensation doled out till 31-12-05 was only Rs. 1,026 crore.

However, the assertion that the VAT experiment has been very successful.

Business houses need the VAT documents that need to get maintained are :

(1) **Tax Invoice :** It is a VAT compliant invoice and will contain details such as if the product is exempt or Vatable, the date of sale, etc.

(2) **Credit and Debit Notes :** These are documents for acknowledging adjustment to purchases and sales and contains up dated details of goods returned, price adjustment and damaged goods.

Modvat : Modvat is modified value added tax.

12. Difference between Public and Private Finance

Public Finance	*Private Finance*
(1) For the state, deficit budgeting is a virtue, particularly during depression. For raising effective demand and the level of economic activity, the state spends more to increase the	(1) Surplus budgeting in a virtue for individuals. It is always good for the individuals to spend less and leave a surplus for the future.

purchasing power. Surplus budgeting may be resorted to during inflation in the economy. In the normal circumstances it is not advisable for the state to have surplus budget, since it may imply heavy taxation and less expenditure on public welfare.	
(2) Elasticity of finance : State is capable of making great changes in public finance with ease and comport.	(2) For individuals, drastic changes in the income and expenditure are very difficult to effect.
(3) Coercive power : The government can use coercive authority, if necessary to raise revenue.	(3) Private individuals cannot use force to get revenue.
(4) Solvency : A State cannot be decalled insolvent since the assets of the state are equal to the total assets of all its citizens.	(4) Private individuals can become bankrupt, when their liabilities exceed the assets.

13. Deficit Financing

When a budget, is prepared in a manner that public expenditure exceed the public revenue it is known as a deficit budget.

A surplus budget may be justified during inflation as an anti inflationary measure. But this policy may prove to be disastrous in a period of economic depression.

In such a period, a policy of deficit financing may be recommended.

Unlike the private finance (for which surplus budgeting is a virtue), the **deficit financing** is a virtue for **public finance**, *i.e.*, for a state Govt. budget, particularly during economic depression.

For increasing the effective demand and the level of economic activity, the state spends more to increase the purchasing power.

In the normal circumstances, it is not advisable for the state to have surplus budgets, since it may imply heavy taxation and less expenditure on public welfare and social infrastructure.

Deficit financing or deficit budget is applicable for the govt. and for this a govt. borrows from commercial banks, RBI, general public (who invest in NSCs, Kisan Vikas Patra etc.) and also from foreign countries etc.

Borrowing by an individual has a limit, but for a govt. of a country there is no limit.

The Govt. needs to borrow for providing subsidies in food, agriculture, and for providing healthcare and educational services for people.

For building infrastructures like roads, railways, electricity generation/supply etc. the govt. also may need to borrow by preparing deficit budget.

PROBABLE QUESTIONS

1. What is public finance? Differentiate between Public and Private finance.
2. Describe in brief the classification of public finance.

3. Illustrate the canons of public expenditure.
4. What are the various sources of public revenue? Which is the most important source?
5. Distinguish between tax revenue and non-tax revenue and between direct and indirect tax.
6. Describe sources of central government revenues.
7. What are various sources of state govt. revenues?
8. What is importance of public expenditure in India?
9. Describe various heads of public expenditure.
10. What is a budget? Discuss importance and types of budgets.
11. Write notes on

    (a) VAT *(b)* MODVAT

    (c) Deficit financing *(d)* Fiscal policy

    (e) Public debt.

CHAPTER

4

BALANCE OF TRADE

1. Balance of Trade
2. Balance of Payment
3. Exchange Control
4. Exchange Rate Mechanism
5. Theory of International Trade
6. GATT and Developing Countries
7. India and WTO
8. International Institutions :

   World Bank

   IMF

   WTO

   ADB

Probable Questions

Balance of Trade, BOP, Measures to Correct Imbalance in BOP, Exchange Rate Management, Role of Exch. Rate System and IMF, IBRD, Asian Development Bank, World Bank, India and WTO.

1. BALANCE OF TRADE

During a given period of time exports and imports may be exactly equal in which case, the balance of trade is said to be balanced. But this is not necessary for those who export and import are not necessarily the same person. Even where exports and imports are canalised through one agency — the state trading corporation in a socialist economy, there is no reason why exports and imports should be equal. If the value of exports of a country exceeds the value of imports, the country is said to experience an export surplus or a favourable balance of trade. If the value of imports exceeds its value of exports, the country is said to have a deficit or an adverse balance of trade.

2. BALANCE OF PAYMENT

Balance of payment is more comprehensive in scope than balance of trade for which it includes not only imports and exports which are visible items but also such invisible items as charges for shipping, banking, insurance, tourist traffic, interest on investments, & gifts etc. A country say India, has to make payments to other countries not only for its imports of merchandise but also for banking, insurance and shipping services rendered by other countries and from such international organisations as the international monetary fund and the World Bank. These are debit items for India since the transactions involve payments abroad. In the same way foreign countries imports goods from India to make use of Indian Shipping, banking and insurance facilities, import Indian films and so on, for all which they make payment to India. These are credit items for India as she receives payments from foreign countries. Balance of payments, it will be seen, gives a comprehensive picture of all transactions including imports and exports.

Balance of Payment is continued on page 191 onwards.

3. EXCHANGE CONTROL

Exchange control relates to government regulation of exchange rates as well as restriction on conversion of local currency against foreign currency.

(a) **Intervention :** For an effective control of foreign exchange rate and foreign exchange market the government should have a central authority viz the central bank which should have complete power and control and regulate the foreign exchange markets. Any individual wanting foreign exchange should purchase it only from the central bank and from no other source. Likewise anyone wanting to sell foreign exchange should sell it only to the central bank. The buying and selling of foreign exchange by a single authority enables the latter to adjust the demand and supply of foreign exchange according to the needs of the country.

(b) **Restriction :** As government intervention in the foreign exchange market has been found a week weapon of exchange control, more powerful weapon has been devised in the form of export restriction. Exchange restriction refers to the policy by which the government restricts the supply of its currency into the exchange market. Exchange restrictions may be of three types.

- Cenrtralise all trading in foreign exchange with the Central Bank.
- Prevent exchange national currency against foreign currencies without the Govt.'s permission.
- Make the foreign exchange transactions through Govt.

4. EXCHANGE RATE MECHANISM

Every country has its own currency. Trade between countries, involves different currencies. The rate at which one currency buys or exchanges for another currency it known as the rate of exchange. In other words, it is the price of one currency in terms of the other country. If, for example, Rs. 45 exchange for one US dollar, it means that Rs. 45 in India what one dollar buys in USA.

In order to reflect the day to day fluctuations in demand and supply in the foreign exchange market Equilibrium exchange rate is determined differently under the gold Standard and Paper currency system.

Exchange rate management plays a role complementary to trade policy. This is on account of the fact that exchange rate movements can be used for correcting the imbalances in the current account of the balance of payments. In India, prior to 1991, the rupee was pegged to the US dollar, pound sterling or a bucket of currencies of India's major trading porters. In July 1991 when the Govt. of India announced major trade and industrial policy liberalisation measures, a two-step downward adjustment of 18-19 per cent was carried out in the exchange rate of the Indian rupee. This was to help the country in increasing the export earnings and thus in tackling the serious imbalances in the balance or payments.

The exchange rate is now largely determined by the market, *i.e.*, demand and supply conditions. However, Reserve Bank intervenes to check excessive volatility in the market. *The objective of exchange rate management has been to ensure that the external value of the rupee is realistic and credible as evidenced by a sustainable current account deficit and manageable foreign exchange situation.*

Kinds of Rates of Exchange

Broadly there are three kinds of exchange rates :

(1) **Spot rate and forward rate :** An exchange rate quoted for the spot transaction is called the spot rate of exchange, while the one quoted for buying and selling currency in future is known as forward rate of exchange.

(2) **Fixed, flexible and floating exchange rates :** When exchange rate is fixed in terms of gold or another currency it is called exchange rate when this rate is fixed for a short period but is changed from time to time, it is known as flexible exchange rate. If exchange rate of the currency of a country is allowed to change and finds its own level, it is known as floating exchange rate.

(3) **Multiple rates :** It is possible that a country adopts more than one exchange rate for its currency, *i.e.*, one exchange rate for exports while another for imports. In such a case the country is following multiple exchange rate system. A special case of multiple exchange rate is the two-tier exchange rate system where Govt. maintains two exchange rates, one for the capital transaction and the other for commercial transactions. The forms is generally lower than the latter.

- **The Role of Exchange Rate System :** The exchange rate system is an important element in any country's financial system. Countries which have floating exchange rates can follow monetary policies independently of other countries. In countries with fixed exchange rate systems, the currency is pagged with one or more currencies. When a country has such a system, it has to align its monetary policy with that of other countries. If India pegs its currency with US dollar, with open capital market, its interest rates will move in tendem with the US.

5. THEORY OF INTERNATIONAL TRADE

(a) Introduction

No country has abundance of all the resources and each country tends to specialise in the production of those goods which it can produce most efficiently with its resources. It then exchanges the surplus production of these produced goods with the surplus production of other countries.

Thus international trade suffers from some natural and artificial barriers.

Each country has its own currency and banking system. Movement of goods between countries is subject to certain government restriction. Inspite of all these factors against international trade, it has been steadily growing.

First two theories are classical theories of International Trade :

(a) According to the principles of absolute advantage, basis of trade between two countries exists when each of these can specialise in the production of a good which it can produce cheaper than the other.

(b) According to the principle of comparative advantage, each country specialises in the production of those goods and services in which it has greater comparative advantage and imports these goods in which it has greater comparative disadvantage.

For example India can produce textile garments at a cost much a lower than sophisticated Air Crafts, therefore, it will produce and exports textiles and import Boeing or AIR Bus air crafts.

Following is also known as **Heckscher-Ohlin** theorem :

(c) According to Modern theory of International Trade, a country specialises in the production of a good, and exports it, which uses more of the relatively abundant factor, and imports those goods which use more of relatively scare factors.

For example, a country having abundant labour but scarce capital, will tend to specialise in the production of labour—intensive goods and tend to import capital intensive goods in exchange. Diamond is produced in S. Africa and cut and polished in India, since this job is labour intensive.

(b) Gains from International Trade

International Trade is beneficial for all the trading partners. The principle of comparative advantage shows that if different countries specialise on the basis of their comparative costs, all the trading countries will be better off compared to a situation where they do not trade all.

Gains from international trade can broadly be classified as Static Gain and Dynamic gains :

***(i)* Static Gains :** Static gains from trade are the increase in well-being of the countries entering into trade with each other.

Both trading partner countries are benefited by specialisation and trade.

The principle of comparative advantage leads to an important conclusion that free trade among nations encourages international specialisation among nations.

Following are the benefits for countries participating in International Trade :

(a) relatively more efficient allocation of resources of the trading partners.

(b) increasing production of goods and services in the countries specialising in the good and services where they enjoy comparative advantage.

(c) product prices find to get equalised among trading partners and

(d) resource prices among trading countries find to get equalised as relative demand for resources finds to adjust so as to correspond with relative demand of goods and services.

***(ii)* Dynamic Gains :** International trade has very significant role to play in economic growth of nations. According to Robertson, international trade is an 'engine' of growth.

Major dynamic gains are as follows :

(a) International trade results in increasing output and income of the nations and thus it leads to economic growth.

Through international trade, the world economy can achieve a more efficient allocation of resources and a higher level of well-being of its people.

(b) The underdeveloped countries can take advantage of the superior technology of advanced countries. It is possible only when the former import capital goods from the latter.

(c) When underdeveloped countries establish trade relations with advanced countries, the former are not only able to procure advanced technology but the latest technical knowhow and managerial skills, which are extremely important for growth.

Thus, if each nations specialises according to its resource endowments and enters into trade with other nations, the world economy and economy of each of these trading partners can realise greater output and income and can maintain a higher level of economic growth.

To the extent that countries are not able to trade freely, they are forced to shift their resources from more efficient (*i.e.* lower costs), production to less efficient (*i.e.* higher cost) production in order to meet their domestic demands.

(c) Limitations of International Trade

Though international trade is beneficial for countries, free trade has not received favour from Govts.

This is because free international trade has following limitations :

(i) Cheap imported goods may destroy local industries manufacturing those goods.

(ii) Specialisation resulting from trade may lead to lop sided growth of the economy.

(iii) If trade is uncontrolled, it may lead to economic handicap in the long-run. For example — a country may export some strategic raw materials (whose supply is limited) in large quantities, thus jeopardising future developments.

(iv) Dependence on other countries may prove fetal in situations like war.

(d) Forms of Trade Restrictions

Following are the main kinds of restrictions on internations trade :

(i) Tariffs or Customs Duties : This is the most common form of trade restriction.' Customs duty is imposed as a percentage of the value of goods being imported either in terms of physical units or in terms of weights in tons.

(ii) Quantitative Restrictions : These restrictions limit the physical quantity of goods to be imported during a given period. For this purpose, generally the system of licensing and quota, are used. Quota limits the total quantity of goods to be imported, while import licensing limits the imports of an individual importer.

The quantitative restrictions have become very common in the recent time.

(iii) Foreign Exchange Restrictions : This involves, control and restrictions of sale and purchase of foreign exchange. Though this system was originally used to mitigate the situation of foreign exchange shortage, over time it has been increasingly used to control and restrict imports.

The general practice under exchange control and regulations is to release foreign exchange on the basis of set priorities of imports of different goods.

Most of the under-developed countries are following an active economic policy, in the sense that there is control and regulation of the economy by the Govt. In such a case, foreign trade control and regulation also becomes one of the instruments of growth and economic development.

Protection is, therefore, used as one of the devices to influence the direction and rate of planned economic development.

Internation Trade is also discussed in Chapter 7 of Business Economics.

(e) Balance of Payments

International balance of payments do not include only export and import of goods and services.

They also consist of :

(i) Buying and constructing plants abroad

(ii) Buying and selling foreign securities

(iii) Loans and grants by the Govt.

(iv) Private gifts and grants

(v) Sale and grant of military aid.

The international balance of payments is a summary information of all the transactions that take place between the notion's residents and residents of all the foreign countries.

It records the nation's purchases from and sales to all other nations and it accounts for any differences between sales and purchases by showing how these have been financed.

Depending on whether it has purchased more or less than what it has sold to the other nations, a country will have balance of payments surplus or deficit.

The balance of payments surplus implies that the nation's exports were more than sufficient to finance the sum of its imports., public and private grants, public and private capital outflows.

The balance of payments deficit indicates the insufficiency of export to finance imports and other capital outflows.

It must be noted balance of trace and balance of payments are not the same. Balance of payments is more comprehensive than balance of trade. Balance of trade is the difference between the import and export of goods by a nation, which is only a part of balance of payments.' "Balance" in balance of trade implies gap between exports and imports.

The Balance of Payments (BOP) is broader in its scope and include trade in merchandise and services. *It is a systematic record of all international economic transaction, visible and invisible, of a country during one year.*

BOP, therefore, presents a better picture of a country's financial transactions with the rest of the world than the balance of trade.

The analysis of BOP is done in terms of two major sub-divisions—current account and capital account.

Balance of Payment BOP
- Current A/c (Exports & Imports + Income & transfer of money to and from abroad *i.e.* Credit & Debit balance)
- Capital A/c (Record of transfers of capital to and from abroad)
- Financial A/c (Record of flow of money into and out of country for investment/deposit in Bank & Financial Institutions)

In a free foreign exchange market, BOP will automatically balance. Why?

A floating exchange rate (US dollar via-a-vis rupee) will ensure that demand for rupee is equal to the supply. It will thus also ensure that the credit on BOP and equal to the debits *i.e.* that BOP balances.

This does not mean that each part of the BOP account will separately balances, but simply that any current account but simply that any current account deficit must be matched by capital and financial account surplus and vice versa.

As the exchange rate (dollar vs. rupee) rises (or appreciates), this will cause imports to be cheaper and exports to be expensive. The current account will move into deficit. There is a movement up along the new demand supply curves until a new equilibrium is reached. At this point, any financial account surplus is matched by an equal current (plus capital) a/c deficit.

Transactions relating to goods, services and income constitute the current account, where as the capital account presents transfers of money and other capital items and changes in the country's foreign assets and liabilities resulting from the transaction recorded in the current account.

(f) Measures to Correct the Imbalances in Balance of Payments

The balance of payments disequilibrium can be corrected by—

(a) Monetary measures which include depreciation/devaluation of domestic currency, deflation and exchange control.

(b) ***Non-monetary measures :*** These consist of import control, export promotion, tariff, quota bilateral agreements and starts trading.

BOP is also discussed in Chapter 7 of Business Economics.

6. GATT, DEVELOPING COUNTRIES AND INDIA

General Agreement on Tariffs and Trade (GATT) was established in 1947 after the Second World War with 23 member countries.

AT GATT Conference in 1964 at Brussels, known as the Kennedy Round, GATT had 62 members and in 1993 Conference known as Uruguay Round these were 123 countries as its member.

Objectives of GATT

The general objective of GATT was to enable member-countries to enter into reciprocal and mutually advantageous arrangements to bring about substantial reduction in tariff as also reduction or removal of other barriers to international trade, and if possible, elimination of discriminatory practices in the sphere of international trade.-

In other words, the general objectives of GATT were :

(i) To bring about improvement in the Standard of living of people in member-countries.

(ii) To encourage full employment and steady and growing level of real income and effective demand.

(iii) To bring about expansion of world trade and world production.

(iv) The enable full use of the world's resources.

The above general objectives are to be achieved through evolving a pattern of world trade based upon multilateral trade and non-discriminatory tariffs with the ultimate objectives of the countries concerned.

7. INDIA AND WTO

WTO in Promotion of World Trade and India

The World Trade Organisation (WTO) was established on 1st January, 1995 and WHO is the embodiment of the GATT' s Uruguay Round results and the successor to the GATT.

WTO has larger membership than GATT, the present number of member's stands at 160 and India is one of the founder members of the WTO. WTO' s headquarter is in Geneva, Switzerland.

WTO's roles in promoting world trade *vis-a-vis* India's advantages as a member of WTO are high lighted through the following prints.

(i) Over 75% of WTO members are developing countries who are willing to adopt economic reforms in their respective countries and India will gain in economic terms by joining WTO.

(ii) WTO promotes world trade and India is in urgent needs of exports and import, therefore, India gains to be part of the multilateral trading system.

(iii) WTO through International Trade Centre (ITC) helps the developing countries like India in formulating and implementing export promotion programmes as well as import operations and techniques.

(iv) WTO provides information and advice on export markets and marketing techniques and assets in establishing export promotion and marketing services and imports training programmes for country' s personnel required to work for these services.

ITC's help is freely available for the least developed countries.

(v) Increases in world trade are substantial especially in the product segments such as textiles, agriculture, forestry, fishery, processed food and beverages and developing countries like India are expected to obtain large gained from these sectors.

(vi) Another important role who plays is that a member country is served from entering into multiple bilateral trade negotiations with other countries for under taking export import activities.

(vii) WTO provides for a multilateral set of rules which ensure greater protection against bilateral pressures or against trade restrictions and member country is benefited by these rules.

(viii) The Uruguay Round Package consisted of several area such as tariffs, textiles and agriculture, those related to market access and India is placed in a favourable position with respect to these areas.

India & WTO is further discussed on Chapter 5.

8. INTERNATIONAL INSTITUTION

(a) World Bank

Also known as International Bank for Reconstruction and Development IBRD) Founded in 1944 and started operating in 1946. World Bank is a specialist agency of the UNO and it aims at assisting in the process of economic development and raising the level of living standard of the world people. It also endeavours to promote private foreign investment. It also helps to maintain long range balance of trade growth and maintain balance of payment equilibrium for member nations.

The management of the bank is similar to that of IMF's, by the Board of Directors.

The bank lends foreign exchange to member nations on consideration of (1) its capability to repay (2) the proposed Project Programme of a nation, which is economically sound. The rate of interest depends on what the bank itself has to pay to borrow at the time the law is made.

The bank has been financing the members nations' projects in agriculture, rural development, education and farm planning which directly affect the well being of masses. It has been able to channel private investments for public development projects in countries.

(b) IMF (International Monetary Fund)

IMF was organised in 1946 and commenced operation in 1947. IMF was set up to administer a "code of fair practice" in the field of foreign exchange and to make short term loans to member countries experiencing temporary deficits in their balance of payments and to enable them to meet these payments without resorting to devaluation of currency or exchange control.

The major functions of IMF are : (1) to function as a short term credit institution; (2) Helps in orderly adjustment of exchange rate; (3) Acts as a reservoir of currencies of all member countries; (4) Acts as a lending institution in foreign exchange.

Each member country contributes for its fund partly in gold and partly in its own currency.

IMF fund has contributed for the expansion of world trade and the institution has provided excellent machinery for consultation in international monetary affairs. In avoiding competitive exchange depreciation, it encourages member nations to declare the par values of their currencies fixed in terms of gold or US dollar.

The IMF has tried its best to adapt itself to the dynamic requirement of the world economy.

(c) WTO

The World Trade Orgnisation (WTO) replaced GATT on January 1, 1995. About 140 countries have since joined WTO which seeks to eliminate trade barriers.

WTO's mission is to open up markets even further and promote a co-operative atmosphere around that world. WTO deals with the global rules of trade between nation. Its main function is to ensure that trade flows as smoothly, predictably, and freely as possible.

Decisions in the WTO one typically taken by consensus among all member countries and they are ratified by members' parliaments.

WTO's agreements are the legal ground rules for international commerce.

WTO's agreements bind governments to keep trade policies within agreed limits for everybody's benefit.

4. ADB (Asian Development Bank)

ADB started operation in 1966 with 31 founder members countries. The objective of forming ADB were (1) to promote harmonious regional growth and co-operation in Asia and—Far East; (2) to help in co-ordinating the plans and policies of the nations of the region with a view to making their economies more balances and viable; (3) to promote investment of public and private capital in the region; (4) to promote foreign trade in the region; (5) to provide technical assistance in implementing development projects.

The management of ADB is patterned on the model of the World Bank, *i.e.*, by the Board of Directors.

India is an important member of ADB and is only next to Japan in term of subscription.

India has been encouraging ADB to develop policies helpful to the poor countries in the region.

PROBABLE QUESTIONS

1. Explain with the help of the principle of comparative advantage, why do countries trade with each other.
2. What do you mean by balance of payment disequilibrium? How can it be corrected?
3. Discuss gains of international trade.
4. Describe the objectives of GATT.
5. What roles does WTO play in promoting international trade? How is India benefited by being a member country of WTO?
6. "Globalisation has helped India to have dominant economy in the world during the last decade illucidate.
7. Discuss about the significance of International trade for a developing country like India.
8. "Human Resource Management must be receptive to the new globalisation Process". Discuss.

CHAPTER 5

ECONOMIC DEVELOPMENT AND WELFARE

- Characteristics of Underdeveloped Economies and Developed Economies
- Development Planning in India
- Pre and Post Liberalisation Planning
- The Indian Capital Market
- Welfare

1. CHARACTERISTICS OF UNDERDEVELOPED ECONOMIES AND DEVELOPED ECONOMIES

The Keynesian theory is applicable to both the under developed and developed countries. First we should try to understand the peculiar problems and the nature of unemployment in the underdeveloped countries and as they are different in the developed countries.

According to the Keynisean theory, the volume of the employment and level of income depend upon the effective demand. This effective demand in turn, depends upon the aggregate demand and the aggregate supply function. The output and the employment mainly depend on the aggregate demand.

Thus, the effective demand leads to more output and employment of the workers thorough the consumption and the investment demand, being two components of the aggregate demand.

The conditions prevailing in the underdeveloped countries are very much different from those of the advanced countries in the world.

There is heavy pressure of the population in the underdeveloped countries, resulting in widespread unemployment, low per capita income and poverty in the economy.

On account of the appalling poverty, the market for the industrial goods is very small, giving little scope to the industrialists for expanding their business activity.

In the underdeveloped countries, due to the lack of job opportunities in the industrial sector, the peasants continue to stick to the small pieces of land, which are inadequate even for their subsistence living.

There is predominance of the agriculture sector in the underdeveloped economies and there is a serious problem of disguised unemployment there.

There is underemployment, chronic and distinguished unemployment in the under-developed countries, due to the shortage of or under utilisation of the capital resources.

On the other hand, the main cause of unemployment in the advanced countries is slackness of the economic activities. During the recession, the demand declines, and the investment activities get discouraged. As a result, the entrepreneurs cut down their production considerably which may cause retrenchment of the labour force rendering them unemployed. This is cyclical unemployment. This problem is overcome by raising the demand for goods and services.

Technological unemployment is also found in the developed countries. The main cause for this unemployment is the use of new techniques of production. When the workers are displaced by the use of new techniques, it results in technological unemployment. But technological unemployment is temporary in nature since as and when the labour force gets the knowledge about the new technique, it gets opportunities of employment.

For the underdeveloped countries, the low capital formation weakens the process of the economic growth.

Due low level of industrial production, the underdeveloped countries spend their precious foreign exchange for importing necessary goods and services from the developed countries.

In the advanced countries, an increased consumption as a result of an increase in the income raises the demand for all types of goods and services. But it is not so, in the case of under developed countries.

For the developed countries, the industrial economy has a rising supply curve to meet the rising demand. The supply curve is fairly elastic here and the producers quickly respond to any increase in the demand for their products, leaving little scope for the inflation.

In the underdeveloped countries predominated by the agricultural sector, the output fails to respond even with the rising prices. The agricultural supply curve is inelastic due to various bottlenecks like the uneconomic size of holdings etc.

Keynes assumption regarding the existence of the excess capacity in the consumption goods industries may be valid for the developed countries. It is possible to expand the income and the output through increase in the investment by utilising the idle capacity in the developed countries. However, what is true for the developed countries may not be true for the underdeveloped countries. There is no scope for increase in the supply of consumption goods in response to increase in the demand for consumer goods at least in the short period in the underdeveloped countries.

Further, since the predominated agricultural sector is the biggest producer of the consumer goods, it is absurd to assume the existence of the excess capacity in the underdeveloped countries. Under such a situation, an increase in the aggregate *demand will only lead to inflation.*

To sum up, the main constraint in the developed countries is the deficiency of demand, while the underdeveloped countries are faced with the problem of shortage of the aggregate supply. The developed countries can easily overcome the problem of unemployment through increased public expenditure or low rate of taxation (liberal fiscal policy). A cheap money policy can also be used to raise the level of investment and hence the economic activity during a depression. However, any inflationary of money through the monetary and the fiscal policy will only generate inflanary trends in the underdeveloped countries due to acute shortage of the capital equipment and the working capital.

Thus, it is true that the Keynes analysis does not have much relevance to the specific problems of the underdeveloped countries, still the tools of analysis proposed and developed by keynes are indispensable even for an underdeveloped country like India.

India and WTO

India was one of the 76 countries that became a member of the WTO on its first day. Divergent views have been expressed in support and against India becoming a member of WTO.

(*a*) Arguments for India's joining WTO.

(*i*) India is one of the few developing countries which has succeed in implementing liberalisation programmes. Over three quarters of WTO members are developing countries in the process of economic reform form non-market system. These countries have chosen to join WTO after careful deliberations in their respective countries. Obviously, they have perceived economic gains for themselves by becoming members. India should not be an exception.

(*ii*) As long as India needs export and import, it makes far more sense to be part of the multilateral trading system of WTO.

(*iii*) By being a member of the WTO, India can benefit from the International Trade Centre jointly operated by the WTO and UN, the latter acting through UNCTAD (UN Conference on Trade and Development).

(*iv*) Another advantage of WTO membership stems from the fact that India is saved from entering into multiple bilateral trade negotiations with other countries.

With the WTO membership, India has the advantage of having trade links with all other member countries without the need of bilateral agreements.

(*v*) WTO provides for a multilateral set of rules which are beneficial to a country like India.

(*vi*) The real importance of the WTO to India was in the role that a dynamic export industry can play in the country's development. Both in terms of job creation, skill development and technological evolution, and opening up to the outside world is essential.

(b) Arguments Against Membership of WTO for India

(1) The claim that the world trade increases substantially and that India's exports will expand considerably is not acceptable to many. Removal of trade barriers will not guarantee expansion in world trade.

(2) WTO alongwith IMF and World Bank represents the interests of developed countries and India as a developing country has blindly walked into the trap laid by these developed countries.

(3) The worst fears expressed about the WTO agreement relate to the steep hike in prices of drugs and agricultural inputs (which items India may need to import eventually). WTO is also discussed in Chapter 7 of Business Economics.

3. DEVELOPMENT PLANNING IN INDIA

(1) India has adopted the mixed economy system and the mixed economy is necessarily a planned economy. It is an economy in which the govt. has a clear and definite economic pan. The public sector will have to operate according to certain priorities and to realise specific social and economic goals. Naturally, the public sector should have an economic plan. At the same time the govt. can not leave the private sector to function in its own unorganized way.

(2) Indian Govt. has to prepare and implement a comprehensive economic plan integrating the private sector with the public sector. It is for these reason that India has adopted development planning since 1951 when the first five year plan was launched.

(3) India has over five decades of development planing and has completed ten five-year plans and the tenth five year plan (2002-2007) had completed on 31.3.2007.

These development and economic plans have been designed to achieve following four important long-term objectives.

- Increase production to the maximum possible extent so as to achieve a higher level of national and per capita income.
- Achieve full employment.
- Reduce inequalities of income and wealth.
- Set up a socialist society based on equality and justice and the absence of exploitation.
- Achieve planned rate investment within a given period.

(4) Massive investments were made in all the five year plans to realise the above objectives.

The following table gives the allocation for the five year plans.

Five Year Plans	*I*	*II*	*III*	*IV*	*V*	*VI*	*VII*	*VIII*	*X*
Heads of Development									
(i) Agriculture & Irrigation	37.0	20.9	20.5	23.3	22.1	22.2	20.2	20.6	10.1
(ii) Power	7.6	9.7	14.6	18.6	18.8	16.7	17.4	18.7	26.5
(iii) Industry	4.9	24.1	22.9	19.7	24.3	26.5	23.7	18.8	19.3
(iv) Transport & Communication	26.4	27.0	24.6	19.5	17.4	16.0	17.1	18.7	21.3
(v) Social Services (Education & Healthcare etc.)	24.1	18.3	17.4	18.9	17.4	18.6	21.6	23.2	22.8
Total	**100.0**	**100.0**	**100.0**	**100.0**	**100.0**	**100.0**	**100.0**	**100.0**	**100.0**

(5) The various administrative controls were exercised by the govt in India in the areas of industrial licensing, product preservation for public sector, MRTP and asset classification of monopolies, product reservation for the small scale sector, Foreign Exchange Regulation Act, tariffs and quotas, the mini-plant fetish, labour market rigidities, development finance and indigenous availability and essentiality.

(6) **The Mini-plant Fetish :** In the 1970s, the govt, began to believe that mini-plants constituted appropriate technology, not with standing strong evidence to the contrary. Such plants were encouraged through fiscal concession and subsidised development finance.

There was, consequently, mushrooming of mini-cement, mini-steel, mini-paper and mini-sugar plant etc.

However, these mini plants were not technically viable, fell short of economies of scales and could only exist under a regime of subsidies and high tariffs etc.

(7) **Indigenous Availability and Essentiality :** In the late 1960s and 1970s, any manufacturer who wanted to import capital gods or components had to satisfy the Directorate General of Technical Development (DGTD) that the item was essential and was not locally available.

Essentiality gave enormous discretionary powers to the officials of DGTD, while indigenous availability means advertising in trade generals.

(8) **The Reforms and the Recovery :** There is a general agrement that the reforms adopted in the New Industrial policy in 1991 have yielded positive results.

Post liberlisation era, GDP rose impressively by 7.2% in 1994-95 and accelerated to 7.5% in 1996-97.

For the first time since 1950, India has achieved a growth rate of over 7%.

A significant contribution to this achievement has come from industry and services.

(9) **National Income and Per Capita Income :** The rate of growth of the national income in an economy is an indication of the pace at which the economy has been growing. A high growth rate indicates that the economy is a developed one. Low growth rate signals that the economy is an under-developing or a poor one.

The development and economic plans in India have progressively resulted in increases in National Income and per capita income. Following table proves this point.

Year	*National Income (Rs. crore)*	*Per Capita Income (Rs.)*
1980-81	1,10,685	1,630
1992-93	5,45,435	6,255
1996-97	9,85,162	10,708

(10) **Control of Population Growth :** In 1976, the population policy in India received a new impetus, when the govt. issued a statement in its national policy. The statement contained several—new measures and it reflected the govt's realisation that the population explosion had reached a critical stage and was proving to be a major stumbling block in its efforts to raise the living standards of the masses.

In 1977, the family planning nomenclature was changed to family welfare and the sixth five year plan listed limited population growth as one of its main objectives. The seventh and eighth plans too did emphasize the need for limited population growth.

4. PRE AND POST LIBERALISATION PLANNING IN INDIA

Pre liberalisation planning phase may be referred to the development planning covering five year plans consisting part of the 8th five year plan till 1994 when the results of reforms and process of liberalisation started showing positive.

And the post liberlisation period i.e. from 1994-95 when GDP (in India) rose impressively by 7.2% and accelerated to 7.5% in 1996-97. For the first time in India since 1951 (*i.e.,* commencement of 1st five year plan), the GDP growth rate of over 7% was achieved.

(a) Objectives of Reforms : Through reforms a country changes from central planning to a market economy.

The main objectives of reforms are as under :

(i) Freely determined prices evolving out of decentralised markets rather than prices controlled by government.

(ii) Property rights and incentives, which the Hungarian economist Janos Kornai argues in his book "The Road to a free economy" are the most important and frequently under emphasized part of a market economy : Decentralising decisions without prices providing incentives through property rights will not create efficiency.

(iii) Competitive markets, so that the price system leads to an efficient allocation of goods, labour and capital.

(*iv*) Freedom to trade at home and abroad, which is needed in order to achieve the efficiencies associated with comparative advantage and economies of scale.

(*v*) A role for government in establishing a policy that keeps inflation under check and that efficiently collects taxes to pay for public goods and provides a social safely net.

(*vi*) A role for non-government organisations, because in a market economy many transaction occur within organisation as, for example when as entrepreneur sets up a new firm to market a new product.

(*b*) there is general agreement that any successful transitions from central planning to a market economy must achieve these features of a market economy.

Thus, the era of reforms and the process of liberalisation commenced in India since July, 1991 with the introduction of New Industrial policy.

The industrial licensing and MRTP Acts were abolished. FERA was replaced with FEMA and the process of privatisation *i.e.*, the process of converting a government enterprise into a privately owned enterprise was adopted.

In order for a market economy to take root, it is necessary that existing state enterprises be privatised.

More and more private investment from abroad (FDI) were encouraged in various sectors of economy and these also brought new technologies and products into the country.

(*c*) Subsequent to 1995 when GATT was replaced by WTO in Geneva, Switzerland, India became a signatory of the liberal trade agreements between the member countries and as a result more and more free markets brought economic freedom for industries.

(*d*) Ever since the adoption of NIP in 1991, the government has been increasingly with drawing from the production field leaving more and more economic space to the private sector to expand its activities.

All the three plan documents (the 8th, the 9th and the 10th) released during the period of the last decade or so have emphasized the role of private sector in future economic development of the country, and the government is ready to play the facilitatory role with necessary investments in infra-structure and social sectors only.

(*e*) As a result of increased productivity and improved capital formation (*i.e.*, larger profits of corporate houses) coupled with the impressive growth in export of goods and services together, with large amount of foreign exchange inflows, India has been in a position to build impressive foreign exchange reserve US $ 250 billion and with the appreciating value of rupee compared to US dollar. India has achieved in 2007 the rare honour of a trillion dollar economy with only a dozen of countries in world joining trillion dollar Economy Club".

5. INDIAN CAPITAL MARKET

(*a*) Stock Market Economics

It is widely believed that there is a strong link between the lowered interest rates and a booming stock market as well as boom in real investment. Thus, it is expected that the cheap money policy helps to keep the stock market on a bullish drift and vice versa.

The policy makers should make the market more transparent to the investors and frame policies to influence the real sector and the financial sector.

Economist keynes in his " Treastise on Money" has stated that there is a close link between lower interest rates, rising stock prices and increasing real investments through larger capital issues and that the cheap money policy would help to keep the stock market bullish.

Bulls are those operators of the stock market who expect share values to go up and make purchases at current prices and enter into contracts for selling the shares when their prices go up.

Bears are those operators of the stock exchange who expect share values to fall and make sales currently, hoping to buy them forward at lower prices, in the falling prices market.

Thus, **Bulls** are interested in share prices going up and **Bears** in their going down.

It is not that bulls or bears control economic policies. There are exogenous factors affecting share prices and their course. These factors are beyond the control of bulls or bears. The ordinary investor is simply interested in buying shares at current prices with a view to making capital gains when share prices go up. It is the prospect of the latter sort, of income that makes ordinary persons buy shares when booms are expected.

P/E Ratio : a company's P/E ratio is computed by dividing the current market price of the share by per share earnings. A company's per share earnings are simply the company's after tax profit dividend by number of outstanding shares.

P/E ratio is also known as earnings Multiple.

$$\text{P/E Ratio} = \frac{\text{Market value per share}}{\text{Earning per share (EPS)}}$$

A high P/E generally indicates that market is paying more to obtain the stock, because it has confidence in company's ability to increase its earnings.

Conversely, a low P/E often indicates that the market has less confidence that the company's earnings will increase rapidly or steadily, and therefore, will not pay an much for its stock.

P/E is best viewed overtime.

- **Equity shares** are ordinery shares which provide the main source of risk bearing capital of a company. The holders of these shares arc the first among all provides of funds to bear the losses. The holders enjoy voting rights at the AGM and are the owners of the company the ordinary shares and not redeemed except in the event of liquidation and therefore provide the most permanent of all long from funds.

  The equity shares are listed in a stock exchange and are the only security which offers ownership rights to its holders.

- **Preference shares** are often considered to be hybrid security because it has certain features common to ordinary shares and certain features common to debentures.

Like debenture interest, the rate of preference dividend is fixed.

Preference share holders have claims on income or assets of the company (prior to holders of ordinary shares).

Like debentures the preference share are redeemable on a fixed maturity date like the debenture holders, the preference share holders usually do not have voting rights.

- **Debentures and Bonds :** These are simply pieces of papers stating the amount borrowed, terms of repayment and rate of interest they are issued in different denomination ranging from Rs 100 to Rs 1000.

  The term of issue of debentures are stated in a document called the debenture trust deed, and are binding on all parties concerned.

  For debentures and bonds, credit rating has to be obtained compulsorily from agencies like CRISIL, irrespective of maturity period.

  The invertors generally find the debentures to be more attractive than the preference shares because unlike preference dividend, interest on debentures must be paid whether or nor there is profit.

- **Warrants :** A warrant entitles its holder to purchase specified number of ordinary shares at specified price, called exercise price, within specified date, called expiration data. These are mostly issued along with debentures as "sweetener" to make the debentures issue more attractive.

- **Global Depository Receipts (GDR) :** The GDR is an instrument used by Indian companies to raise funds from the non resident investors. This is a negotiable certificate in form of depository receipt created by the overseas. Depository Bank outside India against ordinary shares or foreign currency convertible bonds of an Indian company.

  The GDRs are denominated in dollars or other freely convertible foreign currencies and being negotiable, can be listed and traded in any international stock exchange.

- **External commercial Borrowings (ECB) :** ECB's are foreign currency borrowings from international recognised sources such as banks, export credit agencies, suppliers of equipment, foreign collaborators and foreign capital markets etc.

  The ECBs are permitted as source of finance for Indian corporate for expansion of capacity and fresh investment. The borrowers are required to obtain prior approval from RBI, when the loan amount does not exceed US 10 million dollar or equivalent. In other cases, prior approval from Ministry of finance shall be necessary.

- **Treasury Bills :** This is a mode of parking surplus funds rather than raising them. The treasury bills are short term promisery notes issued by the GOI at a discount, *i.e.,* they do not carry explicit rate of interest but their issue prices are set below the face values. The yields from treasury bills therefore, depends on differable between issue price and face value.

  Typical maturity periods for treasury bills are 14, 28, 91 and 364 days and face values may be Rs. 25,000 to Rs. 100,000.

The transury bills are approved securities for the purpose of statutory liquidity Ratio (SLR) requirements.

- **Commercial Bills :** These are negotiable instruments (bills of exchange) drawn by a seller of goods on buyer. The banks provide finance against these bills through discounting. The bank has recourse to drawer and drawee.

  The banks can raise funds through bills purchased (i.e. discounted) by them.

- **Certificate of Deposits (CD) :** CD's are negotiable term deposit receipts issued by commercial banks. These, like treasury bills, are a mode of investing surplus funds rather than raising them.

  Maturity periods can vary from 3 months to 1 year.

  Minimum size of deposit per depositor is Rs. 5 lac and in multiple of Rs. 1 lac there after.

- **Commercial paper (CP) :** These are unsecured notes containing a promise to pay under term stipulated companies with high credit rating borrow through issue of these papers mainly to finance their working capital needs. The main buyers or these notes are banks and mutual funds.

  The main conditions to be fulfilled by the issuer company are :

  (i) Companies with specified credit rating can issue CPs subject to prior approval or RBI.

  (ii) The specified credit rating must be obtained within 2 months before the issue.

  (iii) CPs are issued at discount and they do not carry any explicit rate of interest.

  (iv) Maturity period can very from minimum 15 days to maximum 360 days.

  (v) Minimum issue size is Rs. 25 lacs.

  (vi) NRI's can invest in CP only on non-repatriation basis.

  (vii) CPs can not be transferred by endorsement and delivery.

- **Cost of Capital :** The capital employed by a firm normally comprise equity shares, preferences shares, debts borrowed from commercial banks and financial institutions and also its retained earnings.

  Cost of capital is an important ingredient in capital budgeting and plays a vital role in evaluation of any investment proposal.

  The cost of capital is the minimum rate of return expected by the investors which will maintain the market value of share constant at particular level. The cost of capital depend on the risk involved in the firm, generally the higher will be the cost of capital.

  Thus, the cost of capital is a concept which should be expressed in quantitative terms like ROI (Return on Investment).

  The cost of capital is used as a tool for making financial decision like dividend policy, capitalisation of profits and Right issues etc. The cost of Capital acts as determinant of capital mix in the designing of a appropriate capital structure.

- **Capital Market :** Capital Markets means the market for all the financial instruments, short term and long term, as also commercial, industrial and government paper.

  The capital market is a market where borrowing and lending of long term funds takes place. Capital markets deal in both debt and equity. In these markets productive capital in raised and made available to the corporate. The government both central and states raise money in the capital market, through the issue of government securities. Capital market refers to all the institutes and mechanisms of raising medium and long term funds, through various instruments available like shares, debentures and bonds etc.

2. CONTITUENTS OF CAPITAL MARKETS

Capital markets requires many intermediaries who transfer funds from those who save to those who require these funds for investments.

There are two important operators carried on in the markets.

(1) Raising of new capital

(2) Trading in these securities already issued by the companies.

The important contituents of the capital market are :

(i) The shock Exchange *(ii)* Banks *(iii)* Investment trusts and companies *(iv)* Financial institution or Development Banks *(v)* Mutual Fund *(vi)* Post office saving banks *(vii)* Non-banking financial institutions *(viii)* International financial investors and institution.

The supply in this market comes form savings from different sectors of the economy i.e. sources like individuals, corporate, Governments, foreign countries, Banks, Provident Funds and Financial Institutions.

All these entities contribute to savins in the economy and part of these savings flows in capital market in term of shares, debentures & bonds etc.

Capital Market instruments generally have secondary markets and transaction take place through the stock markets generally.

Transactions in this market are conducted only through authorised dealers.

Economic development of a country is reflected in the stock markets. When companies want to expand or diversity they need capital. This capital can be raised through the capital markets. When economy is growing stock markets are more vibrant.

3. MONEY MARKET CONSTITUENTS

Money market Instruments are :

(1) "T" Bills

(2) Commercial paper

(3) Certificate of Deposits

(4) Money Market Mutual Funds

(5) Repos and Reverse Repos Market.

"T" Bills are introduced to stabiles the money markets. They are sold on the bases of fortnightly auction, but the amount, however is not specified in advance. These bills have been instrumental in reducing the net RBI credit to the government. They have high liquidity and safely.

Money Market Mutual Funds (MMMF)

To enable the small investors to participate in the money market, a money market mutual fund is a conduit through which they can earn market related yield. MMMFs invest the funds collected from the investors in instruments like

(a) Transury bills and government securities

(b) Call/Notice Money

(c) commercial bills

(d) Commercial Paper

(e) Certificate of deposit

Repos and Reverse Repos

Repo/ready forward/purchase (buy back transactional deal in an agreement between a seller and buyer stipulating the sale and dater repurchase of securities at a particular price and a date. It is essentially a short term loan to the seller with securities issued as collateral.

Similarly, the buyer purchases securities with an agreement to sell the same to the seller on an agreed date in future at a prefixed price. For the buyer of the securities it is a reverse rep deal.

3. WHAT IS A MUTUAL FUND?

Mutual fund can be defined as a trust that pools in the savings and funds from large number of investors have a common financial goal. Mutual Funds issue units to investors which represent equitable rights in the assets of the mutual fund.

Mutual fund is a diversified, since its assets are invested in many different securities. Investment in the mutual finds may be in the form of stocks, bonds or money market securities or combination of these.

Mutual funds are professionally managed on the behalf of the share holders and each investor holds a pro-rata share of the port folio entitled to any profits when the securities are sold, but subject to any losses as well.

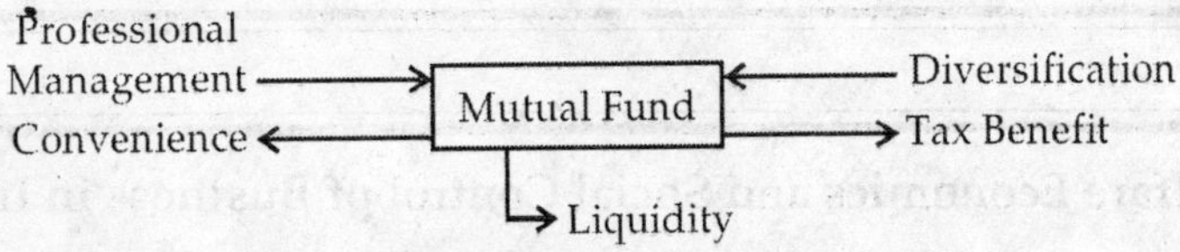

Some useful jargons in Mutual fund are as follows :

- **Portfolio :** Port folio is the group of securities that the fund managers plan to invest. The fund manger can charge the composition of securities.
- **Asset Management Company (AMC) :** The AMC is formed by a group of trustees who has been formed by the board of directors.

  AMC has worth not less than Rs. 10 crores. The AMC invests on behalf of the unit holders, in line with the objectives of the respective schemes.
- **Net Asset Value (NAV) :** The net asset value of the fund is the cumulative market value of the assets fund net of its liabilities. In other words, if the fund is dissolved or liquidated, by selling off all the assets in the fund, this is the amount that the it holders would collectively own. NAV is calculated simply by dividing the net asset value of the fund by the number of units.
- **Open ended and Close end Mutual Fund Schemes :** An open ended scheme is a scheme, in which an investor can buy and sell units on daily basis; the scheme has a perpetual existence and a flexible, ever changing corpus. The investors are free to buy and sell any number of units, any point of time, at prices that are linked to the NAV of the units.

  These schemes are extremely liquid and the funds announce sale and repurchase prices from time to time. These are not listed in stick exchanges and can be only bought and sold to the mutual fund.

  A close-ended scheme is one in which the subscription period for the mutual fund remains open only for the specific period. At the end of this period, the entire corpus is disinvested and the proceeds distributed to the various unit holders. Thus, after final distribution, the scheme ceases to exist.
- **Money Market Mutual Funds :** These are designed as a conduit through which the investors can earn market related yield on the money market instruments. They have to operate within the frame work of RBI guide lines.

  Under the guide lines issued by the RBI, the domestic funds are allowed invest in foreign companies, which have more than a 10% stake in listed Indian companies.

  The regulation also stipulate that there will be a cap of $ 1 billion on the MF industry's overseas investments and an individual MF investments limit of Rs 200 crores.

  The fund is an innovative concept that will allow investors to diversify their investments in blue-chip global equities for the first time.

6. WELFARE

Principles of Welfare Economics and Social Control of Business in India

1. Introduction

Often a distinction is made between the economics of an individual and the economics of a group of people or of society. In the case of the former, economics is the economics of individual welfare, while in the latter it becomes the economics of social welfare. Welfare economics is thus Social-welfare economics.

2. Meaning and Objectives of Welfare Economics

Welfare is a subjective concept and can exist only in the mind of an individual. And Society is in some sense a collection of individuals, social welfare can be conceived of as the summation of individual welfare in some sense.

A.C. Pigou in his book "The Economics of Welfare" states ***"Welfare is a thing of very wide range. There is no need here to enter under a general discussions on its concept, it will be sufficient* to *lay down more or less dogmatically two propositions first that the elements of welfare are category of greater or less."***

Pigou distinguished between social welfare and economic welfare. He defined economic welfare is ***"that part of social welfare that can be brought directly or indirectly into relation with the measuring rod of money."***

Economic Welfare is defined as the satisfaction derived from the use of exchangeable goods and services and can be expressed as a function of goods and services and their relative prices.

Welfare Economics endeavors to formulate propositions by which we may rank on the scale of better and worse, alternative economic situation open to society.

The objective of welfare economics is the evolution of the social desirability of alternative economic states. An economic state is a particular arrangement of economic activities and of the resource of the economy.

Welfare economics is partly a positive and partly a normative science.

Positive approach concerns with what is, was or will be; while normative approach concerns with what ought to be. The statement a government deficit will reduce unemployment and cause an increase in prices is a hypothesis in positive economics, whereas, the statement in setting policy, unemployment ought to matter more than inflation, is normative hypothesis.

Thus, welfare economics is regarded positive in so far as it attempts to explain the outcome of the functioning of the economic system. It is normative in the sense that the very choice of one particular economic situation over others is a value judgement.

***(a)* Social welfare as utilitarianism :** A man's welfare is a subjective thing, as it exists in his mind. Now. a man's welfare at any given time is measured by the amount of satisfaction or utility that he enjoys at that lime. This strives to maximise the satisfaction or utility.

Social welfare can thus be defined simply as the sum of utilities or satisfaction of all the individuals in the society.

This approach to social welfare is known as utilitarianism.

For example, if there are four individuals in the society A. B, C and D, we may write W= Ua + Ub + Uc + Ud. This means, welfare of the society is the sum of the utilities of the four individuals, if the utilities of the individuals increase, the sum of their utilities and hence welfare also will increase.

***(b)* Paretian Welfare Economics :** In Paretian Theory, the question whether utility is measurable or not is of no consequence. If we are able to say merely that social welfare is greater or less in one situation than another, the question of how much greater or less may safely be disregarded. According to Pareto, any change that makes at least one person better off without any body else worse off is an improvement in social welfare.

Conversely, a change that makes no one better off and at least one worse-off is a decrease in social welfare.

It was the distinctive mark of, Pareto's Theorising about 'Optimality' that he assumed only ordinal utility.

Thus, a social welfare function is an ordinal index of the welfare of society and depends upon the utility levels of individuals of the society.

The concept of social welfare function plays an important role in welfare theory,

Pareto optimality is a necessary but not a sufficient condition for welfare maximisation.

Welfare will be maximised at the point where grand utility possibility frontier touches the social welfare function.

***(c)* Amartya Kumar Sen's Social Choice Theory :** Sen, a Nobel Prize recipient in Economics, in his classic work *"Collective Choice and Social Welfare"*, has rejected the Pareto interior mentioned earlier and has brought a generally acceptable ethical considerations in welfare economics.

Sen's greatest contribution in the field of Social Choice Theory is to emphasize decision making on the basis of distributive justice and equity.

In his above mentioned book. Sen argues that ***"The Society in which a person lives, the class to which he belongs, the relation that he has with the social and economic structure of the immunity, are relevant to a person's choice not merely because they affect the nature of his personal interest but also because they influence his value system including this notion of "due" concern for other members of society."*** The insular economic man pursuing his self interest to the inclusion of all other considerations may represent an assumption that pervades much traditional economics, but it is not a particularly useful model for understanding problems of social choice.

Sen's theory on social choice states that social choice should depend not merely on individual oderings, but on their intensities of preference.

This introduction of intensities of preference implies the introduction of cardinality and prepersonal comparison of utility.

As an example, it may be said that if person 1 wants *very* strongly that society should choose x rather than y, while person 2 wants very marginally that y be chosen and not x, then in this two person's world there is a good case for choosing x.

Such interpersonal comparisons of levels of welfare or of marginal gains and losses of welfare of individuals, open up many new possibilities in the field of social choice.

Sen in his above book has discussed a number of possibilities of social choice and it is not possible to discuss all these possibilities in this book.

However, we can get a fair idea of Sen's thinking on the subject of social choice and distributional judgements from his another book "On Economic Inequality".

Sen has imposed five conditions on relation between individual preference or orderings and social preference.

In brief, the first condition permits systematic social choice. The second allows individuals to have any preference pattern. The third establishes a relationship between individual and social references that can be viewed pair by pair. The fourth is similar to Pareto rule. The fifth condition requires that no special importance should be attached to who in particular holds such preference, all at matters being the combination of preferences that are held.

Finally, Sen concludes that all these conditions look reasonable enough but together they rule out distributional judgements.

3. Social Welfare Function

Social Welfare Function is an ordinal index of society's welfare and is a function of the utility levels of all individuals

It is expressed as

$$W = f(U_1, U_2, U_3 \ldots U_n)$$

where U_l is the utility index of the "1" individual.

Social Welfare function is a role by which a social scale of preference can be deduced from individual scales of preferences.

According to Bergson, the value of social welfare function depends on all the variables that night be considered as affecting welfare : the amounts of each and every kind of food consumed by and service performed by each-and every house hold the amount of each and every kind of capital investment undertaken and so on."

Social Control of Business in India and Nationalisation

Ever since Indian planners and government decided to adopt socialistic pattern of society as its aim, the question of nationalisation has continuously assumed importance. The Reserve Bank of India was nationalised in 1948 to meet needs of a government owned Central bank. In 1955, the Imperial Bank of India was nationalised and named as State Bank of India, with a view to help the co-operative movement with rural credit facilities. The life Insurance Companies were nationalised in 1956 on the plea that the private companies were making huge profits at the expense of policy-holders and that these profits can be utilised for building up the national economy.

In 1969, there was a strong controversy over the Social Control of banks and nationalisation of banks. Those who favoured social control of banks suggested that reconstituting the management detailed and strict statutory provisions and close watch over the working of the Commercial banks can serve the desired purpose.

While, those who believed in nationalisation said that "it would be difficult to undertake credit planning (for financing priority sectors) unless the linked control of the industry and banks in the same hands is snapped by nationalisation." (R.K. Hazari).

The nationalisation protagonists pointed to the way the private commercial banks have been functioning which has resulted in ownership and control in a few hands, bank resources largely utilised by the directors at extremely favourable terms and conditions, concentration of wealth and power, indifferent to the needs of rural sector, discrimination against small business units, misuse of funds like hoarding of essential commodities and failure to mobilise savings of the Community. Consequently, 14 major banks deposits of Rs. 50 Crore or more were nationalised in July, 1969.

If one looks at the working of nationlised banks, one finds that there are several advantages which have come in the way of banking industry in India as a result of nationalisation. Since the policies and working of these banks have been more cohesive, harmonious and socially relevant, more favorable conditions have, thus, been created for the proper formulation and implementation of monetary and credit policies in the economy. The nationalised banks have gained tremendously by the Lead Bank Scheme, which avoided unnecessary competition among banks as well as encouraged the banks to expand into new areas.

By following a systematic branch expansion policy the nationalised banks have been able to penetrate not only the rural sector, which was hither neglected but have also helped in progressive reduction in regional imbalances.

By 1992, *i.e.*, 23 years since nationalisation there was an increase of the order 740 per cent in the number of branch offices compared to those in 1969. The total number of branches of the banks in 1992 were 60,649 (compared to 8,262 in 1969), out of which about 58% branches were in rural areas.

The bank advances to agriculture and Small Scale industry increased from Rs. 3,017 crore in 1969 to 1,41.622 crore on December 21, 1992.

Regional imbalance in the banking sector existed in India. Gadgil Committee pointed out that the banking facilities were concentrated in the economically advanced areas of the country.

Since nationlisation of the banks, efforts have been made to rectify this imbalance with partial success. This imbalance can be wiped out only when economic imbalance is corrected.

Govt. of India furthered its policy of nationalisation by taking over the Coal industry, Indian Iron and Steel Company (IISCO) and the foreign companies engaged in the distribution of petroleum.

PROBABLE QUESTIONS

1. Describe the characteristics of an underdeveloped economy.
2. Describe the characteristics of a developed economy.
3. Write the salient features of Development planning in India.
4. What are the objective of Reforms.
5. Write notes on

   (*a*) Bulls (*b*) Bears (*c*) Equity shares

   (*d*) Preference shares (*e*) Debentures (*f*) GDR

   (*g*) External commercial browings (*h*) Treasury Bills (*i*) Commercial Paper
6. What are the constituents of capital market in India?
7. What are various money market constituents? Write their features.
8. What is Mutual Fund? Write about the characteristics of open and close needed Mutual Fund schemes in India.
9. Define welfare. What is the nature of welfare?

QUESTION BANK

ECONOMICS - II

Multiple choice Questions

Group - A

Choose the correct answer from the given alternatives of the following :

1. Under Expenditure method of measuring the N.I., we have

   (*a*) Y= P.O (*b*) Y = W + R + I + P

   (*c*) Y = C + I + G + (X – M) (*d*) Y = W + R + I + P

   where the symbols have usual meanings.

2. "Inflation implies a

   (*a*) High price situation (*b*) Rising price situation

   (*c*) Stable price situation (*d*) Flexible price situation

3. A Keynesian consumption function implies

   (*a*) change in income > Change in consumption

   (*b*) Change in Income = Change in consumption

   (*c*) Change in Income < Change in consumption

   (*d*) Change in savings > Change in consumption

4. In Fisher's Quantity theory of Money, where MV = PT, 'V' implies,

   (*a*) Velocity of circulation of money

   (*b*) Vertical distance

   (*c*) Vertical movement

   (*d*) Vicious circle of poverty

5. 'Net National product can be expressed as

   (*a*) GNP Depreciation (*b*) GNP + Depreciation

   (*c*) MNI – RNI (*d*) GNP + Deprecation

6. Disposable income means

   (*a*) Income before tax payment (*b*) Income after tax payment

   (*c*) Income after consumption (*d*) Income before saving

7. Deficit financing is done, when

   (a) Revenue > Expenditure

   (b) Expenditure > Revenue

   (c) Revenue = Expenditure

   (d) Revenue and expenditure can not be compared.

8. Reserve Bank of India is the

   (a) Commercial bank of India (b) Central Bank of India

   (c) Development Bank of India (d) Industrial Bank of India

9. Demand pull inflation occurs when

   (a) Aggregate demand< Aggregate supply

   (b) Aggregate demand = Aggregate supply

   (c) Aggregate demand> Aggregate supply

   (d) None of these

10. VAT refers to

    (a) Velocity added tax (b) value added tax

    (c) Venture and Taxation (d) Very attractive transportation

11. Macro-economics deals with aspects of

    (a) aggregate (b) Partial

    (c) Individual (d) None of these

12. Net National Product (NNP) is defined as

    (a) GDP Depreciation (b) GNP Depreciation

    (c) GNP Import (d) none of these

13. Stamp duty is a source of revenue for

    (a) Central government (b) State government

    (c) Both central and state government (d) None of these

14. M_3 is defined as

    (a) Currency + Demand deposit

    (b) Time deposit + demand deposit+ Savings Bank Deposit + Currency.

    (c) Demand deposit + currency + time deposit

    (d) None of these

15. IBRD refers to

    (a) Indian Bank for reconstruction and development

    (b) International bank for regulation & development.

    (c) International Bank for reconstruction and development.

    (d) None of these

16. If central bank increases the bank rate then
 (*a*) Inflation can be controlled (*b*) Inflation cannot be controlled
 (*c*) inflation will remain unchanged (*d*) none of these
17. Which country is the largest partner of India's foreign trade?
 (*a*) USA (*b*) China (*c*) UK (*d*) Japan
18. Cost Push inflation occurs when
 (*a*) Aggregate demand curve shifts to right
 (*b*) Aggregate demand curve shifts to left.
 (*c*) Aggregate supply curve shifts to right.
 (*d*) Aggregate supply curve shifts to left.
19. Fiscal Deficit is equal to
 (*a*) total expenditure minus total revenue and capital receipts
 (*b*) Total expenditure minus total revenue receipts
 (*c*) Total expenditure minus revenue receipts and non dept. capital receipts
 (*d*) External borrowing of govt. of India.
20. In case of Fisher's Quantity Theory of money which is correct assumption?
 (*a*) Fall in interest rate?
 (*b*) Constant velocity of circulation of money
 (*c*) Constant price level
 (*d*) Rising aggregate demand
21. ADB has head-quarters in
 (*a*) Korea (*b*) Sri Lanka (*c*) Philippines (*d*) Thailand
22. The word Bank was established in
 (*a*) 1945 (*b*) 1950 (*c*) 1944 (*d*) 1980
23. The head-quarters of world bank is in
 (*a*) Paris (*b*) London (*c*) Washington DC (*d*) New York
24. Speculative demand for money was revealed by
 (*a*) Ricardo (*b*) Samullson (*c*) Keynes (*d*) Smith
25. During inflation
 (*a*) Demand< Supply (*b*) Demand = Supply
 (*c*) Demand> supply (*d*) none of these
26. National Income is computed generally for
 (*a*) 5 years (*b*) 2 years (*c*) 1 Year (*d*) 10 years
27. Comparative advantage is shown first by
 (*a*) Adam Smith (*b*) Keynes (*c*) Ricardo (*d*) Malthes
28. Five-year plan was started in India in
 (*a*) 1950 (*b*) 1947 (*c*) 1951 (*d*) 1948

29. 'Absolute advantage theory of international trade was given by
    (*a*) Adam smith (*b*) Keynes (*c*) Ricardo (*d*) Mathus
30. Internal Debt means
    (*a*) Public loans floated within the country
    (*b*) Obligation of a country to foreign national or government or international institution
    (*c*) both (*a*) and (*b*)
    (*d*) None of these
31. IMF has which of the following main function?
    (*a*) Exchange rate stability
    (*b*) Exchange rate stability with rigidity
    (*c*) Exchange rate stability without rigidity.
    (*d*) Exchange rate stability with flexibility.
32. Sources of revenue for the Union government of India consists of
    (*a*) Tax revenue (*b*) No-tax revenue
    (*c*) Profits of RBUI (*d*) Both (*a*) and (*b*)
33. Revenue deficit is equal to
    (*a*) total expenditure minus total receipts
    (*b*) Total revenue expenditure minus total revenue receipts
    (*c*) Total receipts minus total expenditure
    (*d*) External borrowing of the government.
34. Under "GNP' at factor cost of measuring national income, we have
    (*a*) Y = PO (*b*) Y = C + I + G
    (*c*) Y = W + R + I + P (*d*) Y + C + I + G + (X – M)
35. Indexation is a method of controlling
    (*a*) BOP disequilibrium of a country
    (*b*) Correcting inflation of a country
    (*c*) Correcting fiscal deficits of a country
    (*d*) None of these
36. Fiscal policy means
    (*a*) Change in money supply of the economy
    (*b*) Change in government income and expenditure
    (*c*) Change in expenditure of the government
    (*d*) All of these.

Group - B

Short Answer Type Questions

1. Write down the main objectives and function of IMF.

2. Mention the major sources of revenue of the central government.
3. Define money. What are the functions of money?
4. Explain the functions of WTO.
5. Differentiate between demand pull and cost push inflation.
6. Distinguish between GATT and WTO
7. Define deficit financing.
8. Give an idea of Indian capital Market.
9. State the important functions of RBI.
10. Explain four factors that determine the size of national income.
11. Mention any two functions of WTO. How far the membership of India in WTO would be beneficial for the country?
12. What do you mean by bank rate and open market operation?
13. Distinguish between GNP and GDP.
14. Define M_1, M_2, M_3 and M_4.
15. Mention the characteristics of an underdeveloped country.
16. Write a note on IMF.

Group - C

Long Answer Type Questions

1. To what extent WTO is different from GATT. State the basic functions of WTO.
2. Define money. Highlight the recent condition of Indian money market. Provide some guide lines to improve the condition of the money market.
3. Explain Fisher's Quantity theory of Money. Highlight the limitations of this theory.
4. Define Balance of payment (BOP). List and explain the item that one included in BOP account.
5. Outline the major causes of inflation. Highlight the measures that should be adopted to control inflation in India.
6. Explain briefly the function of commercial Bank. Mention the credit creation process of commercial Bank.
7. *(a)* Given (in Rs.)

Income from wages = 2500	Net inflows = 750
Income from rent = 1800	Direct tax = 800
Total interest received = 2200	Indirect tax= 1300
Corporate profits = 3000	Subsidy = 500
Undistributed profits = 1200	Transfer earning = 450
Corporate tax = 800	Social contribution = 700

Find

(i) Find National Income   *(ii)* Personal Income

(iii) Disposable income   *(iv)* GNP at market price

(*b*) Mention the different methods of meaning N. Income.

8. What is WTO? What are its functions? Mention the benefits of it to India.

9. Explain the comparative cost advantage theory of International trade. How a country will gain from such trade. Give Criticisms.

10. (*a*) Define the concept of inflation.

    (*b*) Distinguish between demand pull and cost push inflation.

11. What is public debt? Describe the money burden and real burden of public debt.

12. (*a*) Define National Income

    (*b*) How can you measure it?

    (*c*) State the difficulties in measuring National income.

13. (*a*) How does planning in pre-liberalisation period differs from that in post-liberalisation period?

    (*b*) Critically evaluate the success of the Indian five years plans in attaining the basic objectives of the plans.

14. (*a*) State the functions of WTO.

    (*b*) Highlight the areas of relevance of WTO agreements in the context of Indian economy?

15. Given GNP_{mc} = 5000 (in Rs.)

    Personal income tax = 1000

    Corporate tax = 800

    Subsidies = 400

    Factor income paid abroad = 800

    Factor income received from abroad= 900

    Undistributed profit = 200

    Indirect tax= 450

    Depreciation = 350

    Compute

    (*i*) GDP_{fc} (*ii*) National income

    (*iii*) Disposable personal income

16. Write notes on any two of the following.

    (*a*) centre state financial relation. (*b*) Inflation

    (*c*) Tariff & quota (*d*) Devaluation

17. What is the need for a central bank of a country? State and explain the function that are performed by Reserve Bank of India.

18. What do you mean by quantity Theory of Money? Explain the Fisher's quantity Theory of Money. Give criticism also.

19. (*a*) State the difficulties in measuring National Income.

(*b*)

	Rs.
GNP	10,436.7
Indirect taxes	703.1
Depreciation	1,393.1
Contribution to social security	746.5
Corporate profit tax payments	353.8
Personal interest income	394.4
Transfer payment to persons	1,288.0
Personal taxes	1,111.9

Calculate National Income, personal Income and personal disposable income.

20. Write notes on any two

(*a*) Public debt

(*b*) Deficit financing

(*c*) GNP & GDP

(*d*) Indian capital Market.

ECONOMICS - III
BUSINESS ECONOMICS

THOMAS ROBERT MALTHUS, 1766-1834

Born : Surrey. England 1766.

Education : Cambridge University, 1784-1788.

Jobs : Parson, Church of England, 1788-1804, Fellow, Cambridge University, 1793-1804, Professor of history and political economy, East India Company College, in Haileybury, England, 1805-1834.

Major Publications : *An Essay on the Principle of Population as It Affects the Future Improve-ments of Society*, 1798; *Principles of Political Economy*, 1820.

Thomas Robert Malthus, called Bob by his dad and Pop by his students, published his *Essay on the Principles of Population* anonymously when he was 32 years old. Very short—only 137 pages—and wonderfully written, this book had an enormous impact on economists, public officials, and even biologists. Its pessimistic idea—that workers would be forever limited to a bare subsistence with intermittent periods of starvation—immediately attracted wide attention and made Malthus famous for all time.

Malthus did not argue that the supply of farmland was completely fixed. He did insist, however, that even if the supply of farmland could be increased through forest clearing, its growth would be far less rapid than population growth. Malthus argued that population growth is geometric, but that the growth of farm production is arithmetic. Thus he wrote :

> *...population, when unchecked, goes on doubling every twenty-five years, or increases in a geometrical ratio.*
>
> *...the means of subsistence increases in an arithmetical ratio. Let us now bring the effects of these two ratios together.*

Taking the population of the world at any number, a thousand millions, for instance, the human species would increase in the ratio of 1, 2, 4, 8, 16, 32, 64, 128, 256, 512, etc. and subsistence as 1, 2, 3, 4, 5, 6, 7, 8, 9, 10, etc. In two centuries and a quarter, the population would be to the means of subsistence as 512 to 10 : in three centuries as 4096 to 13; and in two thousand years the difference would be incalculable....

Malthus did not shy away from giving policy advice based on his theory. For example, he criticized Prime Minister William Pitt's "Poor Bill," which would have paid a small sum each week to workers with children.

I confess, that before the bill was brought into Parliament, and for some time after, I thought that such a regulation would be highly beneficial :... but further reflection on the subject has convinced me, that if... it tend[s] to increase population, without increasing the produce.... a day's labour will purchase a smaller quantity of provisions, and the poor therefore in general must be more distressed.

Pitt was greatly influenced by Malthus's argument : After he heard the argument, he withdrew his support for the bill, arguing that helping the poor in this way would be futile and would only increase the population and lead to more suffering. For many years, the Malthusian prediction was cited as a reason not to give welfare to the poor.

Although Malthus used only elementary biology, his research helped stimulate one of the great discoveries in biology : Darwin's theory of evolution. Darwin wrote in his autobiography that he got the idea of natural selection while reading Malthus.

After Maltus wrote his famous *Essay,* he went on to a career as an economist with broad interests. He was the very first professor of economics (then called political economy) anywhere in the world. He was one of the classical economists, a friend and intellectual opponent of David Ricardo, We can use modern terminology to summarize their main difference : Malthus criticized Ricardo for ignoring short-run economic fluctuations and always focusing on the economy's long-run potential growth path Ricardo criticized Malthus for ignoring the long run growth path and always focusing on the short-run economic fluctuations. One can view the modern theory of economic growth and fluctuations described in this text as combining these two traditions.

Source of quotes : Thomas Robert Malthus, *An Essay on the Principle Population as It Affects the future Improvements of Society,* 1798, pp. 12-13, 50, in *The Works of Thomas Robert Malthus,* Vol. I, ed. E.A. Wrigley and D. Souden (London : William Pickering, 1986).

KARL MARX, 1818-1883

Born : Trier, Germany, 1818.

Education : University of Bonn, 1835, University of Berlin, 1836-1841, University of Jena, doctorate in philosophy, 1841.

Jobs : Editor, freelance journalist, Cologne, Paris, Brussels, 1842-1848, Independent study, freelance journalist, London 1849-1883.

Major Publications : *Communist Manifesto* (with Friedrich Engels), 1848; *Das Kapital*, 1867 (Vol. I); Russian translation, 1868; English translation, 1886.

What led to the rejection of markets and the acceptance of socialism in Russia, China, and Eastern Europe in the twentieth century? Although personal ambition, war, and political repression were factors, the economic writings of Karl Marx in the nineteenth century played a key role.

Karl Marx was an economist and social philosopher, but he was also an eloquent journalist and polemicist. Most of his work as an economist was spent analyzing capitalism. His most famous prediction was that capitalism would eventually die of its own internal contradictions.

Marx originally went to college to study law, but he soon was drawn to the writings of the philosopher Hegel, who characterized history as a struggle between conflicting forces; each idea (thesis) generated its opposite (antithesis), which it then had to contend with until a new thesis (synthesis) was created. This Hegelian view provided Marx with a framework to study the historical development of capitalism.

Marx soon became an outspoken critic of the existing economic and political system in Europe. He spent much of his adult life in London, studying and writing in the archives of the British Museum. Marx eked out a modest living—his wife and children struggling at the brink of poverty—through his journalistic writings and through financial assistance from his long-time friend and collaborator, Friedrich Engels.

Marx's polemical writings were influential. The widely read and often-quoted *Communist Manifesto* was a short pamphlet written in 1848 by Marx and Engels. It was nothing less than a stirring call for a revolution :

A specter is haunting Europe—the specter of communism.... Let the ruling classes tremble at a Communist revolution. The proletarians have nothing to lose but their chains. They have a world to win. Working men of all countries, unite!

Surprisingly, perhaps, Marx and Engels found much to admire in capitalism. They wrote that the *bourgeoisie*— the class that owned or ran the business firms

...has accomplished wonders far surpassing the Egyptian pyramids, Roman aqueducts, and Gothic cathedrals.... [D]uring its rule of scarcely one hundred years, [it] has created more massive and more colossal productive forces than have all preceding generations together.

It is in Marx's economic writings—longer and more ponderous—that his detailed criticism of capitalism is found. In particular, his treatise *Das Kapital* aimed to show why Adam Smith and David Ricardo were wrong in their praise of the market economy. For example, referring to Smith's idea that workers would benefit from increased labor productivity due to the division of labor or to more machinery, Marx wrote in *Das Kapital;*

Adam Smith, by a fundamentally perverted analysis, arrives at [this] absurd conclusion.... In truth, Adam Smith breaks his investigation off, just where its difficulties begin.

Marx argued instead that increases in labor productivity would not benefit workers; capitalists, trying to maintain their profits, would keep workers' wages from rising. But history shows that wages increased by huge amounts in the 150 years since Marx wrote.

Although socialism may have originally seemed like an attractive alternative to the market system, socialism's own severe problems eventually became obvious. Surprisingly, however, Marx wrote almost nothing about how a socialist economy would work. His writings focused entirely on capitalism.

Sources of quotes : Karl Marx and Friedrich Engels, *Communist Manifesto*, 1848, *in Essential Works of Marxism*, ed. A. P. Mendel (New York : Bantam Books, 1961), pp. 1, 44, and 16-17; Karl Marx, *Capital : A Critique of Political Economy* (New York : Modern Library, 1906), p. 647.

CHAPTER 1

INTRODUCTION, CONCEPTS, ECONOMICS—BUSINESS, MANAGEMENT, BUSINESS ECONOMICS

1. Introduction
2. Nature and Characteristics of Business Economics
3. Scope of Business Economics
4. Significance of Business Economics
5. Objectives and Application of Business Economics
6. Micro and Macro Economics
7. Various Issues in Business Economics
8. Economic Models in Business Economics
9. Decision-Making Environment for Business
10. Environment Analysis
11. Industry Analysis

1. CONCEPTS — BUSINESS ECONOMICS

Meaning, Nature, Characteristics, Scope and Significance of Managerial Economics, Objectives and Application, Micro & Macro, Bus. Decisions, Economic Analysis.

1. Meaning of Managerial Economics.

General Economic theory formulates economic theories and principles and derives certain conclusions on the basis of certain assumptions. For instances economic theory of a business firm is based on the assumption of profit maximisation and it seeks to explain how much a firm will produce and at what price it will sell.

But the assumption of profit maximisation makes economic theory of the firm unrealistic as the firm may not be knowing the point of maximum profit or the firm may not be interested in getting maximum profit or may like to expand the business and achieve larger market share. Accordingly economic theory of a firm may fail to provide a satisfactory explanation of what the firm actually does.

Business Economics on the other hand will have to reconcile the theoretical economic theories with actual business practices and reformulate economic theories and practices if necessary. In this sense, managerial economics is pragmatic, while general economic theory is theoretical.

Business Economics serves as a link between economic theory and managerial practice.

Therefore, Business Economics is economics applied in decision-making.

Business Economics is also called Managerial Economics.

A business firm is all the time confronted with problem of allocation of scare resources. Management Economics involves analysis of allocation of resources available to a firm and it is concerned with selection among alternatives.

Managerial economics is concerned with decision making of economic nature. This implies that Managerial economics deals with identification of economic choices and allocation of scarce resources.

1.2 Nature and Characteristics of Business Economics

1.2.1 Nature of Business Economics :

A Business firm will survive and grow if its management is well informed and takes necessary and timely steps with regard to the following.

(a) rapid changes in technological and economic condition.

(b) Fluctuations in demand, supply and prices of relevant goods or services.

(c) Government rules and regulations relevant the specific business.

Business Economics is helpful in deciding the appropriate action in the above cases.

Nature of Business economics as follows :

(i) It gives guidance to management about objectives of a business firm and how they should be set.

(ii) It is micro-economics in character where the unit of study is a business organisation.

(iii) It concentrates on making economic theory more application oriented.

Business economics takes the help of Macro-economics also so as to understand the external conditions which are relevant to the business. Since these conditions are beyond the firm's control it has to adjust itself to the changes in there conditions to survive and grow.

Such external conditions are environmental forces which include domestic and international business condition government policies, political and social situations.

1.2.2 Characteristics of Business Economics

Economics is a branch of science concerned with the problem of allocation of scarce resources and it provides a number of sophisticated concepts and analytical tools to understand and analyse such problems.

Understanding the main features of Managerial economics helps in appreciating the subject in its true perspective.

These characteristic features are as follows :

(i) Business economics is micro-economic in character as it concentrates only on the study of the firm and not on the working of the economy.

(ii) Business economics takes the help of macro-economics to understand and adjust to the environment in which the firm operates.

(iii) Business economics is prescriptive rather than descriptive. It is concerned with the type of decisions that the firm should take in order to prosper, which involves value judgements and not a mere description of behaviour of the firm.

(iv) It is both conceptual and material. It takes the help of conceptual framework to understand and analyse the decision problems and takes the help of quantitative techniques to measure the impact of different factors and policies.

(v) The contents of Managerial economics are based mainly on the "Theory of firm". It is only for the analysis of profits that help is taken of the "theory of distribution".

(vi) Knowledge of Managerial economics helps in making wise choices. Managers continue to face the problem of scarcities and consequently must continue to make choices.

(vii) Business economics being the study of allocation of the resources available for a firm among the activities of the unit, is helpful as it is goal oriented and aims at maximum achievement of objectives.

3. DEFINITION, SCOPE AND SIGNIFICANCE OF BUSINESS ECONOMICS

3.1 Definition

Business Economics is that part of Economics that can be conveniently used to analyse business problems to arrive at rational business decisions.

Business economics is the study of economic theories, logic and tools of economic analysis that are used in the process of business decision-making.

Business economics is concerned with the application of economic principles and methodologies to the decision making processes within the firm. It aims to establish rules and principles to facilitate the attainment of the desired economic goals of management.

According to Spencer and Seigelman, "Managerial economics is the integration of economic theory with business practices for the purpose of facilitating decision making and forward planning by management." Davis and Chang defines managerial economics as "It applies the principles and methods of economics to analyse problems faced by management of a business or other types of organisation and to help find solution that advance the best interests of such organisations."

1.3.2 Scope of Business Economics

The contribution of economics to business decision-making has come to be widely recognised and economics theories and analytical tools which are widely used in business decision-making have crystallised into a separate branch of management studies, known as Managerial economics or Business economics.

Managerial Economics has a close connection with economic theory, operations research, statistics mathematics and the theory of decision making.

Business economics also draws together and relates ideas from various functional areas of Management like production, marketing, finance and accounting, project management, appraisal of investment decision, etc.

A manager has to integrate concepts and methods from all these disciplines and functional areas in order to understand and analyse practical managerial problems.

The following aspects constitute the scope of Business economics.

(i) Objectives of a business firm.

(ii) Demand Analysis and Demand Forecasting.

(iii) Production and cost

(iv) Competition

(v) Output and pricing

(vi) Profit

(vii) Capital budgeting and investment appraisals

(viii) Product policy

(ix) Sales Promotion and Advertising

(x) Marketing strategy and marketing Mix.

1.3.3 Significance of Business Economics

The growing complexity of business decision making has inevitably increased the application of economic concepts, theories and tools of economic concepts, theories and tools of economic analysis and proper decision-making requires a clear understanding of market situations, fundamentals including the business environment.

Managerial economics helps the decisions-making process in the following ways :

(i) It provides a number of tools and techniques and with these a manager can capture the essential relationships that represent the real situation.

(ii) It provides most of the concepts that are needed for the analysis of business problems. Over the years these concepts have proved their value in solving various kinds of managerial problem.

(iii) Concepts of elasticity of demand, fixed and variable costs, opportunity-cost and net present value etc., all help in understanding and solving decision-making problem.

(iv) Managerial economics is helpful in making decision such as the following types.

What should be the optimum Product-mix?

What is the best production techniques?

What is the optimum input-mix?

What is the optimum level of output?

What is the product price?

How much should the firm advertise?

How to make investment decision?

Whether to make or buy an item?

What is the economic order quantity for purchasing an item?

When to delete a product from the product line?

When to add a product in the product line? etc. etc.

(v) In order to take a favourable decision, a manager should be able to analyse problems logically and clearly and in this case managerial economics is helpful.

4. OBJECTIVES AND APPLICATION OF BUSINESS ECONOMICS

1. Objectives and Application of Business Economics

Decision-making involves selection of one option from multiple alternatives. The problem of decision making arises because resources of a business firm in terms of capital, land, labour and management are limited and the management of the firm in order to maximise profit, have to decide the types of raw materials and their sources the types of products that should be produced and sold, pricing policy to be adopted for the products, channels of distribution and the extent of advertising etc.

All the above decisions automatically involve forward planning.

The present day business involves considerable uncertainty and risk. The uncertainty relates to consumers' choice of goods and services, market fluctuations, competitive conditions, forces of demand and supply, Government policies regarding price control, imports and exports, duties and taxation etc.

It is impossible for any business manager to have perfect knowledge about future and to be certain about any and all the conditions affecting the business.

Therefore, a business manager of today has to make decision and undertake forward planning under considerable uncertainty, and any wrong decision may spell disaster for the business.

In this case, managerial economics help the manager in reducing the extent of uncertainties and take proper decision favourable for the firm.

Managerial economics deal with a number of concepts such as demand, supply, production, pricing, competition and business cycles etc.

Managerial economics makes decision process easy and also helps in undertaking forward planning.

Managerial economics is economics applied in business decision making. Managerial economics integrates economic theories with actual business practices.

Economics theories help a decision maker to know what information is necessary to make an intelligent decision, to find the correct solution for a problem and to learn how to process and use the information.

After obtaining the desired information, the manger must analyse. This information and use it in connection with the theoretical and statistical tools available to make the best possible decision under the circumstances.

Business is influence not only by what decision are taken within the firm but also by the general business environment.

While the internal factors are within its control, the external factors like the general economic condition, rate of growth of national income, per capita income region use etc. are outside its sphere of control.

Managerial economics helps understand these external factors and suggest policies which the firm should follow for making the best use of these internal and external factors.

5. MIRCO AND MACRO ECONOMICS

5.1 Nature and Differences — Micro and Macro Economics

Economics

Micro Economics | Macro Economics

Micro economics is concerned with the economics of a business firm where as Macro economics is relevant for economy of a state or a country.

In **micro-economic analysis** the problem of choice is analysed focussing on single individual entities like a consumer, a producer, a seller, a commodity etc.

In **macro-economic analysis** the problem is approached from the angle of totality like national income, national consumption and general inflation rate etc.

Business economics is micro-economic in character and it helps in studying what is going on within the firm, how best to use the available scarce resources between various activities of the firm and how to be technically as well as economically efficient.

Business economics takes the help of macro-economics so as to understand the external conditions which are relevant to the business. Since these conditions are beyond the firm's control, it has to adjust itself to the changes in these conditions to survive and grow.

Micro-economics issues for a business firm are the following :

Type of product, size of the plant, technology for production, product-pricing, product distribution, sales promotion, competition, capacity expansion, diversification.

The micro-economic theories which are concerned for above items are following theory of demand, theory of production, theory of pricing, theory of profit, and theory of capital and investment Decision.

Macro-economic issues for the general business environment in which a business operates are the following :

Economic system of country (*i.e.* capitalist, socialist or mixed), Capita income, Population size, Magnitude of foreign trade, Capital market, Industrial, Monetary and Fiscal Policies, Labour Laws, Political environment etc.

The following categories of Macro economic factors are important for a business decision making :

(i) **Issues related to macro variables :** Economic activities of the country, industrial production and un-employment, investment climate. These factors influence the functioning of a business firm.

(ii) **Issues related to foreign trade :** Imports and exports, foreign exchange rate including reserves, status of international market. These factors influence the functioning of a business firm particularly in the face of globalisation of economy.

(iii) **Issues related to govt. policies :** Fiscal, Monetary, Industrial and Industrial Relations policies of Government are bound to have influence on the functioning of a business firm.

Government policies regarding healthcare, eduction and housing of citizens, if favourable and beneficial attempt to raise standard of living of average citizen and this is likely to benefit the functioning of a business organisation.

(iv) **Other issues related to govt. policies and awareness of business firms :** These issues are infrastructure building such as roads, communication, railways, irrigation, water supply, power stations for supply of electricity, distribution of electivity and water, availability of transport system—and making these facilities easily available for citizens are dependent of Govt. policies.

Also, control of air and water pollution as per Govt. rules and regulation is the primary responsibility of a business firm.

Also, the business organisations should be aware of social responsibilities for their survival and growth and also for fulfilling their primary responsibilities towards the society at large.

2.3 Economic Models and Business Economic

Models create a set of relationship which approximate the real world situation, while at the same time maintaining simplicity as well as mathematical computability so that satisfactory results are obtained when the model is used in decision-making.

The following models are important from the points of view of managerial economics.

(i) **Quantitative models :** In order to investigate the existence of relationship between different variables, statistical data and methods are used. For example, regression analysis helps in statistical inference and prediction.

(ii) **Allocation models :** These models are used to find an optimising solution for given objectives, like profit maximisation, cost minimisation etc.

The allocation problems exist particularly in case of decision relating to production and transportation.

(iii) **Inventory models :** These models help in optimising inventory levels in production system. The main objectives of such models are to find how to minimise the total cost of holding inventories.

(iv) **Queuing models :** These are waiting line models used where arrival of customers or materials is irregular, so that it is difficult to plan exactly the right number of service facilities necessary.

When the business firm is faced with quening problem it will balance the benefit of reducing the waiting time for it or for the customers against the cost of providing extra facilities.

(v) **Simulation models :** Simulation process is used to describe management games. Its purpose into manipulate the operations models in order to provide information about the environment to assist in making decision.

Monte Carle technique is associated with simulation as this permits generations of events or out comes.

(vi) **Network or scheduling models :** PERT/CPM techniques and networks are used for scheduling.

These are used for determining an optimum sequence of performing certain operations with a view to minimising overall time and/or cost.

(vii) **Pay-off matrix models or decision models :** These models provide a meaningful conceptual framework for improved decision making.

In practical case, decision models are of limited usefulness.

These are 4 kinds of pay off matrix models :

—Pay-off matrix under condition of risk

—Pay-off matrix under uncertainly

—Pay-off matrix under certainty

—Pay-off matrix under conflict

2.3.1 Business Economics and Other Disciplines of Study

The study of managerial economics borrows topics from other disciplines such as Mathematics, Statistics, Operations Research and Management theory and Accountancy.

(a) **Mathematics :** A business organisation is concerned with the concepts of tangible factors quantitative analysis such as sales value, demand price, cost and profit etc.

The use of mathematics in the economics analysis provides not only clarity of concepts, but also a logical and systematic framework within which quantitative relationships may be explored.

A business firm is very often interest in maximising sales and profit and minimising cost of operations. Answers for these problems are found out using mathematical tools.

(b) **Statistics :** Statistical techniques are used in collecting, processing and analysing business data, which are required to be finally utilised for economic anaylsis.

Statistical methods such as probability, forecasting techniques and regression analysis etc. are used in business decisions and for finding out economic variables.

(c) **Operations Research (OR) :** OR tools such as linear programming is used for product mix decision, cost-minimisation decision and profit maximisation decision etc.

Goal programming tool of OR is also used in business decision making.

(d) **Management Theory and Accountancy :** Management theory and accounting are the other disciplines which are closely associated with managerial economics.

Management theories bring out the behaviour of the behaviour of the firm in their efforts to achieve certain predetermined objectives.

Accounting is the main source of date regarding the functioning and performance of the firm.

The scope of managerial economics, thus, includes the concepts and topics from all above disciplines of study.

3. DECISION-MAKING AND BUSINESS ECONOMICS, ECONOMY ANALYSIS

3.1 Decision-Making

Business decision-making is essentially a process of selecting the best out of alternative choices.

Decision-making process consists of following main phases :

(i) Defining the objective.

(ii) Collecting and analysing information about all tangible and in tangible factor such as costs, volumes, sales, price, profitability, industrial relations, law-and-order, social and political environment etc.

(iii) Consider and analyse R & D and experimental results.

(iv) Carry out cost benefit analysis for all alternative choices.

(v) Apply personal business sense, intuition and experience factors to analyse positive negative and risk factors for all alternative choices.

After using all the above points, a business manager carries out quantitative analysis and OR techniques for production, marketing and business environment related items and in the this aspect managerial economics is helpful.

Economic theories state the functional relationship between two or more economic variables.

Economics theories facilitate input output analysis, market and business environment analysis and this they help in decision making.

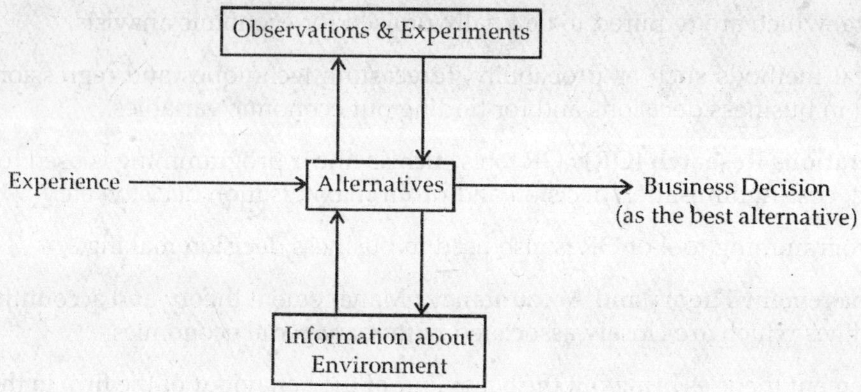

3.2 Business Economics and Business Decision-Making

For a business manager, decision-making involves selection of one option from multiple alternatives. The problem of decision-making arises because resource available to an organisation in terms of capital, land, labor and management are limited and the manager in order to maximise profit, has to decide. The type of raw materials and their sources of supply, the types of products should be produced and sold, the methods of producing the products, pricing of products to be adopted and the mode and extent of advertising and so on.

All the above decisions automatically involve forward planning.

Modern business involves considerable uncertainty and risk. The uncertainty relates to consumers choice of goods and services, market fluctuation, competitive conditions, internal forces of demand and supply, Govt. policies regarding price control, imports and exports, duties and taxation etc.

It is impossible for any business manager to have perfect knowledge about future and to be certain about any and all the condition affecting the business.

Therefore, a manager of today has to make decisions and undertake forward planning under considerable uncertainty, and any wrong decisions may spell disaster for the business.

In this case, Business economics helps the manager to reduce the extend of uncertainties and take proper decision favourable for the firm.

Business economics theories deal with a number of concepts such as demand, supply, production, pricing, competition, business cycles and undertaking new investment etc.

These economics theories make decision process easy and also help to undertake forward planning.

3.3 Economic Analysis

The basic problem with which the management is concerned is economising the scarce resources for achieving maximum objectives.

Economic analysis may be various types and forms :

***(i)* Micro vs. Macro Analysis :** In micro economic analysis the problem of choice is analysed focussing on single individual entities like a consumer, a producer, a seller, a commodity etc.

In macro-economic analysis the problem is approached from the angle of totality like national income, national consumption and general price level etc.

***(ii)* Partial vs General Equilibrium Analysis :** A market is said to be in the position of equilibrium when the values of market variables (price and quantity) show no tendency to change throughout the period of study.

To attain the state of stable equilibrium, the economic problem may be analysed part by part, assuming other things remaining the same. This is partial equilibrium analysis.

By contrast, under general equilibrium analysis the assumption of "other things remaining equal" may be relaxed and inter dependence among variables may be allowed.

***(iii)* Static, Comparative Static vs. Dynamic Analysis :** This has reference to the time dimensions of the analysis of the problem.

A problem may have analysis of following :

(a) At a point of time, allowing no change (static).

(b) At a point of time, allowing once for all change (comparative static).

(c) Over a period of time, allowing successive changes (dynamic).

***(iv)* Positive Vs Normative Analysis :** In positive economic analysis, the problem is analysis in objective terms based on principles and theories.

In normative economic analysis the problem is analysed based on value judgements, and, therefore, the policy prescriptions are explicitly stated.

Business Economics is primarily micro, partial equilibrium type, comparative static and positive in approach, made to elements of macro-economics, general equilibrium, dynamic and normative policy issues.

Positive approach concerns with what is was or will be, while normative approach concerns with what ought to be.

Positive economic analysis (both micro & macro) attempts to develop hypo these which explain why it happened.

In normative (micro) economics analysis one is concerned with problems like what the objectives and policies of business ought to be and how to go about than.

Business economics is concerned with analysis which is prescriptive or normative in nature.

4. ENVIRONMENTAL ANALYSIS

There is evidence that organizations which are good at sensing the environment perform better than those that are not. (D. Miller and P Friesen). However, a major problem is the difficulties that Managers have in understanding the complexity of the environment of a modern organization and relating signals in the environment to likely influences on the organization. Research which has looked at how managers make sense of their environment emphasizes a number of key points : (J. Dutton, E. Walton, E. Abrahamson).

1. Managers have to simplify the complexity of the environment they face. It is not possible for them to operate in terms of perfect knowledge'. Understanding the effect of the simplification processes is important, not least because it shows how analysis using some of the frame work can be *helpful*.

2. Given the complexity of the environment and its influence on the organizations, even if a manager has a very rich understanding of that environment, it is unlikely that he/ she will bring that complex understanding to bear for all situations and all decisions. Rather, and necessarily, the manager will access that part of knowledge. This is called selective attention : the manager selects from a part of his/her total understanding the parts of knowledge which seems most relevant.

3. Managers also use examples and prototypes as away of making sense of, for example, competition. It is not unusual for managers to refer to a dominant competitor rather than a list of competitive characteristics. 'We compete against Japanese—' or 'The service on Singapore Airlines—'are ways of encapsulating quite complex sets of characteristics.

4. Over time, partial representations of reality become very fixed. The Japanese become a generic competitor, Singapore Airlines is competition. The risk is that the 'chunk' of information most often used becomes the only information used. The danger is then that stimuli from the environment are selected out to fit these dominant representations of reality. Information which squares with Singapore Airlines being the main competitor is absorbed, while, information counter this is not. Sometimes this distortion can lead to severe errors as managers miss crucial indicators because they are, in effect, scanning the environment for issues and events that are familiar or at least recognisable.

5. Over time, manager's experience can build up and contribute to a collective know how which is taken for granted in the organization and is referred to as paradigm. This can lead to both a filtering of information and consequently, significant strategic inertia in organizations.

6. There is also evidence that overall, managers tend to be biased towards seeing threats rather than opportunities. Largely because forces which are perceived to have a

potentially high impact on the organizations but to be outside its control are seen threatening. Managers then become sensitive to information which confirms or reinforces such a bias, rather than to other information which counters it. There is therefore a need to find ways of challenging such confirmation of bias.

7. Theoretically, at least, the various functions or parts of an organization scan the environment for signals which can be fed into strategic decision making. However, the evidence is that mid level management tend to have a very parochial outlook. Finance managers scan for financial changes in the environment, marketing managers for changes in the market and so on. So there may be difficulties in building up an overall strategic view of the environment on the basis of such partial outlooks.

The overall picture which emerges is that it is difficult for managers to cope with the level of complexity they face. They must simplify this in order to get on with the job of managing. However, if strategies are to be developed effectively, there have to be means questioning and challenging that which is taken for granted by managers.

Conclusion : The ability to sensechanges in the environment is important because perceived changes in environmental influences signal the possible need for changes in strategy : they throw up opportunities and warn of threats. These can be built into a SWOT analysis. There are some analytical ways in which sensing can be done. It began by warning against the analysis degenerating into a trivial listing of the ways in which different forces affect an organization. The approach is a structured way of avoiding this so as to move towards an interpretation or synthesis, of such forces. The proposed sequence of analysis is as under.

1. Clarify the nature of environment in terms of its level uncertainty, so as to take an initial view on appropriate ways of undertaking analysis.

2. Carrying out an internal audit of environmental influences, beginning at the macro level in order to gain an overall view of the variety of forces at work but also to identify key influences and drivers of change and where useful, to build scenarios for considering future conditions.

3. Focusing more specifically on the forces which determine the nature of competitive environment through five forces analysis.

4. Considering the positioning of the organization in relation to others with which it competes for customers or resources, in order to establish its relative strengths in its market by means of strategic group analysis, market segmentation and attractiveness analysis.

All this should encourage managers to focus on the wider world in which the organization exists rather than on the operational detail of running the organization on a day to day basis. In so doing, it both challenges current thinking and helps identify threats and opportunities that the organization faces. However, driving the development of strategy from an entirely external perspective is not adequate. It is also important to consider resource capabilities and specially strategic competencies of the organization.

5. INDUSTRY ANALYSIS

An industry analysis is intended to help determine the attractiveness of an industry to current and potential participants and to help identify key success factors. The analysis could be conducted for the industry as a whole and for important product markets within the industry. An industry analysis is often conducted along the following dimensions.

1. **Actual and potential industry size.** A knowledge of industry size helps to evaluate investment decision and serves to define market share of the various competitors. In addition to the size of the current market, it is often useful to consider the potential market indicated by usage gap, distribution gap, product line gap, competitive gap etc. which can be filled by finding new uses, finding new users, increasing variety of use, increasing usage frequency, expanding distribution intensity, expanding distribution coverage, adding product line elements, adding product features, penetrating position of other competitors, penetrating position of most direct competitors, etc.

2. **Industry structure.** The intensity of competition in an industry depends on *(a)* number of existing competitors, their commitment to industry, the product differentiation, high fixed costs, and exit barriers, *(b)* threat of potential competitors determined by barriers to entry such as capital investment required, economies of scale, access to distribution channels, and product differentiation, *(c)* substitute products, *(d)* bargaining power of customers and suppliers.

3. **Cost structure.** An understanding of the cost structure of the industry can provide insights into the present and future key success factors. One way to detect key success factors is to analyse the value added in the production stage and observe how it is changing. Another consideration is whether the industry setting makes an experience curve strategy appropriate or even feasible.

4. **Distribution channels.** Access to effective and efficient distribution channels is often a key success factor. The need is to identify alternative channels and trends in their relative importance and then analyse the power relationships in each channel and how they might be changing.

5. **Industry trends and developments.** Industry analysis should be forward looking. Industry trends and events could suggest new growth directions and affect key success factors and portability.

6. **Growth and product life cycle.** The PLC can be applied at the level of product class, product type, application or brand. In attempting to forecast maturity and decline phases, it is useful to consider trends in sales and profits and the advent of reduced product differentiation, price pressures, over capacity, increased buyer knowledge and sophistication, market saturation, replacement demand substitution by product or technology and penetration of usage gap.

The PLC is simple and powerful. However, it is not easily applied. The stages are not easily forecast, or even easily determined. The further product definition (product class, product form, application or brand) to which analysis should be applied is not easy. Even if the stage in life cycle is determined the strategy applications are not always obvious.. There are situations when investment in developing markets is appropriate specially if growth segments can be located and competitors can be purchased at low prices and operated efficiently. The optimal strategy will depend on Co's strengths like strong brand, ability to operate profitably with underutilized assets, flexibility in applying assets and resources, large market share providing economies of scale, established strong relationships with pockets of ending demand. Of price importance is the nature of competitors and their ability to exist.

The belief that growth markets are always attractive is based on assumptions that may not always hold good. These are : *(a)* in growth markets, market share is easier to obtain, *(b)* it is worth more, *(c)* the large share Co. has cost advantage, *(d)* price pressure is less, *(e)* early entry will provide useful experience with technology and *(f)* provide opportunities to prevent competition and create barriers to entry.

INDUSTRY ANALYSIS CHECKLIST

1. How many Cos are there in the industry and what size are they?
2. How concentrated is the industry?
3. To what degree are products substitute?
4. Is the industry growing or contracting?
5. What are relative powers of suppliers, buyers and competitors?
6. What are prevailing competitive strategies?
7. What entry barriers exist?
8. What economies of scale present?
9. What experience curve effects are important?
10. What exit barriers exist? (if any)
11. What important external factors affect competition?

PROBABLE QUESTIONS

1. Define Business Economics. Why it is also called Managerial Economics?
2. Write about the nature and characteristics of Business Economics.
3. What is the scope of Business Economics? Write about the differences between Micro and Macro Economics issues.
4. Highlight about various Economic Models in Business Economics.
5. Illustrate the business decision making environment in Business Economics with examples.

CHAPTER

2

PROFIT

1. Profit and Importance of Profit
2. Meaning and Nature of Profit
3. Functions of Profit
4. Economists' Theories of Profit
5. Profit Policy and Profit Planning
6. Problems in Profit Policy
7. Profit Planning

1. INTRODUCTION

Profit is one of the eight business objectives and is very vital for a business to survive and grow. No business unit can sustain for a long time without profit and high profitability leads to high growth of the unit.

When a business unit operates at such a percent capacity utilisation that it is beyond the breakeven point, then profit is resulted.

The break even point analysis is discussed in details else where in this book. Profit is achieved when the amount on total sales revenue exceeds the total expenditure on manufacturing and overheads; and such resulting amount is the gross profit.

When the items of depreciations, interest and income tax are deducted from the gross profit, the net profit amount is obtained.

Thus, profit is selling price less all expenditures of incurred in manufacturing and making available the product at the customer's place.

Since, selling price is influenced by market conditions, an organisation may not be able to change the selling price in normal circumstances.

Therefore, a business firm has to exercise cost reduction, cost control and waste reduction methods, in order to keep cost of the product as much low as possible. This will result in higher profitability.

2. PROFITS AND IMPORTANCE OF PROFITS

Peter Drucker has suggested eight important areas of business objectives.

1. Marketing
2. Innovation
3. Human Organisation
4. Physical Resources
5. Financial Resources
6. Productivity
7. Social Responsibility
8. Profit Requirement

Profit requirement for a business organisation is so vital for its survival and growth that the management is concerned with making alround efforts for the efficient implementation and control of the above first seven areas of business objectives for the maximisation of the ultimate objective, *i.e.* Profit.

(a) Meaning and Nature of Profit

For an Accountant, profit means the net income from the business. It is calculated by deducting from the total receipts the total expenditure incurred in a business venture.

Economists regard profit as a factor-return like wages, interest and rent. Profit is a return to the entrepreneur for the use of his entrepreneurial ability.

Profit is the reward for the risk an entrepreneur takes in a business.

Profit is also the reward for innovations in production method, products, marketing etc.

(*i*) Relation between Accounting Profit and Economic Profit

$$\pi_A = R - C$$
$$\pi_E = \pi_A - OC$$
$$= R - C - OC$$

π_A = Accounting Profit

π_E = Economic Profit

R = Revenue

C = Explicit Costs (Paid out costs)

OC = Opportunity Costs

Opportunity cost is the income foregone which a businessman could expect from the second best alternative use of his resources.

Since every decision involves a sacrifice of alternatives, the opportunity costs are implied in any decision making.

If opportunity costs are considered then economic profit would find to be less than accounting profit.

(b) Functions of Profit

(i) Profit is a measure of the operational efficiency of the firm.

(ii) Profit is the premium that covers up the cost of staying in business replacement, obsolescence, risk and uncertainty.

(iii) Profit is the source of internal finance. The net retained earning is used to finance expansion and replacement programmes.

(iv) Commercial profitability is an established criteria of project evaluation or appraisal.

(v) Profit reflects the income earning capacity of the firm and thus determines if the firm is capable of discharging social responsibility or not.

(vi) Inter firm comparison, inter industry comparison or product line comparison are all facilitated by the index of profit.

No business firm can function today without having a profit policy because profit plays a crucial role to help decision making.

(c) Economists' Theories of Profit

***(i)* Walker's Theory of Profit :** According to F.A. Walker Profit is the rent of "exceptional abilities that an entreprenuer may possess" over others. Just as rent is the difference between the yields of the least and the most fertile lands, profit is the difference between the earning, of the least and the must efficient entrepreneurs.

***(ii)* Clark's Dynamic Theory of Profit :** According to J.B. Clark, profits arise in a dynamic economy.

A dynamic economy is characterised by *(i)* increase in population *(ii)* increase in capital *(iii)* Multiplication of consumer wants.

The entrepreneurs who take successfully the advantages of changing conditions in a dynamic company make profit.

***(iii)* Knight's Theory of Profit :** According to F.H. Knight, profit is that refresh to uncertainty bearing, Profit arises from the decisions taken and implemented under the conditions of uncertainty. In his view, the profits may arise as a result of decisions concerning the state of market *e.g.* decisions which result in increasing the degree of monopoly, decisions with respect to holding stocks, and decision taken to introduce a new technique.

***(iv)* Monopoly Profit :** Monopoly may arise due to *(i)* economies of scale *(ii)* sole ownership of certain crucial raw materials *(iii)* legal sanction and protection *(iv)* mergers and taken overs.

A monopolist may earn "Monopolist Profit" and maintain it in the long run by using its monopoly powers.

Business and Profit

However, the following three main objectives for a business firm, which help it to survive and grow, will be discussed in this chapter. They are as under :

(i) Profit Maximisation.

(ii) Sales Maximisation.

(iii) Growth Rate Maximisation.

3. PROFIT PLANNING AND MAXIMISATION

(i) Profit Maximisation

The primary objective of any business firm is to try to maximise it's profit. Hence a basic assumption in traditional economic theory is that every business firm acts rationally, and accordingly aims at maximising its profit, subject of course to some of the constraints imposed by government. The entire business economic theory is concerned with the management technique to achieve :

(1) Maximisation of total revenue from sales.

(2) Minimisation cost of production and thus, obtain higher profit.

(3) Maximisation of profit for the business unit.

Normally a business firm is assumed to go for profits both in short and long periods. In case however, the firm is running on losses in the short period, its aim would be to minimise its losses.

In practice the assumption of profit maximisation may not hold good, firm may end at a profit making, but not necessary at maximum profit. For one thing a firm may not know the maximum profit point, for another it may be' satisfied with normal or fair profits. Even if it is possible for a firm to know where it can maximise its profit it may not deliberately follow such a policy due to the following reasons.

To Prevent Potential Competitors : Existence of maximum profit in an industry will be an attraction for new firms to enter in a similar industry and make the market competitive and reduce the profit. A firm could always prefer lower profit than having competitors; for profit maximisation it can aim at the same in the long run. But the real problem is that we cannot objectively state clearly the profit maximising price and output for the firm even for the long period.

(ii) Sales Maximization

The assumption of profit maximisation has been questioned by many modem economists. Berle and Means in their famous book, "The Modern Corporation of Private Property" have argued as fallows :

(a) There is a clearcut separation between ownership and management in a modern corporation (*i.e.* Public Limited Company).

(b) The owners of the company *i.e.* the shareholders are interested in maximising profits.

(c) The managers who run the company and decide corporate policies, have their own motives and aims for the firm, and

(d) The management generate sufficient capital fund for the firm through retained profits and are generally free from the scrutiny of capital markets.

For these points Berle and Means conclude that profit rates are generally higher in owner controlled firms than in manager controlled firms and that professional managers generally ignore profit maximising interest of shareholders.

According to William Baumol every business firm aims at maximising its sales revenue (Price of product × Quantity) rather than its profit. Hence his hypothesis has come to be known as Sales Maximisation Theory.

To Prevent Government Intervention : As high profit is regarded as index of monopoly power and possible exploitation of consumers, the government may intervene whenever the firm has large profits. To prevent government intervention, a firm may follow a policy of less than maximum profit.

To Acquire Consumers Goodwill : A firm may charge less than the maximum price the consumer is willing to pay, this policy is to acquire and maintain the goodwill of consumers.

To Secure Industry Leadership : Often a firm may be willing to sacrifice profit maximisation and instead go in for maximum value of sales in order to acquire industry leadership. When the price leader or the dominant firm fixes high prices with a view to getting high margin of profit, the smaller firms may be tempted to widercat him.

To Check Demand For High Wages : Whenever the trade unions are strong, one method of restraining demand for the wage increase is to restrict profits, for high profits will always be taken as ability to play high wages.

To Retain Image of Efficiency : Whenever a business is run by professionals, the objective would be a steady expansion of sales volume and rising margin of profits rather than maximising profits year after year. This will enable them to retain their image to their shareholders.

Strictly speaking, all the above mentioned constraints do not really intervention or the— assumption of contradict the maximum profit. The prevention of potential competitors or government assumption of industry leadership—these only indicate that in the short period, the firm should not go for high profit. Maximising sales has become an end in themselves and accordingly sales maximisation has become an ultimate objective of the firm. Naturally the management of a firm directs its energies in promoting and maximising sales revenue instead of profit.

The goal of sales maximisation is explained by the management's desire to maintain the firm's competitive position which is dependent on a large extent on us size. Unlike the shareholders who are interested in profit, the management is interested in sales revenue because large sales revenue is a matter of prestige to the management. Besides banks and financial institutions welcome regular growth in sales revenue as a clear indication of the health of the firm. Growing sales revenue also enables the management to pay higher salaries and provide other monetary incentives to the employees which may not be possible, if the firm follows profit maximisation policy.

Baumol however does not ignore the cost of production to be covered and also earn a marginal profit. In fact, he advocates the adoption of a price which will cover the cost and also will yield minimum rate of profit. That is, while the firm is maximising its revenue from sales, it should "earn enough or more than enough profits" to keep the shareholders satisfied.

Baumol's sales maximisation principle is defective in the sense that maximisation of sales revenue without reference to profit has no significance. Baumol practically rejects profit maximisation and advocates sales maximisation but ultimately he ends up in advocating "adequate" profit even if sale maximisation has to be given up.

The chief merit of the "Sales Maximisation Theory" is that it has given another motive to the management of modern corporations besides the profit motive. So long as profit is at a satisfactory level, the management will devote its energy to maximise its sales.

(iii) Growth Rate Maximisation

In modern business, rate of growth of a firm is regarded as a yardstick of corporate success and accordingly, rapid growth of firm is the corner stone of corporate policy. Growth maximisation is, thus, regarded as a major aim of a firm and also an alternative to profit maximisation and sales revenue maximisation aims of a business firm.

The growth of a firm is financed through retained earnings of the firm or through borrowings from the market or through financial institutions or through both. Management normally prefers to finance growth through internal funds-retained profits—because they would not be subject to the scrutiny of the capital market and the interest burden in future may restrict the growth capacity of the company in the future. But how does a firm accumulate large internal funds? Internal retained earnings can only grow through profit maximisation. In other words, the corporate decision to maximise the rate of growth is naturally a decision to maximise profit.

(iv) Social Responsibilities of Business

The concept of social responsibility traditionally is defined in terms of both social and economic goals of business units. Until recent years, much emphasis has been placed only. On the economic objectives of business units which should be efficient in producing goods and services that people want and for which people are willing to pay. If the above objective is done well, it is reasoned that the profits of the business unit could be maximised. Thus, maximisation of profit becomes the dominant goal of business. But today due to a number of reasons much greater emphasis has been placed on the social aspects of organisational obligations to the community as a whole and to the owners of the organisation.

In the past a business which was efficiently using the resources at its disposal was considered as one acting in a socially responsible way. Responsible business was one which was efficiently using the resources available to it. But the current concept not only includes this type of action but much more. **Social responsibility of business is defined broadly as**

"responsibility to customers, shareholders and the community". The current concept of social responsibility may be defined from two points of view, namely, the conceptual and specific corporate social program.

(*a*) *Conceptual* : According to Kenneth Andrews, social responsibility refers to "the intelligent and objective concern for the welfare of society that restrains individual and corporate behaviour from ultimately destructive activities, no matter how immediately profitable and leads to the direction of positive contributions to human betterment, variously as the latter may be defined." According to this definition the promoters of business should give weightage to the social interest of the people in the community, in their process of decision making.

(*b*) *Specific Corporate Social Programme* : Social responsibilities of business may be defined as an operational level, in terms of specific programmes which a corporation may undertake such as education, medical care, employment and training, pollution abatement, culture and art, civil liberty and equal opportunity while speaking of social responsibilities, of business, many people including promoters of business feel that the pursuance of such a concept will ultimately result in a reduction of short range as well as long range profits. This is not necessarily so. For instance, if a business concern assures equity, morality and justice in the selection, training and promotion of employees, that such a concern may well improve its productivity and morale and in turn profits. If a business enterprise replaces a more dangerous machine, it not only avoids accident hazards, but also raises it productivity per man hour. However, some social programmes may reduce the profit of business concerns.

4. CONCEPTS OF PROFIT

Prof F.H. Knight, a noted authority on the theory of profit states "Perhaps no beam on concept in economic discussion is used with a more buildings variety of well-established meanings than profit". Profit is the income received by the organiser on entrepreneur. A firm makes profit when it receives a surplus after it has paid its interest on borrowed capital wages to labourers and rent for land. It Is equal to the difference between total revenue (received by selling a commodity) and total cost of production. Let us take an example to explain profit. Suppose that a firm is producing 10,000 pens a year. It sells them at the rate of Rs. 10 per pen. The total revenue or total income will be equal to Rs. 1,00,000 (10,000 units × Rs. 10). To calculate profit it should estimate its cost of production. Suppose that its expenses come to Rs. 70,000.

		Rs.	Rs.
Total Revenue from Sales			1,00,000
(*a*) Wages of labour	=	25,000	
(*b*) Raw materials	=	25,000	
(*c*) Interest on capital	=	10,000	
(*d*) Rent of business premises	=	10,000	
∴ Total Cost	=		70,000
∴ Total Profit	=		30,000

Profit in the above illustration is the difference between total revenue and total cost of production.

Small businessmen generally include only explicit cost while calculating total cost of production. The excess over explicit cost is regarded as profit. Properly speaking, this is gross profit. The organiser should include in his cost. *(a)* wage for his own labour; *(b)* interest for his own capital; *(c)* rent for his own land and business premises; and *(d)* depreciation of machinery & buildings etc. These costs are implicit costs and they should be deducted from gross profit. The balance or surplus may be known as net profit. This can be summarised as follows :

Gross Profit = Total revenue – Total explicit cost

Net Profit = Total revenue – (Total explicit cost + Total implicit cost).

= Gross Profit – Total implicit cost.

This distinction can be explained with the help of an example. Let us assume that a firm is receiving a total, revenue of Rs. 1,00,000 in 1989 from the sales of 10,000 pens at a price of Rs. 10/- percent.

Suppose that is explicit cost of production in 1989 are :

(a) Rent of business premises = Rs. 10,000

(b) Interest on bank loans = Rs. 10,000

(c) Wages and salaries = Rs. 25,000

(d) Raw Materials = Rs. 25,000

Total explicit or paid out cost = Rs. 70,000

Suppose that the implicit costs of the firm in 1989 are :

(i) Wages for the personal labour of the organiser = Rs. 5,000

(ii) Interest for his own capital = Rs. 1,000

(iii) Depreciation of machinery and equipment = Rs. 2,000

(iv) Taxes paid to the Government = Rs. 2,000

Total implicit cost = Rs. 10,000

Now, Total revenue – Total explicit cost = Gross profit

In our examples :

Total Revenue = Rs. 1,00,000

Total explicit cost = Rs. 70,000

∴ Gross Profit = Rs. 30,000

Now the firm has to deduct its implicit cost also, so as to arrive at net profit.

Gross Profit = Rs. 30,000

Total implicit cost = Rs. 10,000

∴ Net Profit = Rs. 20,000

Net Profit is the income received by the organiser after all the factors of production (including those contributed by the organiser himself) are paid off. This is the income which he receives for his services.

In a big joint-stock company calculation of gross benefit and net profit is made in a simple and straight manner. These are not-explicit and implicit costs for a large firm all costs are infact, explicit costs for it. The large firm calculate its gross profit by talking the difference between total revenue and total cost. Then from its gross profit, the firm deducts two expenses *viz.*,

(a) Depreciation on its machinery and plant and *(b)* direct takes paid to the government (known as corporation take or company profits tax) : the balance is known as net profit. In other words,

(a) Gross profit for a large firm

= Total revenue – Total Cost.

(b) Net Profit for a large firm

= Gross profit – (Depreciation + Taxes to the Govt.)

of the commodity in question, etc. 'Such an increase in demand will lest to a rise' in price of the product, and if cost of production remains the same, profit will arise. On the other hand, supply of a commodity or service may charge because of the introduction of a new process or cheapening of a raw material on improvement in transport, etc. Economists speak of two types of changes which can affect an economy, *(a)* general changes which are common to all the firms in an industry and sometimes common to all the industries in the country; these are changes over which no individual firm or industry has control and *(b)* special changes which are deliberately introduced by individual firms in order to earn a profit.

(a) General Changes

Some changes affect demand only, while others affect supply only and get others both demand and supply. A change in fashion in favour of a commodity will increase the demand for it and all the firms which are producing that commodity will get profit. On the other hand, the cheapening of a raw material or improvement of transport in a region will help to reduce the cost of production of a commodity and, assuming demand to be constant, will lead to larger margin of profit for all the firms in the industry or in the region. A war, an inflation, a business depression, etc., cause changes in a modern economy which lead to profits or losses through influencing demand and supply simultaneously. For instance, during an inflation all prices and costs go up but prices rise faster than costs because most of the costs are contractual and fixed in nature and do not consequently rise as fast as prices.

5. INNOVATIONS AND PROFIT

There are some dynamic changes which are introduced by individual firms themselves. Such changes may take diverse forms such as an invention of a machinery the introduction of a new conorodity or a new variety of an old product introduction of a new method of selling and advertisement, etc. All these changes are collectively called innovations. Whenever an innovation is introduced, it necessitates a new combination of factors which by reducing cost below the prevailing price, causes profit to emerge. In many cases an innovation may not lead to a reduction of cost but may attract more customers and thus increase the total amount of profits.

All the economic progress which we observe in a modern economy is the result of technical progress, which in turn is due to introduction of innovation in the fields of agriculture industry, transport, communication, medicine etc. The motive for introducing an innovation which leads to economic progress is to obtain profit. Profit, therefore is the cause of innovations, and if the innovations than out to be successful, the result will also be profit. Thus, profit is at once both the cause as well as the effect of innovations, and therefore is the cause and affect of economic progress too. This is illustrated in the following figure :

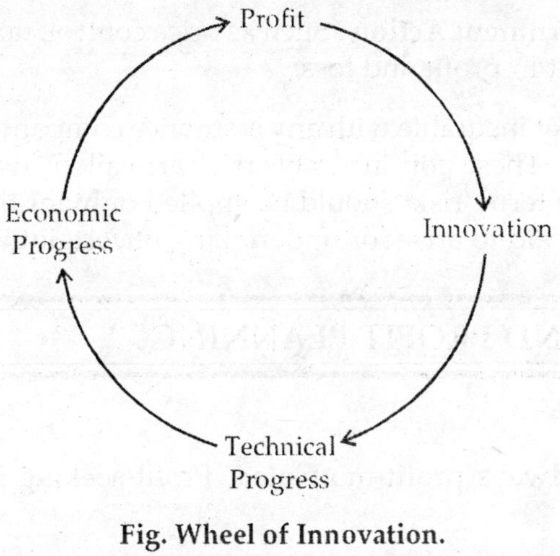

Fig. Wheel of Innovation.

6. PROFIT AS A REWARD FOR RISK AND UNCERTAINTY BEARING

Profit is attributed to risk taking by the entrepreneur. The expectation of profit is a necessary prerequisite for understanding any new venture by the entrepreneur. The greater the risk the higher must be the expected gain in order to Induce an entrepreneur to start a business. Every business is more or less speculative and unless the risk bearer is amply rewarded to Bernard Hawley "the profit of an undertaking is the reward for risk and responsibilities by the entrepreneur. The concept of profit as reward for risk taking confirms to the common motion which relates profit to risk taking.

It is interesting to observe that profit arises not only because risks are borne by the entrepreneurs but because the superior entrepreneurs are able to reduce them. Further it is not very risk that can account for the emergence of profit. According to Prof. Frank H. Knight risks inherent in any business are of two kinds—insurable risks and non insurable risks. Those risks which can be calculated statistically and thus insured with an insurance firm are called insurable risks. These are again of two types : *(a)* risks of loss of property due to earthquake, fire, flood and other natural calamities and *(b)* risks of dishonesty such as robbery, buglary, theft etc. The insurable risks are not the responsibility and worry of the organiser, because by paying insurance premium he is absolved of this worry. Thus insurance premium becomes a definite part of the entrepreneur's cost of production and hence enters into price.

However, there are certain non insurable risks of modern business which are not capable of being reduced to statistical measurement and are not borne by insurance companies. These risks must of necessarily be borne by the entrepreneur himself if he has to carry on production. These non insurable risks are as follows :

(a) **Risk of Competition :** Arise when more rivals enter the industry or because of development of some other new and completive products.

(b) **Technological Risks :** Arise from the possibility of machinery becoming obsolete clue to discovery of new processes.

(c) **Business Cycle Risks :** Arise because of occurrence of business depressions when price falls much more than costs.

(d) **Risk due to Government Action :** Such as price control, tax policy, import and export restrictions etc. may result in profit and loss.

The above risks are not insurable with any insurance company and hence are undertaken by enterprises themselves. These non-insurable risks are called "uncertainties" by Prof. Frank Knight. In his opinion the term 'risk' should be applied only for those risk which are known and unforeseen. Profit is said to arise for undertaking uncertainties of a business.

7. PROFIT POLICY AND PROFIT PLANNING

(1) Introduction

A business firm is always profit-motivated. Profit-seeking is the motive force of any business undertaking.

Market economy is, thus, profit-oriented. Thus, the classical economists have regarded profit maximisation as the sole objective of the business firm in a capitalist economy. In economic theory, the basic, assumption is that though a rational firm seeks to maximise profit, profit-seeking is not the only objective of a business. In reality, profit is not an end in, itself. But the survival of the business, of course, depends on the firm's ability to earn some profit so as to keep it alive, which may not be or need not be the maximum.

Even form an egalitarian point of view, profit is not a sinful act. Reasonable profit is the righteous reward of the entrepreneur for his entrepreneurial and organisational activity. As such, a rational profit policy and planning is important for a modern business firm.

(2) Profit Policy : Profit Restraint

In practice, firms rarely seek to maximise profits. Most firms have many goals of primary importance other than profit. Instead of maximisation of profit thus, the firms are interested in putting a limit on their profits. There are several reasons for limiting or controlling profits.

1. Maintaining Business Goodwill : A policy of limiting profit may be followed by firm in order to win appreciation of consumers and earn business reputation and maintain business goodwill in the market. By keeping a low profit margin, the firm may create a good impression on the consumers and enjoy their patronage. Thus, in an inflationary situation, by restricting the profit margin, the firm may be in a position to maintain a stable price for its product which will definitely fetch consumers' appreciation. Further, keeping a high profit margin and higher prices may also involve the danger of consumer resentment. To avoid this, it is considered a wise policy to keep a low profit margin and maintain business goodwill.

2. Wage Consideration : It the firm maintains high profits, trade unions will demand high wages, which may inflate costs and further complicated the management problem. Thus, to avoid such happenings and to maintain good labour relations profit control is imperative.

3. Avoiding High Taxation and Government's Intervention : High profits may attract high taxation. Again, high profits may be taken as in index of monopoly power which may attract government's attention and investigation and its eventual control. The government may, through price control, regulation of profit intervene etc., so the firm may consider it to be a wise policy aim at less than possible maximum profits.

4. Avoiding Risk : The risk element tends to be high under profit maximisation. Thus, to minimise risk, it is imperative not to go in for maximisation of profits but be satisfied with a reasonable profitability of the business venture.

5. Obstructing Potential Competition : High profitability of the business may attract new competitors to enter the field and share the market. Thus, only a fair profit may be earned by the concerned firm to discourage new entry in its production line. As Joel Dean puts it : "Competitors can invade the market as soon as they discover its profitability, find ways to shift the patents, and make the necessary development outlays in production design, production plant, technique and market penetration." For this reason, a firm may not want to show profit earnings in the business but depict a gloomy picture so that newcomers are discouraged from entering the market.

6. Goal of Domination and Leadership in the Market : If the firm aims to dominate the market and acquire leadership, it may seek to maximise sales and capture the market rather than maximise its profits.

7. Enlightened Self-interest of Survival : The firm in its own interest, for survival, would wet limits on its profits and try to see that its existence becomes permanent in the market so that it can earn a regular flow of business income in the long term. It also implies considerations to prevent loss instead of maximum return.

8. Idealism and Service Motivation : A firm may adopt an idealistic approach and service motivation, so that it will not go in for profit maximisation and instead would like to serve the nation in a reasonable manner. The firm's ideal may be to provide more employment with better wages. It may look into the welfare of its workers more than the self-interest of profit maximisation. A businessman with philanthropic ideas and attitudes always tends to control the profits of his organisation.

9. Liquidity Preference : For a comfortable position in the business liquidity, *i.e.*, possession of cash is very important. Liquidity of the firm is also depending upon the positive ratio of current assets to current liabilities.

Especially, in banking business greater emphasis is placed on liquidity rather than profitability. A bank arranges its assets in the ascending order of liquidity and descending order of profitability.

8. PROBLEMS IN PROFIT POLICY

Though a firm may seek to pursue many other objectives than profit; profit does become a part of the game. Usually, the firm does make budgeting for obtaining a planned rate of profit and would certainly try to improve its profit performance over time, though it may not aim at profit maximisation. In practice, a firm seeks to earn a target rate of return on its investment. It, thus, encounters two major problems in determining its profit policy.

(1) What should be the reasonable rate of profit? and

(2) How to determine it?

Thus, the basic problem of profit policy is to determine a profit standard through the target rate of return on investment.

Criteria for Acceptable Profit Rate or Rate of Return on Investment

Various criteria may be applied to determine the rate return on investment and decide the most acceptable rate of profit.

These may be enlisted as follows :

(1) Competitive Rates of Profit : The firm in its profit policy may consider the rates of profits earned by other firms in the same industry of the rates prevailing in other related industries in similar economic business conditions.

(2) Historical Profit Rate : The firm may look into its past earnings in normal times and determine the planned rate of return for the future course of operation. The firm has to examine the impact of historical rate of profit on equity capital in the past, dividends to share holders and the degree of competitive men in the market.

(3) Sufficient Earning to Protect the Equity : The rate of return on investment should adequately protect the interest of the present share holders, so that it has no problem in raising new equity capital for further expansion.

(4) Plough Back of Profit Rate : The rate of return may be such that it can adequately finance growth through internal resources, *i.e.*, by plough back of profit.

9. PROFIT PLANNING

In modern business profit earning is not an easy task. Profitability and success of the business depends on the firms accurate business planning and operation.

Profit planning is essential in the wake of many constraints limitations and uncertainties of modem business conditions.

Profit planning is an art as well as science. It is the sign of a good business which can make profit consistent with myriad of risk elements encountered and this is only possible with an appropriate profit planning.

To earn profit one has to face risks and one who deals with risks successfully can make profit. To deal with the risks and to avoid losses one has to plan. It is the essence of profit planning.

To earn profit one has to face risks and one who deals with risks successfully can make profit. To deal with the risks and to avoid losses one has to plan. It is the essence of profit planning.

Profit planning is an integral part of business policy and planning. Profit policy is programmed through profit planning. Profit planning gives a concrete shape to the profit-policy of the firm. Profit policy is an ideal. Profit planning is a time bound action to fulfil this ideal.

Profit is the difference between total sales revenue and total cost of production. Thus, in profit planning, to regulate the profit, sales volume and input quantity (or cost of production) are to be manipulated. In modem business, profit are, thus, controlled by adopting many sophisticated techniques such as break-even analysis, cost control, profit volume analysis and linear programming.

PROBABLE QUESTIONS

1. Write about importance of profit for a business firm.
2. What are the objectives of business?
3. What are various types of profit? Describe their relationships.
4. What are various function of profit?
5. Write about various theories of profit.
6. What do you mean by "profit policy?" What are various problems in profit policy?
7. Highlight the concept of policy of profit maximisation.

CHAPTER 3

THE IS-LM MODEL

1. IS-LM Model—Significance
2. Characteristics of IS & LM Curves
3. Properties of IS & LM Curves
4. Business Cycle — Meaning, Definition and Types
5. Phases of Business Cycle
6. Adjusting Business Plans to Cyclical Situations
7. Business Cycle and Business Strategies
8. Business Cycle and Unemployment, Money, Interest Rates and Prices
9. Monetary Policy and Fiscal Policy
10. Business Cycle Stabilisation Policy
11. Comparison between Fiscal and Monetary Policies

1. Significance

The IS-LM model emphasises the interaction between the goods and the financial markets. Income affects spending which in turn determines output (GNP) and Income (GNI). Financial market is influenced by income and income is influenced by interest rate; *i.e.*, higher interest rates lower spending and thus at lower interest rate invest demand increases and equilibrium level of goods output increases. Thus, spending, Interest rates and Income are determined jointly by the equilibrium in the goods and financial markets. It is the shorthand expression of equality of investment and saving and LM is the short hand expression of equality of money demand (L) and Money supply (M).

2. The Derivation IS Curve

IS is (–) ve sloping curve; the diagram high lights the concept that at higher interest rate, both income and output levels fall and at lower interests rates both income and output level increase.

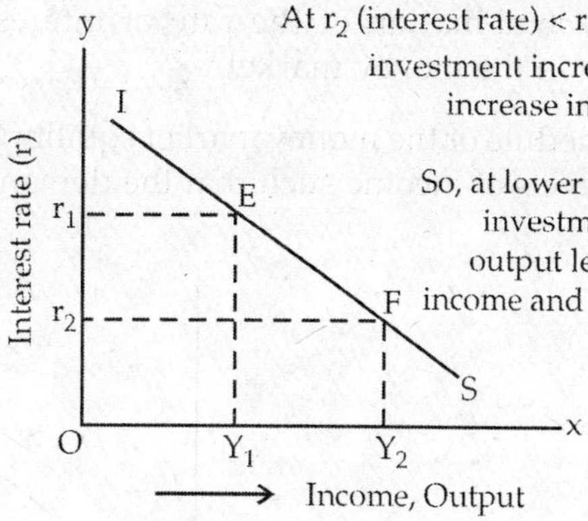

At r_2 (interest rate) < r_1 demand for investment increases causing increase in output level

So, at lower interest rates investment rises and output levels rise and income and employment also rise.

3. The Derivation of LM Curve

LM curve is a (+)ly sloped curve.

L_1 & L_2 are demand for money curves correspond to two different income levels.

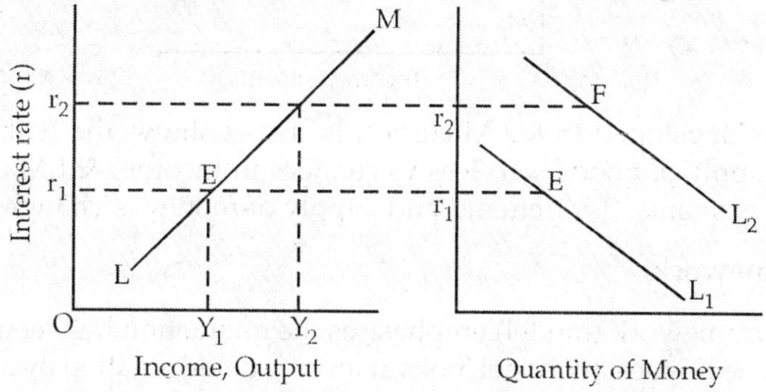

The LM curve is a locus of points showing alternative combination of the rate of interest and the level of income that bring about equilibrium in the money market.

LM curve is the Money Market equilibrium schedule which shows all combination of **interest rates** and **levels of income** such that the demand for money is equal to supply.

4. Characteristics of IS & LM curves

IS-LM Model continues to be used for macro economic studies. The main reason is that it provides a simple and appropriate framework for analysing the effects of monetary and fiscal policies changes on the demand for output and interest rates.

The commodity market equilibrium schedule is IS curve (schedule). It shows combination of interest rates and levels of output such that planned (desired) spending (expenditure) equals income. 'I' denotes autonomous investment and the investment function states that the lower the interest rates, the higher is the planned investment.

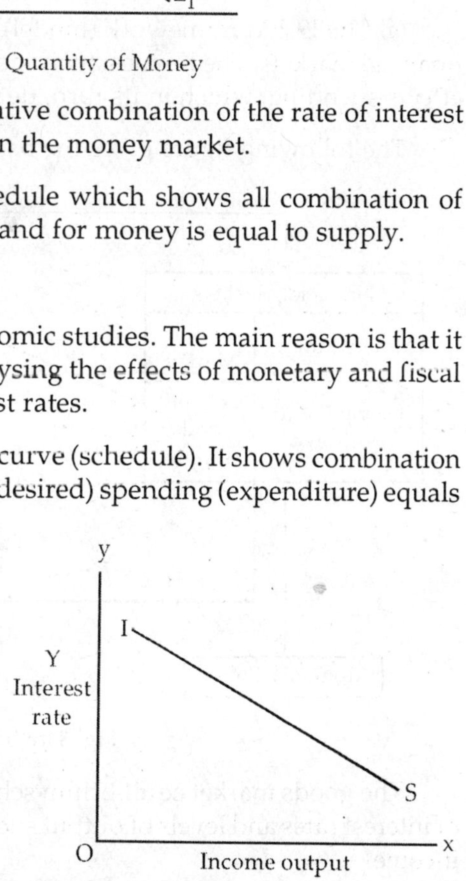

IS curve is negatively sloped because a higher level of interest reduces investment spending, thereby reducing aggregate demand and thus the equilibrium of income. The steepness of curve depends on the interest elasticity of investment.

IS curve is shifted by changes in autonomous spending. The LM curve is a locus of points showing alternative combination of the rate of interest and the level of income that bring about equilibrium in the money market.

LM schedule or the money market equilibrium schedule shows all combination of interest rates and levels of income such that the demand for money is equal to its supply.

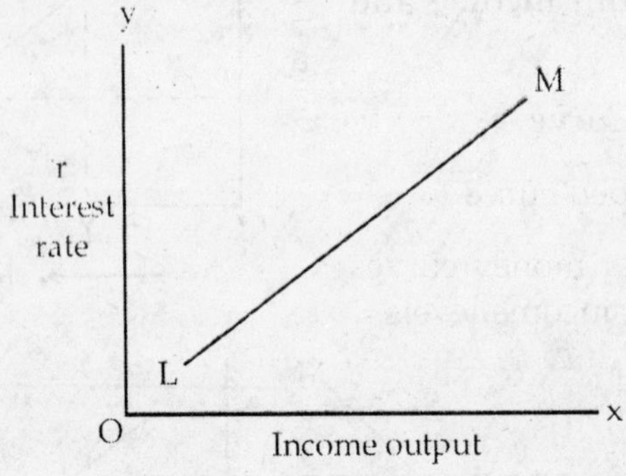

Prof. J.R. Hicks developed IS & LM curves. Is curves shows the real sector of economy (for demand and supply of goods/services vs changes in Income) & LM curves demand the monetary sector of economy (for demand and supply of money is changes in interest rates).

5. The IS-LM Framework

(a) The IS-LM framework (model) emphasises the interaction between the goods and the financial markets. The Keynesian model looks at income determination by arguing that income effects spending, which in its turn, determines output (GNP) and income (GNI).

The following figure gives the basic structure of the IS-LM model.

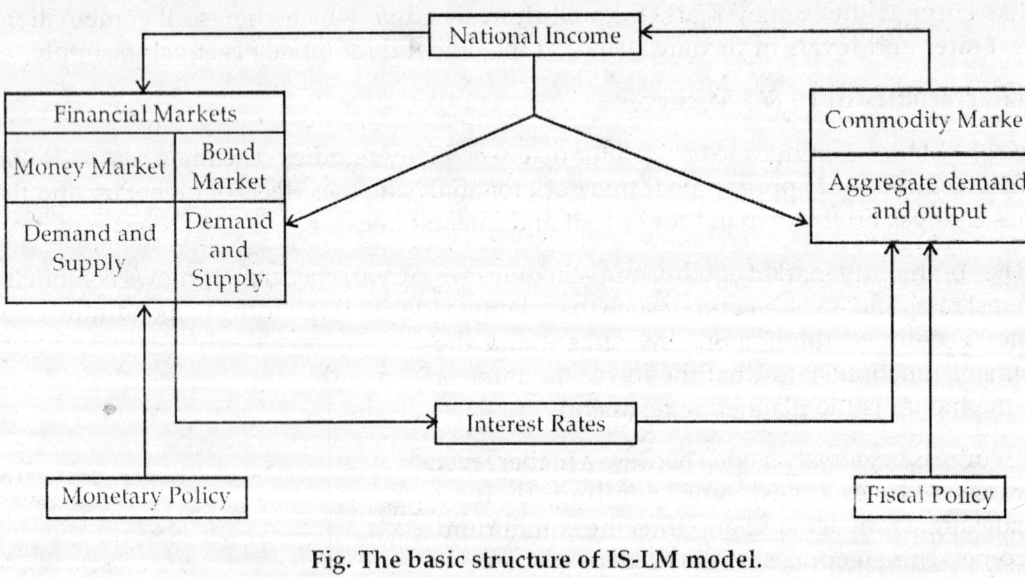

Fig. The basic structure of IS-LM model.

The goods market equilibrium schedule is the IS curve (schedule). It shows combinations of interest rates and levels of output such that planned (Desired) spending (expenditure) equals income.

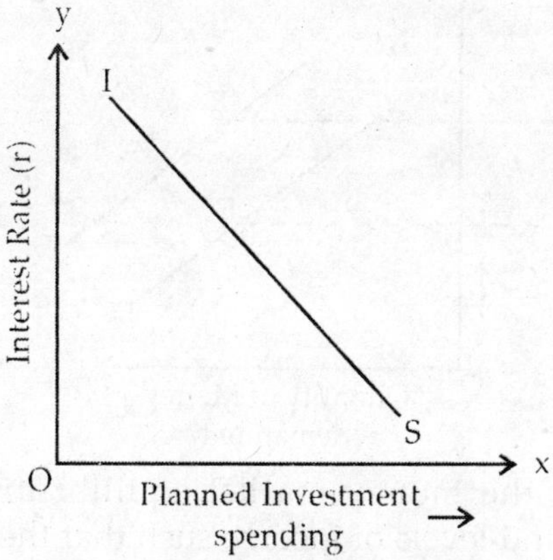

Fig. The Investment Schedule.

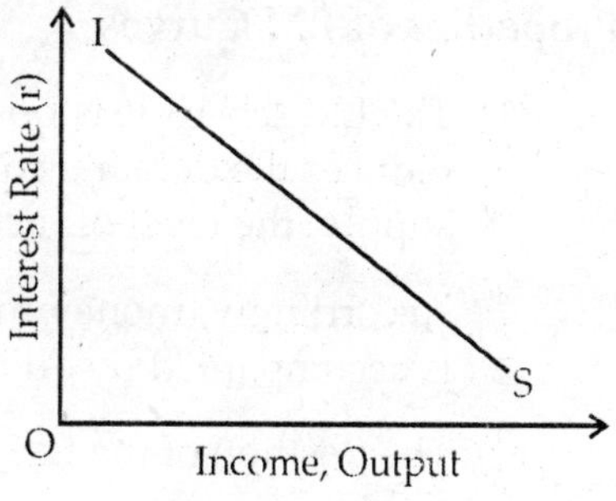

(b) Diagram on the right shows a typical investment (demand) schedule. It shows the planned level of investment (spending) at each rate of interest.

Higher interest rates lower the planned rates of investment spending.

(c) The IS curve is locus of points showing alternative combination of interest rates and income (output) at which the commodity market clears. That is why the IS curve is called the commodity market equilibrium schedule.

(d) Properties of IS curve :

(1) **The slope of the IS curve :** The IS curve is negatively sloped because a higher level of the interest rate reduces investment spending thereby reducing aggregate demand and thus the equilibrium level of income The slope (steepness) of the curve depends on the interest elasticity of investment multiplier. If autonomous opening increases, IS curve shifts to right with reduction in saving.

(2) **The position of the IS curve :** The position of the IS curve depends on the level of auto-nomous spending. Investment spending which is independent of both income and the rate of interest is autonomous investment. If autonomous spending increases, the IS curve will shift the right. Autonomous spending may be investment spending or government expenditure.

(3) The IS curve is the schedule of combination of the interest rate and the level of income such that the goods market is in equilibrium.

(e) Money market Equilibrium and the LM curve the financial market refers to the market in which money, bonds, stocks and other forms of income earning assets are traded.

The higher the rate of interest, the lower the quantity of money demanded, at a fixed level of income. An increases income raises the demand for money.

The LM curve is a locus of points showing alternative combination of the rate of interest and the level of income that bring about equilibrium in the money market.

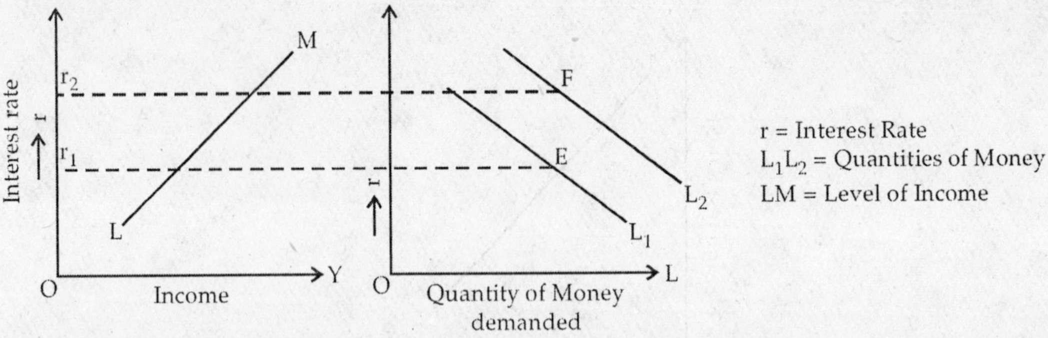

LM schedule (curve) is the money market equilibrium schedule which gives all combination of interest rates and levels of income such that the demand for money is equals to its supply.

Properties of LM Curves

(1) The LM schedule is positively sloped. This means that an increase in the interest rate reduces the demand for money to maintain the demand for money equal to the fixed supply, the level of income has to rise.

Accordingly, money market equilibrium implies that an increase in the interest rate is accompanied by an increase in the level of income.

(2) The position of the LM curve. An increase in money supply shifts the LM curve to the right.

(3) At all points to the right of LM curve, there is an axes demand for money and at points to its left, there is an excess supply of money.

(4) An increase in the quantity of money in circulation or decreases in demand for money shifts the LM curve to the right side.

(f) **Use of IS-LM Model :** The IS-LM model continues to be used (since its introduction in 1939 by J.R. Hicks) for macro economic studies. The main reason is that it provides a simple and appropriate framework for analysing the effects of monetary and fiscal policy changes on the demand for output and interest rates.

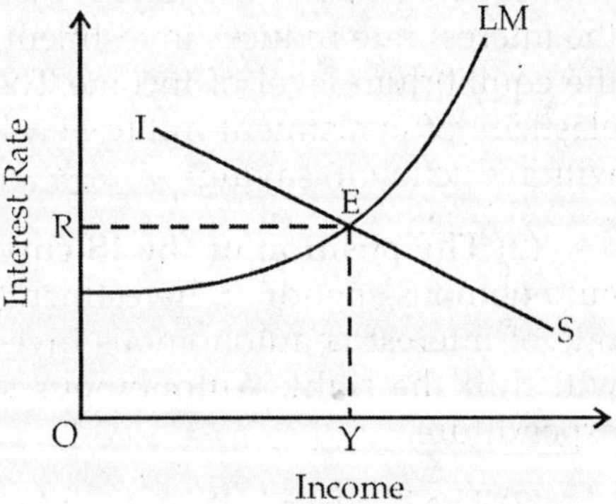

Fig. Income Equilibrium Position.

(g) General Equilibrium—Products & Money markets. Figure shows an equilibrium position where IS and LM curves interest each other at point E relating to Y level of income to R interest rate this combination of income level and interest rate leads to simulatenous equilibrium in goods market (of saving instruments) and the money market (of demand and supply).

This general equilibrium position persits at a point of time of given price level. If there is any deviation forms the equilibrium position, certain forces will act and react in such a manner that the equilibrium will be restored.

6. (Business Cycle, Adjusting business plans to Cyclical situations) Unemployment, Money, Interest Rates and Prices

(1) Business Cycle : Meaning, Definition and Types of Business Cycle.

Business cycle or trade cycle refers to the fluctuations in economic activity occurring regularly in the capitalist societies. Business cycles or Trade cycles are the wave like fluctuations in economic activity as reflected on the basic economic variables like employment, income, output and price levels. These fluctuations are cyclical in nature.

The business cycle in the general sense may be defined as an alternation of periods of prosperity and depression of good and bad trade.

Definition : According to John Keynes "A trade cycle is composed of periods of good trade characterised by rising prices an low unemployment percentages, alternating with periods of bad trade characterised by falling prices and high unemployment percentages.

Thus, business cycles are cyclical fluctuations characterised by alternating wages of expansion and contraction. They do not have a fixed rhythm, but they are cycles in that the phases of contraction and expansion recur frequently and in fairly similar pattern.

In other words Business cycles are the wave—like fluctuations in economic activity as reflected in the basis economic variables like employment, income, output and price level.

There are main two types—minor cycle—duration of which may have average duration or 40 months and major cycle may consist of 2 to 3 minor cycles.

Regarding durations of minor and major business cycle there various opinions of economists.

(2) Phases of Business Cycle :

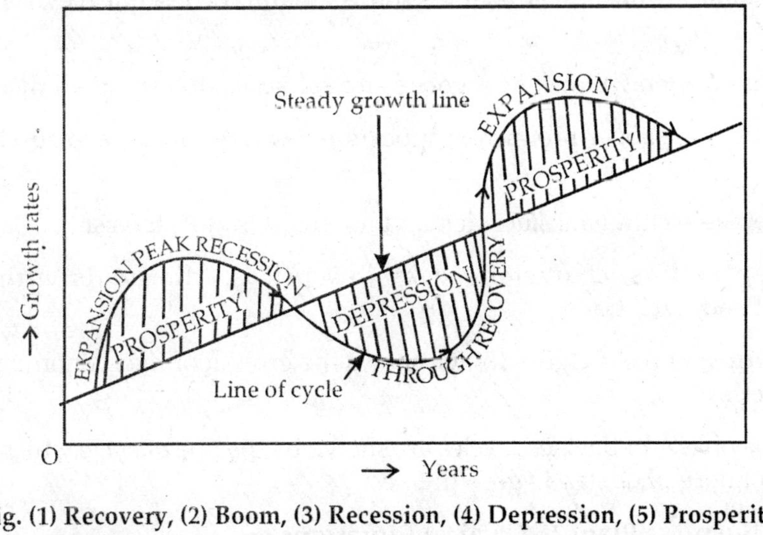

Fig. (1) Recovery, (2) Boom, (3) Recession, (4) Depression, (5) Prosperity.

A business cycle is typically divided into 4 phases as above.

(1) Recovery is the revival of economic activity : This is the phase of revival of demand for goods and services. The economic activity as a whole increases slowly. The upward movement of business activity is slow, production picks up construction activity is revived and there is gradual rise in employment.

(2) Prosperity : During this phase there is rapid cumulative movement of prices, employment, income and production. The prices and general business activity is above normal.

Total output starts growing at a rapid pace due to higher investment and employment.

During this phase there is great incentive for new investment, even though interest rates, wage rates and raw material prices are bus higher.

The peak of prosperity may lead to over-optimism in business psychology resulting in over-full employment of resources and raw material, and therefore, leading to inflationary rise in prices. If it happens, it indicates the end of prosperity phase and advent of recession in the very near future.

This phase of boom has inherent seeds of recession in the form of structural constraints of the economy.

(3) Recession : When the business cycle takes a downward turn from the stage of prosperity, the state of recession is said to have set in. Recession phase of business cycle is characterised by fall in prices, restrictions of bank loans, a sharp increase in interest rate and fall in investment.

Production falls, unemployment increases, and inventory stocks accumulate.

If not controlled in the beginning by timely monetary and fiscal measures by Govt, which can sustain investment at a high level, recession may give way to even a more grave situation, called depression.

(4) Depression : If unchecked, depression is a natural consequence of the recessionary crisis.

In this phase, general demand for goods and services fall faster than their production.

The phenomenon of over-production appears and workers in large so numbers are thrown out of work.

Banks reserves accumulate since demand for credit is at its lowest.

Depression is thus, characterised by low prices, idle funds with banks, mass unemployment and slack trade.

Line of Normal or Steady growth line shows the growth of the economy when there are no business cycles.

The various phases of business cycles are shown by the line of cycle which moves up and down the line of normal or steady growth line.

(3) Adjusting Business Plans to Cyclical Situations

(A) Meaning & Significance : Business cycles, especially the violent fluctuations in economic activities, cause not only harm to business but also misery to human beings by creating unemployment and poverty during the depression period.

Economists and the Government have felt concerned with the consequences of business cycles and suggested various ways and means to control economic fluctuations.

The experience of the Great Depression of 1930s and Keynesian revolution in mid-1930s assigned a big role to the Government in maintaining economic growth and preventing unemployment and business fluctuations. Therefore, the government interventions with the economy all over the world increased in a big way.

The government in free enterprise economics not only entered the production of commodities and services but also adopted a number of fiscal and monetary measures to control and regulate the private economy and prevent violent economic fluctuations.

The Govt. in developing countries like India assumed the role of a key player in economic growth, employment and stabilisation.

While advanced countries faced depression during 1980s with growth rate as low as 2 to 3 per cent developing countries like India faced double-digit inflation, in addition to unemployment and balance of payment crises.

The major stabilization problem in the developing countries is the problem of controlling prices and in the developed countries, preventing growth rates from sliding further down.

The stabilisation issue remains an important today as ever.

Stabilisation : Therefore adjusting business plans to cyclical situations leads to stabilization which broadly means preventing the extremes of ups and downs, particularly depression, in the economy without preventing or obstructing the process of economic growth.

Stabilisation should permit a reasonable degree of flexibility for self-adjusting forces of the economy.

The two most important and widely used economic policies to achieve economic stability are *(i)* fiscal policy and *(ii)* monetary policy.

Fiscal Policy—This is announced by Finance Ministry G.O.I. from time to time. Bank interest rates, Import & Export policies, changes in Excise duties and custom duties and export benefits are worked out and announced by G.O.I. from time to time.

Monetary Policy—Banking operations play a vital role, By expanding and contracting credit creation, changing discount rates, and the ratio between deposits and cash reserves, the banks can change the volume of money supply in economy, and this, contribute to the cyclical phenomenon. This is done by Reserve Bank of India.

(B) Business Cycles *vis-a-vis* Business : Certain phases of a business cycle have favourable affects on business, but on the whole the cyclical fluctuations have an adverse effect on the business operations.

During recovery and prosperity phases, a business firm gains because demand, prices, and profits increase, And, during recession, a business firm loses due to the opposite effects.

But, the cyclical fluctuations need full understanding of the process of change and the business acumen should make appropriate adjustments quite frequently.

Even when the business is passing through the phase of prosperity, the firm starts experiencing sharp rises in prices of raw materials, rental rates, wage costs, discount rates etc. Near the peak of prosperity phase, the firm finds markets highly competitive.

The following phase of recession lands the firm in even greater difficulty. Demand falls and old orders cancelled, prices fall and inventory level goes up significantly during this phase. Banks call back their credits. Many a time, firms have to sell their goods even at a less price so as to meet their obligations.

The element of fixed costs to the firm is also a major contributor to loss, because the variable factors like labour, raw material, fuel etc. can be relatively easily adjusted to changes in demand. A lot of capacity remains a excess during the phase of depression.

Though firms can make necessary adjustments to overcome the ill-effects of a business cycle, this is not always easy and without cost (due to time-lag between occurrence and adjustment).

Attempts are made to reduce the ill-effects of cyclical fluctuations.

The suggested remedies are of two types :

***(i)* The Preventive Measures :** Which tend to eliminate the causes that breed economic crises.

Different business cycles call for separate remedies to remove the basic cause of maladjustments.

The following preventive measures of general nature may be recommended.

(a) The complete equilibrium between demand and supply in business is possible if appropriate information is available at the right time.

(b) Taking due care that *(i)* inventories do not increase or decrease, *(ii)* financial commitments do not exceed financial resources, *(iii)* plant and equipment increase at a steady rate.

(c) The fixed cost per unit of output should not be allowed to go up.

(d) During depression, there is lack of demand, and the firms should be careful in accepting orders, which can be ruinous for the firm.

***(ii)* Curative Measures :** These are important to smoothen cyclical fluctuations. These measures are as follows :

(a) Proper monitoring of costs and their reduction can help in overcoming the problem of recession.

(b) Improvement quality and other characteristics of product can also produce good results.

(c) Sale and Marketing strategies are changed to adjust to new situations.

(*d*) A business firm can formulate and implement a suitable strategy for a new product during the period of depression, in order to benefit at the recovery phase.

(*e*) In order to tide over the difficult time of depression, a firm can utilise a part of its retained earnings.

(C) Business Cycles vs. Unemployment, Money, Interest Rates and Prices

Two types of policies are pursued by a country to combat inflation and recession (*i.e.* inflationary and deflationary tendencies) in the economy.

These are called stabilisation policies, which include (*i*) Monetary Policy and (*ii*) Fiscal Policy.

(*i*) Monetary Policy : It refers to the credit control measures adopted by Reserve Bank of India.

These are Quantitative or general controls and Qualitative or Selective controls.

Quantitative or general controls include Bank rate variations open market operations and varying reserve ratios. They aim at regulating the overall level of credit in the economy through the commercial banks. Bank rate is the minimum lending rate at which the central Bank discounts bills and securities held by commercial banks.

By raising bank interest rate, Central Bank makes borrowing costlier. This reduces the money like money supply in the economy, resulting in the reduction in demand for goods and services and this checks the price rise.

Also Central bank sells securities in the open market and thereby reduces reserves of commercial banks which reduces credit in the market and this reduction in money supply helps in checking price rise. Chances in reserve ratio can help combat inflation

The part of deposits which a commercial bank has statutorily to keep with the Central bank as deposit is called the reserve fund.

In order to reduce the credit by the commercial banks, many a time the central bank increases the percentage of deposits. Increase in reserve ratio reduces the bank advances, thereby reducing demand for goods and services, and checks price rise.

Selective credit controls are used to encourage or discourage specific types of credit for particular purposes.

In order to check the speculative activity in the economy, the Central Bank changes the margin requirements to be charged by commercial banks on these activities.

In recessionary conditions, the central bank should use monetary policies in the opposite direction to control recessionary forces. The Central Bank should lower the bank interest rate, thus, making borrowings by commercial banks cheaper, which in turn lower their lending rates, resulting in greater demand for credit.

This would encourage investment, output, employment, income and demand.

Consequently, prices would start rising.

Similarly, in open market, the Central Bank should buy securities thereby raising money supply in the economy, whose impact would also be an increase in investment, output, employment, income and prices.

The central bank can also use the instrument of reserve ratio to combat recessionary conditions.

Lowering reserve ratio would lower reserves of commercial banks which would encourage greater lending, thus reviving economic activity.

(ii) **Fiscal Policy :** Fiscal Policy refers to the deliberate changing of taxes and governmental spending for the purpose of keeping the actual GNP close to tine potential full employment GNP. If the potential GNP is exceeded it causes inflation, while if the actual GNP falls short of the potential it causes recessionary conditions.

(D) Recovery and Prosperity Phases

(a) When inflation is due to excess purchasing power in relation to the amount of goods and services available in the economy, the basis remedy for controlling inflationary conditions is to drain scar away excess purchasing power. In such a case, fiscal policy should aim at taking rupees out of the income-expenditure stream. As a result of this the aggregate demand will reduce, leading to control of price rise.

This is done in two ways : *(a)* To restrain or reduce government spending and create a surplus budget (where tax revenue exceeds govt. expenditure).

The cutback on govt. expenditures would reduce aggregate demand originating in the public sector.

(b) To increase taxes on business and consumers without increasing Govt. expenditure. Its impact would also be to create surplus budget and dampen the aggregate demand.

However, both the approaches can also be used simultaneously.

(c) **Recession :** To combat recessionary conditions, just the opposite kind of fiscal policy measures need to be adopted.

The Govt. should aim to generate fiscal deficit by either increasing Govt. expenditure, or decreasing taxes or both.

In recession, the economy suffers from unemployment as well as low level of output and aggregate demand.

To give boost to aggregate demand, there is need to pump purchasing power in the economy. By increasing aggregate demand, the unused capacity and unemployed labour can be employed.

4. Trade Cycle and Crashing of Boom

Hawtrey argues that a trade cycle is nothing but small scale replies of an outright money inflation and deflation. The upward phase of a trade cycle—revival prosperity and boom—is brought out by an expansion of money and bank credit and also by increase in the velocity of circulation of money supply. On the other hand, the downward swing of the business cycle is nothing but monetary deflation.

Expansion of bank loans is made possible by the fall in the rate of interest, which induces the merchants to increase their stocks and the banks to grant loans more liberally. The merchants begin to place more orders with manufacturers who, with the object of executing the orders increase production by employing more resources in production. There is greater demand for factors of production all round and consequently either income and employment leading to further increased demand for goods. In course of time a cumulative upward trend is set in motion.

As the volume of business expands and factors of production are rendered fully employed, prices rise further and induce further upward business, expansion resulting in inflationary conditions or boom conditions. However this boom crashes when this banking authorities suspend their policy of credit expansion.

4. *(a)* The sudden crashing of the boom requires an explanation. The banks suspend credit and call on the borrowers to return the loans either because they are afraid that the phase of business expansion has reached the maximum point beyond which they cannot give any more loans or because they are afraid that that phase of business expansion has reached maximum point and hence downward trend may set up in the immediate future. Now sudden suspension of credit facility by the bank comes as a bolt from the blue for till the last; minute the entrepreneurs and merchants have been enjoying the liberal policy of the bank and now contrary to their expectations, they receive sudden notices of immediate call back, of loans advanced to them. To meet the sudden calls from banks they have to dispose of their stocks at any price the can repay bank loans.

5. 'Keynes' Theory of Trade Cycles

Keynes never worked out a pure theory of trade cycles, though he made significant contributions to the trade cycle theory. Keynes states "The trade cycle can be described and analysed in terms of fluctuations of the marginal efficiency of capital relativity to the rate of interest".

According to Keynes the level of income and employment in a capitalist economy depends upon what he calls effective demand comprising total consumption expenditure and investment expenditure changes in *the* total expenditure will imply change in effective demand and will lead to changed in income and employment in the country. Therefore, **in the Keynesian system fluctuations in the total expenditure are responsible for fluctuations in business activity.**

Lengthening of the process of production is brought about by increase in money supply which causes the market rate of interest. Shortening of the process of production is brought about by decline in the supply of bank money which raises the market rate of interest. Therefore, the failure of the banking system to keep the supply of money constant is responsible for business cycles.

The basic weakness of Hayek's approach is its emphasis on the rate of interest and complete neglect of such real factors as technological changes and innovations influencing volume of investment. Further according to Hayek, the sole cause for if change in the volume of investment is the charge in the lower market rate of interest relative to equilibrium rate of interest.

6. Over Saving and Under Consumption Theory

This is one of earliest of business cycles theory and names of Malthus, Max and Hobson are associated with this theory. The main constants of the theory can be stated as follows :

In a free capitalist society, the rich people has large incomes but they are unable to spend all their incomes and hence they save automatically. Thus savings are usually invested in the industry and hence that increase the volume of goods produced. At the same time, the majority of people in the country have law incomes and consequently have low prosperity to consume. Thus consumption is not, increasing correspondingly as a result the market is glatted with goods and depression logically should follow, unless prices fall to a very low level—low enough to allow the goods to be carried off the market. The fundamental idea of under consumption arises.

7. Over Investment Theory

Prof. Von Hayek has developed a theory of business cycles in terms of monetary over investment and consequent over production. According to him there is natural or equilibrium rate of interest at which demand for loanable funds is equal to supply of funds through voluntary saving, at the same time there is also the market, rate of interest based on demand for and the supply of loanable funds in the market. Hayek's thesis is that so-long as the market rate of interest is the same as the natural rate of interest, there will be stability in business condition that any disparity between the two, will lead to business fluctuations. For instance, a fall in the market rate of interest below the natural rate will lead to more investment and thus an upward swing in business activities. On the other hand a rise in market interest over the natural rate of interest will lead to a fall in investment and therefore a downward swing in business activity.

Now the market rate of interest may fall below the natural rate of interest, because of an increase in money supply, in excess of demand for the same. This increase in money is brought about by the banks lending to entrepreneurs through whom it eventually reach the consumers as factor owners. The increased money supply is made available to the entrepreneurs by lowering the rate of interests. There is a spurt of investment activity. The demand for capital goods increases and accordingly their prices goes up. As a direct consequence of this rise of capital goods prices, there is a diversion of resources from the production of consumption goods to the production of capital goods—resulting in the reduction of the supply of consumer goods. But this situation cannot continue for long, for increase in the production of capital goods, the higher prices for them will result in larger income for the sector owners who, in turn can normally be expected to increase their consumption of goes. The demand for consumption goods also rise and their prices will too go up. There will now be competition between capital goods and consumption goods industries for scarce resources. Naturally, the prices of factor services will go up raising the cost of production of capital goods industry. The profit margins of capital goods industry will therefore become unattractive. At the same time the banking system decides to reduce the rate of credit expansion by raising the market rate of interest above the equilibrium rate, causing investment to fall abruptly.

Hayek's basic thesis can now be summarised as follows—After rating stage of prosperity and depression are due to lengthening and shortening process of production brought about by a change in money supply which causes a change in market rate of interest away from the natural rate of interest.

8. Comparison between Monetary Policy and Fiscal Policy

Monetary policy is the deliberate effort by the central bank to influence economic activity by variation in money supply. Credit availability and interest rates consistent with the specific national objectives.

In framing monetary policy for an economy the central bank is guided by price stability exchange stability, full employment and maximum output including a higher growth rate of the economy.

Fiscal policy was first recommended by Keynes after the great Depression of the 1930s as an effective measure to check inflation and subsequently, fiscal policy became a powerful tool for economic development.

Fiscal policy involves desiguing the tax structure, tax revenue and public expenditure in such a way that the objective of full employment is achieved.

Fiscal policy may be used to minimise the effects of business cycles and to maintain stable price levels.

The broad objectives of Fiscal policy are mobilisation of resources economic development and growth, reduction of disparities of income, expansion of employment, price stability and correction of is equilibrium in balance of payments.

Thus, the main constituents of fiscal policy and public expenditure, taxation and public borrowing.

Fiscal policy is an important instrument in the hands of the government to meet its financial requirements and relates to the management of finance by the government.

On the other hand, Monetary policy refers to the policies pressured by the central bank to regulate the growth of money and credit in the economy.

Even though two policies are interdependent and the fiscal policies of the government guides the directions of monetary policy.

PROBABLE QUESTIONS

1. What is meant by the Trade Cycle? Explain the process of boom, the depression and the recovery.
2. Explain the view that the Trade Cycle is purely a monetary phenomenon.
3. Why is controlling trade cycles necessary? Describe the major stabilisation policies.
4. Write the significance of
   (a) Monetary Policy
   (b) Fiscal Policy.
5. What is the significance of IS-LM Model? Describe characteristics of IS & LM curves.
6. Draw graphs and explain the relationships of interest rate, income, output and investment etc.
7. Write about the properties of IS & LM curves.

CHAPTER 4

BUSINESS AND ECONOMIC MODELS

1. Forecasting Methods
2. Regression Analysis and Regression Equation
3. Popular Trend Methods of Forecasts
4. Game Theory
5. Inventory Models

1. FORECASTING METHODS

Various economic forecasting techniques are available; these are both quantitative and qualitative.

The following factors are to be considered for the economic forecasts :

(i) The time into the future that one must forecast.

(ii) The degree of accuracy required.

(iii) The lead time available before arriving at a decision.

(iv) The quality of data and the nature of relationships available.

(v) The benefit expected *vis-a-vis* the associated cost for a particular techniques of forecast.

Forecasting is a system model and both micro and macro system are considered for a forecast various subsystems in system model are inputs output, constraints, conversion methods etc.

2. Macro economic forecasting includes predicting economic aggregates such as inflation, unemployment GDP growth, short term interest rates and trade flows.

(a) Qualitative techniques of economic forecast includes :

- Expert opinion and Delphi method
- Survey

(b) Quantitative techniques of economic forecast includes :

- Time Series Analysis
- Barometric Method
- Trend projection or curve fitting or extra polation techniques are known as point and interval estimates.

Macro economic forecasts are used for a state observation and Micro economic forecasts are used for a company.

Types of economic forcasts are Micro and Macro forecasts and short time and long time forecasts.

Point and interval estimates are extra polating the trend line. This is a quantitative technique and is based on the fundamental assumption that future events will follow an established trend observed in the past.

In this case, data in collected at different points in time and time-series data in used for the purpose.

A typical time series has four major components such as :

A secular trend : Represents the long-term direction and average movement in the time series.

Cyclical fluctuations : Which usually follow variation in the growth of the economy.

Seasonal variation : caused by changes in weather condition and social habits (*i.e.* Durga puja, diwali etc.)

Random (unsystematic) variations : Such as wars, crop failure, natural calamities and changes in taste and preference of consumers.

Above time-series variations are plotted in graph as follows :

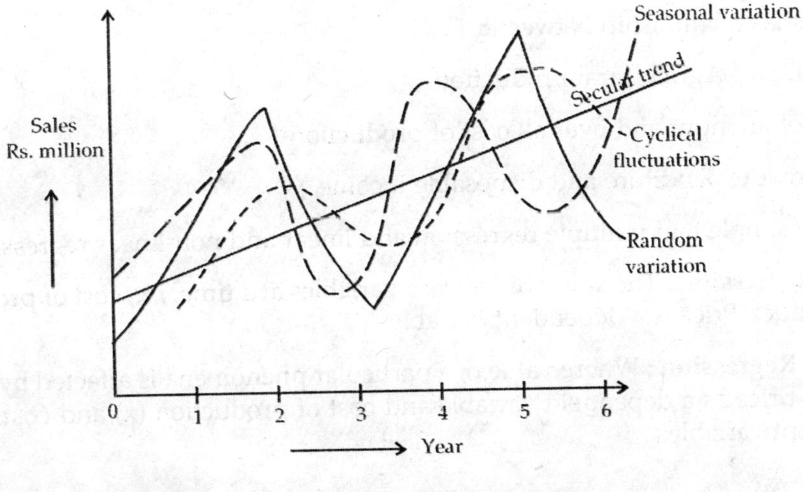

3. ECONOMETRIC MODELS FOR ECONOMIC FORECAST

The statistical methods used in forecasting can be broadly classified into two categories, *i.e.*, time series model (distributed earlier) and econometric models the primary distinguishing characteristics of econometric models is the use of an explicit structural model that attempts to explain the underlying economic relations.

Econometric models have three major advantage for forecasting purposes.

Firstly, econometrics require analysis to define explicit casual relations (*i.e.* cause and effect relation).

Secondly, such models permit analysts to consider the sensitively of the variable to be forecasted. Using estimated values, it is possible to determine which of the variables are most important in determining changes in the variables to be forecasted.

Thirdly, this approached can easily be used for computer simulation. A simulation model basically permits researchers to consider alternative projection based on hypothetical conditions.

4. DELPHI MODEL

Developed by Rand Corporation USA, this techniques draws on the expertise of a panel of specialists and consensus is arrived at. The result is a pooled judgement. Each member from inside and outside is an expert in the field. The co-ordinator provides a series of written questions and receives the feedback. Feedbacks are compiled and a forecast is made. This is expensive and time consuming method.

5. REGRESSION ANALYSIS

It deals with correlation between two variable 'Regress' means moving backwards. Sir Francis Galton used it for the study of heredity. Regression is the measure of average relationship between two or more, variables in terms of the original units of the data.

It establishes relationship between :

—Rainfall and Agricultural production

—Prices of an input and over all cost of production

—Consumer expenditure and disposable income

There are simple and multiple regression and linear and non-linear regression.

Simple Regression : The study of any two variables at a time, *i.e.*, cost of production and price of a product. Price is a dependent variable.

Multiple Regression : Where value of a particular phenomena is affected by multiplicity of factors, *i.e.*, price as a dependent variable and cost of production (x) and cost of advtg (y) are independent variables.

Price is expressed as $z = f(x, y)$.

Regression Equation

Line of regression of y or x is the line which gives the best estimate for the value of y for any specified value of x, in the least square sense. The equation of regression line y on x is given by

$$\frac{y-\bar{y}}{6y} = r\frac{x-\bar{x}}{6x}$$

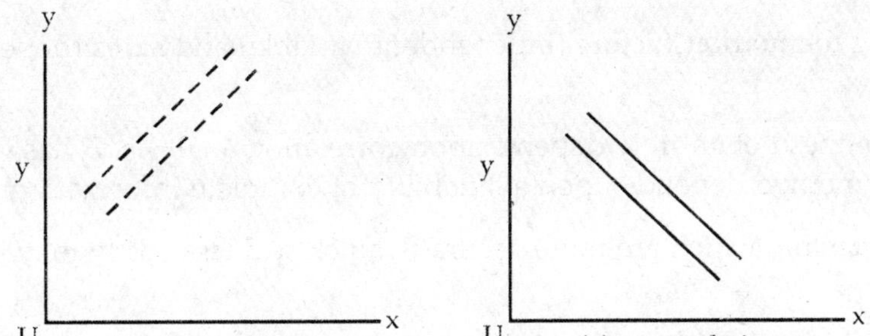

(+)ve correlation x (–)ve correlation x

where r = correlation coefficient $-1 \le r \le +1$.

and when $r = 0$, there is no correlation.

$-1 < r < 0$ —means (–)ve correlation

i.e., $r = -0.9$ show high degree of (–)ve correlation

and $r = -0.1 \rightarrow$ low degree (–)ve correlation.

Similarly $0 < r < +1 \rightarrow$ shows (+)ve correlation

$r = +0.9 \rightarrow$ high (+)ve correlation

$= +0.1 \rightarrow$ low (+)ve correlation

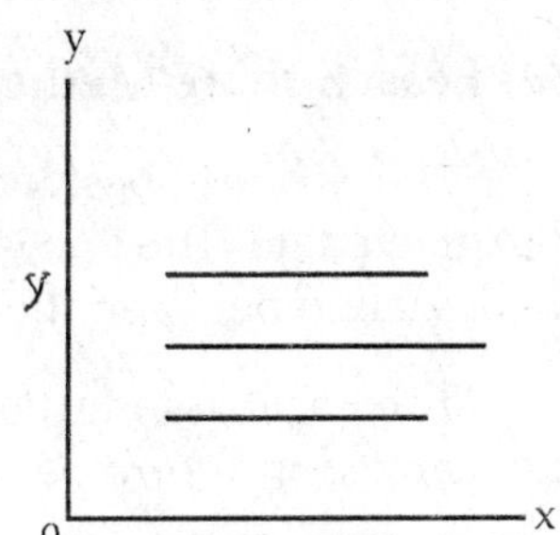

No correlation x

6x, 6y = standard deviation of x and y

$$6x = \sqrt{\frac{\sum x^2}{N} - \bar{x}^2} \text{ and } 6y = \sqrt{\frac{\sum y^2}{N} - \bar{y}^2}$$

$\bar{x}, \bar{y} \rightarrow$ mean values, $N \rightarrow$ nos. of readings.

6. EXPERT OPINION

Various consultancy agencies have entered into the field of sales. The consultancy agencies have specialised experts in the respective field. This includes dealers, trade associations etc. They may conduct market researches and possess ready-made statistical data. Firms may make use of the opinion of such experts. These opinion may be carefully analysed by the company and a sound forecasting in made.

In this method specialised knowledge is used and more accurate forecasts are made.

However, the success of forecast depends on competancy of experts and reliability of data used.

7. ECONOMETRIC MODEL BUILDING

This is a mathematical approach of study and is an ideal way to forecast sales. This method is more useful for marketing durable goods. It is in the form of equation, which represent a, set of relationship among different demand determining market factors.

By analysing the **market factors** (independent variable) and **sales** (dependent variable), sales are forecasts.

This system does not entirely depend upon correlation analysis. It has great scope, best adoption or this method depends upon availability of complete information.

The market factors which are more accurate, quick and less costly may be selected for a sound forecasting.

8. POPULAR TREND METHOD OF FORECAST

Popular trend methods of forecasts are :

(a) Least square Method *(b)* Moving average method

(a) Least Square Method

This is one of best method of determine trend. In most cases, we try to fit a straight line to the given data. The line is known as 'Line of best fit" as we try to minimise the sum of squares of deviation between the observed and the filled values of the data.

The basic assumption here is that the relationship between the various factors remains unchanged in future period also.

If Y is the demand and X the period for a certain item,

then $Y = a + bx$ —linear relationship a and b can be estimated with the help of past information about x and y.

If x and y are the deviation of X and Y (variance) from respective means, the least square estimates of a and b are given by

$$\hat{a} = \frac{\Sigma y}{n} \quad \& \quad \hat{b} = \frac{\Sigma xy}{\Sigma x^2} \qquad n = \text{nos. of observations}$$

The calculation of Σy, Σxy and Σx^2 can be done with the help of given data on Y and X.

(b) The Moving Average Method

This method can be used to determine the trend values for given data without going into complex mathematical calculation. The calculations are based on some predetermined period in weeks, months, years etc. The period depends on the nature or characteristics in the time series and can be determined by plotting the observation on graph paper.

The moving average is an average of some fixed or predetermined number of observation (given by period) which moves through the series by dropping the top item of the previous averaged group and adding the next item in each successive average.

9. REGRESSION ANALYSIS — NUMERICAL PROBLEM

Problem 1 : From the following results, obtain the two regression equations and estimates the yield of crops when the rainfall is 22 cms and the rainfall when the yield is 600 kgs.

	Yield in kgs	Rainfall in cms
Mean	508.4	26.7
SD	36.8	4.6

Correlation coefficient between yield and rainfall is 0.52.

Solution : Let the yield of crops and rainfall be respectively denoted by y and x.

Then $\bar{x} = 26.7$ $\quad \bar{y} = 508.4$ $\quad$ and $\quad r = 0.52$

$6x = 4.6$ $\quad 6y = 36.8$

Equation of line of regression yield (y) on rainfall (x) is

$$\left(\frac{y-\bar{y}}{6y}\right) = r\left(\frac{x-\bar{x}}{6x}\right) \quad \text{or} \quad \frac{y-508.4}{36.8} = 0.52\left(\frac{x-26.7}{4.6}\right)$$

or $$y - 508.4 = \frac{36.8 \times 0.52}{4.6}(x-26.7) = 4.16(x-26.7)$$

$$= 41.6x - 111.072$$

or $$y = 4.16x + 508.4 - 111.072 = 4.16x + 397.328$$

The most likely yield of crop (y) when the rainfall x = 22 cms is given by

$$y = 4.16 \times 22 + 397.328 = 91.520 + 397.328 = 488.85 \text{ kgs}$$

Equation of the line of regression x on y is :

$$\left(\frac{x-\bar{x}}{6x}\right) = r\left(\frac{y-\bar{y}}{6y}\right) \quad \text{or} \quad \frac{x-26.7}{4.6} = 0.52\frac{y-508.4}{36.8}$$

or $$x - 26.7 = \frac{4.6 \times 0.52}{36.8}(y-508.4) = 0.065(y-508.4)$$

or $x - 26.7 = 0.065\,y - 33.046$

or $x = 0.065y + 26.7 - 33.046 = 0.065\,y - 6.346$

The most likely estimate of rainfall (x) corresponding to yield Y = 600 is given by

$x = 0.065 \times 600 - 6.346 = 39.00 - 6.346 =$ **32.654 cms.**

Problem 2 : The following is the demand of room coolers in five towns during the year 2005. Fit a regression line of y and x and estimate the demand of coolers for a city of population 50 lacs.

Town	A	B	C	D	E	
Population (lacs) (x)	4	6	7	10	13	$\bar{x} = 8 = \frac{\sum x}{n}$
Demand for room coolers (y)	40	60	50	70	90	$\bar{y} = 62 = \frac{\sum y}{n}$

Soln. : Find out 'r' correlation coeff. from the following equation

$$r = \frac{\sum xy - \frac{(\sum x . \sum y)}{n}}{n\,\partial x \partial y}$$

here $n = 5$

$$\text{and} \quad \partial x = \sqrt{\frac{\sum x^2}{n} - \left(\frac{\sum x}{n}\right)^2} \quad \text{and} \quad \partial y = \sqrt{\frac{\sum y^2}{n} - \left(\frac{\sum y}{n}\right)^2}$$

$\partial x = 3.16$ and $\partial y = 17.20$, $r = 0.957$

The regression equation of y on x is

$$y - \bar{y} = r\frac{\partial x}{\partial y}(x - \bar{x}) = 0.957 \times \frac{17.20}{3.16}(x - \bar{x})$$

or $y - 62 = 5.22(x - 8)$ or $y = 62 + 5.22(x - 8)$

For x = 50 lacs, the estimated demand for coolers will be $y = 62 + 5.22(50 - 8)$

= 281.211 or 282 coolers **Ans.**

10. EXPONENTIAL SMOOTHING METHOD (FOR DEMAND FORECAST)

This method eliminates the necessity of keeping extensive records of historical data (like involving average method) and also tries to screen out the irregularities in the demand pattern.

The method allows for trend and takes into considerations the short term fluctuation in the determination of the forecast.

Exponential smoothing is a weightage average of the observations and here the most recent observation is assigned the highest weightage and it decreases in geometric progression as we move towards the older observations.

Exponential smoothing method is considered to be more realistic than moving average method where past observations carry just as much weight as the latest.

The fundamental concept of exponential smoothing method is that :

New estimate = Old estimate of latest actual demand + ∂ (latest actual demand – old estimate of latest actual demand)

$$Ft = \partial D_t + (1 - \partial)F_{t-1} = F_{t-1} + \partial e_t$$

where, F_t = Forecast at time t

D_t = Actual demand at time t

F_{t-1} = Forecast at time (t – 1)

∂ = Smoothing Coefficient (value between 0 and 1)

$e_t = (D_t - F_{t-1})$

Procedure :

1. Find error by subtracting the recent average from the latest incoming observation.
2. Multiply error e_t by ∂. This is the correction to be applied to the past average.
3. Add correction (∂e_t) to the past average, F_{t-1}. This gives new average F_t as the forecast for the next period.
4. Value of ∂ lies between 0 & 1.

Problem 1 : Exponential smoothing method – Numerical Problem. Forecast the demand for the following series by exponential smoothing method.

Period	1	2	3	4	5	6	7	8	9	10	11	12
Actual demand	10	12	8	11	9	10	15	14	16	15	14	15

Consider $\partial = 0.1$ and then compare the forecasts for $\partial = 0.7$

Solution :

Period	*Actual demand*	$\partial = 0.1$			$\partial = 0.7$			*Remarks*
		F_{t-1}	F_t	e_t	F_{t-1}	F_t	e_t	
0			10			10		
1	10	10	10	0.00	10.00	10	0.00	
2	12	10	10.20	2	10.00	11.40	2.00	$F_t = F_{t-1} + \partial e_t$
3	8	10.20	9.98	–2.20	11.40	9.02	–3.40	& $e_t = D_t - F_{t-1}$
4	11	9.98	10.08	1.02	9.02	10.41	1.98	
5	9	10.08	9.97	–1.08	10.41	9.42	–1.41	
6	10	9.97	9.97	0.03	9.42	9.83	0.58	
7	15	9.97	10.47	5.03	9.83	13.45	5.17	
8	14	10.47	10.82	3.53	13.45	13.84	0.55	
9	16	10.82	11.34	5.18	13.84	15.35	2.16	
10	15	11.34	11.71	3.66	15.35	15.11	–0.35	
11	14	11.71	11.94	2.29	15.11	14.33	–1.11	
12	15	11.94	12.25	3.06	14.33	14.80	0.67	

Now we calculate MDA = $\frac{\Sigma|e_t|}{12}$ = 2.42 for ∂ = 0.1 and 1.62 for ∂ = 0.7.

Since MDA for ∂ = 0.7 is lesser than MDA for ∂ = 0.1, ∂ = 0.7 gives better forecast.

11. GAME THEORY

(1) Game theory and its importance in business.

(2) Construction of game theory models.

(3) Solution of two person zero sum games.

(4) Game theory & limitation.

(5) 2-Person, Non-zero sum games.

(1) Game Theory and its Importance

The game theory is a technique which introduces a table known as 'Pay offs Matrix". Showing the expected values for various out comes to determine the best way to play against the opponent. The object is not to find the best answer, but to minimise the maximum (known as minimax) risk or reduce your chance of losing.

Suppose a manufacture is trying to decide whether it is worth while for him to cut the price of him product. The answer will depend on what is competitor will do.

There are 4 possible choices :

1. He cuts his price, the competitor keeps his price contract.

2. He cuts the price, the competitor also cuts the price.

3. He helps him price constant, the competitor cuts the price.

4. He keep his price constant the opponent keeps his price constant.

Thus the manufacturer has to analyse all these outcomes with the help of game theory which shows the profitability under each situation from which the manufacturer can make a final choice.

In the game theory, the decision makers are known as 'players', the choices are called strategies and the preferences of the decision makers called "pay offs".

If the sum of pay off is zero, the same is said to be zero sum, but where the sum of pay offs is not zero, there are called "non-zero-sum game".

The use of 'pay of matrix' for expressing the problem and evaluating various decision can have important implication for business or industries but to make theory really practicable, the analyses should have lot of imagination and know new development of the science.

Thus, the game theory is the mathematical theory based on which strategy steps are taken to win a game played in a conflicting situation to maximise the benefits or to minimise the loss or damage.

A game is an activity between two opposing person or parties.

The activity is governed by set of rules and is carried out by each party.

Each party initiates series of steps base of on its respective strategy and tries to convert the situation to be of a nature which ensures success to itself.

Characteristics of Games

(i) The situation is competitive.

(ii) There are a finite number of competitors or players.

(iii) Each competitor has a finite number of stategies.

(iv) The game is said to be played when both competitors initiate action based on their chosen strategies.

(v) Every game leads to an out come.

(vi) Every outcome has stakes *i.e.* payment given and taken.

Assumption in a Game

(i) The existence of conflict.

(ii) The existence of a set of rules.

(iii) A desire to dominate the other.

(iv) Parties act in good faith employing fairmeans.

(v) Rationate and intelligent moves are planned and are made.

(vi) No international gap or communication gap exists between parties.

(vii) Decisions once taken are not reverted.

(viii) Simultaneous application of strategies by both parties.

(ix) Pay-off is paid before the game.

Following terms are used :

Strategy : It is plan of action executed by each player to win the game.

Strategies is of two types pure strategy and mixed strategy.

Pure Strategy : This is a predetermined plan of action based on which gems are played and which does not change during the game.

Mixed Strategy : This is a case when the strategy is changed while the game is in progress.

Players : Competitors who play the game.

Pay-off : Outcome of the game is known as pay-off.

Pay-off Matrix : This is a table showing the outcome of the game when different strategies are adopted.

Value of Game : This is the maximum guaranteed gain to player. A (maximising player) if both players use their best strategies.

Fair Game : Game is said to be fair when the value of the game is zero.

Solution of a Game : When the best strategies of both players are found and the value of the game is determined, we say that the game is solved.

Maximum : Maximum value of the minimum pay-off in each row.

Minimum : Minimum value of the maximum pay-off in each column.

Saddle Point : This is the value of elements 'K' in a pay-off matrix, which is the minimum of its row as well as the maximum of its column, *i.e.* minimum = maximum.

Game with Saddle Point (pure strategy games) : A game in which the maximum for A = minimax for B. This is called a game with a saddle point. These are also called pure strategy games. IT there are more than one saddle point, then there will be more than one solution.

Value of Game : Pay-off at saddle point is called the value of the game (V). If maximum = V, then minimax = $\overline{V}$, V and $\overline{V}$ are called upper and lower values.

Fair Game : A game is said to be fair when $V = \overline{V} = 0$.

Strictly Determinable Game : A game is said to be strictly determinable if $|V| = |\overline{V}|$.

2. Construction of Game Theory Model

(a) Consider the following matrix

A \ B	Y_1	Y_2	Y_3	Row minimum
X_1	1	2	3	1
X_2	4	5	6	4
Column maximum	4	5	6	

X_1 and X_2 are strategies used by player A, Y_1, Y_2 and Y_3 are strategies used by opponent player B.

Maximin = 4 (maximum of row minimum)

Minimax = 4 (Minimum of column maximum)

∴ Maximin = Minimax

Hence, the above pay-off matrix is called game with a saddle point. Here the saddle point is 4, at element (2,1) in the pay-off matrix *i.e.* (X_2, Y_1).

(b) Consider the following table :

A \ B	Y_1	Y_2	Y_3	Y_4	Row minimum
X_1	4	2	4	3	2
X_2	2	–4	2	0	–4
X_3	3	–6	4	2	–6
X_4	4	–2	2	1	–2
Column maximum =	4	2	4	3	

Maximin = Maximum of row minimum = 2

Minimax = Minimum of column maximum = 2

∴ Maximin = Minimax = 2

Hence, the above pay-off matrix is called same with multiple solutions as saddle points at elements (1, 2), (2, 1), (2, 3), (3, 4) and (4, 3).

Problem 3 : You are setting a plant to produce a new product. You have five alternative methods of mfg. from which selection may be done. But profit depends on one of the experimental automatic packing M/C which will be successful. There is 50-50 chances that either one or the other will be successful but definitely not both. Depending on which one is successful, prepare the matrix for the five methods.

The main problem is that you have to select and start installing the method of manufacture before you know which packing M/C will work about.

Select the suitable method to assure the maximum profit.

Production Method	*Profit/Unit Rs.*		*Row Minimum*
	Packing M/C A	*Packing M/C B*	*Z*
1	1.00	1.30	1.00
2	2.40	0.80	0.80
3	1.80	1.40	1.40
4	1.60	1.20	1.20
5	2.20	1.10	1.10
Coln. maximum =	2.40	1.40 Rs.	

Solution : Maximin = Maximum of Row minimum = 1.40

& Minimax = Minimum of column maximum = 1.40

∴ Maximin = Minimax

Hence, above pay-off matrix is a game with a saddle point at element (3, 2) equal to Rs. 1.40 for production Method 3 and packing M/C B.

∴ Select, packing M/C B for production Method 3. **Ans.**

(3) Two Persons Zero Sum Games

Consider the following model

Player A	Player B	
	Strategy Y_1	Strategy Y_2
Strategy X_1	A wins 3 Points	A wins 4 Points
Strategy X_2	B wins 2 Points	B wins 3 Points

Many management situation are depicted by two-person games. In the above table A and B, are competitors of equal intelligence and ability.

Each has a choice of 2 strategies. Each known the outcome of a combination of their strategies.

From the table, we notice that A is placed in an advantageous position, because he always gets one point more than B what ever be the strategy employed by B. So long as A maintains strategies X_1. Hence, strategy of A is fixed *i.e.* X_1. Throughout the game.B knows his disadvantage. His objective in this game is to minimise his loss.

To minimise his loss, he must choose strategy Y_1.

Thus, there is no uncertainty about the respective strategies, taken by both sides. In each game. A wins by 3 points and B loses by 3 points.

If B has played strategy Y_2, he would have lost 4 points, which he would not want to do.

Point 3 in the saddle point.

Gain of A = +3

Gain of B = –3

Sum = 0

Since, the sum of gains of A and B equals Zero, this is called two persons zero sum game.

The above table is written in a conventional from as follows. This is also called rectangular game.

This matrix is called pay-off matrix or pay out matrix.

A \ B	Y_1	Y_2
X_1	③	4
X_2	2	3

In the conventional matrix form, the outcome of game, is term of pay-offs of one player (*viz.* A) is depicted. For example, row with positive sign is indicative of the gain of A and second row with negative sign, indicates of the loss of A.

By implication, A's loss = B's gain

(a) **Two-Person Zero Sum Game :** A game with two players, where the gain of one player equals the loss to the other to known as a two person zero sum game. It is also called a rectangular game because their pay off matrix is in the rectangular form.

Characteristics are :

(1) Only two players participate in the game.

(2) Each player has finite number of strategies to use.

(3) Each specific strategy results in a pay-off.

(4) Total pay off to the two players at the end of each lay is zero.

Notes :

Saddle point : A saddle point is a position in the pay-off matrix where the maximum of row minimum coicides with minimum of column maxima.

The pay off at the saddle point is called the value of the game.

If maximumvalue is $\underline{Y}$ the minimax value is $\bar{Y}$ and the value of game is Y.

Game is fair : A gain is said to be fair if maximin value = minimax value= 0.

i.e. if $\bar{Y} = \underline{Y} = 0$.

Game is strictly determinable : A game is strictly determinable, if maximin value = minimax value ≠ 0.

$$\underline{Y} = Y = \bar{Y}$$

Problem 4 : Solve the game where pay off matrix is given below.

Player B

Player A

A_1	B_1	B_2	B_3
A_2	1	3	1
A_3	0	4	–3
	1	5	–1

Solution :

Row Min

1

–4

–1

Coln. Max. 1 5 1

Maximin = 1 = Minimax = 1.

Saddle point exists : The value of the game is the saddle point which is 1.

The optional strategy is the position of Saddle point and is given by (A_1, B_1), (A_1, B_3) and (A_3, B_1) → multiple saddle points.

Problem 5 : For what value of the game with the following matrix is strictly determinable?

$$\text{Player A} \quad \begin{array}{c|ccc|} & \multicolumn{3}{c}{\text{Player B}} \\ A_1 & B_1 & B_2 & B_3 \\ A_2 & \lambda & 6 & 2 \\ A_3 & -1 & \lambda & -7 \\ & -2 & 4 & \lambda \end{array}$$

Solution : Ignoring value of λ, pay off matrix is given by

$$\begin{array}{|ccc|c} & & & \text{Row minimum} \\ \lambda & 6 & 2 & 2 \\ -1 & \lambda & -7 & -7 \\ -2 & 4 & \lambda & -2 \\ \hline \text{Col. maximum} \; -1 & 6 & 2 & \end{array}$$

Since the game is strictly determinable maximin = minimax ≠ 0 $\underline{Y} = Y = \overline{Y}$

Maximin = 2 = $\underline{Y}$

Minimax = –1 = $\overline{Y}$

∴ –1 > l ≤ 2. **Ans.**

Problem 6 : Determine which of the following two person zero sum games are strictly determinable and fair. Given the optimum strategy for each and player in the case of strictly determinable games.

(a) Player B

$$\text{Player A} \quad \begin{array}{c} \\ A_1 \\ A_2 \end{array} \begin{array}{c} \begin{array}{cc} B_1 & B_2 \end{array} \\ \begin{bmatrix} -5 & 2 \\ -7 & -4 \end{bmatrix} \end{array}$$

(b) Player B

$$\text{Player A} \quad \begin{array}{c} \\ A_1 \\ A_2 \end{array} \begin{array}{c} \begin{array}{cc} B_1 & B_2 \end{array} \\ \begin{bmatrix} 1 & 1 \\ 4 & -3 \end{bmatrix} \end{array}$$

(minimax) = $\underline{\underline{Y}}$ = Max (–5, –7) = –5

(maximin) = Y = Min (–5, 2) = –5

Solution : Player B

$$\text{Player A} \quad \begin{array}{c} \\ A_1 \\ A_2 \end{array} \begin{array}{c} \begin{array}{cc} B_1 & B_2 \end{array} \\ \begin{bmatrix} -5 & 2 \\ -7 & -4 \end{bmatrix} \end{array} \begin{array}{c} \text{Row Min} \\ -5 \\ -7 \end{array}$$

Coln. Maximum –5 2

∴ Maximin = –5 and Minimax = –5

∴ Maximin = Minimax = –5

Hence the value of the game is –5. The optimal strategy is the position of saddle point given by (A_1, B_1) or element (1, 1).

The game is not fair since $Y = \bar{Y} \neq 0$.

(b) Player B

$$\begin{array}{lc} & \begin{array}{ccc} B_1 & B_2 & \text{Row Min} \end{array} \\ \text{Player A} \begin{array}{c} A_1 \\ A_2 \end{array} & \begin{bmatrix} 1 & 1 \\ 4 & -3 \end{bmatrix} \begin{array}{c} 1 \\ -3 \end{array} \end{array}$$

Col. Maximum 4 1

and Maximin = 1.

Minimax = 1.

Since $\underline{Y} = \bar{Y} = 1 \neq 0$, the game is strictly determinable, the value of game is 1. The optimal strategy is (B_1, A_1), (B_2, A_1) in element (1, 1) and (1, 2).

Problem 7 : Solve the game where pay off matrix is given below

$$\begin{vmatrix} -2 & 0 & 0 & 5 & 3 \\ 3 & 2 & 1 & 2 & 2 \\ -4 & -3 & 0 & -2 & 6 \\ 5 & 3 & -4 & 2 & -6 \end{vmatrix} \quad \begin{array}{c} \text{Row Minimum} \\ -2 \\ 1 \\ -4 \\ -6 \end{array}$$

Col. Maximum 3 3 1 5 6

Maximin = 1 & Mini – Max = 1

∴ Maximin = Minimax

value of game is 1 and there is one saddle point at element (2, 3) which is the optimal strategy.

Problem 8 : Determine which the following two person Zero-sum games are strictly determinable and fair. Give optimum strategy for each player in the case of strictly determinable games.

(a) $\begin{bmatrix} -5 & 2 \\ -7 & -4 \end{bmatrix}$ *(b)* $\begin{bmatrix} 0 & 2 \\ -1 & 4 \end{bmatrix}$ *(c)* $\begin{bmatrix} 5 & 0 \\ 0 & 2 \end{bmatrix}$ *(d)* $\begin{bmatrix} 1 & 1 \\ 4 & -3 \end{bmatrix}$

Problem 9 : Consider the game G with the following pay-off.

$$\begin{array}{cc} & \text{Player B} \\ \text{Player A} & \begin{bmatrix} 2 & 6 \\ -2 & \mu \end{bmatrix} \end{array}$$

(a) Show that G is strictly determined whatever be the value of μ.

(b) Determine the value of G strategies (1, 1) (2, 2) elements.

4. GAME THEORY

Game theory deals with the process of competitive interaction. Game theory may be defined as a body of knowledge that deals with making decisions when two or more intelligent and rational opponents are involved under condition of conflicts and competition."

Instead of making inferences from the past behaviour of the opponent "the approach of game theory is to seek to determine a "rival's most profitable counter strategy to ones own "best" moves and to formulate the appropriate determine measures.

For example, if two firms are locked up in a war to maintain their market share, then a price cut by the first firm will invite reaction from the second firm in the nature of a price-cut. This well, intern, affect the sales and profits of the first firm which will agains have to develop a counter-strategy to meet the challenge from the second firm.

The game, will thus go on. Game theory helps in determining the "best" course of action for a firm in view of the expected counter moves from the competitors. The competition in the game are called players.

4. *(a)* Limitations of Game Theory

The important limitations are :

1. The assumption that the players have the knowledge about their own pay-off and pay-off of others is unrealistic. He can make only make a guess of his own and his rivals' strategies.
2. As the number of players increases in the game, the analysis of gaming strategies become increasingly complex and difficult. For many players in an oligopoly situation game theory may not be helpful.
3. The assumption of maximum and minimax show that the players are risk averse and have complete knowledge or the strategies. There do not seem practical.

   However, **inspite of its limitation game theory provides insight into the operations of oligopoly markets.**

   Game theory gives insight into several less-known aspects which arise in situation of conflicting interests. For example, it describes and explains the phenomena of bargaining and coalition formation.

Game Theory Application

(1) Game theory works well in case of management and trade union agreements in which collective bargaining aspect is important.

(2) Game theory is also applicable for coalition of political parties such as in 2003-2004 UPA & left front coalition in the centre.

5. THE 2-PERSON, NON-ZERO SUM (OR NON CONSTANT SUM) GAMES

Unlike Zero-sum games where are firm's loss is necessarily the other firm's gain the *vice versa*, the non-zero-sum games refer to a situation where there exists a jointly preferred outcome the existence of a jointly preferred outcome means that both players may be able to increase their pay-offs through some form of co-operation or agreement concerning the actions to be chosen.

Non-constant-sum games are divided into

(i) Co-operative games *(ii)* Non-cooperative game

(i) **Co-operative games :** In this, the players are assumed to be rational to realise that it is mutually advantageous to cooperate on any and every action which is likely to benefit at least one of the players without affecting the other adversely.

(ii) **Non-cooperative game :** The most popular form of a non-cooperative game is known as the prisoner's dilemma. In this game there is no communication between the participants and no way to reach or enforce agreements. Due to lack to communication and trust they are in a worse off situation than they could have been.

6. GAME THEORY—PRISONERS' DILEMMA AND COALITION POLITICS

Game Theory attempts to capture human behaviour empirically in strategic situations, in which an individual's success in making choices depends on the choices of others.

The most common, example cited in game theory relates to the "Prisoners' Dilemma".

Suppose, the police arrest two people who have committed armed robbery together. But there is not enough evidence to book them.

However, there is enough evidence to send them jail for auto theft for two years.

The chief inspector makes the following offer to each prisoner separately.

(a) If one prisoner confesses to the robbery, he goes scot free but the other prisoner gets ten years jail.

(b) If both confess to robbery, they get five years each.

(c) If neither confesses, then each gets only two years jail just for auto theft.

This is seen as optimal solution and the least damaging for both.

In coalition politics the political parties would ideally look for an optimal solution based on the game theory.

In 2009 Lok Sabha election, the Congress party and its allies in Bihar (*i.e.* Lalu-Pasowan combine) and UP (*i.e.* Mulayam Singh Yadav's Samajbadi Party are caught in a situation which is taken to the prisoner's dilemma.

Congress Party's going alone in Bihar created a three cornered contest, *i.e.* congress, Lalu Pasawan and Nitish BJP & in UP, Congress, SP and Mayawati also a three cornered contest.

The congress's ego as a national party and its near-term goal of retaining power at the centre have made it go alone.

Intuitively, politicians may be very good at game theory but there are instances when they have misread the situations.

5. INVENTORY MANAGEMENT

1. Norms for Inventory

The norms for inventory could be set by either the top management or the materials management department. The top management usually sets monetary limits for investment in inventories. That materials department then has to allocate this investment to the various items and ensure the smooth operation of the company. It would be worthwhile if the inventory norms (limits) in consulation with the materials department. The norms thus evolved should specific and quantified. The achievement of the targets set is the responsibility of the materials department.

In the setting up of the norms, the involvement of persons who are directly responsible for maintain is very desirable. Other departments involved in setting the norms are finance, production, marketing and materials control. The norms of inventory should be converted to specifically spell out parameters like the number of stockouts permitted, the sales to inventory ratio and inventory to consumption ratio.

(a) **Inventory Decisions :** There are two basic inventory decisions a manager must take in order to effectively manage inventories. These are :

(1) Quantity of an item should be ordered when the inventory is replenished (2) when should the inventory be replenished?

For (1) → Use 6 types EOQ models described later.

For (2) → Order Point or Re-order levels = ROL = Safety stock + Reserve Stock + Buffer Stock.

= Average Consumption Rate × Average Lead time

= dP. /week × Nos. of weeks

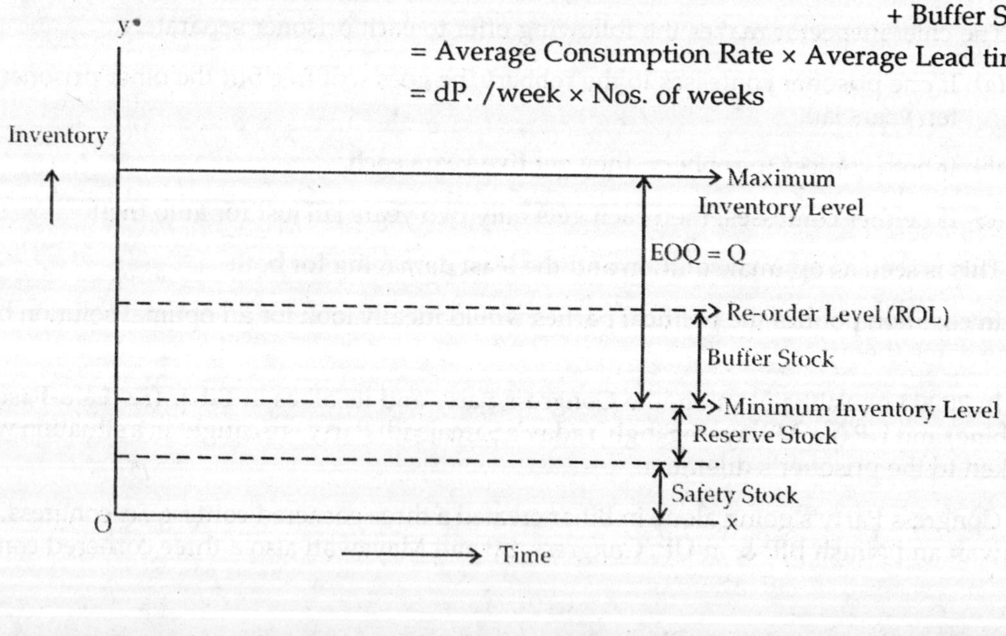

2. Cost of Ordering

Every time an order is placed for stock replenishment certain costs are involved, and, for most practical purposes it can be assumed that the cost per order is constant. The ordering cost co- may vary, dependent upon the type of items, raw material like steel against production components like casting. However it is assumed that an estimate co can be obtained for a given range of items. The cost of ordering co includes :

(i) Paper work cost, typing and despatching an order.

(ii) Follow-up cost the follow up required to ensure timely supplies—includes the travel cost for purchase follow up, telephone, tedex and postal bills.

(iii) Costs Involved in receiving the order, inspection, checking and handling of the stores.

(iv) Any set up cost of machines if charged by the supplier, either directly indicated in quotations or assessed through quotations for various quantities.

(v) The salaries and wages to the purchase department. This is relevant for consideration if the purchasing function is carried out at the same level with the existing staff. If the level of purchasing activity decreases significantly, obviously a proportional amount of personnel will be transferred to other departments.

If the level of purchasing increases, the extra load will be tackled by paying overtime to the existing staff or by recruiting new personnel. The additional cost can be viewed as the marginal cost of orders. The ordering cost in a typical Indian firm is around Rs. 100 per order but experience shows that this cost varies considerably depending on the efficiency of the purchase department.

3. Cost of Inventory Carrying

The cost Co is measured as a percentage of the unit cost of the item. This measure therefore gives a basis for estimating what is actually costs a firm to carry stocks. This cost include *(i)* interest in capital *(ii)* insurance and tax charges, *(iii)* storage cost—any labour, excluding handling of receipts of new orders—the cost of provision of storage area and facilities like bins, racks etc. *(iv)* allowance for detoriation or spoilage, *(v)* salaries to stores staff and *(vi)* Obsolence. The inventory carrying cost varies and in a typical Indian industry is about 30 percent A major portion of this is accounted for by interest on capital which depends on the fiscal policies of the government. A few firms differentiate the cost as fixed and variable cost. in the analysis of and use of mathematical formula, only the variable costs of ordering should be considered are fixed cost will be constant irrespective of the number of orders placed or inventory carried.

Static : One time supply or demand.

Dynamic : Continuous and repetitive supply or demand.

Certain : Quantity is known for supply or demand.

Risk : Quantity of supply/demand known over a probable range of value.

Uncertain : Qnty of supply/demand not known.

4. Understocking Cost or Overstocking Cost

Understocking cost, Ku, is the cost incurred when an item is out of stock. It includes the cost of lost production during the period of stock out and the extra cost per unit which might have to be paid for an emergency purchase.

Overstocking cost is the cost (Ko) for a specific period of time. The time varies in different contents—it could be the lead time of procurement or the entire life time of a machine. In the case of one time purchases overstocking cost would be : Purchase Price – Scrap price.

5. Economic Order Quantity (ECQ)

Inventories are built to act as a cushion between supply and demand. The supply could be a one time supply (static) or a continuous repetative one (dynamic). The demand on its part could be totally known (certain), be known over a range of probable values (risks) or be totally unknown (uncertain). Thus six different inventory models can be perceived.

Model		*EOQ*	*Supply*	*Demand*
EOQ—I	1.	I	Static	Certain—order on EOQ quantity.
	2.		Static	Risk (Probabilistic)—Consider costs of overstocking & understocking
	3		Static	Uncertain (Not Known)—is used under a "uncertainty purchase system"
EOQ—II	4.	II	Dynamic	Certain—Consider cost of overstocking and Understocking
EOQ—III	5.	III	Dynamic	Risk—Consider costs of overstocking and understocking & ICC & OC.
	6.		Dynamic	Uncertain—does not exists.

Out of those six possible inventory models, the static certain model is very obvious. The supply is one time and the quantity is known. Hence allowing for the, lead time, the quantity can be ordered so that it is received when needed. The dynamic uncertain model do not exist for the very reason that a situation which is dynamic and repetitive case to be uncertain after a certain lapse of time. The static uncertain modal is based on regret matrix which is discussed in detail in the chapter on purchasing under uncertainty. The three remaining models, then are static risk, dynamic certain and dynamic risk.

The cost relevant for consideration in these three models are :

Table

Inventory	*Understocking Cost*	*Overstocking Cost*	*Inventory Carrying Cost*	*Ordering Cost*
Static-Risk	✓	✓	—	—
Dynamic Certain	—	—	✓	✓
Dynamic Risk	✓	✓	✓	✓

(a) **Static Risk Model :** This model is useful for project purchases and purchase of capital and insurance spares. Examples of this category are publication of calenders, dairies, year books, buying capital spares etc. which are one time decision, but the quantities can be estimated in the probability values. The cost relevant for consideration are the understocking and overstocking. It is pointless to consider the supply side cost as the purchase is not repetitive. The optimal stocking policy in this situation is to stock upto level "S"—S denotes service level—where F(S) is the cumulative probability of demand upto "S" is equal to $\frac{K_u}{K_u + K_o}$.

The EOQ for this model thus is $\frac{K_u}{K_u + K_o}$. ...(1)

(b) **Dynamic Certain (EOQ) Model :** The Cost relevant for consideration in this model are cost of ordering and inventory carrying. Since the demand is certain the understocking and overstocking cost, becomes irrevalent for consideration. The EOQ is equal to $\sqrt{\frac{2MCo}{SCc}}$

where EOQ = $\sqrt{\frac{2MCo}{SCc}}$.

M = Annual Demand of the item

S = Unit Cost of the item

Co = Ordering Cost

Cc = Carrying Cost

(c) **Cost Sensetivity Analysis :** The Economic order quantity is given by $\sqrt{\frac{2MCo}{SCc}}$ where values of Co & Cc are estimated as averages for all the items the stores. The averages are used for convenience in designing an inventory model. It can be proved that these estimates are useful for practical consideration. This is done by carrying out a cost sensitivity analysis.

(d) **Derivation of EOQ :** Let the annual demand be "M" (determinastic). Let Co be the cost of ordering and Cc the inventory carrying cost and S\unit price of an item.

The total ordering cost when the orders placed in quantity Q = $\frac{M}{Q}$Co.

Inventory Carrying Cost is = $\frac{Q}{2}$S.Cc

The total annual cost is = $\frac{M}{Q}$Co + $\frac{Q}{2}$S.Cc.

For Cost be minimum.

$$\frac{dC}{dO} = O = \frac{-M}{Q^2}.CO + \frac{1}{2}SCc$$

$$\text{or,} \qquad \frac{M}{Q^2}CO = \frac{1}{2}S.Cc.$$

$$Q^2 = \frac{2MCo}{SCc}$$

$$\text{or,} \qquad Q(\text{Optimum}) = EOQ = \sqrt{\frac{2MCo}{SCc}}$$

The graphical representation of EOQ is shown in Fig.

Numericals—Inventory Models

Problem 1 : For a leading biscuit manufacturing organisation the annual demand for corrugated boxes is 20,000 of the cost of placing an order is Rs 100 and the inventory carrying cost is 20 percent. The price per box is Rs 10.

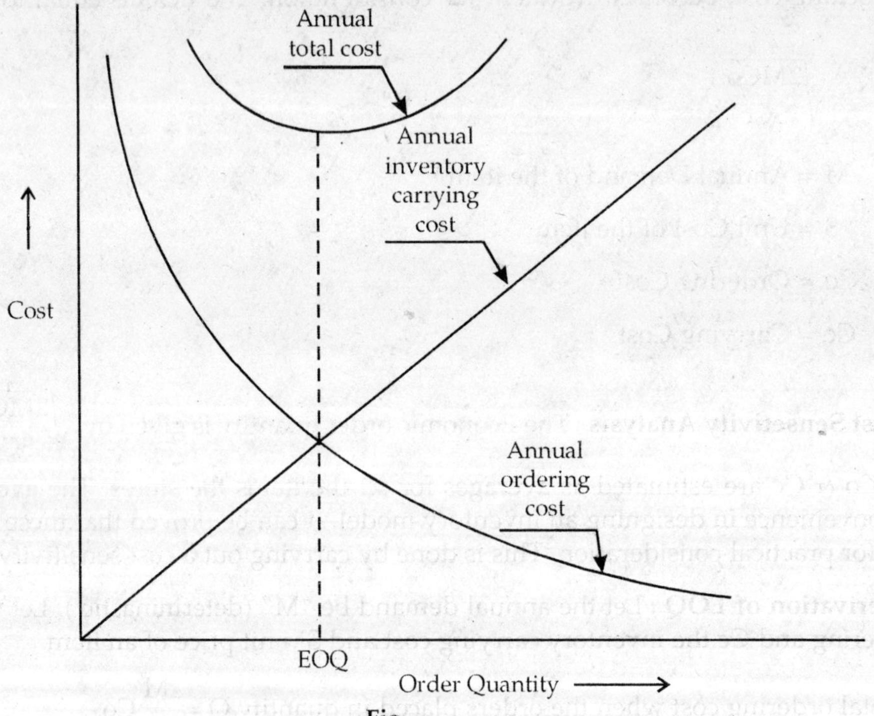

Fig.

Find out the economic ordering quantity and nos of orders to be placed in a year.

Solution : $EOQ = \sqrt{\frac{2MCo}{SCc}}$ Here $M = 20{,}000$

$Co = \text{Rs. } 100$

$= \sqrt{\frac{2 \times 20{,}000 \times 100}{10(0.20)}}$ $S = \text{Rs. } 10$

$Cc = 20 \text{ per cent} = 0.20$

= 1440 Nos.

Economic ordering quantity = 1440 units

Nos. of $P.O_s$ to be placed in a year $= \frac{20,000}{1440} = 14.4 = 15$ nos.

Problem 2 : An Automobile company buys a lot of 1000 axles which is a 3 month supply the price per axle is Rs. 250 and the ordering cost in Rs. 300. The inventory carrying cost is estimated at 20% of unit value. What is the total annual cost of the inventory policy being followed at present?

Determine the economic order quantity.

Solution : Co = Rs. 300. Ordering cost

Annual demand = M = 1000 × 4 = 4000 axles.

Inventory Carrying Cost = Holding Cost = 250 × 0.20 = Cc

Q = Number units per order = 1,000 = Rs. 50.

Total Annual Cost = Annual Ordering Cost + Annual Holding Cost

$$= \frac{M}{Q} Co + \frac{Q}{2} (SCc)$$

$$= \frac{4,000}{1,000} \times 300 + \frac{1,000}{2} \times 50$$

= Rs. 1,200 + Rs. 25,000

= Rs. 26,200.

$$EOQ = \sqrt{\frac{2MCo}{SC_c}} = \sqrt{\frac{2 \times 4,000 \times 300}{50}} = 215 \text{ axles} = Q_1$$

The total annual cost at EOQ

$$= \frac{M}{Q_1} \times Co + \frac{Q_1}{2} SC_c = \frac{4,000}{215} \times 300 + \frac{215}{2} \times 50$$

= 5,600 + 5,350 = Rs. 10,950/-

There, Annual saving by ordering axles on EOQ norms instead of 1000 axles per order.

= Rs. 26,200 – Rs. 10,950 = Rs. 15,250.

Problem 3 : A Hospital needs 50,000 disposable Syringes a year the ordering cost Rs. 200 and unit procurement price Rs. 10 the inventory carrying cost is 20%.

(1) Determine EOQ

(2) Find out total annual cost of inventory.

Solution : $EOQ = \sqrt{\frac{2MCo}{SC_c}} = \sqrt{\frac{2 \times 50,000 \times 200}{10(0.20)}} = \sqrt{10 \times 10^6}$

= 3162 units = Q **Ans.**

Total Annual inventory cost (Rs.)

$$= \frac{M}{Q} Co + \frac{Q}{2}(SC_c)$$

$$= \frac{50,000}{3162} \times 200 + \frac{3162}{2} \times 10(0.20)$$

$$= 3163 + 3162$$

$$= \text{Rs. } 6325 \qquad \textbf{Ans.}$$

PROBABLE QUESTIONS

1. What is a forecast? What are various methods of forecasts?
2. What is regression analysis. Develop a regression equation of Y on x.
3. What do you understand "point and interval estimates"?
4. What is significance of game Theory? What is "Prisoner' Dilemma" in same theory?
5. What are various types of inventories? What are various inventory models? Write their characteristic.
6. Derive the formula for EOQ both graphically and mathematically.

CHAPTER 5

OPTIMISATION : CONCEPT OF SLOPE, DERIVATIVES, CONSTRAINED OPTIMISATION

1. SLOPE

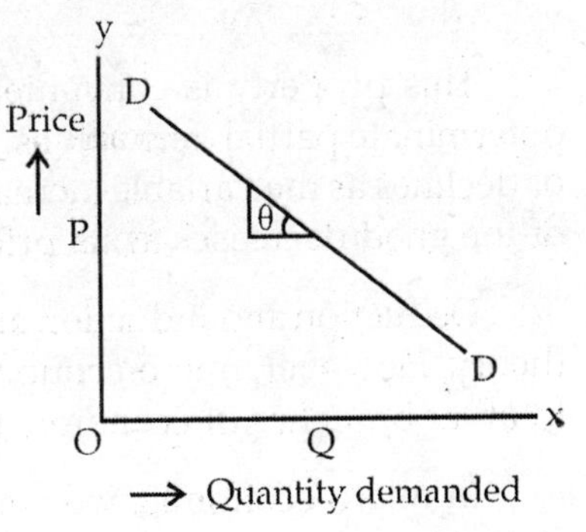

Graphs are drawn two dimensional coordinates, *i.e.*, x and y co-ordinates to represent the relationships between two variables. The constant and uniform relationship's between two variables are shown in straight line with equations Y = a + bx or y= a – bx.

Slope is represented by tan θ, where θ is the angle as shown in the following graphs.

The graph between price and quantity demanded is shown by demand curve DD with a negative slope or –tan θ this mean, if price of a commodity increases, the quantity demanded reduces.

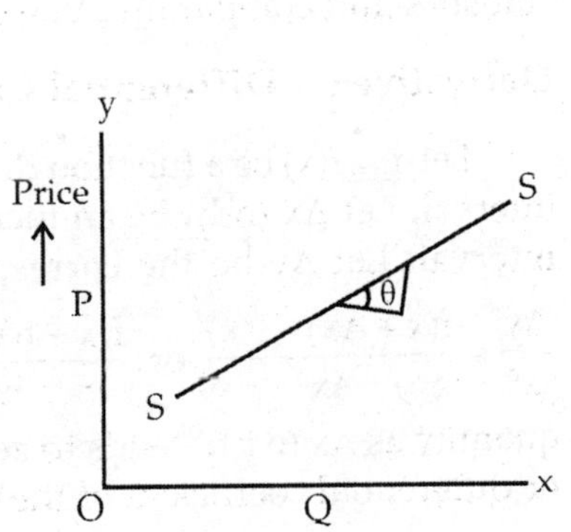

On the otherhand :

The graph between price and quantity demanded is shown by supply curve SS with a positive slope or + tan θ. This means, if quantity demanded increases the price will increase with supply of the commodity.

In Economics, slope is the property or plotted points on the curve or graph of a function. In geometry, slope = $\frac{\text{Vertical Length}}{\text{Horizontal Length}}$, *i.e.*, represents steepness of a line. For the non-linear curve like ISO quantity, the slope is measured as $\frac{OA}{OB}$ by drawing tangent AB.

This slope represents MRTs, *i.e.* Marginal Rate of Technical substitution, *i.e.* the rate at which K and L are being substituted. Also, slope = $\frac{\Delta y}{\Delta x}$, Δ or delta represents small change.

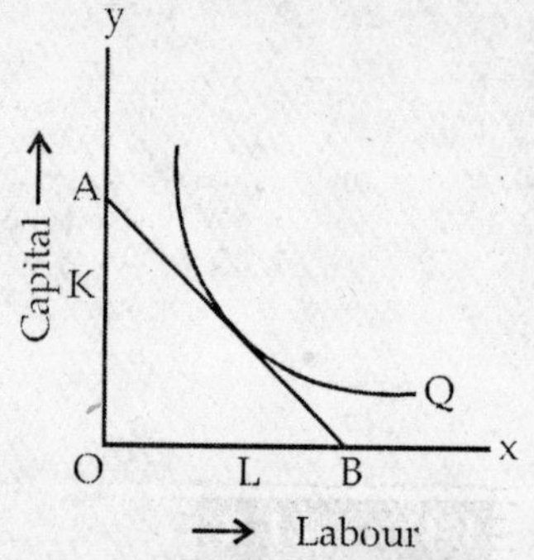

Thus, the slope of a curve stands for the rate of change of one variable. In relation to a unit change in the associated variables. In a straight line the slope is constant indicating proportionate change.

2. DERIVATIVES

The average change in demand due to a small partial change in any variable can be measured by the partial derivative of the demand function. Thus,

$$\frac{\partial q_i}{\partial p_i} = \varphi_i = \frac{\Delta q_i}{\Delta p_i} \quad \text{as} \quad \Delta p_i \to 0 \quad \text{(Price effect)}$$

$$\frac{\partial q_i}{\partial y} = \varphi_y = \frac{\Delta q_i}{\Delta y} \quad \text{as} \quad \Delta p_i \to 0 \quad \text{(Income effect)}$$

This property is convenient, and so we usually assume that the demand function has determinate partial derivatives. The sign of partial derivative shows whether demand increases or declines as the variable increases. Thus, if Q_1 is negative it shows that the quantity demanded of the good decreases as its price increases.

Deduction and induction are complementary modes of inference that are used in economic theory, However, micro-economic theory gives greater emphasis to deductive reasolving than to other branches of economic theory.

In micro-economic, we construct deductive models of explanation and use the tools of statistics and comparative statistics to analyses the properties of models.

Derivative (or Differential Coefficient) of a Function

Let Y = f(x) be a function defined in a certain interval and x be a fixed interior point of this interval. Let Δx (orh) be an increment of x such that x + Δx (or x + h) lies within the stated interval. Let Δy be the corresponding increment of y = f(x). Then the incremental ratio $\frac{\Delta y}{\Delta x} = \frac{f(x + \Delta x) - f(x)}{\Delta x}$ or $\frac{f(x+h) - f(x)}{h}$ is a function of Δx (or h). If this ratio tends to a finite quantity as Δx (o r h) tends to zero from either side, the finite quantity is called the derivative or differential coefficient of the function y = f(x) w.r.t. x at the point x.

Two notations used for derivative are *(i)* $\frac{dy}{dx} = \frac{d}{dx}f(x)$ *(ii)* $y' = f(x)$. The process of finding the derivative is called differentiation. To differentiates f(x) w.r.t. x means to find the derivative of f(x) w.r.t. x.

3. RULE OF FINDING MAXIMUM AND MINIMUM VALUES OF A FUNCTION

(1) Find $\frac{dy}{dx}$ for the given function $y = f(x)$

(2) Find the values of x for $\frac{dy}{dx}$ is zero. Let these be $a_1, a_2, a_3, \ldots$

Method 1

Take the first value a_1, if $\frac{dy}{dx}$ is positive for $x < a_1$ and negative for $x > a_1$, the function has a maximum at $x_1 = a_1$.

If $\frac{dy}{dx}$ is negative for $x < a_1$ and positive for $x > a_1$, the function has a minimum at $x = a_1$.

Similarly, test the other values $a_2, a_3, \ldots$ of x found in step (2).

Method 2

(3) Find $\frac{d^2y}{dx^2}$.

(4) Put $x = a_1$ in $\frac{d^2y}{dx^2}$, If the result is negative, the function has maximum value x = a, and the maximum value is y = f(a), If by putting x = a, in $\frac{d^2y}{dx^2}$, the result is positive, the function has a minimum value at $x = a_1$ and minimum value is $y = f(a_1)$. Similarly, test the other values $a_2, a_3, \ldots$ of x found is step(2).

Numericals

4. Examine the nature of the total cost function $TC = a(x - 5)^3 + b$, where x is quantity produced and a and b are positive constants.

Solution : $\frac{d(Tc)}{dx} = \frac{d}{dx}\left\{a(x-5)^3 + b\right\} = 3a(x-5)^2 > 0$ for $x \neq 5$ & $= 0$ for $x = 5$

Hence Tc is rising with a stationary point at x = 5.

$$\frac{d^2(Tc)}{dx^2} = \frac{d}{dx}\left\{3a(x-5)^2\right\}$$

$= 6a(x - 5) < 0$ for $x < 5$ hence Tc is concave-down for $x < 5$

and > 0 for $x < 5$ hence Tc is concave up for $x > 5$

and $= 0$ for $x = 5$, hence Tc has a point of inflexion at $x = 5$

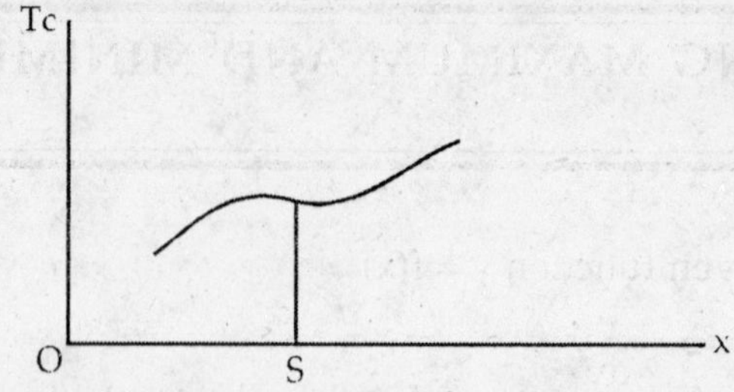

Thus, Tc is rising with a point of intersection on at x = 5 and concave down before and concave up after x = 5, as shown in the diagram.

5. If the sides a rectangle are x and y, express the perimeter P and area A interim of x and y. Prove that, among all the rectangles with fixed perimeter P, the square is the one with maximum area.

Solution : In terms of x and y, we have

$$P = 2(x + y) \qquad ...(i)$$

$$A = xy \qquad ...(ii)$$

From *(i)* we have $y = \frac{P}{2} - x \qquad ...(iii)$

Substituting the value of y in *(ii)*, we have

$A = x\left(\frac{P}{2} - x\right) = \frac{P}{2}x - x^2$, which is to be maximised.

For maxima and minima

$$\frac{dA}{dx} = 0 \Rightarrow \frac{P}{2} - 2x = 0 \Rightarrow x = \frac{P}{4}$$

Also, $\frac{d^2A}{dx} = -2 < 0$

Hence, the area A is maximum when $x = \frac{P}{4}$

$\therefore \; y = \frac{P}{2} - \frac{P}{4} = \frac{P}{4}$ from *(iii)*

Thus, $x = y = \frac{P}{4}$ for maximum A. Hence the area of the rectangle for a given perimeter is maximum when sides are equal *i.e.* the rectangle is a square.

6. APPLICATION OF DERIVATIVES IN ECONOMICS

In the field of economics, derivatives have great application in finding the cost function, revenue function, profit function etc.

Few application are as under :

(1) Demand Function : It is a relationship between demand of the quantity and price P of a commodity.

Mathematically expressed as $q = f(\phi)$ where $P > 0, q > 0$ is the demand function.

(2) Supply Function : If x be the amount of supply when p is the price, then supply function is given by $x = f(p)$ where $x > 0, p > 0$. The supply curve is a rising curve in which $\frac{dx}{dp} > 0$ *i.e.* (+)ve.

(3) Cost function : If C(x) is the total cost, f(x) the variable cost, and 'd' the fixed cost when the output is x units, then $C(x) = f(x) + d$ where $x \geq 0$.

Here the fixed cost d is independent of the total level of output x *i.e.* it remain constant at all levels of output.

$$\text{Average Cost (AC)} = \frac{\text{Total Cost}}{\text{Output}} = \frac{f(x)+d}{x}$$

$$\text{Average Variable Cost (AVC)} = \frac{\text{Variable Cost}}{\text{Output}} = \frac{f(x)}{x}$$

$$\text{Average Fixed Cost (AFC)} = \frac{\text{Fixed Cost}}{\text{Output}} = \frac{d}{x}$$

(4) Revenue Function : If x units be sold at Rs. p per unit, then the total revenue or total turnover.

$R(x) = px$ where $p > 0$ and $x > 0$.

(5) Profit Function : Profit function P(x) is the difference between the total revenue and total cost

i.e. $P(x) = R(x) - C(x)$ where $x > 0$

(6) Production Function : Production of a firm depends upon several economic factors like investment (K), labour (L) and raw materials (R) etc.

Thus, Production = f(K, L, R)

(7) Price Elasticity of Demand : It is defined as the ratio or the proportionate change in quantity demand to the proportionate change in price.

Thus, if the quantity demanded changes from x to $x + \Delta x$ and price change from p to $p + \Delta p$, then the

$$\text{Price elasticity of demand} = ed = \lim \frac{\Delta x / x}{\Delta P / p}$$

$$ed = \frac{P}{x} . \lim_{\Delta P \to 0} \frac{\Delta x}{\Delta P} = \frac{P}{x} . \frac{dx}{dP}$$

Unusually, the demand curve has a negative slope at all prices *i.e.* if price increases, the quantity demanded decreases and therefore $\frac{dx}{dp}$ is negative at all prices.

When $e_d > 1$, the demand is elastic.

& $e_d < 1$, the demand is inelastic.

(8) Income Elasticity of Demand : If x = quantity demanded, y = income per head in a group of people, then income elasticity of demand

$$e_y = \frac{y}{x}.\frac{dx}{dy}.$$

This gives the elasticity of quantity demanded in response to a change in income.

$e_y > 1$, then the goods are luxury goods

$e_y < 0$, then the goods are inferior goods

$0 < e_y < 1$, the goods are necessity goods.

(9) Equilibrium Price and Quantity : Equilibrium price is the price at which quantity demanded = quantity supplied.

Monopoly price is the price at which the profit is maximum. It can be shown that the price at the point of equilibrium is the same as monopoly price.

(10) Marginal cost, Marginal Revenue and Average Revenue Marginal cost in defined by

$$MC = \lim_{\Delta \to 0} \frac{\Delta c}{\Delta x} = \frac{dc}{dx}$$

where c(x) is the total cost when output is x.

If R(x) = total revenue when x units are sold at a price p per unit, then marginal Revenue is

$$MR = \lim_{\Delta \to 0} \frac{\Delta R}{\Delta x} = \frac{dR}{dx} \quad \text{where } R = px$$

$$AR = \text{Average Revenue} = \frac{R}{x}$$

11. A firm produces x tones of output at a total cost C(x)

$$= \text{Rs.}\left[\frac{x^3}{10} - 6x^2 + 70x + 11\right]$$

Determine in terms of x *(i)* the average cost *(ii)* Average variable cost *(iii)* Average fixed cost.

Find the value of each of the then at the level of output of 10 tonnes.

Solution : Total cost $C(x) = \frac{1}{10}x^3 - 6x^2 + 70x + 11$

$$\text{Average Cost} = AC = \frac{C(x)}{x} = \frac{1}{10}x^2 - 6x + 70 + \frac{11}{x}$$

$$\text{Average Variable Cost} = \text{AVC} = \frac{\frac{1}{10}x^3 - 6x^2 + 70x}{x}$$

$$\text{and Average Fixed Cost} = \text{AFC} = \frac{1}{10}x^2 - 6x + 70 = \frac{11}{x}$$

At the output level of x = 10 tonnes

$$\text{AC} = \frac{1}{10}(10)^2 - 6 \times 10 + 70 + \frac{11}{10} = \text{Rs. } 21.10$$

$$\text{AVC} = \frac{1}{10}(10)^2 - 6 \times 10 + 70 = \text{Rs. } 20$$

$$\text{AFC} = \frac{11}{10} = \text{Rs. } 1.10 \quad \textbf{Ans.}$$

12. A demand function is given by $xp^n = k$ where n and k are constants calculate the price elasticity of demand.

Solution : We have $xp^n = K$ or $x = xp^{-n}$ $\therefore \frac{dx}{dp} = -nkp^{-n-1}$

$$\therefore \text{ed} = \text{price elasticity of demand} = -\frac{p}{x}.\frac{dx}{dp} = -\frac{p}{Kp^{-n}}x(-nKp^{-n-1}) \quad \textbf{Ans.}$$

13. The total cost function of a commodity is given by $C(x) = 0.5\,x^2 + 2x + 20$ where C denotes total cost and x denotes the quantity produced.

Find the average cost and the marginal cost.

Solution : Average Cost = AC = $\frac{C(x)}{x} = 0.5x + 2 + \frac{20}{x}$

$$\text{Marginal Cost} = \frac{dC}{dx} = \frac{d(0.5x^2 + 2x + 20)}{dx} = x + 2$$

14. If $C = 0.05\,q^2 + 16 + \frac{100}{q}$ is the manufacturer's average cost function what is the marginal cost when 50 units are produce also interpret the result.

Solution : Total cost = C(x) = Average Cost × Quantity Produced

$$= \left[0.05q^2 + 16 + \frac{100}{q}\right] \times q = 0.05q^3 + 16q + 100$$

$$\therefore \text{Marginal Cost} = \text{MC} = \frac{dC}{dq} = \frac{d}{dq}(0.05q^3 + 16q + 100)$$

$$= 0.15q^2 + 16.$$

At $q = 50$, $\frac{dC}{dq} = \text{MC} = 0.15(50)^2 + 16 = 375 + 16 = 391$ **Ans.**

Interpretation : If the production is increased by 1 unit from q = 50 to q = 51 then the cost of additional unit is Rs. 391 (if cost c in Rs.)

Constrained Optimisation

Optimisation is maximising or minimising with limited resources, maximising revenue, maximising sales, maximising productivity and maximising profits with resource of man power capital and raw materials being limited.

Similarly, minimising the cost of production with controlled resources leads to the least unit cost of production.

A business organisation aims at optimisation on the above basis to remain profitable.

The problems of maximisation and minimisation are solved with the help of calculates but without any constraints involved in the process of decision making. In reality, however, the management is faced with certain constraints. Some of the problems faced by management are minimisation of cost subject to output constraint or maximising revenue subject a certain level of profit etc. Constraints in the form of legal, environmental and behavioural act as limiting factors in making decision.

We should deal this concept by restricting the number of constraint to one only. More than one constraint will make the treatment complicated.

Suppose, Cost function is $C = 10L + 4K + 300$ ...(1)

L, K are labour and capital and c = Cost.

If management wants to minimise cost subject to level of output (Q) equal to 100 units. Output is a function of capital and labour is given by

$$Q = 10L^{0.5}K^{0.5} \qquad \text{...(2)}$$

or $100 = 10L^{0.5}K^{0.5}$ or $L^{0.5}K^{0.5} = 10$ or $L = \dfrac{100}{K}$

Substituting in eqn. (1) for $L = 10^2 \times K^{-1}$

We get, $C = 10 \times 10^2.K^{-1} + 4K + 300 = 10^3K^{-1} + 4K + 300$ ...(3)

Applying the first order condition for optimisation in solving for K

$$\frac{dC}{dk} = -\frac{10^3}{K^2} + 4 = 0 \quad \text{or} \quad -\frac{10^3}{K^2} = -4 \quad \text{or} \quad K^2 = \frac{10^3}{4}$$

$\therefore \; K = 5\sqrt{10}$ units

To check whether this value of K minimise cost, we apply the second order condition *i.e.*

$$\frac{d^2C}{dk^2} = \frac{10^3}{K^3} = 10^3K^{-3} \qquad (\textit{i.e.}\text{ whether } \frac{d^2C}{dk^2} > 0)$$

for $K = 5\sqrt{10}$ $\quad \dfrac{d^2C}{dx^2} > 0$

Hence, the second order condition is satisfied.

Substituting $K = 5\sqrt{10}$ in eqn. (2) for Q = 100 to get L which minimises cost

$$10L^{0.5}(5\sqrt{10})^{0.5} = 100$$

or $L = 2\sqrt{10}$ units

∴ The firm should use $2\sqrt{10}$ and $5\sqrt{10}$ units of labour and capital respectively for an output of 100 units. This use of inputs will minimise the cost.

and To get the minimum cost,

we substitute $2\sqrt{10}$ & $5\sqrt{10}$ for in eqn. (1)

$$C = 10L + 4K + 300$$

$$= 10 \times 2\sqrt{10} + 4 \times 5\sqrt{10} + 300$$

$$= 20\sqrt{10} + 20\sqrt{10} + 300 = 40\sqrt{10} + 300$$

Note : For optimisation technique in case of more than one constraint, we have to use the method of **Lagranjan multipliers** for solving the problem of constrained optimisation.

Constrained Optimisation

While maximising profits, if the firm faces no resource constraints, this is case of contained optimisation. In real sense, however, business managers face resource constraints and such problems of profit maximisation or cost minimisation one solved by constrained optimising techniques using Linear programming constrained optimisation by substitution and lagrangian multiplier principles.

***(a)* Constrained optimisation by substitution :** The process of solution involves two steps :

(i) Express one of the variables in term of the other and solve the constraint equation for one of variables (x or Y) and

(ii) Substitute the solution into the objective function to be maximised and solve it for other variable.

***(b)* Constrained optimisation by Lagrangian multiplier method :** This method is used to solve the optimisation problem of a complex nature and these which can not be solved by the substitution method.

The basic approach of the Lagrangian multiplier method is to form a Lagrangian function by combining the objective function and the constraint equation and then solve it by the partial derivative method.

The greek letter "λ" is used for solving the Lagrangian function and is called Lagrangian multiplier.

Thus, constrained profit maximisation and constrained cost minimisation problems are solved by lagrangian multiplier method.

***(c)* Linear Programming :** The basic purpose of operations Research (OR) is to optimise the resources. Resources are in the form of men, materials, machines, money and time Linear programming (LP) is a technique of OR. The basic objective of LP is to minimise the cost or maximise the profit. This is called the "objective function."

There are restrictions in the conversion process such as the availability of materials, or machinery or manpower or available time for operations, etc. These are called "constraints".

There are many variables in a system or a given problem. Some are known, some are unknown, some of them are controllable, others are not. The range of certain variables are restricted, some are not LP deals with the problems in which the relations between those variables are linear. The term "programme" means a 'plan of actions'.

Because of above reasons, the method of solving such problems is called linear programming solution.

Definition : LP is a versatile mathematical technique in OR and a plan of action which solves a given problem involving linearly related variables in order to achieve the laid down objective in the form of minimising or maximising the objective function under a given set of the constraints.

Basic Solution : These are instances where number of unknown 'p' are more than the number of linear equations 'q' available. In such cases, we assign zero value of all surplus unknowns. These will be 'N' such unknown. With these values, we solve 'q' equations and get values of 'q' unknowns.

Such solutions are called basic solutions.

Basic Variables : The variables whose value is obtained from the basic solutions is called basic variables.

Non-basic Variables : The variables whose values are assumed as zero in the basic solution are known as non basic variables.

Solution : A solution to a LPP is the set of values of the variables which satisfies the set of constraints of the problems.

Slack Variables : Linear equations are solved through the equality form of equations. Normally, constraints are given in the less than or equal to (≤) form.

In such cases, we add the appropriate variables to make it an equality (=) equation. The variables added to constraints to make it an equality equation in LPP are called slack variables and often denoted by the letter 'S'.

PROBABLE QUESTIONS

1. What do you understand by "slopes" and "derivatives" illustrate with examples.
2. Write about the rules of finding maximum and minimum values of a function.
3. Write about of the application of derivatives in economics.

4. What is constrained optimisation? How is it helpful for a business organisation?
5. Write notes on :
   (a) Constrained optimisation by substitution;
   (b) Lagrangian Multiplier method.
6. Importance of Linear Programming & its application for solving business problems.

CHAPTER

6

BREAK EVEN ANALYSIS FOR MANAGERIAL DECISION-MAKING

1. Break-Even Point (BEP)
2. Importance of BEP
3. Important Features on BEP Analysis
4. BEP Calculations
5. Assumptions in BEP Analysis
6. Safety Margin, Effect of Change in Price and Change in Costs etc.
7. $\frac{\text{Profit}}{\text{Volume}}$ Ratio or $\frac{P}{V}$ Ratio
8. Whether to Accept an Order or Not
9. Make or Buy Decision
10. Numericals

1. BREAK-EVEN POINT

The break-even point means the level of output or sales at which no profit or less is achieved,

It indicates the position at which marginal profit or contribution is just sufficient to cover fixed over heads.

In other words, a business is said-to break-even when its income equal its expenditure.

When production exceeds the "Break-Even Point" the business makes a profit and when it is below the "Break-Even Point," the business mans losses.

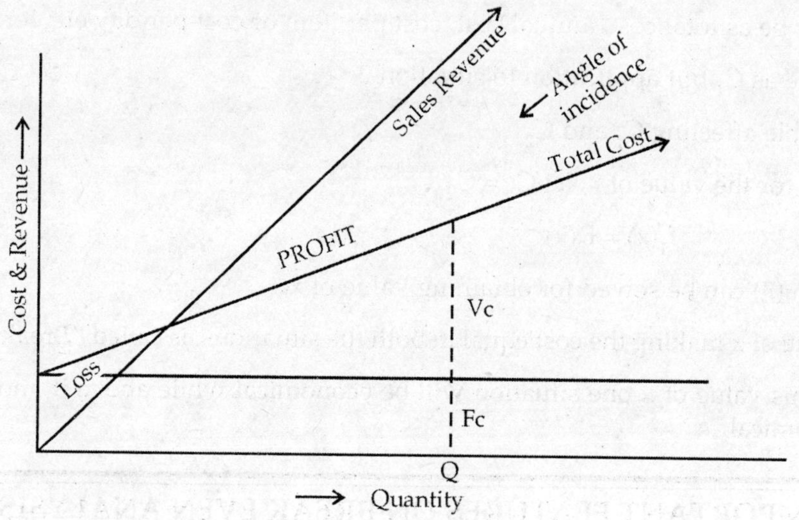

Fig. Graphical Method.

(a) Importance of BEP

Variable costs such as raw materials, energy, maintenance spares and casual labour and fixed costs with insurance premium, interest on borrowed capital, salaries & wages and administrative overhead, the former vary with output and the latter is fixed.

A manager faces the problem of finding out the capacity or production at minimum level he should maintain to avoid loss.

BEP capacity is such that at this point there is no loss or profit.

If the firm produces higher tan BEP capacity it can generate profit from operation.

Usually, the manager will attempt to operate at 100% capacity if there are no constraints.

At full capacity of production, the minimum average cost will be obtained and profit will be maximised.

(b) Break-Even Point Theory

The breakeven point of any two variable situations is the point or the value at which they become equal as the result of a common variable.

There are following two methods to obtain break-even point.

(i) Mathematical method

(ii) Graphical method

***(i)* Mathematical method :** Let cost be the common variables in two situation 1 & 2, then cost equation will be

$C_1 = f_1(x)$ ...... a function of (x) ...(1)

$C_2 = f_2(x)$ ...... another function of (x) ...(2)

C_1—may be as total cost, annual cost, cost per item or cost per day etc. for situation 1.

C_2—same as C_1 but application to situation 2

x—variable affecting C_1 and C_2

To solve for the value of x, let $C_1 = C_2$

i.e. $f_1(x) = f_2(x)$ ...(3)

Equation (3) can be solved for obtaining value of x.

The value of x making the cost equal in both the situations, is called "Break Even Value".

Below this value of x one situation will be economical while above it another situation will be economical.

2. SOME IMPORTANT FEATURES ON BREAK EVEN ANALYSIS

(i) Angle of Incidence

It is the angle at which income line (sales line) cuts the total cost line. If the angle is large, it is an indication that profits are being made at a high rate, on the other hand, if the angle is small it indicates that less profits are being made and are achieved under less favourable condition.

(ii) Margin of Safety

It is the output at full capacity minus the output at "Break Even Point". It is expressed as percentage of output at full capacity.

If the margin of safety is small, a small dup in production capacity will reduce. The profit to a great extent.

$$\text{Margin of Safety} = \frac{\text{Output at full capacity} - \text{output at B.E.P.}}{\text{Output at full capacity}} \times 100$$

(iii) Contribution

It is the difference between sales price and variable cost. It is also called Marginal as Marginal Profit or Gross Margin

The marginal profit provides the contribution towards fixed cost and profit.

Contribution = (Sales – Variable Cost) which in turn will be equal to fixed cost + Profit.

(iv) Break-Even Point Calculations

S = Sales Price, V = Variable cost, F =Fixed cost

P = Profit

Now $S = F + V + P$

or $S - V = F + P$

At B.E.P. $P = 0$

$\& S - V = F$

Multiply both sides by S

$S(S - V) = FS$

$$\therefore S = \frac{FS}{S-V} = \frac{F}{\frac{S-V}{S}} = \frac{\text{Fixed Cost}}{\text{Contribution per unit}}$$

$$\& \text{ Sales at B.E.P.} = \text{Rs. } \frac{FS}{S-V}$$

$$\& \text{ Nos. of Units at B.E.P.} = \frac{\text{Fixed Cost}}{\text{Contribution / Unit}}$$

$$= \frac{\text{Fixed Cost}}{\text{Marginal Profit Unit}}$$

(v) Assumptions in Break Even Analysis (Also drawbacks of B.E.P.)

The various assumptions that underline in this technique are given as under :

(a) It is assumed that over the entire range of volume of production all costs are perfectly variable.

(b) It is assumed that over the entire range of volume of production all costs are absolutely fixed.

(c) It is assumed that with the physical volume of Production all revenues are perfectly variable.

(d) The volumes of sales and Production are equal.

(e) It is assumed that for multi-product output, the product-mix should be stable.

(vi) Application or uses of B.E.P.

It can be used to determine the following :

(a) Safety margin with proposed volume

(b) Quantity needed to have desired profit

(c) Effect of change in price

(d) Effect of change in costs

(e) Whether to accept an order or not

(f) Whether to make or buy

3. (a) Safety Margin

It refers to the extent to which the firm can afford to decline in sales upto the BEP. It is expressed by percentage ratio of sales over BEP volume to the sales volume.

$$\therefore \text{ Safety Margin} = \frac{\text{Sales Volume} - \text{Sales at BEP}}{\text{Sales Volume}} \times 100$$

(b) Quantity Needed to have Desired Profit

It is given by

$$\text{Target Quantity} = \frac{\text{Fixed Cost} + \text{Target Profit}}{\text{Contribution Per Unit}}$$

(c) Effect of Change in Price

Sometimes, management/Mktg. Mgr. is required to consider whether to reduce price of a product or for selling bulk quantity of product.

Management/Mktg. Mgr. has to consider the following facts in this regard.

If the sale price is reduced, then contribution margin will reduce and this will increase, the sales value But this increased volume may or may not receive increase in demand because it depends on elasticity of demand.

As the sale price is reduced, BEP shifts towards right side *i.e.* towards larger quantity side.

$$\text{At B.E.P.} \quad Q = \frac{F+P}{S-V}$$

for reduced sales price S_1, Quantity is Q_1

$$Q_1 = \frac{F+P}{S_1 - V}$$

Therefore, Marketing Manager has to obtain a supply order for Q_1 quantity at reduced price level S_1 where $S_1 < S$.

(d) Effect of Change in Costs

(i) Change in variable cost *(ii)* Change in Fixed cost.

***(i)* Change in V.C. :** Variable costs may change due to change in prices of input materials/ energy or due to higher losses.

$$\text{At BEP} \quad Q = \frac{F+P}{S-V}$$

for change in $V \to V_1$ & $Q \to Q_1$, also $S \to S_1$

$$Q_1 = \frac{F+P}{S_1 - V_1} \qquad (S1 - V1)\text{—Change in contribution}$$

If the sales volume remains same, *i.e.* $Q_1 = Q$

$$\therefore \frac{F+P}{S_1 - V_1} = \frac{F+P}{S-V} \qquad \text{or } S_1 - V_1 = S - V$$

$$\text{or } S_1 = S + (V_1 - V)$$

S_1 is new selling price to maintain present profit.

Due to increase in variable cost *i.e.* increase in Vc will shift BEP right to give higher Q.

Thus higher quantity is to be sold to maintain the present profit with no change in price of Product.

***(ii)* Change in Fixed Cost :** Fixed cost may change due to an increase in staff executive remuneration, taxes, insurance & building rent etc. or overhead expenses.

This in turn will bring change in B.E.P., if the sale price is unchanged.

$$\text{At BEP} \quad Q = \frac{F+P}{S-V} \qquad \ldots(1)$$

$$\text{for} \quad F \rightarrow F_1 \qquad Q \rightarrow Q_1$$

$$Q_1 = \frac{F_1 + P}{S-V} \qquad \ldots(2)$$

$$\therefore Q_1 - Q = \frac{(F_1 + P) - (F + P)}{S-V}$$

$$= \frac{F_1 - F}{S-V}$$

$$\text{or } Q_1 = Q + \frac{F_1 - F}{S-V}$$

If Q is unchanged then there is change in Sales price, then $S_1 = S + \frac{F_1 - F}{Q}$

(iii) $\frac{P}{V}$ ratio is known $\frac{\text{Profit}}{\text{Volume}}$ ratio

$\frac{P}{V}$ is given by

$$\frac{P}{V} = \frac{\text{Sales Price} - \text{Variable Cost}}{\text{Sales Price}} \times 100$$

Sp = Selling price (unit) P = Profit

$$= \frac{Sp - Vc}{Sp}$$

V = Volume

$$= \frac{\text{Contribution}}{Sp}$$

Vc = Variable cost per unit

$$\therefore \text{Contribution} = \frac{P}{V} \times Sp$$

We can write

1. $\frac{P}{V}$ ratio = $\frac{\text{Change in contribution}}{\text{Change in Sp}}$

2. $\frac{P}{V}$ ratio = $\frac{\text{Change in Profit}}{\text{Change in Sp}}$

4.4.2 WHETHER TO ACCEPT AN ORDER OR NOT

If extra capacity to produce a product is variable then some times management has to decide whether to accept another order at a price which less than the initial selling price.

For example, a plant is operating on its 50% full capacity. A buyer offered to buy 4000 units at Rs. 5.00 per unit while the average cost Rs. 6.00. Now the problem is whether to accept this order or not.

The other details of the product are

Total capacity	= 20,000 units	
Present output	= 10,000 units	
Direct Matl. cost	= Rs. 10,000 – Re. 1/pc	Direct cost
Direct Labour	= Rs. 10,000 – Re. 1/pc.	Rs. 2/pc.
Fixed costs	= Rs. 40,000	

In this question, one can find that additional cost of making these 4000 units is Rs. 4000 for material cost and Rs. 4000 for labour cost (total Rs. 8000) and the revenue from Sales would be 4000 × Rs. 5 = Rs. 20,000. Thus, the concern will save = Rs. 20,000 – Rs. 8,000 = Rs. 12,000.

So, it would be profitable to accept anything more than Rs, 2 per unit, which is the direct cost per unit.

There is only danger that, if other consumers come to know that this product is being sold at a lower price, they may also demand supply at the lower price.

These fire, in such case acceptance order should be kept secret.

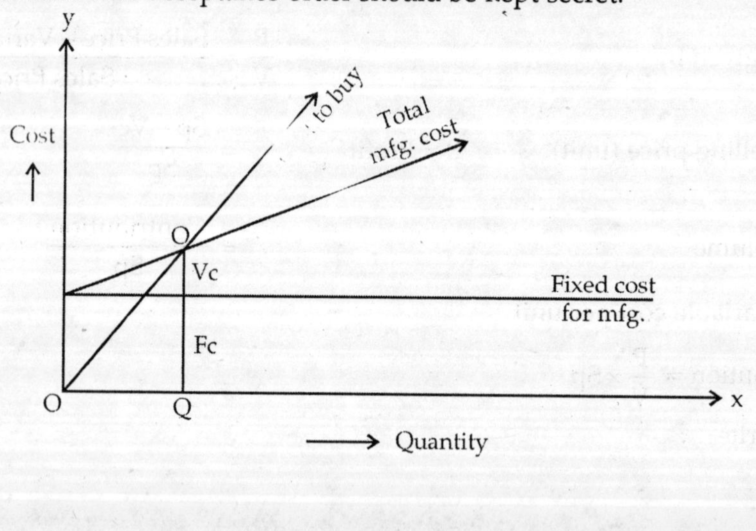

4.4.3 Whether to Make or Buy (Ref. above diagram)

$$Q = \frac{\text{Fixed Cost}}{\text{Purchase Cost - Variable Cost}}$$

Upto Q quantity—it is economical to buy the product.

Beyond Q quantity—it is economical to manufacture item in house.

Example 1 : The fixed costs of a company are Rs. 3, 50,000. The net sales amount to Rs. 6,00,000 annually. The direct costs are 35% of sales in rupees. Determine the following :

(i) The Break-Even Point in terms of Sales rupees

(ii) The Sales required to earn a profit of Rs. 80,000.

$$(i)\ \text{BEP} = \frac{F}{1-\frac{V}{S}} = \frac{3,50,000}{1-\frac{0.35\times 6,00,000}{6,00,000}}$$

$$= \frac{3,50,000}{0.65} = \text{Rs. } 5,38,461.53 \quad \textbf{Ans.}$$

(ii) Profit Rs. 80,000

Sales = ?

$$\text{Sales} = \frac{F+P}{1-\frac{V}{S}} = \frac{3,50,000+80,000}{1-0.35}$$

$$= \frac{4,30,000}{0.65} = \text{Rs. } 6,61,538.46 \quad \textbf{Ans.}$$

Example 2 : A lathe m/c costing Rs. 10,000 can produce components at the rate of 6 pieces per hour and another automatic lathe costing Rs. 20,000 can produce 20 pieces per hour. The operator on either of the m/c is to be paid at the of Rs. 1. 50 per hour. Determine the minimum number of pieces which will change the cost situation in favour of the automatic m/c.

Solution : First situation :

Cost of lathe m/c. Rs. 19,000

Production = 6 pcs./hour

Operator rate = Rs. 1. 50/hour

Second situation :

Cost of automatic lathe = Rs. 20,000

Production = 20 pcs/hour.

Operator rate = Rs. 1. 50/hr.

Let N be the production pieces at which cost equation are equal.

$$\text{Thus, } 10{,}000 + \frac{N}{6} \times 150 = 20{,}000 + \frac{N}{20} \times 1.50$$

$$\text{or,} \quad \frac{N}{6} \times \frac{3}{2} - \frac{N}{20} \times \frac{3}{2} = 20{,}000 - 10{,}000 = 10{,}000$$

$$\text{or,} \quad \frac{3N}{12} - \frac{3N}{40} = 10{,}000$$

$$\text{or,} \quad \frac{3N}{4}\left(\frac{1}{3} - \frac{1}{10}\right) \frac{3N}{4}\left(\frac{10-3}{30}\right)$$

$$\text{or,} \quad \frac{3N}{4} \times \frac{7}{30} = \frac{7N}{4} \times \frac{1}{10} = 10{,}000$$

$$\text{or,} \quad 7N = 10{,}000 \times 40$$

$$\therefore \; N = \frac{10{,}000 \times 40}{7} = 57{,}142.86$$

or 57,143 pieces

It means if production is more than 57,143 pieces then automatic lathe m/c will be economical.

Example 3 : The fixed costs for the year 2000 are Rs. 500, 000 and variable cost per unit is Rs. 25. The estimated sales for the period are valued at Rs. 15,00,000. Each unit sells at Rs. 150. Determine.

(i) B.E.P.

(ii) Rs. 12, 00,000 will be the likely sales turnover for the next budget period, calculate the estimated contribution and profit.

(iii) If a profit target of Rs. 6, 50,000 has been budgeted, compute the sales turnover required.

F = Fixed Cost = 5,00,000

V = Variable cost Rs. 25/ unit

S = Selling cost = Rs. 150/ unit

$$\textit{(i)}\ \text{Break-Even Point} = \frac{F}{1 - \frac{V}{S}}$$

$$\text{BEP Quanty} = \frac{F}{S - V} = \frac{F}{S\left(1 - \frac{V}{S}\right)}$$

$$\text{or } Q \times S = \text{BEP Sales} = \frac{F}{1 - \frac{V}{S}} = \frac{5{,}00{,}000}{1 - \frac{25}{150}} = \frac{5{,}00{,}000}{1 - \frac{1}{6}} = \frac{5{,}00{,}000 \times 6}{5}$$

= Rs. 6,00,000 **Ans.**

$$\textit{(ii)}\ \text{Sales Turnover} = \frac{\text{Fixed Cost} + \text{Profit}}{1 - \frac{V}{S}} = \left(1 - \frac{V}{S}\right) = \frac{5}{6}$$

$$= (\text{Fixed Cost} + \text{Profit}) \times \frac{6}{5} \text{ from (1)}$$

or Sales Turnover $\times \frac{5}{6}$ – Fixed Cost + Profit

$= 12,00,000 \times \frac{5}{6} - 5,00,000 = \text{Profit}$

or, $10,00,000 - 5,00,000 = \text{Profit}$

$\therefore$ Profit = Rs. 500,000.

Now estimated contribution

$$S = \frac{\frac{F+P}{S-V}}{S} \text{ or } \frac{F+P}{S-V} \times S$$

or $S - V = F + P$

or Contribution = F + P = 5,00,000 + 5,00,000

= Rs. 10,00,000 **Ans.**

(iii) If Profit is Rs. 6,50,000, then Sales = ?

$$\text{Sales} = \frac{F+P}{1-\frac{V}{S}} = \frac{5,00,000+6,50,000}{5} \times 6$$

= Rs. 13,80,000 **Ans.** $\left[\left(1-\frac{V}{S}\right) = \frac{5}{6}\right]$

Problem 10 : The fixed costs for the financial year 2000-2001 are Rs. 40,000. The sales for this period are Rs. 100,000. The variable cost per unit is Rs. 2.00. Selling price of each product is Rs. 10 and the number of units involved coincides with the expected volume of output.

Construct the Break Even Chart and determine.

(a) Break-Even Point

(b) How many minimum product should be sold to earn profit?

(c) Profit earned at a turnover of Rs. 80,000.

(d) Margin of Safety

(e) Angle of incidence

PROBABLE QUESTIONS

1. What is Break Even Point?

   (a) What is its significance.
2. What are the draw backs in BEP analysis?
3. Highlight the following concepts:

   (a) Angle of incidence

   (b) Margin of safety

   (c) Contribution

   (d) $\frac{P}{V}$ ratio
4. Describe the effects of chance in price on BEP.
5. Describe the effects of change in costs on BEP.
6. What do you mean by "Make or Buy decision"?

CHAPTER 7

ECONOMIC CONCEPTS FOR MANAGERS : COMPETITIVE ADVANTAGE, EXCHANGE RATES, TRADE RESTRICTIONS, BOP, WTO

1. Exchange Rate
2. Kinds of Rates of Exchange
3. Foreign Exchange Concept
4. Abritage and Transaction
5. FERA and FEMA
6. Fluctuations in Foreign Exchange Rates
7. Competitive Advantage
8. International Trade
9. Gains from International Trade
10. Trade Restrictions
11. Balance of Payments (Prop.)
12. Current Account and Capital Account
13. Measures to Correct Imbalances in BOP
14. WTO

1. EXCHANGE RATE

Every country has its own currency. Trade between countries, involves different currencies. The rate at which one currency buys or exchanges for another currency in known as the rate of exchange. In other words, it is the price of one currency in terms of the other currency. If, for example, Rs. 40 exchange for one US dollar, it means that Rs. 40 in India what one dollar buys in USA.

In order to reflect the day to day fluctuation in demand and supply in the foreign exchange market. Equilibrium exchange rate is determined different under the gold standard and paper currency system. Kinds of rates of exchanges are described later.

Exchange rate management plays a role complementary to trade policy. This is on account of the each that exchange rate movements can be used for correcting the imbalances in the current account of the balance of payments. In India, prior to 1991, the rupee was pegged to the US dollar, pound sterling or a market of currencies of India's major trading postea Rs In July 1991 when the Govt of India announced major trade and industrial policy liberalisation measures a two-step downward adjustment of 18-19 percent was carried out in the exchange rate of the Indian rupee. This was to help the country in increasing the export earnings and thus is tackling the serious imbalances in the balance of payments.

The exchange rate is now largely determined by the market *i.e.* demand and supply condition. However, Reserve Bank interviews to check excessive volatility in the market. The objective of exchange rate management has been to ensure that the external value of the rupee is realistic and credible as evidenced by a sustainable current account deficit and manageable foreign exchange situation.

Kinds of Rates of Exchange

Broadly there are three kinds of exchange rates :

(1) Spot rate and forward rate : An exchange rate quoted for the spot transaction is called the spot rate of exchange while the one quoted for buying and selling currency in future is known as forward rate of exchange.

(2) Fixed, flexible and floating exchange rates : When exchange rate is fixed in terms of gold or another currency, it is called fixed exchange rate when the rate is fixed for a short period but is changed from time to time, it is known as flexible exchange rate. If exchange rate of the currency of a country is allowed to change and finds its own level, it is known as floating exchange rate.

(3) Multiple rates : It is possible that a country adopts more than one exchange rate for its currency *i.e.* one exchange rate for exports while another for imports. In such a case the country is following multiple exchange rate system. A special case of multiple exchange rate is the two tier exchange rate system where Govt maintain two exchange rates, one for the capital transaction and the other for commercial transaction. The former is generally lower than the latter.

***(a)* The Role of Exchange Rate System :** The exchange rate system is an important element in any country is financial system countries which have floating exchange rates can follow monetary policies independently of other countries. In countries with fixed exchange rate system, the currency is pegged with one or more currencies. When a country has such a system, it has to align its monetary policy with that of other countries. If India pegs its currency with US dollar, with open capital market, its interest rates will move in London with the US.

Foreign Exchange : Concept of Spot rate, forward rate, Abritage, transaction brief introduction to FERA and FEMA.

(b) **Foreign Exchange :** Rate of exchange and exchange control.

Every country has its won currency trade between countries involves different currencies. The rate of which one currency buys or exchanges for another currency is known as the rate of exchange. It is the price of alone currency in terms of the other currency.

Just like any other price, exchange rate in also determined by the forces of demand and supply. In the foreign exchange market there prevails an equilibrium rate of exchange. In order to reflect the day to day fluctuation in demand and supply in the foreign exchange market, a market rate of exchange occurs which revolves round the equilibrium or norma rate of exchange. Equilibrium exchange rate is determined differently under the gold standard and paper currency system.

Unlike other markets, the foreign exchange markets do not have a physical trading floor. It is primarily an over the counter market which means that instead of face to face deals, the transaction take place through electronic communication media like telephone, fax or computer networks.

Exchange control's relate to the government control on exchange rate and conversion of domestic currency into foreign currency.

In the direct method of exchange control the Govt or the central Bank (*i.e.* RBI in case of India) intervenes where as in the indirect method, the regulation of foreign exchange rate is the use of custom duties and quantitative restriction like quotes. These have an impact in term reducing demand for foreign goods, and there by making exchange rate favourable for the country.

The other indirect method used in varying the interest rate in the country. For example, if interest rate increases in India. It would attract short term capital form abroad. Consequently, demand for rupee will increase, resulting in raising. The exchange price of the rupee. Opposite would be the effect, it interest rate in lowered.

(c) **Kinds of rates of exchange :** Broadly, there are three kinds of exchange rates :

(i) Spot rate and forward rate : An exchange rate quoted for the spot transaction in called the spot rate of exchange, while the one quoted for buying and selling currency in future in known as forward rate of exchange.

These rates are discussed later in this chapter.

Fixed, flexible and floating exchange rates. When exchange rate is fixed interims of gold on another currency, it is called fixed exchange rate. When this rate is fixed for a short period but is changed from time to time, it is known as flexible exchange rate.

If exchange rate of the currency of a countries is allowed to change and find its own level, it is known as floating exchange rate.

(iii) Multiple rates : It is possible that a country adopts more than one exchange rate for its currency *e.g.* one exchange rate for exports while another for imports. In such a case the country is following multiple exchange rate system.

In such a two ten exchange rate system the Govt. may use one for the capital transaction and the other commercial transaction. The former is generally lower than the latter.

***(d)* Spot and forward Transactions (Rates) :** A forwards transaction involves an agreement where by one agrees to buy or sell foreign currency at a future data at a pre-determined rate. The pre-determined rate, called the forward rate, is different from the rate ruling on day of agreement.

The later rate is called the spot rate, which applies to spot transaction. In a spot transaction, the seller under takes to deliver the foreign currency within 2 business days. The different between the spot rate and forward rate in either premium or discount. The difference is called premium, when the forward rate (direct quote) exceeds the spot rate (direct quote).

The difference is called discount, when the spot rate exceeds the forward rate.

Like the spot rates, the forward rates are also determined by market forces, but an ideal forward rate balances the interest and inflation rate differentials between countries.

Consider an exporter who receively an order from USA to supply certain equipment for $ 1,00,000 on 01-04-2004. The relevant spot rate per dollar on that day was Rs. 48. However, since the normal delivery time was 2 months, the exporter was expecting to receive the dollars only 2 months down the line on 31-5-2004. This means, instead of selling the dollars at Rs. 48 per dollar on 01-04-2004, he would sell them at spot rate ruling on 31-05-2004, which could be higher or lower than Rs. 48. If the spot rate is lower, say Rs. 47 per dollar the exporter. This loan can be higher if the spot rate falls further.

The exporter could cover himself against the above possibility of loss by entering in to a 2 months forward contract with a bank on 01-04-2004 to sell $ 1,00,000 on 31-05-2004 at a price determined on 01-04-2004. The rate, at which the forward contract can be entered into, is the forward rate.

If the forward rate in Rs. 47.80 the forward discount in Rs. 0.20 (Rs. 48-Rs. 4700) and the exporter can be sure of realising Rs. 47, 80,000 from his dollar on 31-5-2004 what every happens to spot ration that day.

Likewise, if the forward rate is Rs. 48.30 per dollar, the forward premium is Rs. 0.30 (Rs. 48.30 Rs. 48) and the exporter can be sure of realising Rs. 48,30,000 from his dollars on 31-5-2004.

Though the forward contract protects against adverse movements of exchange rates, it also prevents the exporter from gaining out of favourable movements, which is dony be interesting into certain special contracts called option contracts". The discussions on the "opinion contracts" are beyond the scope of this chapter.

The expressions "Hedging " refers to action designed to guard against risk which is involved in the foreign currency transaction. It is possible to hedge against such risks by forward transaction, which have been explained above.

***(e)* Abritage and Transaction :** A business can enter into foreign currency transaction mainly in two ways. First by undertaking projects in other countries and second through exports and imports. In case of foreign projects a business exposes itself to certain special risks *viz.*, political, cultural and economic etc., including transaction and transaction.

The translation, transaction and economic risks arise mainly from exchange rate fluctuations. In case of exports and imports, the principal risk in transactions risk.

The principle players in the foreign exchange market are large international banks and major international corporations. The banks make the market, which means they make two ways quotes for foreign currencies, one the buying or bed rate and the other the selling or asking rate.

The banks may enter into transaction with individuals, companies or other banks. The market in which banks, trade with each other is called the inter-bank market.

The Indian foreign exchange market is a controlled market in which the reserve bank of India is the key player. The other participants of this market are banks and the business under takings.

Business undertakings in India can buy and sell only as much foreign currencies as they need for actual transactions. In other words, speculations in foreign currencies are not permitted in India.

Under section 10 of Foreign exchange management Act (FEMA), 1999, none other tan the persons authorised by the Reserve Bank of India can deal in foreign exchange in India. The person so authorised are required to comply with directions and orders issued by RBI from time to time. They are also to follow the rules frammed by the foreign exchange dealers association of India (FEDAI).

Foreign exchange quotations may be direct quote or indirect quote.

A direct quote is the amount of domestic currency equivalent to one unit of foreign currency (*i.e.*, 1 US dollar = Rs. 45) where as, an indirect quote is the amount of foreign currency which is equivalent to one unit of domestic currency (*i.e.* Rs. 1 = dollar).

Thus, Indirect quote is the reciprocal of direct quote.

(f) **FERA & FEMA : (**FERA) Foreign Exchange Regulation Act, 1973 was meant to govern the inflow of foreign capital in India. The most essential element in the Act is section 29, which provides for permission, general or specific, by the foreign companies from the reserve bank of India in case of following.

(1) In case the company wants to carry on existing or new activities trading, commercial or industrial in nature.

(2) If it wants to acquire wholly or partly any under taking or its parts.

(3) If it wants to purchase any Indian company.

(4) If it wants to open branches, offices or other places of business in India.

Under the Act, all Foreign Companies and Indian Companies with non-resident investments exceeding 40 per cent are required to get the approval of RBI for undertaking business activities in India.

In 1991, the Govt. of India had amended FERA Act so as to allow 51% equity participation by all foreign companies.

FERA Amendment, 1993 gave rise to FEMA (Foreign Exchange Management Act), 1999.

Continuing with its policy to make FERA more relevant to economic needs, the Govt. of India had promulgated the ordinance amending the provisions of FERA, 1973.

The ordinance of January 8, 1993, debates nine sections, amends 19 sections and adds two section to FERA, 1973.

FEMA, 1999 came into existence replacing FERA, 1973 and under this Act, only the RBI is authorised to deal in foreign exchange in India as described earlier.

(g) **Causes of Fluctuations in Foreign Exchange Rates :** The various theories of exchange rate determination, seek to explain only the equilibrium or normal long period exchange rates.

Market rates (or day-to-day rates) of exchange are subject to fluctuations in response to the supply of and demand for international money transfers. In fact, there are various factors which affect or influence the demand for and supply of foreign currency which are ultimately responsible for the short-tern fluctuations in the exchange rate.

Important among these are :

(i) **Trade Movements :** Any change in imports or exports will certainly cause a change in the rate of exchange. If imports exceed exports, the demand for foreign currency rises; hence the rate of exchange moves against the country. Conversely, if exports exceed imports, the demand for domestic currency rises and the rate of exchange moves in favour of the country.

(ii) **Capital Movements :** International Capital movements from one country for short periods to avail of the high rate of interest prevailing abroad or for long periods for the purpose of making long-term investment aborad.

Any export or import of capital from one country to another will bring about a change in the rate of exchange.

(iii) **Stock Exchange Operations :** These include granting of loans, payment of interest on foreign loans, repatriation of foreign capital, purchase and sale of foreign securities etc. which influence demand for foreign funds and through it the exchange rates.

(iv) **Speculative Transactions :** These include transactions ranging from anticipation of seasonal movements in exchange rates to the extreme one *i.e.* flight of capital. In periods of political uncertainty, there is heavy speculation in foreign money. There is scramble for purchasing certain currencies and some currencies are unloaded.

Thus speculative activities bring about wide fluctuations in exchange rates.

(v) **Banking Operations :** Banks are the major dealers in foreign exchange. They sell drafts, transfer funds, issue letters of credits, accept foreign bills of exchange etc.

These operations influence the demand for and supply of foreign exchange, and hence the exchange rates.

(vi) **Monetary Policy :** An expansionist monetary policy has generally an inflationary impact, while a contractionist policy tends to have a deflationary inflation. Inflation

and deflation bring about a change in internal value of money. This reflects in a similar change in the external value of money. Inflation means a rise in the domestic price level, fall in the internal purchasing power of money and hence a fall in exchange rate.

(vii) **Political Conditions :** Political stability of a country can help very much to maintain a high exchange rate for its currency, for it attracts foreign capital which causes the foreign exchange rate to more in its favour.

On the contrary, Political instability causes a panic flight of capital from the country, hence the home currency depreciates in the eyes of foreigners and consequently, its exchange rate falls.

2. COMPETITIVE ADVANTAGE

Michael Porter, Professor of Harvard Business School in his book "The Completive Advantage (1990)" has stated that following four attributes of a business foster strong competition in both inside and outside of country of location.

(i) **Factor conditions** : Skills, Technology, Capital formation, Infrastructure

- Skill of employees are improved through education, training and development
- Technology upgradation and development need to be carried out by adopting R & D activities in the company. Modern technology may also be procured from the advanced countries together with meaning proper arrangement for technology absorption in the company.
- Capital formation should be productive.
- Infrastructure includes electric power generation, water supply & drainage, roads, railways, airports & sea ports facilities.

(ii) **Demand Condition** : Demand conditions are favoured by sizeable population with good disposable income, proper demographic characteristics etc.

(iii) **Related & Supposing Industries** : Development of ancillary industries to support large scale industries like petro-chemicals, motor vehicles, railway locomotives and air crafts manufacturing etc.

(iv) **Firm Strategy Structure and rivalry** :

- Strategy of Business Firm : To gain competitive advantage through new product development, higher economy scale of operation, Maximising productivity, Production of goods/services of the superior quality and at the lowest unit cost of production, product differentiation and incorporating superior marketing techniques.

- Structure & rivalry : The interfirm rivalry for the business is influenced by the factor shown below :

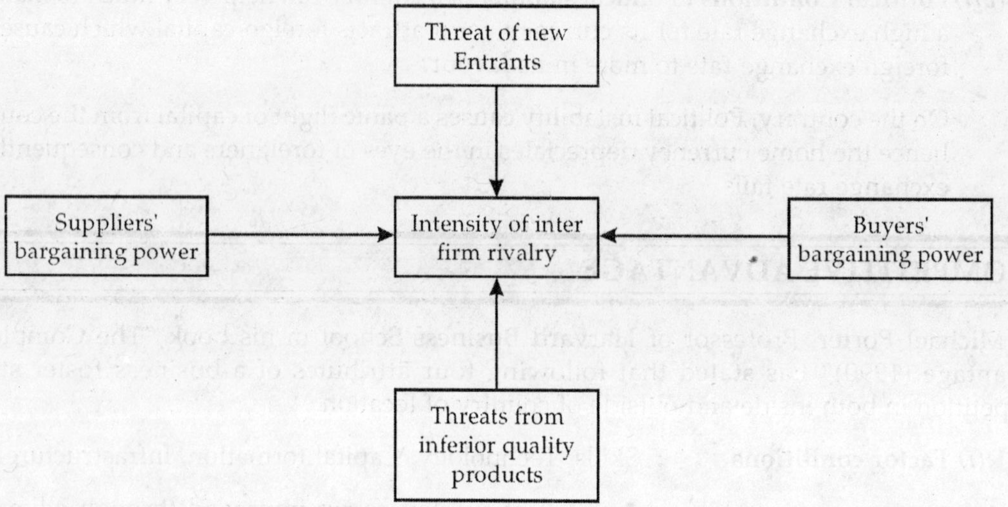

(a) Important Factors for Economic Growth :

These four factors are :

(1) **Human Resource and its Quality :** Example Japan, Singapore, Honkong are the countries which have achieved competitive advantage by developing the quality of human resource *i.e.* giving importance to education and health care systems.

(2) **Natural Resources :** Countries like UAE, Kuwait have abundant crude petroleum as natural resources to help them achieve competitive advantage.

(3) **Capital Formation *i.e.* Capital Productivity :** Countries like China, South Korea and India have invested in infrastructures for helping industrial growth.

(4) **Technological Progress :** Advanced countries like USA, UK, France and Japan have achieved competitive advantage through technological development and progress. These above four factors consist of four wheels of economic growth.

3. THEORY OF INTERNATIONAL TRADE

(i) Introduction

No country has abundance of all the resources and each country tends to specialise in the production of those goods which it can produce most efficiently with its resources. It then exchanges the surplus production of these produced goods with the surplus production of other countries.

Thus international trade suffers from some natural and artificial barriers.

Each country has its own currency and banking system.' Movement of goods between countries is subject to certain government restrictions. Inspite of all these factors against international trade it has been steadily growing.

First two theories are classical theories of International Trade :

- According to the Principle of Absolute-Advantage, basis of trade between two countries exists when each of there can specialise in the production of a good which it can produce cheaper than the other.

- According to the principle of comparative each country specialises in the production of those goods and services in which it has greater comparative advantage and imports these goods in which it has greater comparative, disadvantage.

  For example—India can produce textile garments at a cost much lower than sophisticated Air Crafts, these fire, it will produce and export textiles and imports Boeing/AIRBUS air crafts.

Following is also known as Heckscher-Ohlin theorem :

- According to Modem theory of International Trade, a country specialises in the production of a good, and exports it, which uses more of the relatively abundant factor, and imports those goods which use more of relatively scarce factors.

- For example, a country having abundant labour but scarce capital, will tend to specialise in the production of labour—intensive goods and will tend to against import capital intensive goods in exchange. Diamond is produced in S. Africa and cut and polished in India, since latter job is labour-intensive.

(ii) Gains from International Trade

International Trade is beneficial for all the trading partners The principle of comparative advantage shows that if different countries specialise on the basis of their comparative costs, all the trading countries will be better-off compared to a situation where they do not trade all.

Gains from International Trade can broadly be classified as static Gains and Dynamic Gains :

Static Gains : Static gains from trade are the increase in well-being of the countries entering into trade with each other.

Both trading partner countries are benefited by specialisation and trade.

The principle of comparative advantage leads to an important conclusion that free trade among nations encourages international specialisation among nations.

Following are the benefits for countries participating in International Trade :

- relatively more efficient allocation of resources of the trading partners

- increased production of goods and services in the countries specialising in the goods and services where they enjoy comparative advantage.

- product prices find to get equalised among trading partners and

- resource prices among trading countries find to get equalised as relative demand for resources finds to adjust so as to correspond with relative demand of goods and services.

Dynamic Gains : International trade has a vary significant role to play in economic growth of nations. According to Robertson, International trade is an 'engine' of growth.

Major dynamic gains are as follows :

- International trade results in increasing output and income of the nations and thus it leads to economic growth.

  Through international trade, the world *economy* can achieve a more efficient allocation of resources and a higher level of well-being of its people.

- The underdeveloped countries can take advantage of the superior technology of advanced countries. It is possible only when the former import capital goods from the latter.

- When underdeveloped countries establish trade relations with advanced countries, the former are not only able to procure advanced technology but the latest technical knowhow and managerial skills which are extremely important for growth.

Thus, if each nations specialises according to its resource endowments and enters into trade with other nations, the world economy and economy of each of these trading partners can realise greater output and income and can maintain a higher level of economic growth,

To the extent that countries are not able to trade freely, they are forced to shift their resources from more efficient (*i.e.* lower cost), production to less efficient (*i.e.* higher cost) production in order to meet their domestic demands.

(iii) Limitations of International Trade (Trade Restrictions)

Though international trade is beneficial for countries free trade has not received favour from Govts.

This is because free international trade has following limitations :

- Cheap imported goods may destroy local industries manufacturing those goods.
- Specialisation resulting from trade may lead to lop sided growth of the economy.
- If trade is uncontrolled, it may lead to economic handicap in the long run. For example—a country may export some strategic raw materials (whose supply is limited) in large quantities, thus jeopardising future developments.
- Dependence on other countries may prove fetal in situations like war.

(iv) Forms of Trade Restrictions

Following are the main kinds of restrictions on internations trade :

- **Tariffs or Customs duties :** This is the most common form of trade restriction Customs duty is imposed as a percentage of the value of goods being imported either in terms of physical units or ink terms of weights in tons.

- **Quantitative Restrictions :** These restrictions limit the physical quantity of goods to be imported during a given period. For this purpose, generally the system of licensing ana quota are used. Quota limits the total quantity of goods to be imported, while import licensing limits the imports of an individual importer.

  The quantitative restrictions have become very common in the recent time.

- **Foreign Exchange Restrictions :** This involves control and restrictions of sale and purchase of foreign exchange. Though this system was originally used to mitigate the situation of foreign exchange shortage, over time it has been increasingly used to control and restrict imports.

The general practice under exchange control and regulations is to release foreign exchange on the basis of set priorities of imports of different goods.-

Most of the underdeveloped countries are following an active economic policy, in the sense that there is control and regulation of the economy by the Govt. In such a case, foreign trade control regulation also becomes one of the instruments of growth and economic development

Protection is, therefore, used as one of the devices to influence the direction and rata of planned economic development.

International Trade is also discussed in Chapter 4 of Economics II (Macro Economics).

(v) Balance of Payments

International balance of payments do not include only export and import of goods and services.

They also consist of :

- Buying and constructing plants abroad
- Buying and selling foreign securities
- Loans and grants by the Govt.
- Private gifts and grants
- Sale and grant of military aid.

The international balance of payments is a summary information of all the transactions that take place between the nation's residents and residents of all the foreign countries.

It records the nation's purchases from and sales to all other nations and it accounts for any differences between sales and purchases by showing how these have been financed,'

Depending on whether it has purchased more or less than what it has sold to the other nations, a country will have balance of payments surplus or deficit.

The balance of payments surplus implies that the nation's exports were more than sufficient to finance the sum of its imports, public and private grants, public and private capital outflows.

The balance of payments deficit indicates the insufficiency of export to finance imports and other capital outflows.

It must be noted balance of trade and balance of payments are not the same Balance of payments is more comprehensive than balance of trade,^ Balance of trade is the difference between the import and export of goods by a nation, which is only a part of balance of payments,' "Balance" in balance of trade implies gap between exports and imports.

The balance of Payments (BOP) is broader in its scope and include trade in merchandise and services, It is a systematic record of all international economic transaction, visible and invisible, of a country during one year.

BOP, therefore, presents a better picture of a country's financial transactions with the rest of the world than the balance of trade.

The analysis of BOP is done in terms of two major sub-divisions—current account and capital account.

- **Current Account :** Import and export of goods and services + invisible amounts *i.e.* foreign travels & NRI remittances.
- **Capital Account :** All international transactions related to scale & purchase of assets which includes corporate shares & debentures, government securities & deposits in commercial banks and real estates etc.
- **Balancing the Accounting :** Reflecting the double entry book keeping procedures the aggregated balance or payments account must balances. In fact, any current account deficit is wiped out either by borrowing or by reducing foreign assets. Thus, the balance of international payments as a whole must by definition show a final zero balance *i.e.*

Current Account Balance	+	Capital Account Balance	+	Official Reserve Account Balance	=	0

Thus, the overall balance of payments must balance *i.e.* the deficit in one area implies a surplus in another. If a country suffers from a deficit in its current account balance it must generate an off setting surplus on the sum of its capital account & official reserve account balance.

Transactions relating to goods, services and income constitute the currant account, where as the capital account presents transfers of money and other capital items and change's in the country's foreign assets and liabilities resulting from the transaction recorded in the current account.

(vi) Measures to Correct the Imbalances in Balance of Payments

The balance of payments disequilibrium can be corrected by—

- Monetary measures—which include depreciation devaluation of domestic currency, deflation and exchange control.
- Non monetary measures—These consist of import control, export promotion, tariff, quota bilateral agreements and state trading.

BOP is also discussed in Chapter 4 of Economics II (Macro Economics).

(vi) GATT, Developing Countries and India

General Agreement on Tariffs and Trade (GATT) was established in 1947 after the Second World War with 23 member countries.

At GATT Conference in 1964 at Brussels, known as the Kennedy Round, GATT had 62 members and in 1993 Conference known as Uruguay Round these were 123 countries as its member.

Objectives of GATT

The general objective of GATT was to enable member-countries to entar into reciprocal and mutually advantageous arrangements to bring about substantial reduction in tariff as also reduction or removal of other barriers to international trade, and if possible, elimination of discriminatory practices in the sphere of international trade.

In other words, the general objectives of GATT were :

- To bring about improvement in the Standard of living of people in member-countries.
- To encourage full employment and steady and growing level of real income and affective demand.
- To bring about expansion of world trade and world production.
- The enable full use of the world's resources.

The above general objectives are to be achieved through evolving a pattern of world trade based upon multilateral trade and non-discriminatory tariffs with the ultimate objectives of the countries concerned.

WTO in Promotion of World Trade and India

The World Trade Organisation (WTO) was established on 1st January, 1995 and WTO is the embodiment of the GATT's Uruguay Round results and the successor to the GATT.

WTO has larger membership than GATT, the present number of member's stands at 140 and India is one of the founder members of the WTO. WTO's headquarter is in Geneva, Switzerland.

WTO's roles in promoting world trade vis-a-vis India's advantages as a member of WTO are high lighted through the following prints :

(i) Over 75% of WTO members are developing countries, who are willing to adopt economic reforms in their respective countries and India will gain in economic terms by joining WTO.

(ii) WTO promotes world trade and India is in urgent needs of export and importy therefore India gains to be part of the multilateral trading system.

(iii) WTO through International Trade Centra (ITC) help the developing countries like India in formulating and implementing export promotion programmes as well as import operations and techniques.

(iv) WTO provides information and advice on export markets and marketing techniques and assets in establishing export promotion and marketing services and imports training programmes for country's personnel required to work for these services.

ITC's help is freely available for the least developed countries.

(v) Increases in world trade are substantial especially in the product segments such as textiles, agriculture, forestry, fishery, processed food and beverages and developing countries like India are expected to obtain large gains from these sectors.

(vi) Another important role WTO plays is that a member country is served from entering into multiple bilateral trade negotiations with other countries for undertaking export—import activities.

(vii) WTO provides for a multilateral set of rules which ensure greater promotion against bilateral pressures or against trade restrictions and a member country is benefited by these rules.

(viii) The Uruguay Round Package consisted of several area such as tariffs textiles and agriculture, those related to market access and India is placed in a favourable position with respect to these areas.

WTO is also discussed in Chapter 5 of Economics II (Macro Economics).

PROBABLE QUESTIONS

1. Explain with the help of the principles of comparative advantage, why do countries trade with each other.
2. What do you mean by balance of payments disequilibrium? How can it be corrected?
3. Discuss gains of international trade.
4. Describe the objectives of GATT.
5. What role does WTO Play in promoting international trade? How is India benefited by being a member country of WTO?
6. "Globalisation has helps India to have a dominant economy in the world during the last decade"—Elucidate.
7. Discuss about the significance of International Trade for a developing country like India.
8. "Human Resource Management must be receptive to the new globalisation process"—Discuss.

CHAPTER 8

INDIAN ECONOMIC OVERVIEW

1. India as an Underdeveloped Economy
2. India as a Developing Economy
3. India as a Mixed Economy
4. Various Sectors of Indian Economy
5. Indian Economy Since Economic Reforms in 1991
6. Dark Sides of Indian Economy in the 21st Century
7. The Brighter Sides of Indian Economy in the 21st Century
8. Current Status of Indian Economy

1. INTRODUCTION

Presently India is a developing country. Though Indian economy no longer suffers from stagnation as it did under the British, the development since independence has not been spectacular. India had opted for a planned capitalist development, and accordingly built up a mixed economy.

During the British rule, the economic policies of the British rulers were largely responsible for the country's economic backward ness.

The economic planning as practised in India over the past five decades and the development of the public and private sectors were meant for moving a stand still economy in keeping with its characteristics as a mixed economy.

The salient features of Indian economy can be broadly discussed under the following three heads, *i.e.* *(a)* India—An underdeveloped economy *(b)* India—A developing economy *(c)* India—A mixed economy.

(a) India—An Underdeveloped Economy

The following important features of an underdeveloped economy are present in the Indian economy.

(1) Low per capita income : The US per capita income (2005) US $30,000 china $ 1600 India < $ 1000, Nov., 2007—PCI US $ 1000.

(2) Inequitable distribution income and high incidence of poverty : High incidence of poverty BPL about 30% population (mostly tribal and rural per capital earning $ 1 dollar or less undernourishment & child mortality rates high. Similarly, the income between the rich & poor—is high.

(3) Predominance of agriculture :

In 1811—UK's 38.3 % population dependent on Agriculture

In 2007—India 70% (about) " " " " "

Prevalence of distinguished employment in India.

(4) Rapita population growth : Let 1950-2000 India population has troubled to cross 1 billion mark current growth rate @ 20% is higher then world standard.

(5) Low Level of Human Development : UN'S HDI 2002 India HDI 0.595 compared to Norway (first) 0.956, USA 0.939, Japan 0.938, UK 0.936, France 0.932, China 0.745, Sri Lanka 0.740, Bangladesh 0.509, Elthiopia (Africa) 0.359 India's HDI Rank is 127 among 170 country with Norway 0.956 & Ethiopia 0.359.

HDI elements are average life span, knowledge (literary level) and standard of living (per capita income).

(6) Wide spread unemployment : Educated and uneducated employment rates are high unemployment in India is chronic and results from structural defects in the economy.

These is high industrial in employment also.

(7) Poor capital formation : Leads to scarity of capital.

Growth in economy comes for servings and investments. Due to scarcity of capital growth has been stagular or poor (barring recent growth rate of 8%).

(8) Technological backwardness : Currently except IT sector the other technology spheres—there is lack of innovation practically no new technological development.

(b) India a Developing Economy

Economic development in India has broadly two aspects

1. Quantitative 2. Structural

(i) Quantitative estimate for National Income trends

→ Rise in NNP 1950-51 → Rs. 1,32,367 crore
2003-04 → Rs. 12,66,005 crore

Thus over 53 years of economic planning the trend rate of growth of national income was around 4.35% per annum. This is more moderate result.

→ Rise in Per Capital Income (PCI)—This is considered a better growth index than former.

PCI → 1950-51 Rs. 3,687 (at 1993-94 price level)

PCI → 2003-2004 Rs. 11,798

Average growth rate of PCI between 1950-2003 has been 3.3-3.5% per annum.

(ii) Structural changes : Structural changes indicate that the process of development is continuing sin independence. Even though speed of change in slow.

→ Significant changes in sector distribution of domestic product An important index of development is steady decline in the importance of agriculture.

In 1950-51—The share of agriculture in GDP → 59.2% (1993-94 Price level)

In 2005-06— " " " " GDP → 20% (at current price level)

3. Sectors in India Economy

Primary sector—Agriculture

Secondary sector—Industries Mining, construction & electricity etc. This is known as industrial sector.

Industrial sector —	1950-51	13.3% GDP	[at 1993-94 price level]
	2002-03	27.3% GDP	
	2005-06	26% GDP	

Tertiary Sector—Trade, Transport, Commn. & Services—known as services sector.

Services sector —	1950-51	27.5% GDP
	2002-03	50.7% GDP
	2005-06	54% GDP

(iii) Slowly changing occupational distribution of population. In a developing economy, occupational distribution of population steadily changes in favour of secondary and tertiary sectors. This happens as result of decline in the importance of agriculture from which transfer of population to other sectors takes place.

In 1951—69.7% population depended an agriculture

1991—64.9% " " " " "

(iv) Growth of basic capital goods industries : Under the 2nd five year plan a high priority was accorded to capital goods industries which is pre requisite to over all growth of economy.

Iron, steel, heavy chemical Fertilizers, heavy Engg, Machine Tools, Locomotive, Aluminium, Electrical, Egypt, Petroleum products, industries were developed during economic plan periods.

(v) Expansion is social overhead capital : Social overhead capital broadly includes transport facilities, Irrigation system, Energy production units, Educational institution. Healthcare system etc. The development of these create favourable condition for growth and result in better standard of living.

Education has not expanded at a desired rate, as a result even now 35% of people in India are illiterate. This is a sign of back wardness.

(vi) Progress in the banking and financial sector : Bank nationalisation → 1969 → more credits to small & large industries and 3 sectors of economy.

Opening of stock exchange and SEBI

Entry of foreign banks, Mutual funds (morgan Stauby, Menil Lynch etc.)

Insurance—privatisation and private domestic and foreign companies entry in the insurance field.

(c) India—A mixed Economy

Mixed economy with a dominant private sectors

Services : Insurance, Air Lines, Banking, Financial market

Industries : Petroleum, Fertilizer, Cement, Steel

Sun rise industries : IT, Software, BPOs (ITES)

Public sector : Nava Ratna Status for some PSUs. Sick industries being diverted or privatised.

NIP (New Industrial Policy) : 1991 various physical controls have been withdrawn.

2. INDIAN ECONOMY SINCE ECONOMIC REFORMS IN 1991

(a) Macro Economic Performance

The economic reforms introduced in 1991 have put Indian economy on a higher growth path. We have an opportunity to accelerate poor growth further and take of into a ghihg growth trajectory.

The trend rate of growth of GDP was 5.6 per cent per annum during the thirteen year period since the reforms, compared to 5.9 per cent during the six year period from 1985-86 to 1990-91.

Inflation was higher upto 1996 since the reforms as compared to pre-reform period. Thereafter, it had distinctly slowed down.

Since the structural reforms have adversely affected poor in many countries, it was expected to happen in this country also after the reform process was initiated in mid 1991.

According to the noted economist Jagdish Bhagvati and other the economic growth improved significantly as a result of the economic reform since 1991 which in turn has reduced poverty although it has also increased the income inequality.

Since the reforms there has been a significant increase in inward foreign direct investment.

The average rate of industrial growth over the post reform period (1990/91-2003/04) is at 5.2 per and it is at 9 per cent in the year 2006.

The economy is now more open and the share of merchandise imports plus exports in current GDP at market prices has gone up to 17.6 per cent in 1990s as against 12.4 per cent during 1985-1990.

Balance of trade position has also shown some improvement and the countries foreign exchange reserves are more than adeguata for 15 months import requirement compared to one month's in 1990-91.

India's central Govt. fiscal deficit as a proportion to GDP has marginally declined in the post reform period, and the revenue deficit during 2005-06 ad 2006-07 are showing a declining trend.

Since the reforms there has been a significant increase in inward foreign direct investment over the previous decade.

3. INDIAN ECONOMY IN 2006-07 AND BEYOND

(a) The Darker Side of the Economy

The economy land scape of India has undergone tremendous change with visible signs of growth momentum in all sectors. However, growth perse, is not sustainable unless the benefits of the growth are widespread. Moving to the next level of economic development requires our growth model of bring in inclusive growth so that the world becomes a better place to live in.

This has been reiterated by the Approach paper to the 11th-five-year plan with a vision of broad based and inclusive growth. World wide, inclusive growth has received recognition with the nobel peace prize being conferred to Prof. Mohd. Yunus and the Grameen Bank of bangladesh for enabling large population groups to find ways to break out of poverty.

While Indian economy has shown an average growth of 8.1% in the last 3 years, the benefits have not equitably percolated to the different sequents of our society, especially to those in the lower rungs of socio-economic ladder.

The rural and agricultural sector, in particular, has not gained the desired momentum of growth and development.

Nevertheless, the high growth has raised the expectation of the people for better delivery of core public services like health care education water supply and electricity etc.

If these expectation are not, satisfied, if will result in social disorder due to prevalent social disparity.

India still suffers from substantial poverty with 34.7% of population subsist unless than US # 1 a day, 79.9% live on US $ 2 per day. About 214 million people are chronically food insecure and 50% of children (mostly tribal and rural) are undernourished and 68 out of 1000 die before the age of one year.

For inclusive growth to be a reality, government intervention in the form of institutional and legal support to poor is warranted.

Even though the Indian Parliament has passed in Feb., 2006 the Historical National Rural Employment Guarantee Act (NREGA) that guarantees 100 days of wage employment in a year to every rural household whose adult members are willing to do unskilled manual work, the actual implementation and the benefits are to be judged in future.

Since the last decade, the phenomenal growth of IT and ITES in India, more and more talented scientists, Engineers and Technologists are attracted towards, these sectors due to much higher monetary compensation compared to the universities, Research Institution and Higher Educational Institutions.

As a result, there is drying up of basic research in science and technology which is likely to diminish the development in the scientific and technology spheres that could help the country to develop a complementary and or alternative source of economic growth in the event of BPO bonanza, which is dependent upon demands placed by foreigns, runs its course in future.

(*b*) The Brighter Side of the Economy

The Indian economy is racing along and GDP has climbed to about $ 690 billion (Rs. 3,20,200 Crores) in 25 up from about $600 billion in 2003. At the current speed and with 8 percent growth becoming the norm, Indian economy is salted to touch $ 1 trillion by 2010. In the year 2006, the manufacturing and services sectors are registering the growth rates of 9 and 10 percent respectively. Manufacturing BPOs, IT and Softwares and over all exports in India are driving the economy at a much brisker pace of economic growth. New factories manufacturing motor cars to mobile phones, computers to washing machines, steel to tractors are coming up in the country side. Out sourcing is growing at 30% annually and India is famously a world beater in this.

Global manufactures are looking into the future and finding a serious demographic squeeze facing china, because of its one child policy and turning to India which is likely to have more young workers aged 20 to 24 years by as early as 2013. The international Labour Organisation predicts that by 2020, India will have 116 million workers in this age bracket to China's 94 million.

But by far, the biggest question mark hanging over the rise of manufacturing in India lies in the whether the country has enough roads, ports and electricity generating plants to move huge quantities of goods and power the factories that make them.

The clearly visible speed breakers for Indian economic progress are agriculture, power and rural sector.

It is clear that the infrastructure is not keeping pace at any where near the speed that is required to cope with all this fast growth. The world case is of course, electricity, which needs to grow at 10 per cent annually just to keep pace with the increasing demand.

Unless, these are sustained improvements in budget performance, the government will not have the fiscal space to improve the infrastructure and undertake the social expenditure needed to broaden the inclusiveness of the growth process.

However, India's strength lies in its flourishing entrepreneurial spirit and this has resulted in the existence of a vibrant and dynamic private sector.

The shape of Indian Economy was projected by the planning commission is given below :

The Shape of the economy

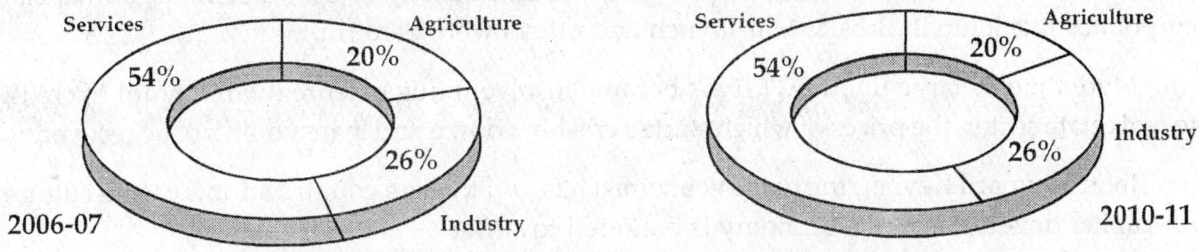

Sector-wise break up as projected at the end of the 11th Plan by the Planning Commission

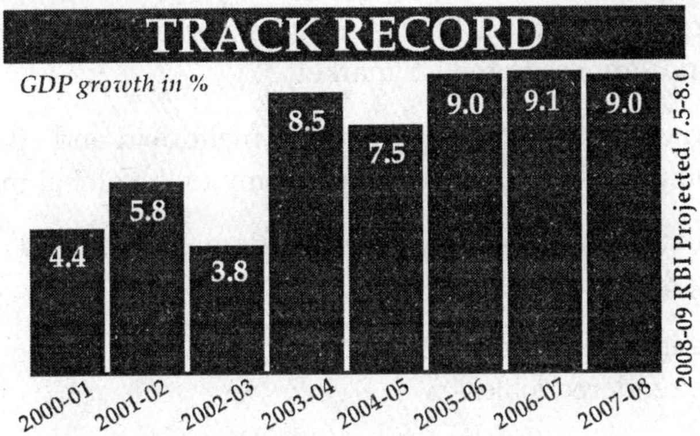

Fig. India's GDP growth rates

in 2007-08

MIXED BAG

Industry	% change over previous year			
	06-07	07-08	06-07(Q4)	07-08(Q4)
Agri, foresty & fishing	3.8	4.5	4.9	2.9
Mining & quarrying	5.7	4.7	8.2	5.9
Manufacturing	12.0	8.8	12.8	5.8
Electricity, gas & water supply	6.0	6.3	5.4	5.6
Construction	12.0	9.8	12.2	12.6
Trade, hotels, transport & comm.	11.8	12.0	11.6	12.4
Financing, insurance realty & biz service	13.9	11.8	13.4	10.5
Community, social, personal services	6.9	7.3	5.1	9.5
GDP	9.6	9.0	9.7	8.8

4. THE STATE OF INDIA ECONOMY 3RD QUARTER OF 2008

The US economic crisis became public in the 2nd quarter of 2008 when large financial corporates like lehman Bros & Marilllynch and others went bankrupt.

More than 30 large financial MNCs became insolvent due to lenregulated grant of credit to real estate sector, the prices of which started crashing down and loans could not be recovered.

John Meynard Keyner, the noted economist has said that is a country adopts casino culture for capital development, its economy is bounded to suffer.

The US sever recession of 2008 is country to 1930-33 great depression.

Most European countries, china, Brazil and others enjoy major export oriented benefits by exporting goods and services to the US market.

These are countries mostly affected by the US meltdown and so also India which has pushed a globalisation process by opening its economy to the global market.

Even though Indian economy growth is mostly domestic demand oriented due to global meltdown Indian mfg & services sectors are also badly affected.

IT sector whose export earnings to US was substantial, has been badly hit and large nos of personal have been rendered jobless.

G.O.I. has taken Steps to cut CRR for supplying funds to the market 0.5% cut in CRR supplies Rs. 20,000 crore to the economy.

Other measures are proposed to be taken are reducing excise duties & sales taxes which would boost the mfg/ services sectors by reducing cost of production and stimulating demand for goods/services.

It is recommended that G.O.I could invest a portion of Rs. 250 billion foreign exchange reserve to build infrastructures in electricity generations, roads, ports, & air ports which would create substantial employment and for the present and would pacilitate coming up of industries and services in future. At this junction government should resort to increase expenditure spending to stimulate demand.

IMF has estimated that by 3rd quarter of 2009 the global economic recession will be over.

5. INDIA ECONOMY—2008

1. We are thrilled that India has a constellations of billionaires and that over companies have set their rights on buying some of the world's oldest and most prosecutions brands. We exult that despite the economic meltdown in the west, our mammoth middle class still marches on into malls, taken flights with gay a bandon and buys apartments at prices that their parents could not have dreamt of in their wildest dreams.

This is one India

Another India lurks in the shadow of this flittering growth where debt-ridden farmers kill them selves every day in despair, and poverty forest thousands of children to drop out of school. Where the future of many is pegged to a good monsoon this year and rising prices are a huge concern. Where people still suffer from hunger everyday and die of diseases that can be easily cured.

(a) The world's largest economies, 29th July, 2008

India : The India economy is the 12th largest in the world. That is India's GDP stands at $ 1.171 Trillion. However, in purchasing power parity, India is the world's fourth largest economy. Its GDP in PPP terms is $3.092 billion. These are the year 2007 figure, recently released by the **world bank.**

PPP—is an economic theory that estimates the amount of adjustment needed on the exchange rate between countries in order for the exchange to be equivalent to each currency's purchasing power.

India is one of the four test growing economies in the world, yet its annual per capita income remain quite low at $950 or about Rs. 40,000 That puts India in the 160th spot.

Incidentally, world bank's figures show that the world's GDP is at $54.347 trillion and India accounts for just over 2 percent of global GDP.

The world's largest economics

1. **United states :** GDP is at 13.82 trillion account for more than 25% of global GDP. On "PPP" terms it the world's leading economy but on PCI basis (PCI = $ 46,040) begs it at the 15th spot.

2. **Japan :** GDP $ 4.377 trillion, 2nd largest world economy on ppp terms it is ranked 3rd at $4.283 trillion & PCI basis ($37,670) it is ranked 25th.

3. **Germany :** 3rd largest economy with GDP at $3.297 trillion, PPP terms it 5th largest (42.752) & PCI ($38,860) it is 23rd.

4. **China :** Asian giant world's 4th largest economy, GDP $ 3.281 trillion, PPP terms $ 7.055 trillion, it is ranked 2nd in world. PCI ($2630 per years) is still low.

5. **UK :** GDP $ 2.728 trillion, world's fifth largest economy "PPP" basic ($ 2.082 trillion) it is ranked 7th PCI ($ 42,740) is impressive, a rich nation & ranked 19th in the spot.

6. **France 7. Italy 8. Spain 9. Canada 10. Brazil 11. Russian Federation**

Demographic characteristics of India as on 2008-09 India has a very young workforce, an essential requirement for a vibrant economy. The advanced countries are worried because of their aging population and dwindling workforce. They are out sourcing work to countries like India India's population growth of around 2 per cent which is more than the population of some countries.

INDIAN ECONOMY AT A GLANCE

Current State of Indian Economy—2009

Due to the delayed and deficient monsoon in the most parts of the country, India has been experiencing one of the word droughts in the recent decades and food is likely to be in short supply. About 60 per cent of the population who depend on agriculture and allied activities for their livelihood are going to experience a substantial reduction in their earnings millions of small farmers and landless wage workers may possibly starve, quite a few will commit suicide, some may die out of malnutrition.

Even after 60 years' of independence, India's agriculture still remains a gamble in the monsoon, output fluctuates in frightening proportion with the vagaries of the rain god's—mood. India's agriculture, even though might provide livelihood for three-fifth of the country's population, its contribution to the nation's GDP is a paltry. One-fifth or less. The rate of growth in this sector may be in the negative this year.

The other side of he economy which is receiving equally wide coverage in the media concerns movements in India's gross domestic product. The government of India has officially announced that our GDP this year is to grow at a rate exceeding six percent. And this is at the backdrop of a global recession, the worst after the Great Depression of 1930s. The growth rate in the USA is zero, in the West Europe, too, it is barely positive. While such is the daunting picture in most of the rest of the world, India has by and large held on to its growth targets. The services sector continues to be buoyant and the growth in the manufacturing sector has been showing encouraging. Tata Steel's Indian operation has exhibited encouraging profitability, but its merged entity the Anglo Dutch Steel Company Corus Steel has produced substantial loss for the last two quarters of financial year.

Foreign exchange is rolling in, almost qushingly is as many expatuate Indians are closing down their accounts in the crash prone American banks and sending money home. The foreign exchange reserve is very comfortable at over 265 billion US dollar. The stock market is booming because of these cumulative factors, the sensitive index has crossed 17000 mark for the first time in the last 16 months and is likely to touch 20,000 mark very soon.

Sixty-odd years of independence have produced very odd sorts of links and non-links in the economic sphere. The economy, as measured by wise grammarians, expands and supposedly prospers. This prosperity does not, however, touch the nation's majority. The economy bursting at the seam invites foreign experts to come and partake of the feast sumptuously spread before them. The nation's majority is left out of this bobanza, which is a non-link.

Besides above, the 2009 Human Development Report (HDR) has placed India at the 134 rank out of 182 countries in the world, Norway, Australia and Iceland are this year's top three ranked countries as per the Human Development Index (HDI), whereas Nigeria (West Africa) Afghanistan and Sierr Leone are bottom three ranked countries. HDI is a summary measure of well-being based on life expectancy, literary, school enrolment and GDP per capita.

HDR is published annually by the United Nations Development Programme (UNDP). However, this year's HDR is based on data till 2007, before the current global downturn.

PROBABLE QUESTIONS

1. Describe the salient features of Indian economy during the first decade of the 21st century.
2. Highlight India as an underdeveloped economy.
3. Highlight India as a developing economy.
4. Highlight India as a Mixed economy.
5. What are three sectors of India's economy and what are their respective contributions to GDP since 1950 to 2008?
6. Highlight Indian Economy Since Economic Reforms in 1991.
7. What have been the dark sides Indian economy in the non millennium?
8. What are the brighter sides of the economy in the new millennium?

QUESTION BANK

Business Economics
Multiple Choice Questions
Group - A

Choose the correct answer from the given alternatives of the following :

1. Profit is maximised only when
   (*a*) Slope of MR curve > slope of MC curve (*b*) Slope of MC = Slope of MR
   (*c*) Slope of MC curve> slope of MR curve (*d*) none of these
2. Curve maintains equilibrium in
   (*a*) Money market (*b*) Product market
   (*c*) Labour market (*d*) None of these
3. LM curve is obtained by equaling
   (*a*) Money demand and money supply (*b*) Income and expenditure
   (*c*) saving and investment (*d*) none of these
4. Marginal costs are closely related to
   (*a*) fixed costs (*b*) variable costs
   (*c*) total costs (*d*) none of these
5. The opportunity cost of a factor of production with specific use is
   (*a*) Very high (*b*) infinite (*c*) zero (*d*) constant
6. When economy is caught into liquidity trade monetary policy is
   (*a*) effective (*b*) infective (*c*) neutral (*d*) none of these
7. Break even point implies
   (*a*) TR = TC (*b*) TR > TC (*c*) TR ≤ TC (*d*) none of these
8. In 1930, there was great
   (*a*) depression (*b*) recession (*c*) expansion (*d*) none of these
9. GATT was replaced by
   (*a*) IMF (*b*) World bank (*c*) WTO (*d*) None of these
10. The comparative advantage theory is developed by

(*a*) Adam Smith (*b*) Amarty Sen

(*c*) David Ricardo (*d*) none of these

11. IS curve is related with

(*a*) goods market (*b*) labour market

(*c*) money market (*d*) None of these

12. Profit is the difference between

(*a*) TR and TC (*b*) TFC and TVC (*c*) AC and MC (*d*) None of these

13. Economic profit will be

(*a*) greater than accounting profit (*b*) less than accounting profit

(*c*) equal to accounting profit (*d*) none of these

14. Economic instability is caused by the functional of the

(*a*) aggregate supply (*b*) agree data demand

(*c*) both (*a*) and (*b*) (*d*) none of these

15. Fiscal policy deals with

(*a*) Government expenditure (*b*) Tax structure

(*c*) Both (*a*) and (*b*) (*d*) Supply of money

16. The comparative advantage doctrine is an analysis

(*a*) trade barrier (*b*) gains from trade

(*c*) both (*a*) and (*b*) (*d*) none of these

17. Exchange rate system can be divided into

(*a*) rigid and flexible category (*b*) fixed and variable category

(*c*) Fixed and flexible category (*d*) none of these

18. WTO stands for

(*a*) World treaty organisation (*b*) world trade organisation

(*c*) Western Treaty organisation (*d*) none of these

19. If annual demand is 1600 units, EOQ is 400 units, then the number of purchase order is

(*a*) 4 (*b*) 5 (*c*) 6 (*d*) 7

20. If the game is a fair one is game theory then value of same will be

(*a*) 3 (*b*) 4 (*c*) 0 (*d*) 6

21. According to schemter, profit arises because

(*a*) managers can anticipate risk (*b*) economy is dynamic in nature

(*c*) managers can introduce innovations in manufacturing techniques

(*d*) managers can exhibit monopoly power.

22. When economy is in the liquidity trap, fiscal policy is

(*a*) effective (*b*) ineffective (*c*) neutral (*d*) none of these

23. SDR stands for

(*a*) specific drawing rights (*b*) special drawing rights
(*c*) special drawings regulations (*d*) special drawing regulations

24. Multi collinearity is defined as
(*a*) explanatory variables are not interdependent
(*b*) these exists no relationship between
(*c*) these exists no relationship between the explanatory variables
(*d*) none of these

25. IS curve maintains equilibriums
(*a*) Money market (*b*) product market
(*c*) labour market (*d*) none of these

26. When CRR increases, money supply in constant the economy.
(*a*) increases (*b*) decreases
(*c*) remains constant (*d*) none of these

27. Monetary policy means
(*a*) change in government expenditure
(*b*) change in money demand in the economy
(*c*) change in money supply in the economy
(*d*) change in tax structure

28. Constrained optimisation means
(*a*) maximising sales volume (*b*) maximising profit
(*c*) minimising total cost (*d*) all of these

29. Regression analysis was advocated by
(*a*) Amartya sen (*b*) David Ricardo
(*c*) Francis Galton (*d*) None of these

30. Business cycle is caused by
(*a*) Fluctuation in government revenue
(*b*) fluctuation in government expenditure
(*c*) fluctuation in economic variables in an economy
(*d*) none of these

Group - B

Short answer Questions

1. Define business economics. Highlight the nature and scope of business economics.
2. Define WTO. Write main function of WTO
3. Find out
(*a*) PV ratio and
(*b*) BEP from the following information

Selling price = Rs. 50 Cost price = Rs. 40

Fixed cost = Rs. 5,000

4. Distinguish between balance to trade and balance of payment
5. A firm's annual inventory requirement is 1600 units. Assume that is acquisition cost is Rs 50 per order. The carrying cost is expected to be Rs. 1 per unit per year. Determine the economic order quantity and the number of order.
6. State the main purpose of demand forecasting.
7. Distinguish between tariff and Quota.
8. Mention the limitation of Break-even Analysis.
9. Define and draw and LM Curve.
10. Suppose firm has following total revenue and total cost function.

    $TR = 300q - 3q^2$ & $T_c = 500q + 50q + 2q^2$

    Find the quantity of output that maximises firm's total profit.
11. Define fiscal and monetary policy. What do you mean by open market operation?
11. What are the assumption of profit maximisation?
12. Explain what you mean by points of IS curve? What is a speculative money demand?
13. The utility function is given by

    U = xy, Budget constraint is given by $100 = xP_{x+y}P_y$. Find the demand for good x and good y.
14. What are various methods of Economic forecasts?
15. Why is controlling trade cycles necessary?
16. Define EOQ equation mathematically.
17. What is the significance of Regression Analysis?
18. What are various types of profits write their relationship?
19. Write short notes on the present state of Indian economy.
20. Discuss the significance of game theory for competitive situation.

Group - C

Long Answer Questions

1. State the purpose of demand forecasting. Describe its uses and limitations in the organisation.
2. Discuss the methods of derivation of IS & LM curves. Mention the role of these two curves in the simultaneous determination of equilibrium rate of interest and income.
3. The utility function is $U = x^3 + y^3$, where maximum utility generated is 72. If price of $x(P_x)$ is 5 and price of $y(P_y)$ is 20, find the money income of the consumer.
4. Define business cycle. What are different phases of a business cycle? How is private business affected during the different phases?
5. Discuss the present position of Indian economy from the point of view of overall development of the various sector of our economy.

6. Given :

The production function $Q = f(x_1, x_2)$ and Cost function $C= x_1x_1 + x_2x_2$

Find out the following :

(a) Maximum output subject to cost constraint.

(b) Minimum cost subject to output constraint using L agranjan multiplier.

7. What are the main objectives of Business Economics? Explain the various situations when the principles of Business Economics are applied. How are Business decisions affected by Economic results? Give examples.

8. What are the causes of business cycles? Discuss about types of business cycles and major stabilisation policies to control business cycles.

9. Determine the equilibrium rate of interest and income in an IS-LM framework. Explain how this equilibrium rate of interest and income changes when

(a) Government expenditure increases

(b) money-supply increases

10. Given the following :

Year	*Sales (Rs.)*	*Profit (Rs.)*
1	80,000	10,000
2	90,000	14,000

Determine (i) P/V ratio

(ii) Total fixed cost

(iii) Break Even point

(iv) Required sales in order to make a profit or Rs 19,000.

11. Define Balance of payment. Briefly discuss about India's Balance of payment position recently.

12. (a) The cost of placing of an order is Rs 50. It is estimated that 300 units will be sold in the next twelve months. Price per unit is Rs 15 and the inventory carrying cost is 20/-. Find the EOQ. Also determine the size of average inventory.

(b) Annual Sales of a company are given below :

Year	1995	1996	1997	1998	1999
Sales (1000 rupees)	45	56	78	46	75

Forecast the amount of sales in 2002.

13. Following are the data of ABC company

Sales : Rs. 2,00,000

Variable cost : Rs. 12,00,000

Fixed cost : Rs. 60,000

Compute (i) the P/V Ratio (ii) the break even sales (iii) the manager of safety.

14. (a) Define constrained optimisation. Derive the condition of output maximisation subject to cost constraints.

(*b*) The cost equation of the firm $C = 5x + 10y$ while the production function is given by $q = xy$. Find the minimum cost of producing 50 units of output.

15. (*a*) Find the optimum commodity purchases by a consumer whose utility function and budget constraints are $U = q_1^2 q_2^2$ and $4q_1 + 8q_2 = 96$ respectively.

(*b*) Find the profit maximising output and price given the following revenue and cost function $R = 1000q - 2q^2$ and $C = q^3 - 59q^2 + 1315q + 2000$.

16. (*a*) Described the main objective and function of world trade organisation.

(*b*) The inutility function is $U = x^3 + y^3$ where the maximum utility is 72. If price of $x(P_x)$ is 5 and price of $y(P_y)$ is 20, find the money income of the consumer.

17. Describe the nature and characteristics of international trade. What is the importance of foreign exchange in international trade?

18. (*a*) Describe the main characteristics of an underdeveloped and developing economics.

(*b*) Write about the nature of mixed economy. Status of India at the current situation.

19. (*a*) What are the elements involved in ordering cost and inventory carrying costs?

(*b*) Draw graphically and explained the "EOQ" condition.

20. (*a*) Business economics is economics applied in decision making" Discuss.

(*b*) Discuss about economic analysis in relation to business economics.